MASTERING **MACRO** PHOTOGRAPHY

DAVID TAYLOR

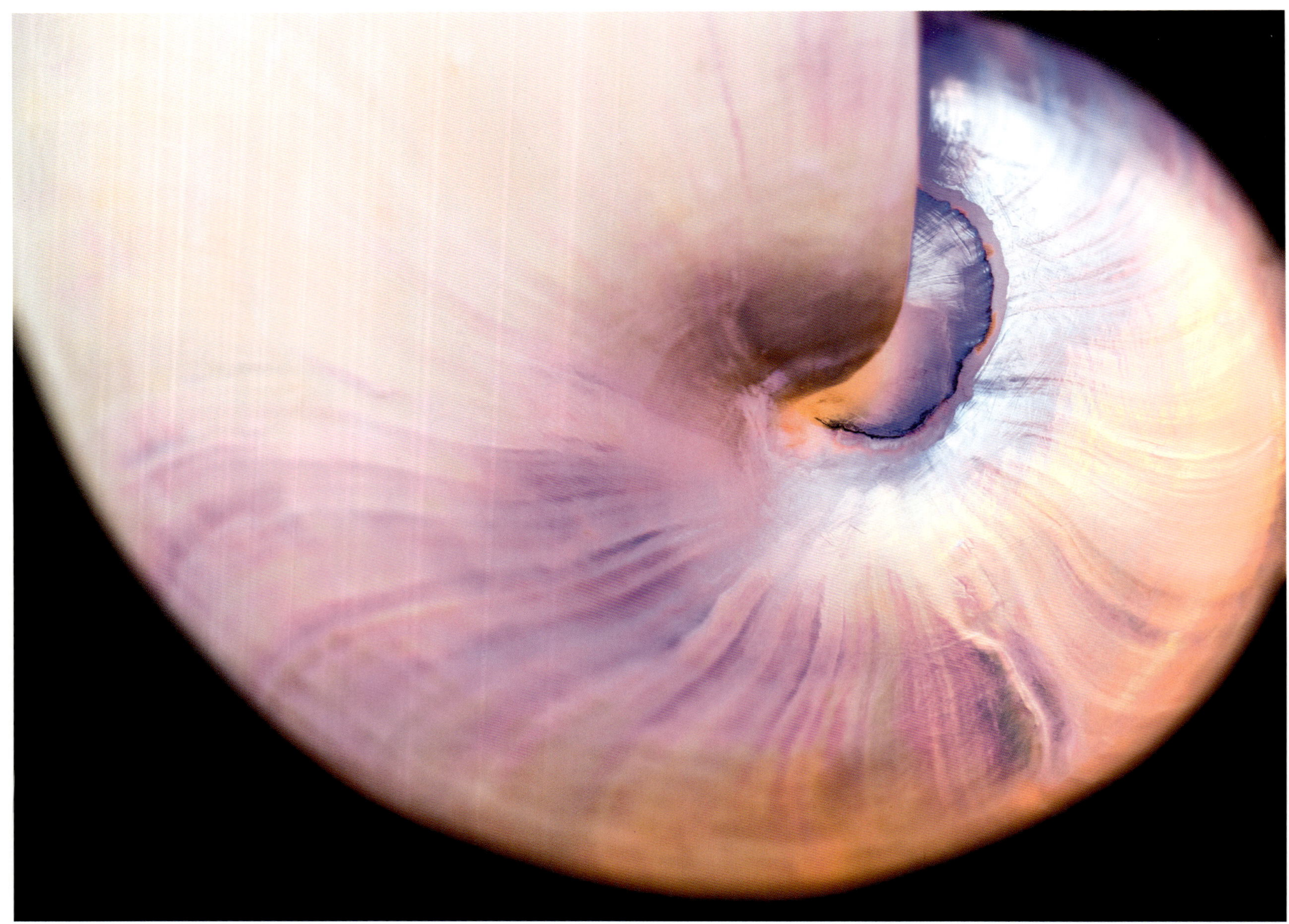

Above: Curves are powerful compositionally. They form a
natural pathway for the eye to wander through an image.
The destination point at the end of the curve would typically
be the sharpest part of the picture—it would look odd if this
area were out of focus. In this image of a pearlescent shell,
the line of the curve is reinforced by natural patterns in the
shell pointing to the center of the curve.

Focal length: 35mm lens

Aperture: f/4.5

Shutter speed: 4 sec.

ISO: 400

MASTERING **MACRO**
PHOTOGRAPHY

DAVID TAYLOR

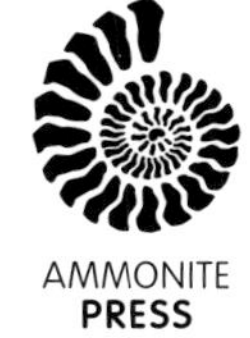

AMMONITE
PRESS

First published 2017 by
Ammonite Press
an imprint of Guild of Master Craftsman Publications Ltd.
Castle Place, 166 High Street, Lewes, East Sussex, BN7 1XU, United Kingdom

Reprinted 2022

British Library Cataloging in Publication Data:
A catalog record of this book is available from the British Library.

Publisher: Jason Hook
Art Director: Robin Shields
Editor: Chris Gatcum
Designer: Luke Herriott

Typeface: Helvetica Neue
Color reproduction by GMC Reprographics
Printed in China

Contents

Introduction

The human eye is a miracle of evolution, capable of switching focus from the far distance to an object within arm's reach almost instantaneously. However, the human eye also has its limitations, such as being able to resolve ultra-fine detail. Fortunately, what nature didn't provide has been more than made up for by science—specifically, the study of optics.

A notable pioneer in the use of optics to magnify detail was the British scientist, Robert Hooke, whose work with microscopes led to the publication of *Micrographia* in 1665. Hooke's meticulous drawings of fleas and other insects showed details never seen before, making the publication the scientific sensation of its day.

Today, we do not need to make drawings because we have photography. Close-up and macro photography is extremely popular, and understandably so—the delight (and occasional revulsion) at seeing details that are normally hidden is just as strong today as it was in the 17th century.

In fact, it is currently a golden age for macro photography. Not only has sophisticated computer software led to new imaging techniques, but modern technology has provided photographers with a head-spinning array of cameras, lenses, and accessories that make it easier than ever to record ultra-fine, close-up detail.

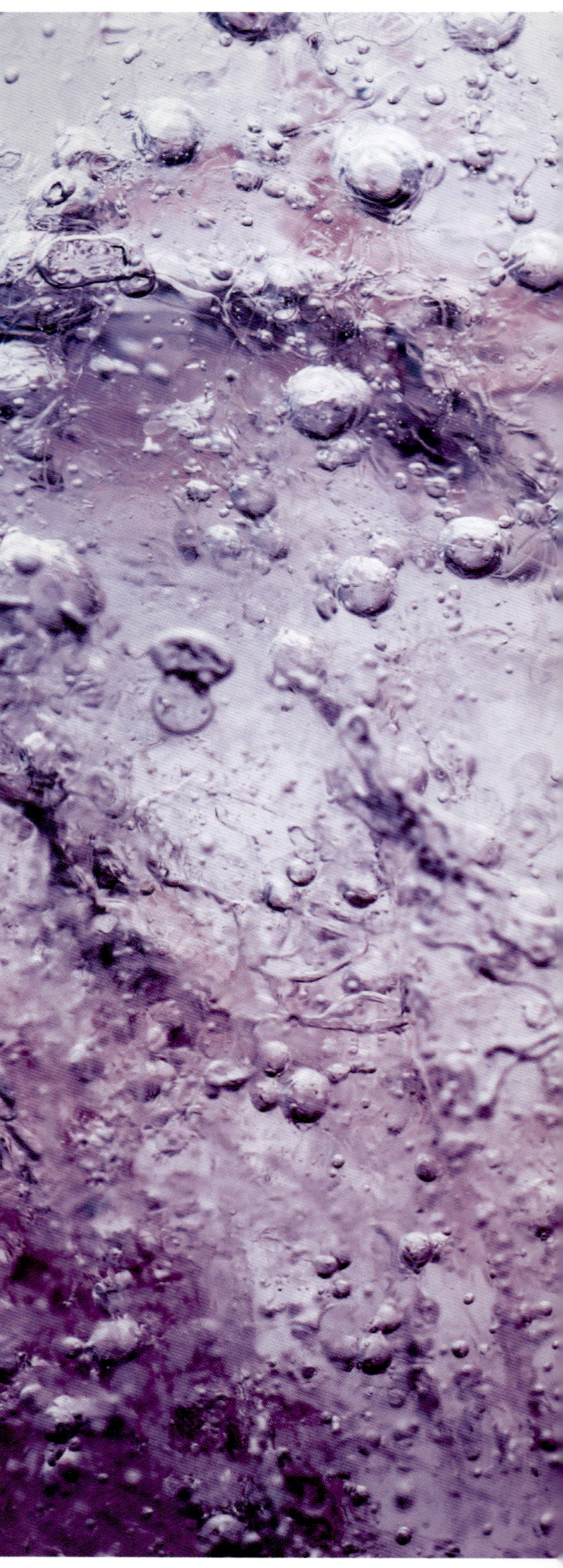

Right: A fascinating aspect of macro photography is that it reveals structure in everyday objects that is normally invisible to the eye. This macro image of ice shows that it isn't uniform throughout: bubbles reveal how the freezing process trapped air that percolated through the water until it solidified, while the deep magenta color shows that a stain leached through the water as well. To show these details the ice was illuminated from behind with an off-camera flash.

Focal length: 100mm macro lens (with 20mm extension tube)
Aperture: f/29
Shutter speed: 1/250 sec.
ISO: 100

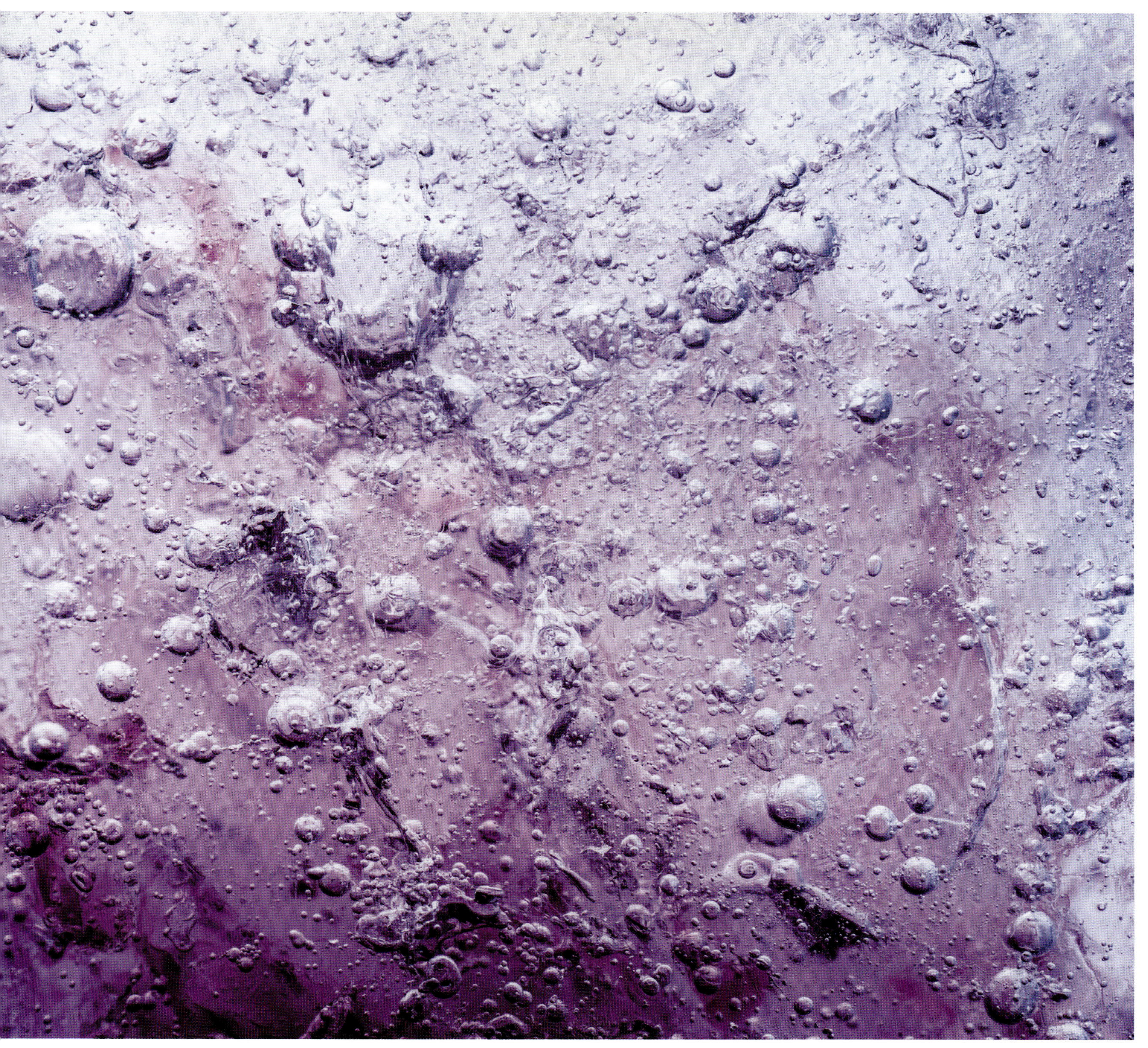

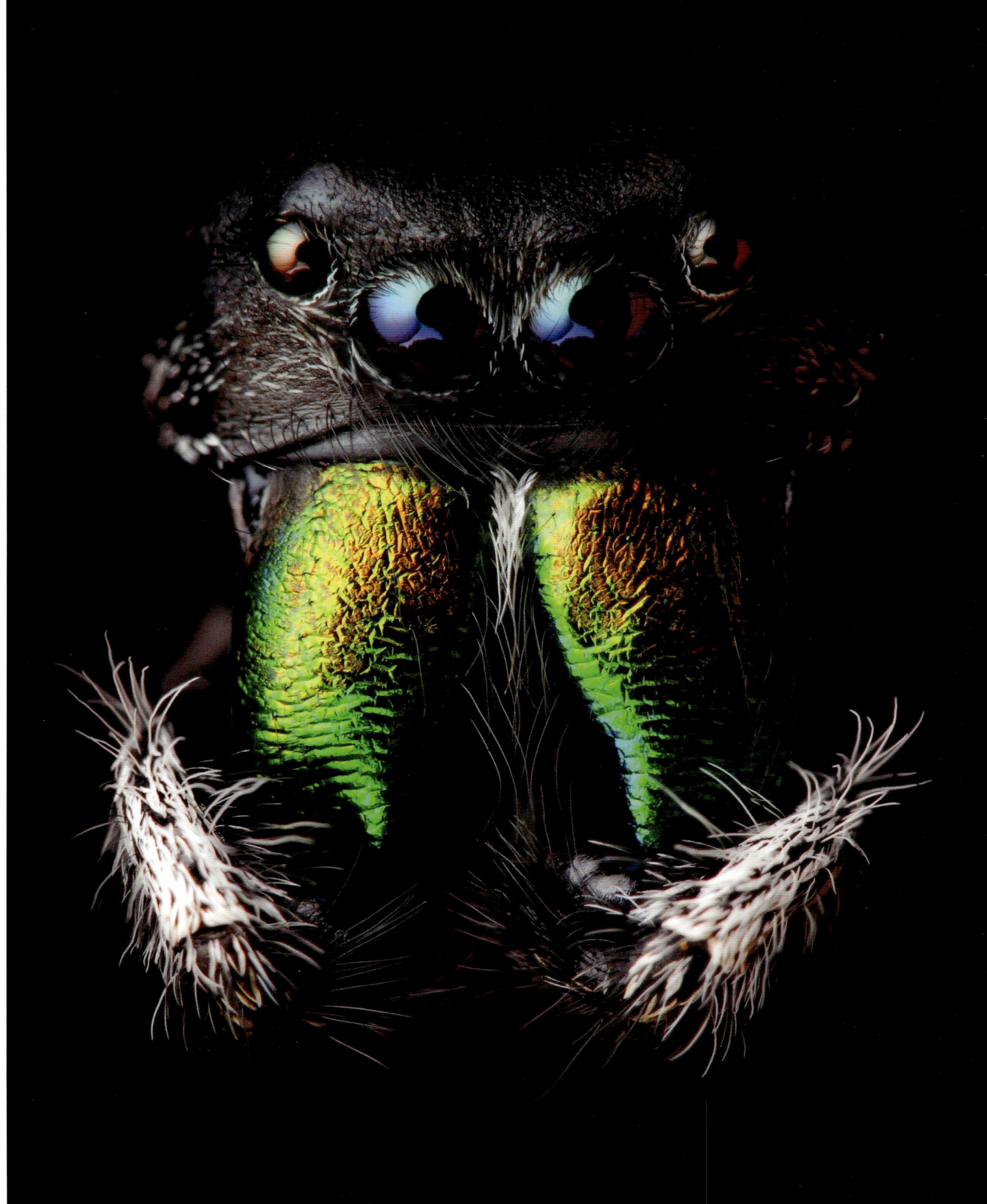

Left: Macro and close-up photography isn't as strict a genre as landscape or portraiture is, so there are many different subject types that can be shot using macro techniques. Having said that, photographers who regularly shoot macro often specialize. For example, by specializing in insects or arachnids—such as this jumping spider—you can learn behavioral patterns that will increase your chance of photographic success.

Focal length: 100mm macro lens (with extension tube)

Aperture: f/14

Shutter speed: 1/160 sec.

ISO: 800

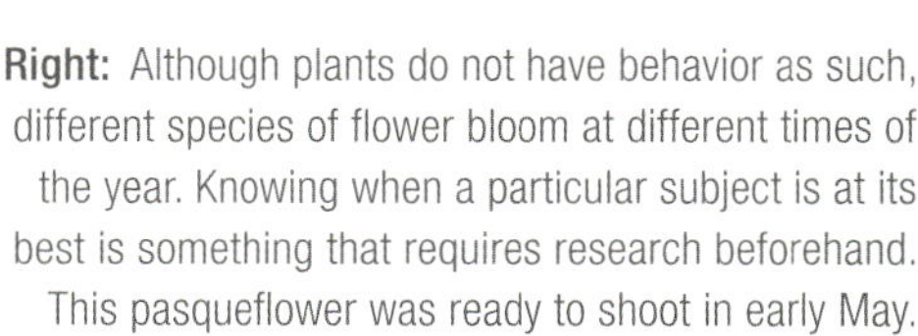

Right: Although plants do not have behavior as such, different species of flower bloom at different times of the year. Knowing when a particular subject is at its best is something that requires research beforehand. This pasqueflower was ready to shoot in early May.

Focal length: 100mm macro lens

Aperture: f/4.5

Shutter speed: 1/250 sec.

ISO: 400

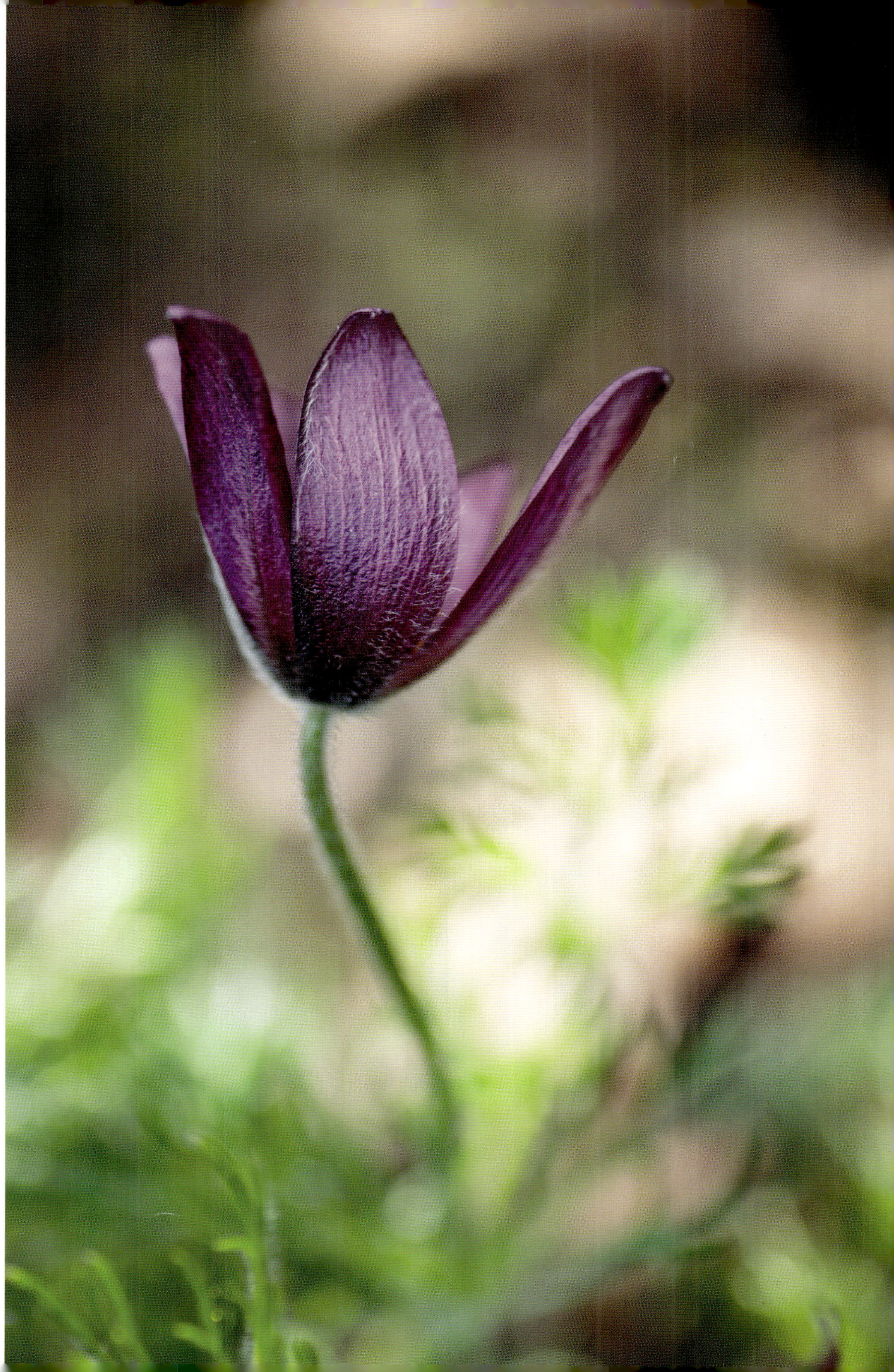

Chapter 1
Equipment

Photography starts with a camera and a lens. The sophistication of this combination will have some bearing on what sort of close-up and macro photography you can achieve, as well as how easy (or otherwise) it is to get acceptable results. However, photography isn't just about cameras and lenses, especially when it comes to close-up and macro photography. There are other accessories that will make an exploration of the close-up world easier and more rewarding. This chapter covers cameras and these extra accessories; lenses and similar equipment will be covered in detail in chapter 2.

FULL-FRAME CAMERAS

A full-frame camera has a sensor with the same dimensions as a 35mm frame of film (36 x 24mm). This is just one of many different sensor sizes used in digital cameras, but it is broadly seen (rightly or wrongly) as the "gold standard" to which other sensor sizes are compared. For more details see page 34.

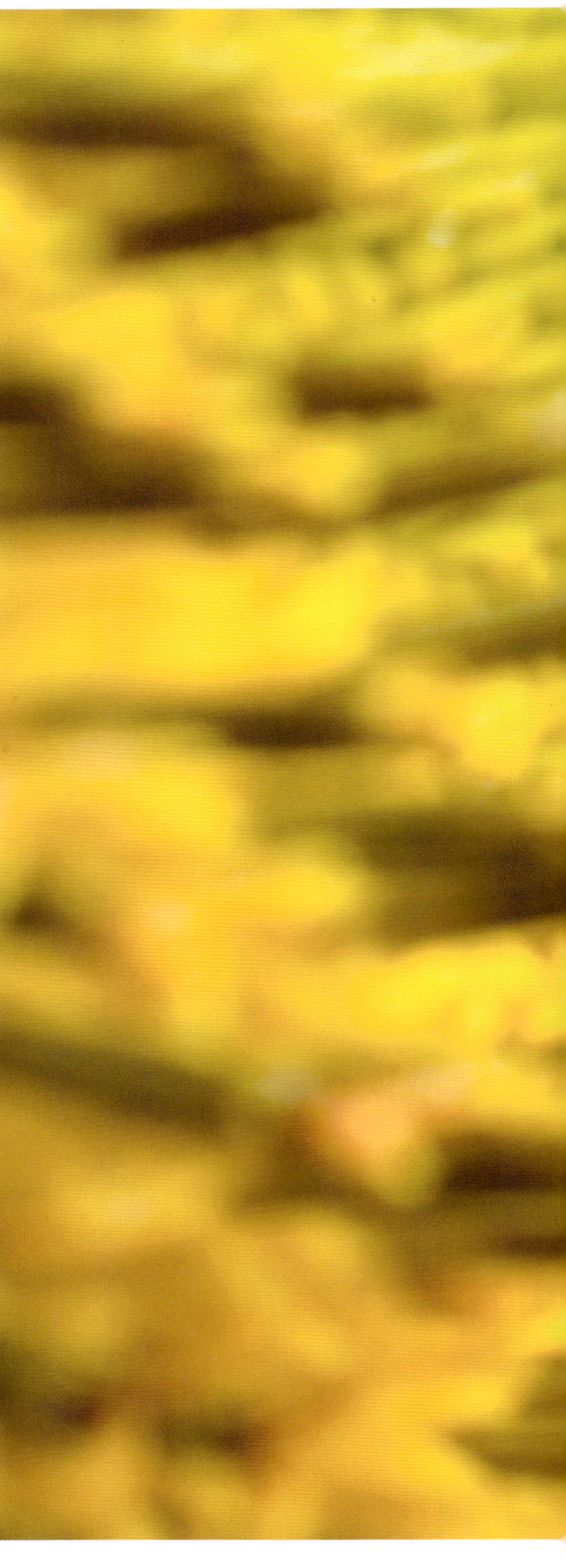

Right: This photograph of a pollen-covered worker bee was shot using a full-frame digital single lens reflex (DSLR) camera and remotely triggered external flash. However, the combination is heavy and bulky, so is not for everyone. When I want to carry less equipment, I use a small Micro Four Thirds system camera instead. This has different capabilities, so I need to tailor how and what I shoot depending on the camera I am using.

Focal length: 100mm macro lens

Aperture: f/16

Shutter speed: 1/250 sec.

ISO: 400

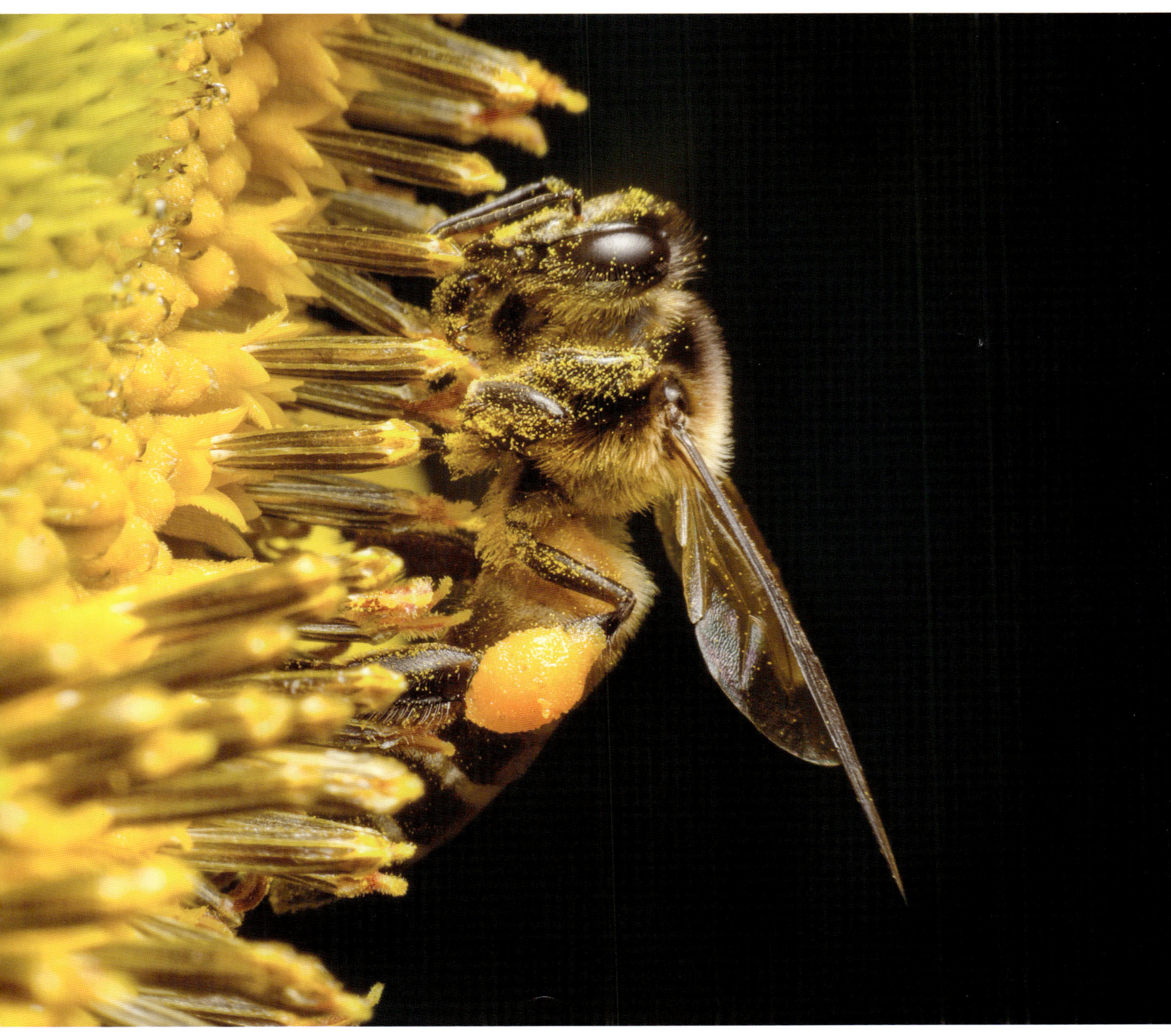

Cameras

There are two broad categories of camera: non-system and system. Non-system cameras are an "all-in-one" solution to photography. They feature a built-in lens that cannot be removed and often lack useful connections such as a flash hotshoe.

In comparison, a system camera is just one component in a photographic range that includes lenses, flash units, and a plethora of other useful extras, such as remote-release cables and battery grips. Because of these optional lenses and accessories, system cameras are far more easily modified to shoot macro imagery, but this doesn't mean that non-system cameras are a non-starter when it comes to shooting close-up photographs.

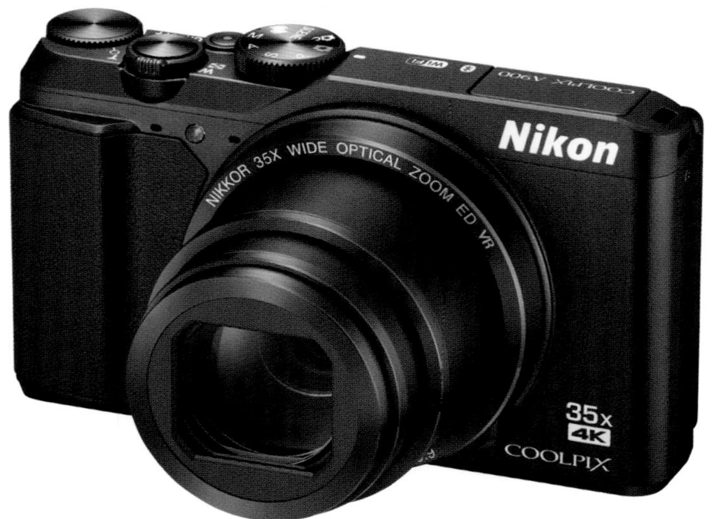

Above: There is a wide range of compact cameras, which target different users. The most useful for "serious" photographers are cameras such as this Nikon A900, which has features that are ideal for macro work, such as full control over the exposure.
© Nikon

Non-System Cameras

The category of non-system camera includes compact cameras and cellphones, which typically house sensors that are far smaller than those found in system cameras. This is partially due to cost (small sensors are cheaper to produce than large sensors), and also partially because it enables the cameras to be physically small and light. This makes non-system cameras easy to carry around, so they're ideal for a more spontaneous approach to photography.

The downside to a small sensor is that the dynamic range is smaller and image noise more pronounced—particularly at higher ISO settings—when compared to the larger sensors found in system cameras. Many non-system cameras also limit how much control you have over aspects of shooting such as exposure or focusing or, at best, bury the required functions deep in their menu systems. This can make shooting a frustrating affair if fine control of an image is desirable, which is generally the case when creating macro imagery.

BRIDGE CAMERAS

Bridge cameras got their name because they are seen as a "bridge" between compact-style and system cameras. Although the lens is fixed, the zoom range is usually large, and many cameras of this type feature a filter ring on the lens, making the use of close-up lenses possible (see pages 38–39). Bridge cameras also tend to offer a similar level of control to a system camera, including the ability to shoot Raw. However, they usually have a small sensor size, which means they suffer from some of the same problems as compact cameras, namely noise and a limited dynamic range.

MACRO MODE

Non-system cameras frequently feature a "close-up" or "macro" focusing mode that allows the lens to focus very closely. However, the focusing distance can vary with focal length—the closest focus distance is usually at the widest focal length.

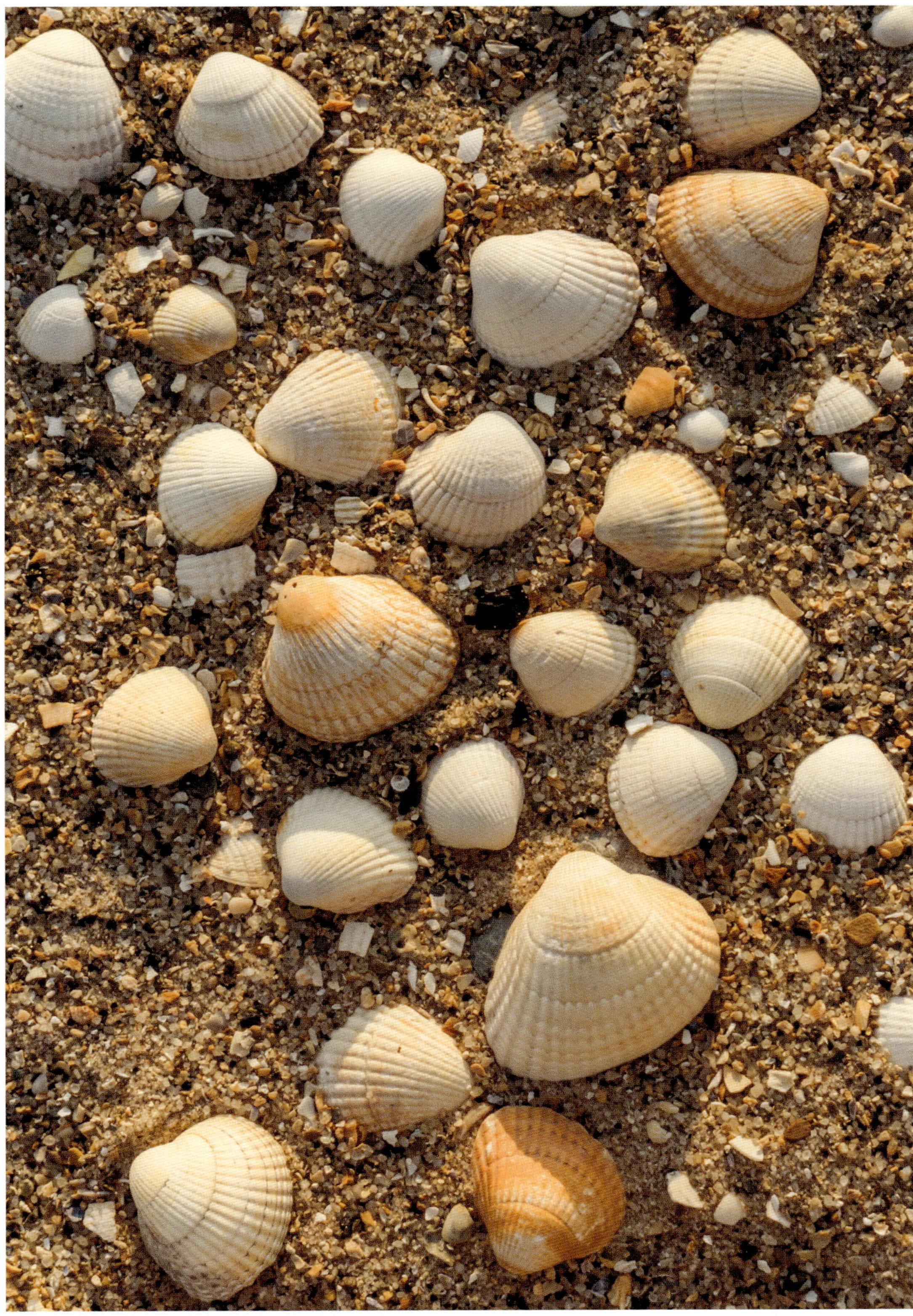

Left: Compact cameras and cellphones are ideal when carrying a full bag of camera equipment would be a chore. Both camera types will make a useful visual "notebook" that will let you try out compositions or serve as an *aide memoire* before you perhaps return with a larger, better-specified camera.

Focal length: 15.7mm

Aperture: f/7.1

Shutter speed: 1/80 sec.

ISO: 80

System Cameras

System cameras let you fit a lens that suits your chosen way of shooting and it is this flexibility that gives this type of camera its appeal. It also means that you can expand your lens range as your needs change over time. If you decide you want to shoot macro, for example, you could fit either a macro lens or an accessory that adds close-up capabilities to a standard lens, as outlined in the following chapter.

There are two popular types of system camera: Digital Single Lens Reflex (DSLR) cameras and Mirrorless cameras (also commonly referred to as "Compact System Cameras" or CSCs). DSLR cameras use a reflex mirror inside the camera body to direct light from the lens through a pentaprism to an optical viewfinder. When the shutter button is pressed down the mirror swings out of the way to reveal the shutter mechanism. The shutter then opens to expose the sensor to light. At the end of the exposure the shutter closes and the mirror swings back down into place.

Modern DSLRs also feature a Live View mode, in which the mirror swings up, the shutter opens, and a live feed from the sensor is directed to the LCD on the rear of the camera.

DSLRs range in size and complexity from small, lightweight, consumer-friendly models to bulky professional-specification models. As they are generally based on older film-based camera systems many "legacy" accessories, such as manual-focus lenses, are often still compatible, providing an alternative to modern accessories.

The second type of system camera is the mirrorless camera. As the name suggests, this type of camera does not have a reflex mirror, which makes the potential size of the camera far smaller and lighter. Mirrorless cameras also do not have optical viewfinders. Instead, a live feed from the sensor is shown either on the rear LCD or through an electronic viewfinder (EVF). The main drawback of relying entirely on an electronic display is that the battery life of mirrorless cameras is relatively poor compared to DSLRs.

The lack of a mirror also means that the flange focal distance—the distance from the mounting flange to the sensor—is far smaller than it is with a DSLR. With a suitable adaptor it is therefore possible to fit virtually any lens designed for a DSLR onto a mirrorless camera. This opens up a wide range of possibilities when you are shooting macro, as you can pick and choose lenses or lens accessories from virtually any camera system ever produced. With a few notable exceptions, autofocus (AF) functionality isn't carried through the adaptor, but as you'll see in chapter 3, this perhaps isn't as big a drawback as you'd imagine.

Another benefit of mirrorless cameras (and something that is increasingly being featured in DSLRs) is built-in Wi-Fi that enables you to stream a live feed from the sensor directly to your cellphone or tablet. This is incredibly useful for certain subjects such as insects, as it means you can set your camera up in a suitable location and then withdraw to reduce the risk of disturbing any subject that moves into your camera's view.

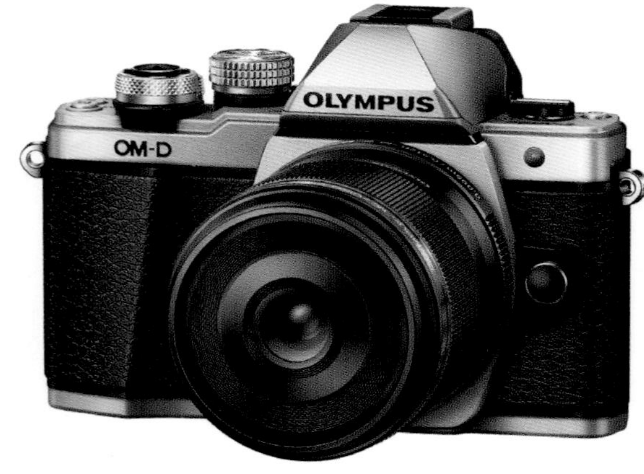

Above: Mirrorless cameras either rely entirely on a single rear LCD to display images and shooting information or house an EVF in a DSLR-style hump (as here) or to one side of the camera body like a rangefinder camera.
© Olympus

RANGEFINDER

A third type of system camera is the rangefinder camera, which is notably produced by the German company Leica. In a rangefinder camera the optical viewfinder is offset and does not provide a direct view through the lens. Composition is achieved through the use of guidelines in the viewfinder that vary in size according to the lens used. Rangefinder cameras are generally not ideal for macro photography, as parallax error—the difference between what the viewfinder sees and what the lens sees—makes the guidelines less accurate the closer the subject is to the camera. However, modern Leica digital rangefinders, such as the company's M11, also offer Live View, which makes macro photography easier.

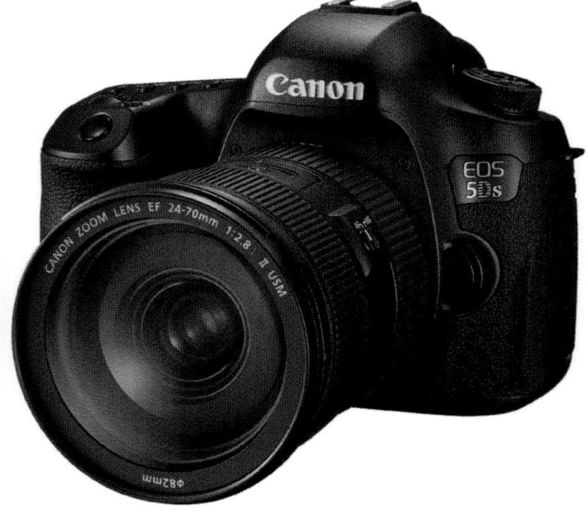

Above: Many DSLRs, such as Canon's EOS 5Ds, are backed up by an expansive range of accessories and can also use many items that were originally designed for the manufacturer's film SLRs.
© Canon

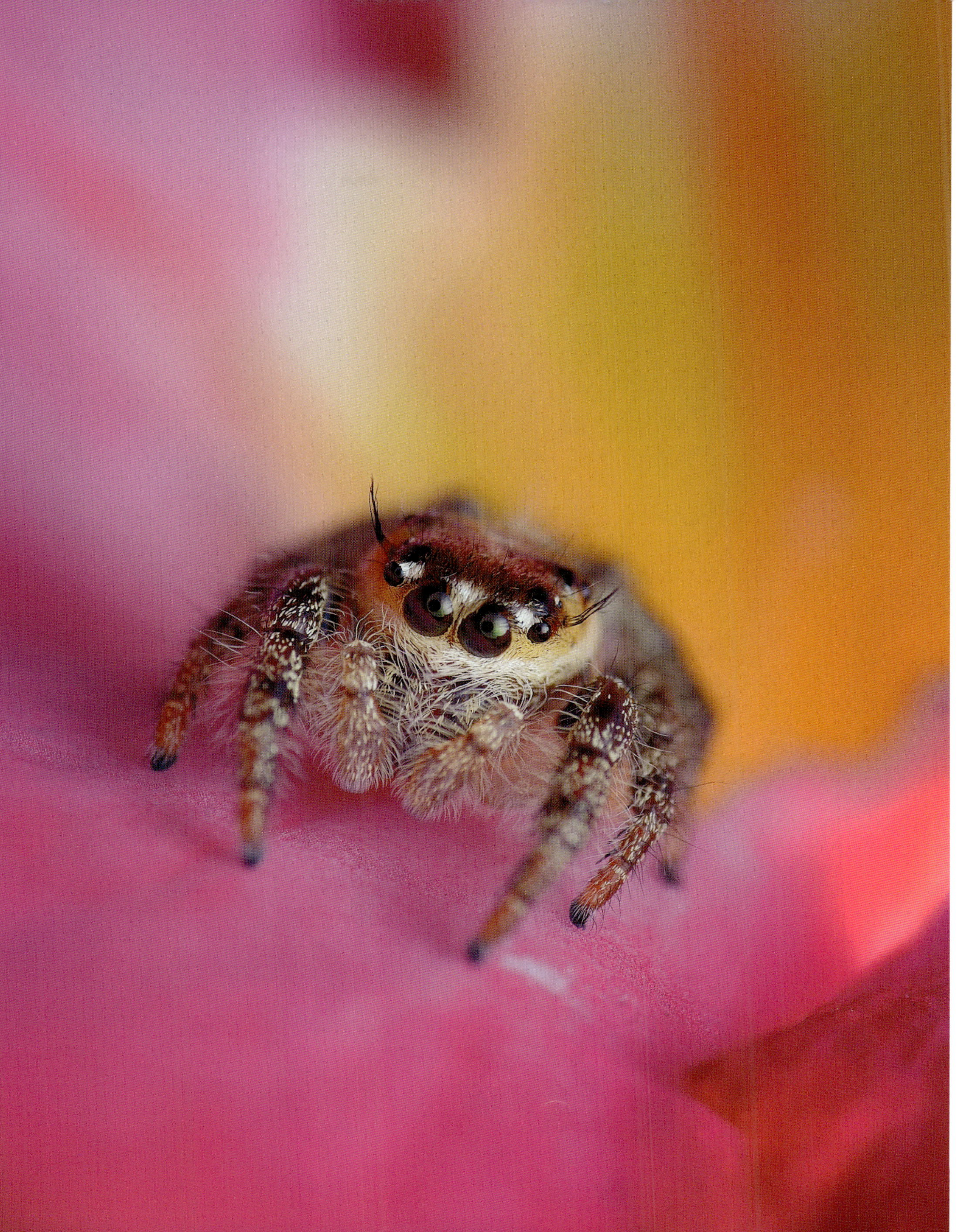

Left: System cameras
allow the use of other
equipment such as bellows,
extension tubes, and
reversed lenses (see page
40), as well as lighting such
as external flash. Flash
in particular is useful to
the macro photographer
who shoots fast-moving
subjects such as this
jumping spider.

Focal length: 100mm macro lens
(with extension tubes)
Aperture: f/14
Shutter speed: 1/200 sec.
ISO: 400

Camera Support

Shooting macro imagery is a real test of your photographic technique. Minimizing camera shake is perhaps one of the greatest challenges you will face, but supporting your camera—rather than handholding it—is the simplest solution.

Tripods

Choosing a tripod can be a difficult decision, as there are a number of factors that need to be considered, depending on your style of shooting, the type of subjects that most interest you, the equipment you use, and your budget. Ideally, a tripod should be as heavy as possible, as that makes a tripod more stable. However, heavy tripods are invariably more difficult to carry: this is not an issue if you only ever shoot in a studio, but will be important if your preference is for shooting outdoors. Metal tripods are generally the heaviest type commonly sold and plastic the lightest. Carbon-fiber tripods offer a perfect (if expensive) compromise between the two.

The height that a tripod can be set to is another important factor to consider. In most cases, a tripod should be tall enough so that your camera can be used at eye level without having to raise the center column (this is because raising the center column raises the center of gravity, making a tripod less stable). However, this may be less important if your subjects are typically found close to the ground, as is the case with most flowers and fungi. In this instance a tripod that allows you to splay the legs out wide or that has a center column that can be inverted or rotated 90° relative to the tripod's legs will be more useful, as it will let you shoot from close to ground level.

Below: For this shot I removed my tripod's center column and re-inserted it upside down—the resulting photograph was also upside down, but that is something that can be rectified easily during postproduction.

Focal length: 100mm macro lens

Aperture: f/22

Shutter speed: 5 sec.

ISO: 100

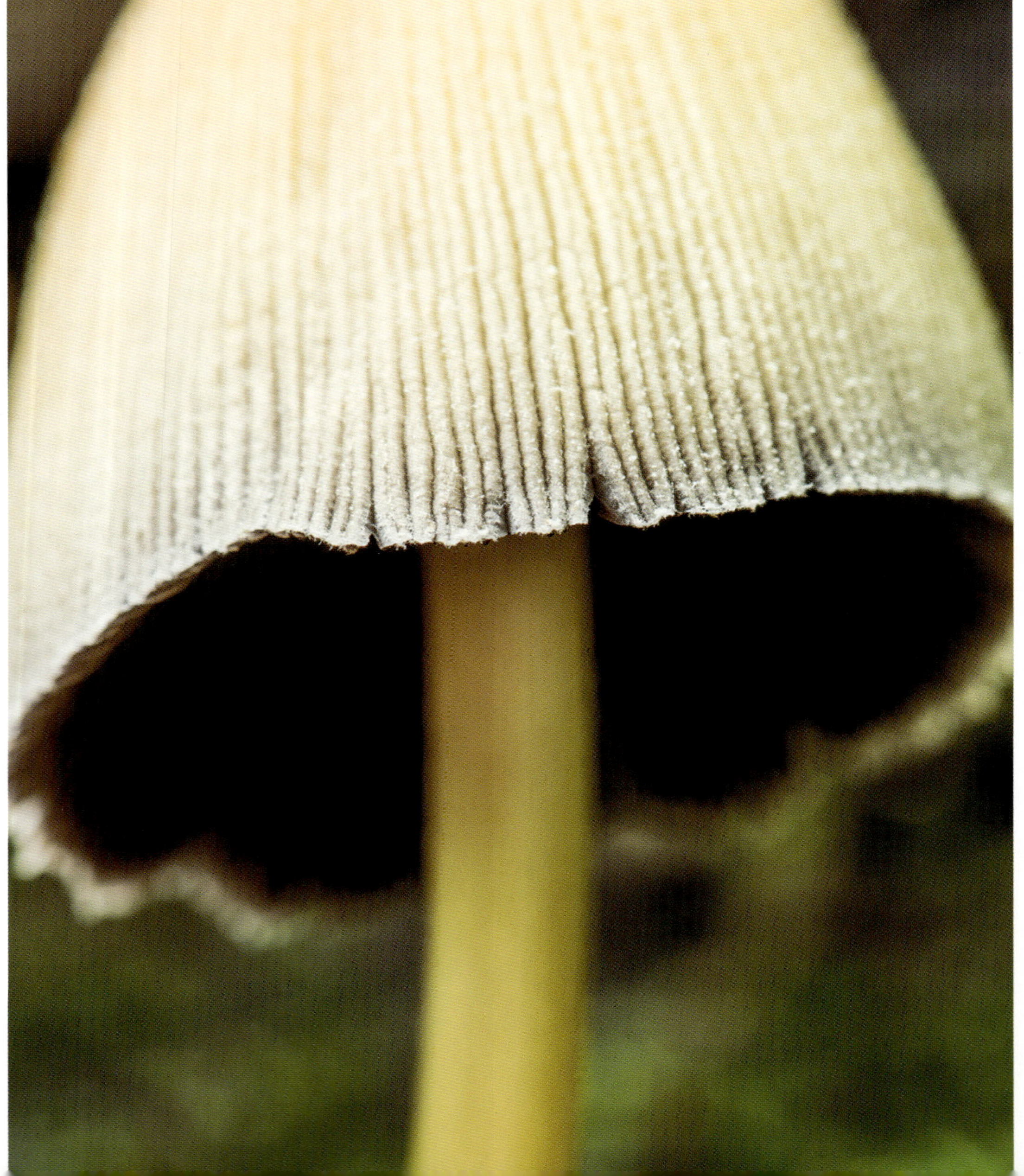

Tripod Heads

Tripods either come with a head that is fitted permanently, or as a set of "legs" that allow you to fit a separate head of your choosing. Although the former is more convenient, the latter lets you choose exactly the type of head that suits your needs, or even swap heads depending on the type of photography you're doing at any particular time.

There are essentially three types of tripod head to choose from: three-way heads, ball heads, and geared heads. Three-way heads let you adjust the angle of the head by moving and then locking one or a combination of levers: as the name suggests, movement is available in three axes.

Ball heads let you move the camera freely in any direction by loosening and then locking a ball-and-socket joint. This makes ball heads quick to use, but they are also less precise when you want to make small adjustments.

The third type of tripod head—a geared head—is similar to a three-way head, but it is not necessary to lock the head once you've adjusted it. Instead, gears are used to control the movement, which makes them very precise. This is great for macro work, although geared heads are typically heavier, bulkier, and more expensive than both three-way and ball heads.

Adjustment Rails

An almost essential piece of equipment for macro photography is an adjustment rail. This fits between a tripod and your camera and allows you to make very fine adjustments to the position of your camera relative to your subject. The simplest adjustment rails let you move the camera backward or forward, while more complex adjustment rails allow lateral movement as well (a good set of adjustment rails will have a measurement scale on it in both directions so you can move the camera's position very scientifically if necessary). Adjustment rails are particularly useful when using techniques such as focus stacking, as outlined on pages 124–125.

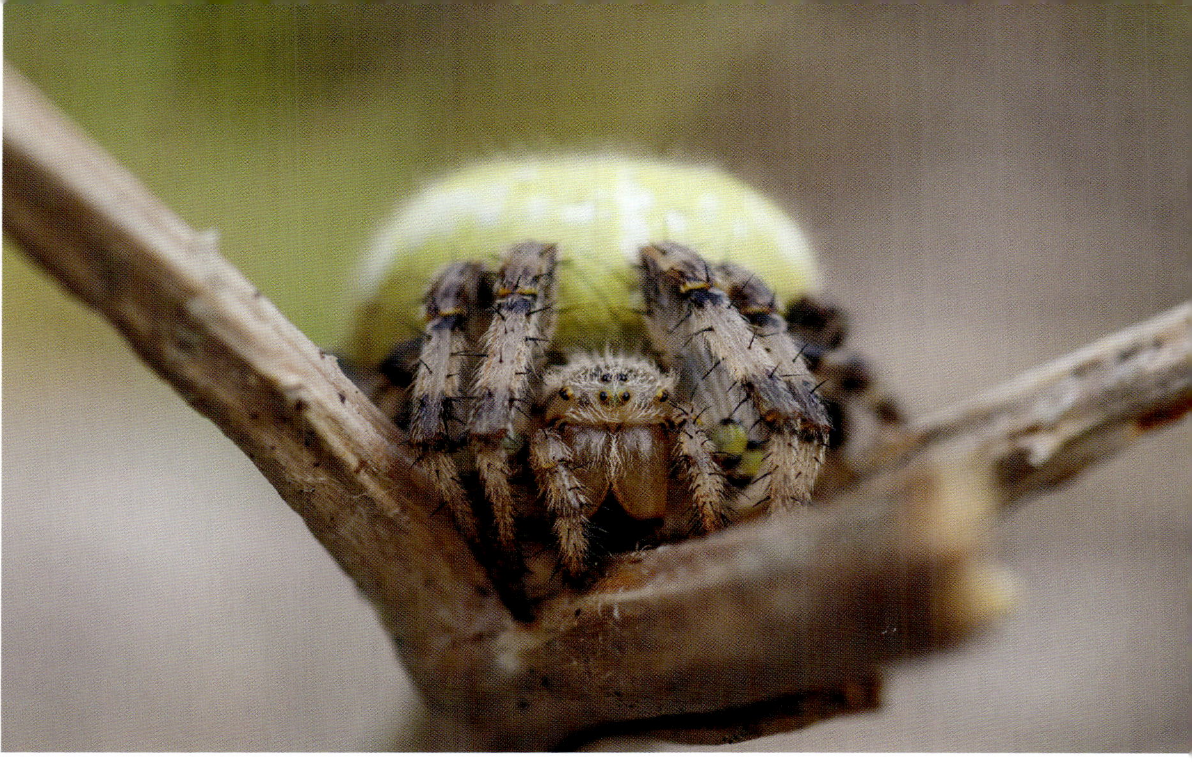

Above: It is far easier to fine tune your focus with an adjustment rail than using the focusing ring on a lens. To start with, focus is roughly set using the lens and the adjustment rail is then racked backward or forward until the focus falls in the correct place.

Focal length: 100mm macro lens

Aperture: f/16

Shutter speed: 1/160 sec.

ISO: 800

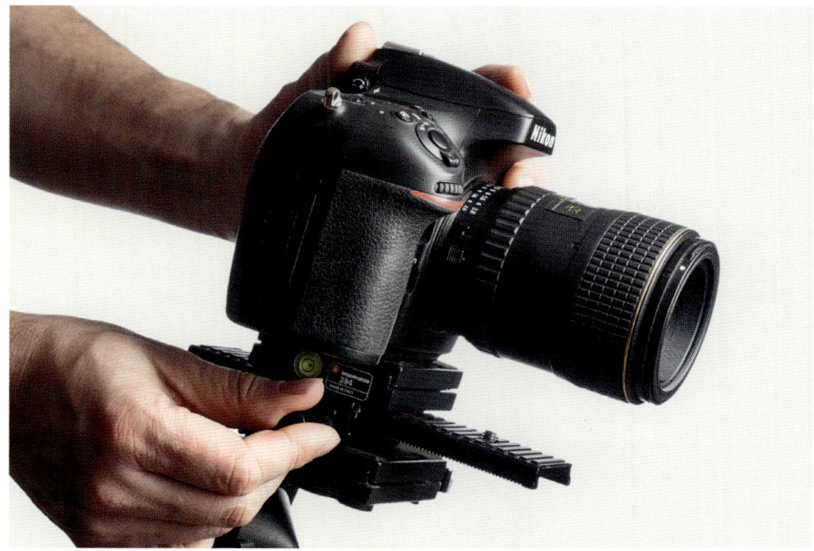

Left: An important benefit of an adjustment rail is that it lets you easily fine tune both composition and focus.

Lighting

As you'll see later in the book, shooting close-up
and macro images often involves the use of small
apertures to maximize depth of field. Adding light
to a scene is an easy way to allow fast shutter
speeds to be employed, which is often necessary
when you are handholding a camera and/or your
subject is likely to move. The other method of
increasing the shutter speed is to increase the ISO
setting on the camera, but this has drawbacks in
terms of noise and dynamic range.

Flash

Most cameras feature a built-in flash and this
would initially seem the most obvious solution
when it comes to illuminating a close-up scene.
Unfortunately, the built-in flash (and a flash added
to the hotshoe of the camera) isn't ideal. All on-
camera flash—where the flash head points toward
the subject—is a frontal light, which tends to flatten
images, making them look less three-dimensional.
For close-up photography, built-in flash also has a
tendency to cast a shadow over your subject due
to the proximity of the flash to the lens: the longer
the physical length of the lens, the greater the risk
of this happening.

   Adding an external flash is therefore a better
option, especially if it can be triggered away from
the camera. For more information about flash and
flash techniques see chapter 5.

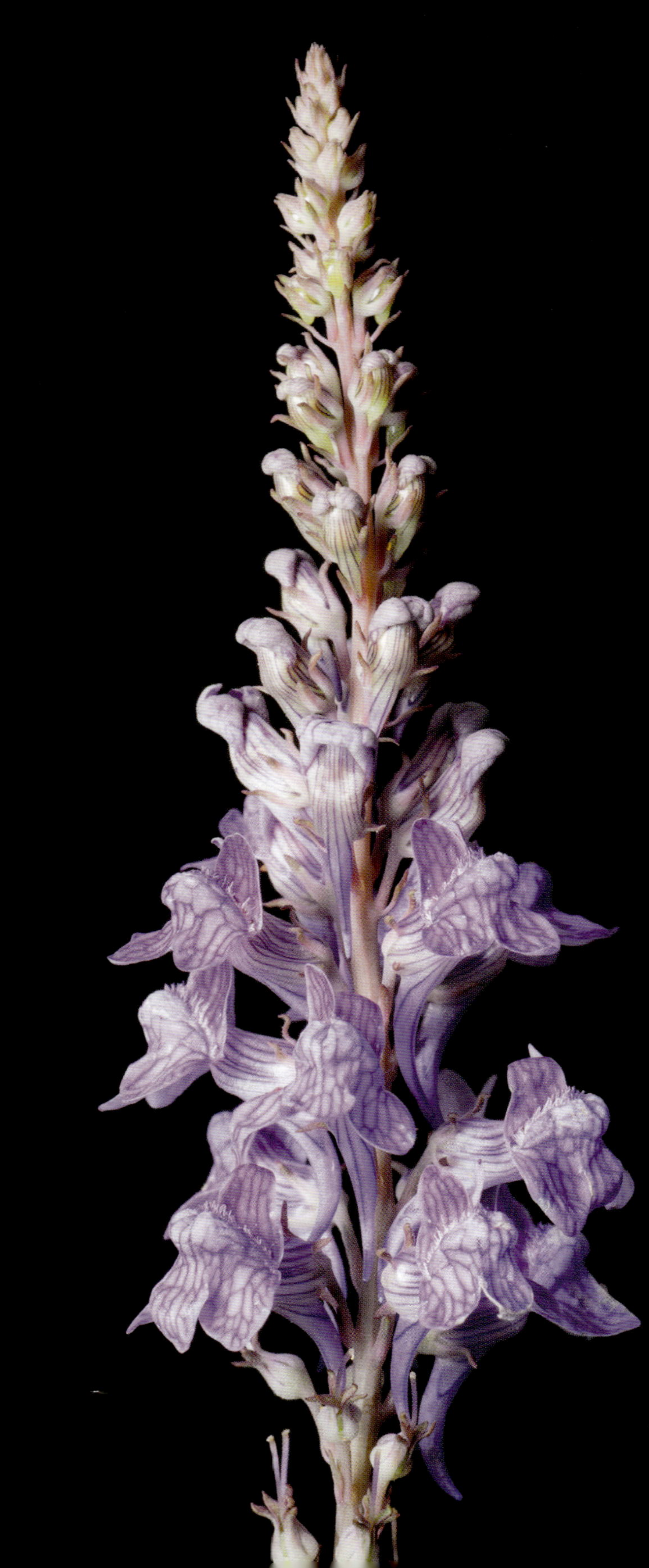

Right: Flash is useful in virtually every shooting situation.
This image may look like a studio shot, but it was actually
shot outdoors at midday. In this instance the flash was set
to overpower the ambient light, which has produced
the dark background.

Focal length: 100mm macro lens

Aperture: f/29

Shutter speed: 1/320 sec.

ISO: 400

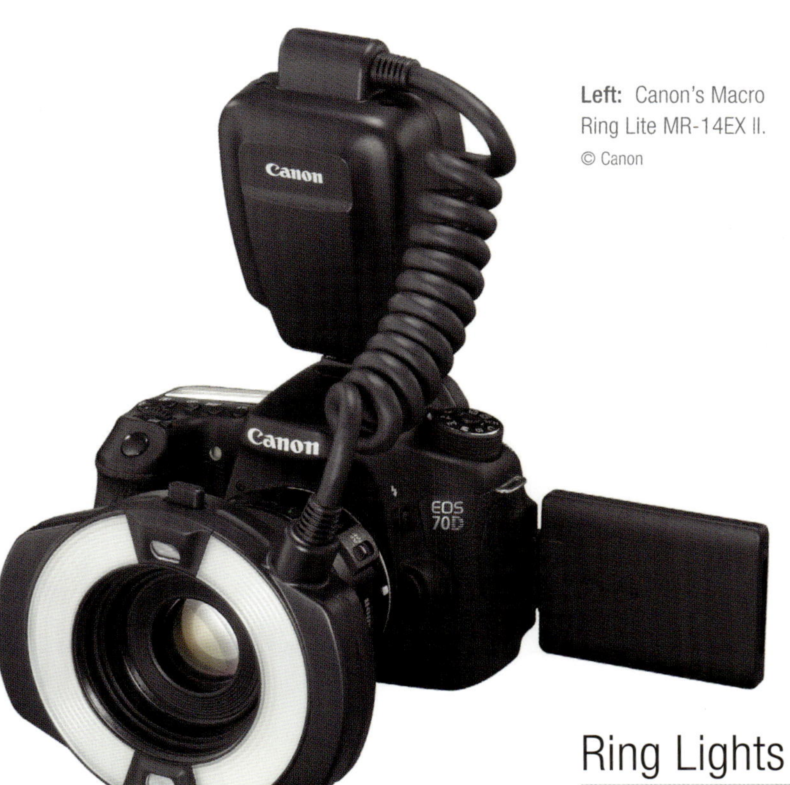

Left: Canon's Macro Ring Lite MR-14EX II.
© Canon

Ring Lights

A ring light is a circular flash (or, more typically now, a ring of LED bulbs) that attaches to the filter thread of a lens. This produces a soft light that illuminates close-up subjects evenly. For many subjects—such as flowers—this is ideal, but as there are typically few shadows it can make photographs look slightly flat.

Some LED ring lights let you turn off one side of the light, which goes a long way to creating more interesting light. Although this option isn't available with flash-based ring lights, covering up one side of the flash with opaque tape will work.

Twin Flash

A twin flash system consists of two small flashes that are mounted on either side of the lens using a bracket attached to the lens filter thread, or less frequently, the lens hood mount. The advantage of a twin flash system over a ring light is its flexibility: the angle and power of both flashes can usually be adjusted independently for greater control over the lighting direction and ratio.

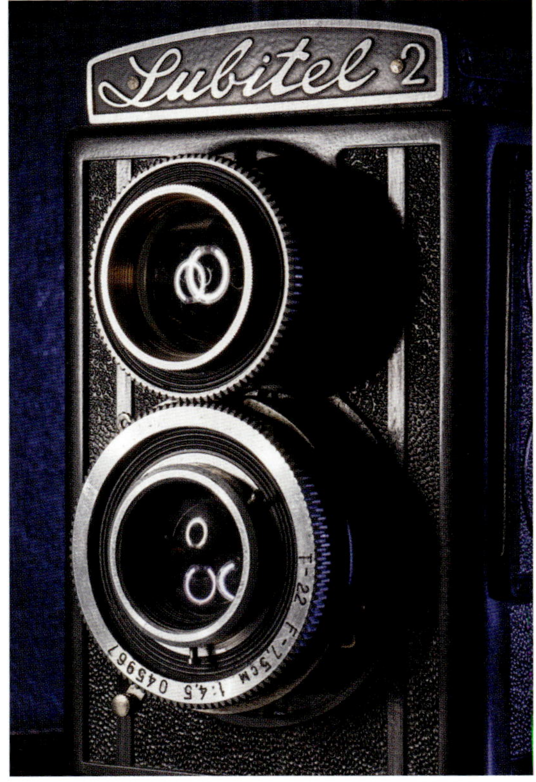

Above: The main drawback of using ring flash is the circular highlights created in reflective subjects.

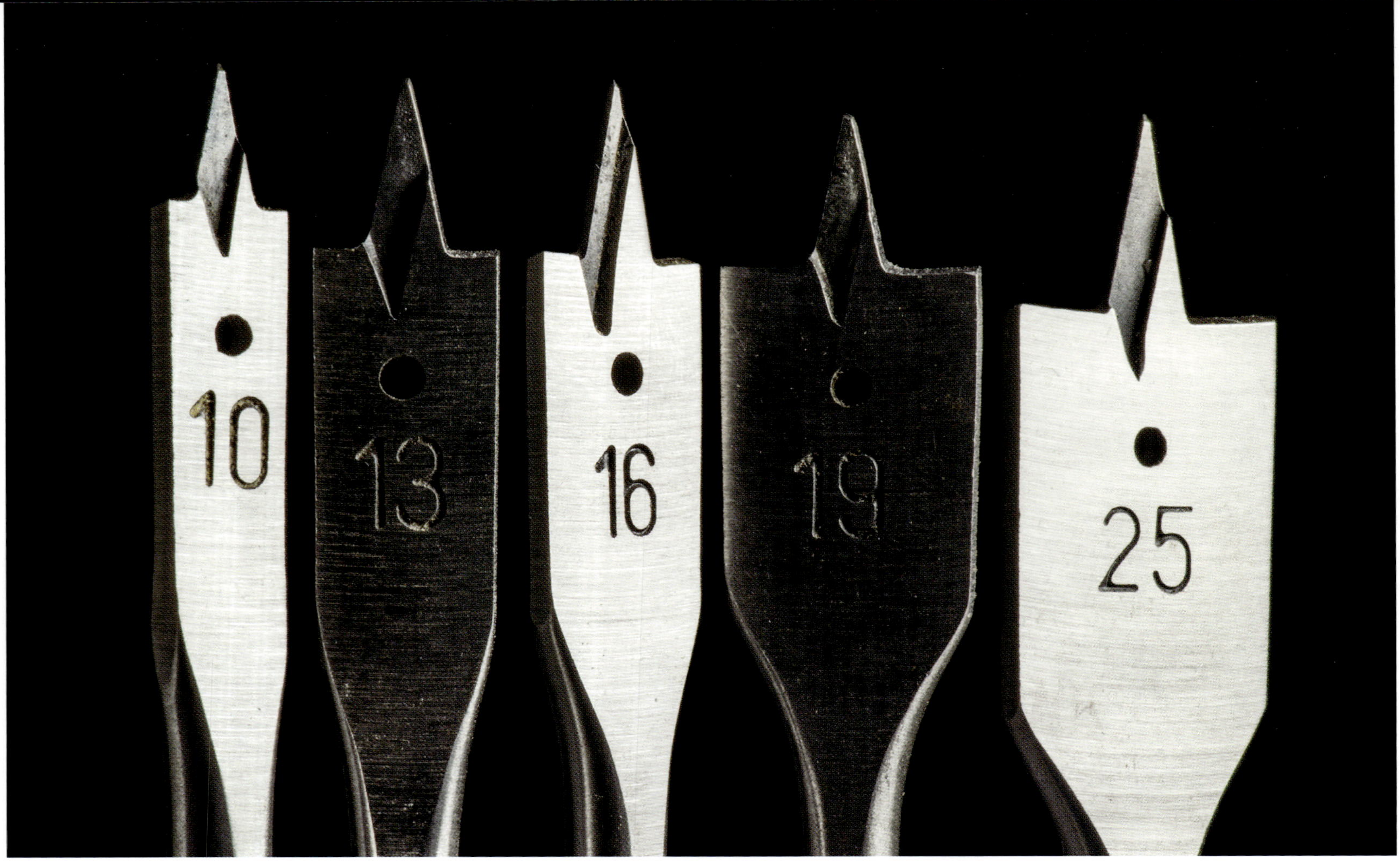

LED Lighting

One of the benefits of flash is that it provides an intense burst of light from a very small package. However, the development of LED lighting is increasingly providing photographers with an alternative. LED lighting is available either as a ring light or in panel form, with the size of the panel determining the number of LED bulbs and therefore the maximum intensity of the light output.

Like flash, LED lighting stays relatively cool, so it can be used close to a subject without running the risk of damaging delicate subjects. However, as LED lighting is a continuous light source it has two key advantages over flash: you can quickly see how light falls across your subject and you can more easily set the correct exposure before shooting. This enables you to make adjustments to the lighting without the need to shoot test shots.

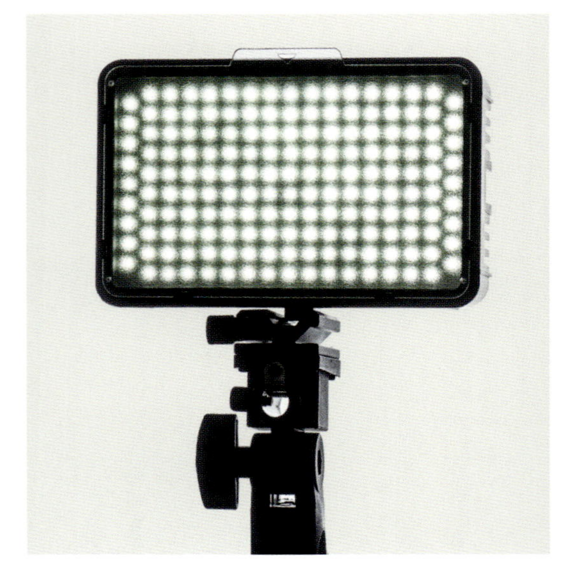

Above & right: Continuous LED lighting is particularly useful when setting up subjects with complex shiny or reflective surfaces. The ability to see how the reflections change as you move your lights is a big time-saver.

Focal length: 100mm macro lens

Aperture: f/40

Shutter speed: 1/4 sec.

ISO: 100

Studio Lighting

Traditional continuous studio lighting uses either tungsten (incandescent) or fluorescent bulbs, both of which have advantages and disadvantages. Tungsten lighting produces a warm light (typically 3200K—see pages 110–111) that is similar to domestic incandescent light bulbs in terms of its color, while fluorescent bulbs produce a cooler, more neutral light (typically between 5000–5600K), which is closer to the color temperature of midday sunlight and flash.

A single tungsten studio light is relatively underpowered, particularly when compared to large, professional flash. Tungsten bulbs also get hot and can damage delicate subjects if brought into close proximity for any length of time. Conversely, fluorescent lighting is far cooler in terms of its running temperature and the bulbs last far longer. The downside is that it is initially far more expensive to purchase fluorescent lights than tungsten.

Diffusers & Softboxes

Bare flash, studio lighting, and the sun on a cloudless day are all point light sources. The light from a point light source emanates from a relatively small area and produces light that is typically hard and creates high contrast (see pages 98–99). To soften the light, the area that the light appears to emanate from needs to be increased, which is when diffusers and softboxes are useful.

A diffuser is made from a white, translucent material that is placed between the point light source and the subject. With flash, diffusers are generally fitted directly onto the flash itself. Larger light sources (such as the sun) can be softened by positioning a diffusing screen over the subject, so the light doesn't reach it directly.

A softbox is essentially a large box-shaped diffuser into which a flash or studio light is mounted. This again softens the light that falls onto the subject, lightening shadows and reducing contrast. When using either a diffuser or softbox there is a degree of light loss that must be compensated for when setting exposure.

Reflectors

A reflector is a sheet of reflective material that is used to "bounce" light from a light source into the shadows of the subject, reducing contrast. Commercial reflectors are typically circular and can be bought in a variety of sizes and reflective surfaces: white reflectors do not modify the color of the light; silver reflectors are also neutral in color, but produce a harder, more intense reflected light; and gold-colored reflectors add a warm tint to the reflected light, enhancing any warm colors in the subject.

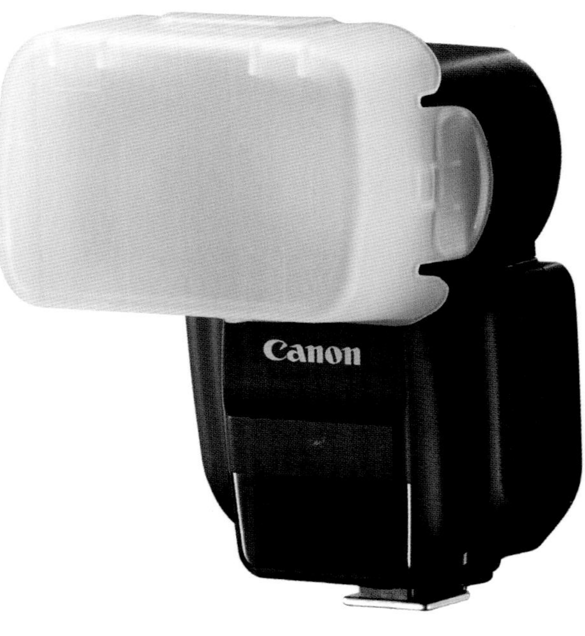

Above: A Canon 430 EX III Speedlite fitted with a diffuser.
© Canon

Scanners

Although cameras are most closely associated with macro photography, a flatbed scanner can also be used to produce striking close-up imagery (the technique is known as "scanography"). This is particularly suited to flat objects or objects that can be squashed down, rather than three-dimensional subjects, as depth of field and the illumination from the scanner's lamp are both limited.

The key specification that determines how successfully a scanner can be used is its optical resolution. This is measured in dots per inch (dpi) or dots per centimeter (dpcm). This figure tells you how many pixels can be captured for every inch or centimeter of the subject being scanned: the higher the dpi/dpcm figure set at the time of scanning, the greater the fine detail that the scanner will be able to resolve.

Another important specification is a scanner's DMax figure, which shows the scanner's dynamic range (see opposite). A higher DMax is preferable as it means the scanner will be better able to capture more tonal information from the shadows through to the highlights.

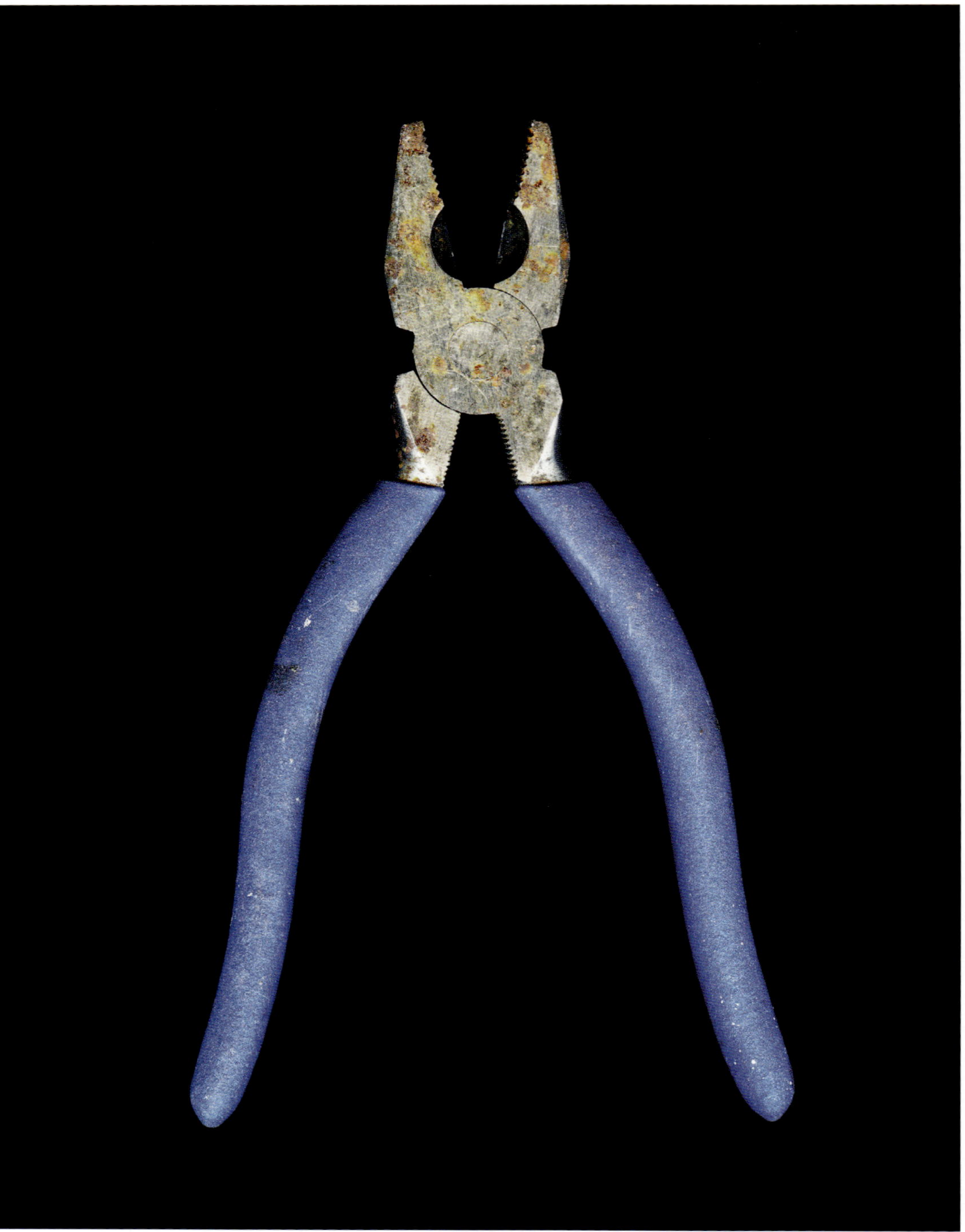

Above: An important element of scanography images is the background behind the subject. All scanners have a white surface built into the lid of the scanner, but draping black velvet over your subject or even placing a black-lined box over it can create a black background. To add a colored background you can drape colored cloth over the subject, but the limited range of the scanner's lamp can result in these colors looking "muddy."

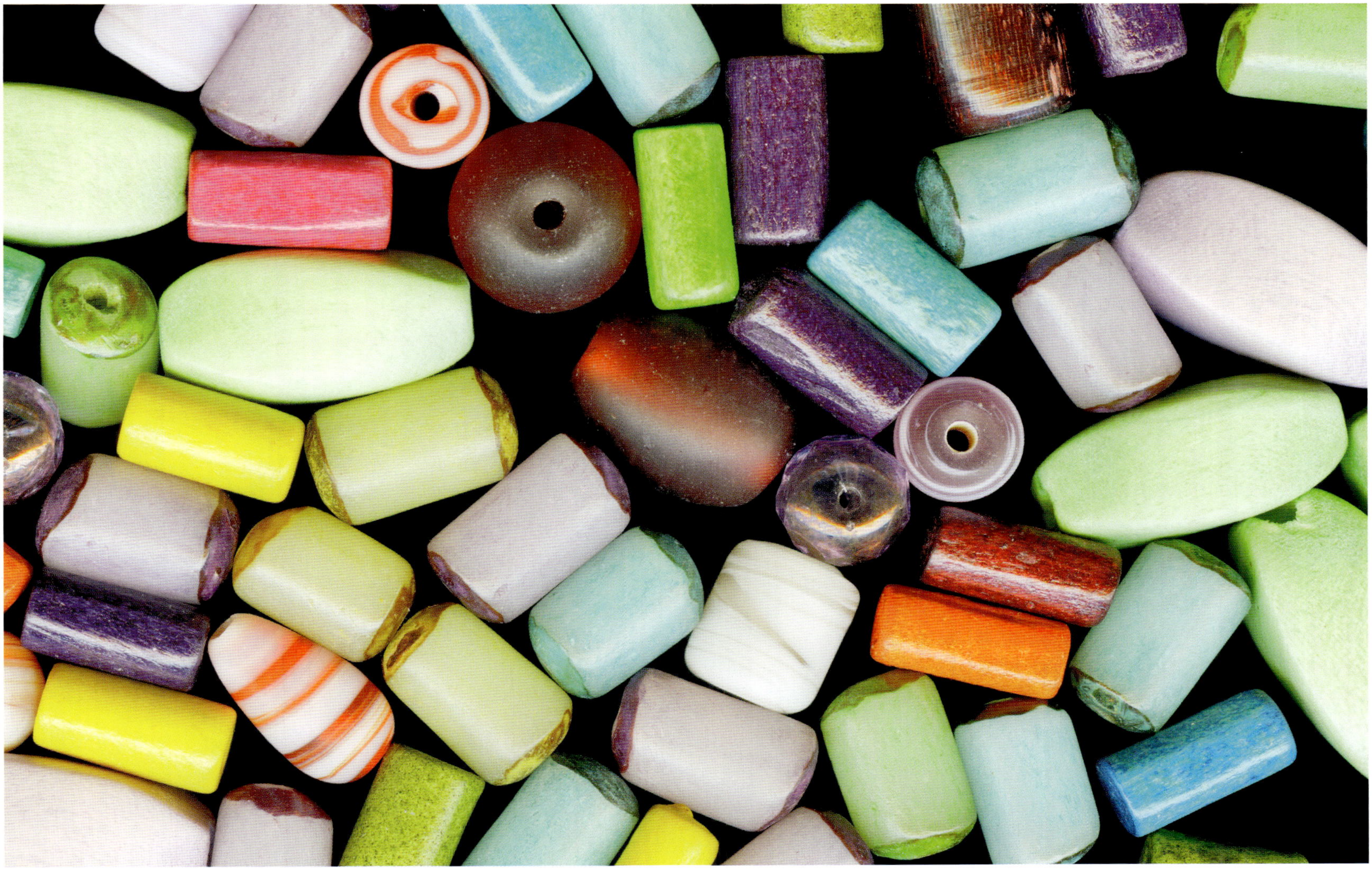

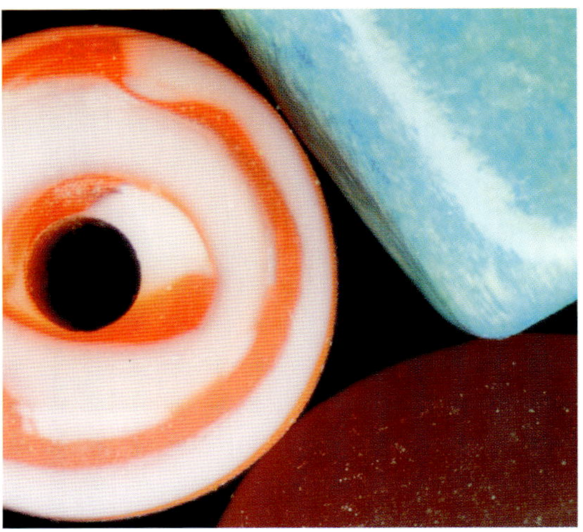

Above & left: These beads were laid directly onto the glass bed (the "platen") of the scanner and scanned at 6400ppi (approximately 2500ppcm). The resulting file measured more than 11,000 pixels across, which was more than enough to extract smaller details (left) at a respectable reproduction size.

DYNAMIC RANGE

Dynamic range describes how well a digital sensor (in a camera or scanner) can retain detail in both the shadows and highlights of the object it is imaging. The wider the dynamic range, the better able the sensor is at recording detail in the shadows and highlights simultaneously.

Microscopes

There are a number of different types of microscope, the most common of which is the compound microscope. This type of microscope features two lenses: the eyepiece and objective lenses. The objective lens, placed closest to the subject, magnifies and focuses an image up into the eyepiece tube of the microscope. All but the cheapest microscopes let you swap between two or five objective lenses to vary the degree of magnification. The eyepiece lens further magnifies the image projected by the objective lens (microscopes can be monocular and have only one eyepiece or binocular with two).

The subject is typically mounted on a glass slide, which is held in place below the objective lens on a platform known as the "stage." Illumination is typically provided either by a mirror or lamp underneath the slide, so subjects need to be naturally translucent or thinly sliced until they are translucent. Some microscopes feature lamps that illuminate the subject from above, allowing more solid, three-dimensional subjects to be viewed, but depth of field issues make it hard to view subjects that are too three-dimensional.

In all cases, focusing is achieved by turning a knob to vary the distance between the stage and the objective lens. This is another good reason why three-dimensional objects are less suitable as they can be crushed if the stage and objective lens are brought too close together.

Attaching a camera to a microscope will let you create images at magnifications far in excess of those possible with standard camera equipment. The objective lenses in microscope vary between models, but 10x to 1000x magnification is usually possible.

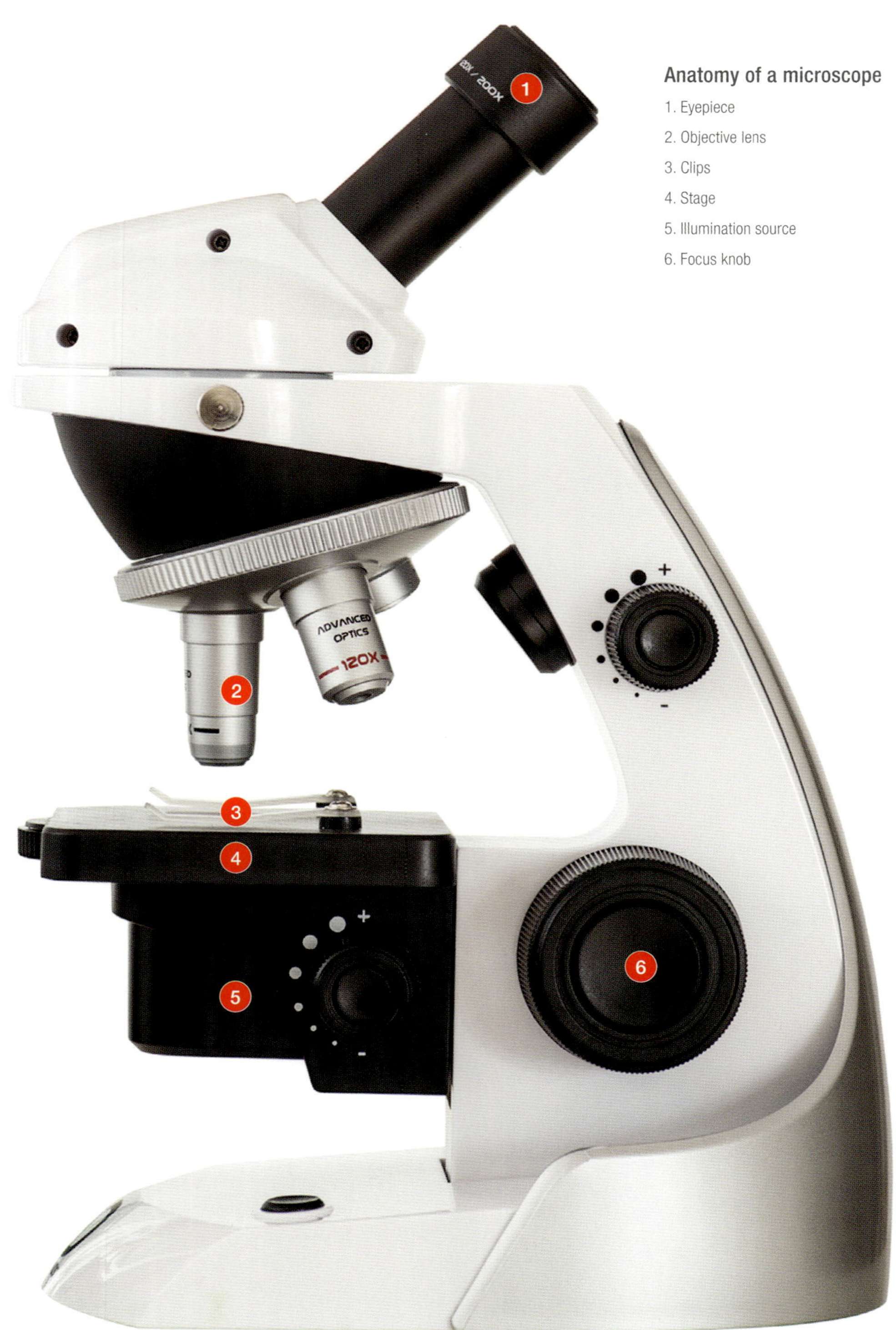

Anatomy of a microscope

1. Eyepiece
2. Objective lens
3. Clips
4. Stage
5. Illumination source
6. Focus knob

Filters

A filter is a sheet of glass, plastic, or optical resin that affects the light that passes through it in a pre-determined way. Filters can be bought in one of two forms: as circular screw-in filters that fit directly to a lens via a thread, or in a rectangular form that slots into a filter holder fitted to the lens via an adaptor ring. Both filter types have their advantages and there is no right or wrong answer as to which to use. In fact, many photographers mix and match according to the particular filter type, getting the best of both worlds in the process.

Filters can also be grouped into two broad categories: effects filters that add a creative effect to an image, such as a "starburst," and exposure-control filters, which are arguably more useful on a day-to-day basis.

Neutral Density Filters

Exposure-control filters reduce the amount of light that reaches the sensor. This effectively mimics shooting under lower light levels, which enables longer shutter speeds and/or larger apertures than would otherwise be possible to be used. Exposure-control filters can be colored so that the light is tinted, although for a more naturalistic image, neutral density (ND) filters are preferable, as they will not color the light.

ND filters are sold in a variety of strengths and can be used singly or stacked to vary the degree of exposure control. ND filters are most typically used to blur subject movement, especially in landscape photographs where they will affect the appearance of running water and wind-blown foliage. They are less useful for macro photography.

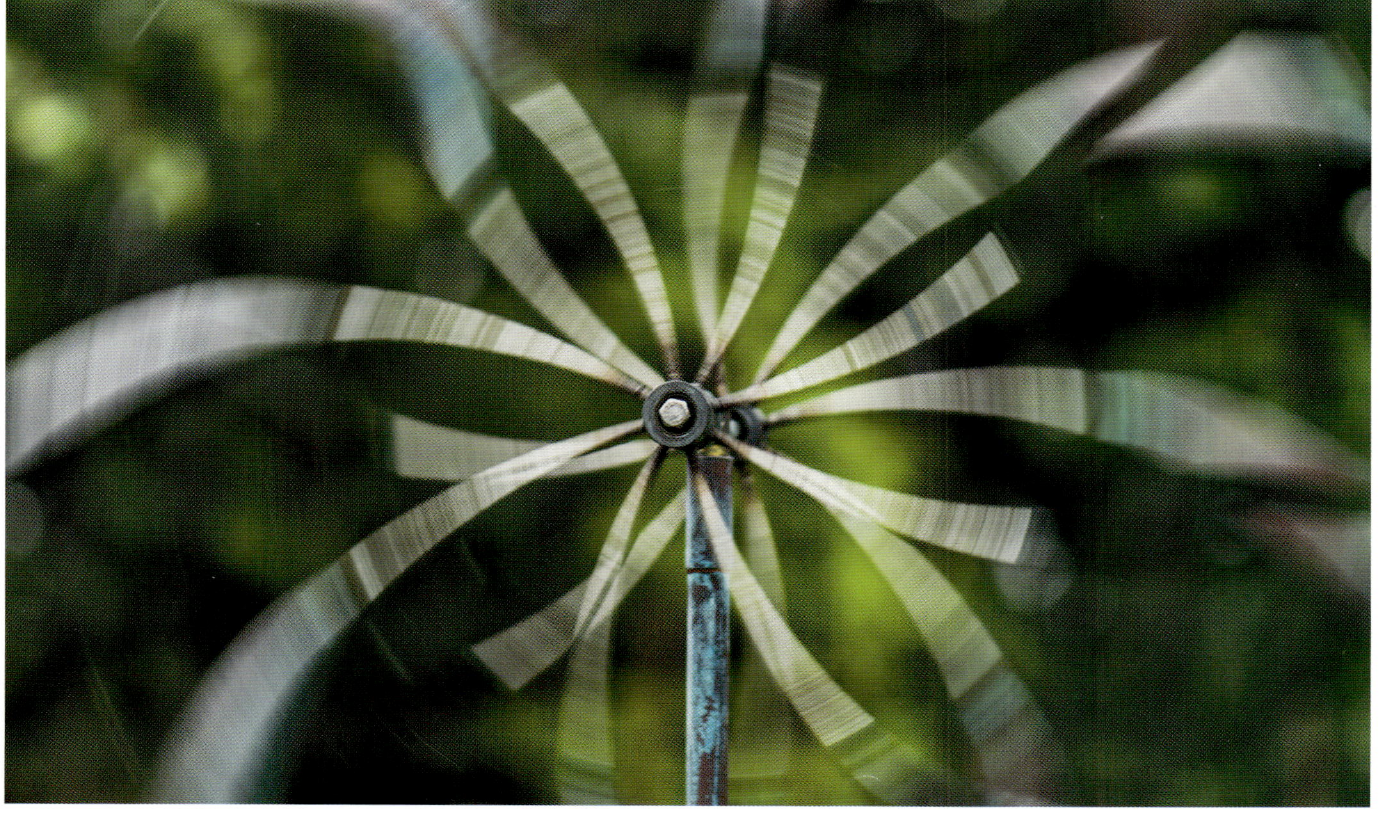

Left: ND filters are particularly useful when you want to combine a long shutter speed with a large aperture and the ambient light levels are high.
Focal length: 85mm
Aperture: f/1.8
Shutter speed: 1/13 sec.
ISO: 100

Polarizing Filter

A polarizing filter is another useful exposure-control filter, although it does more than simply restrict the amount of light passing through it. The most useful effect in terms of macro photography is the filter's ability to reduce the surface glare of non-metallic subjects. This effect only works at a particular angle—at roughly 35° to the surface being photographed—but is incredibly useful when it comes to removing the milky sheen seen on wet rocks or glossy still-life subjects. To control the effect, polarizing filters are turned via a ring until the required amount of adjustment has been achieved.

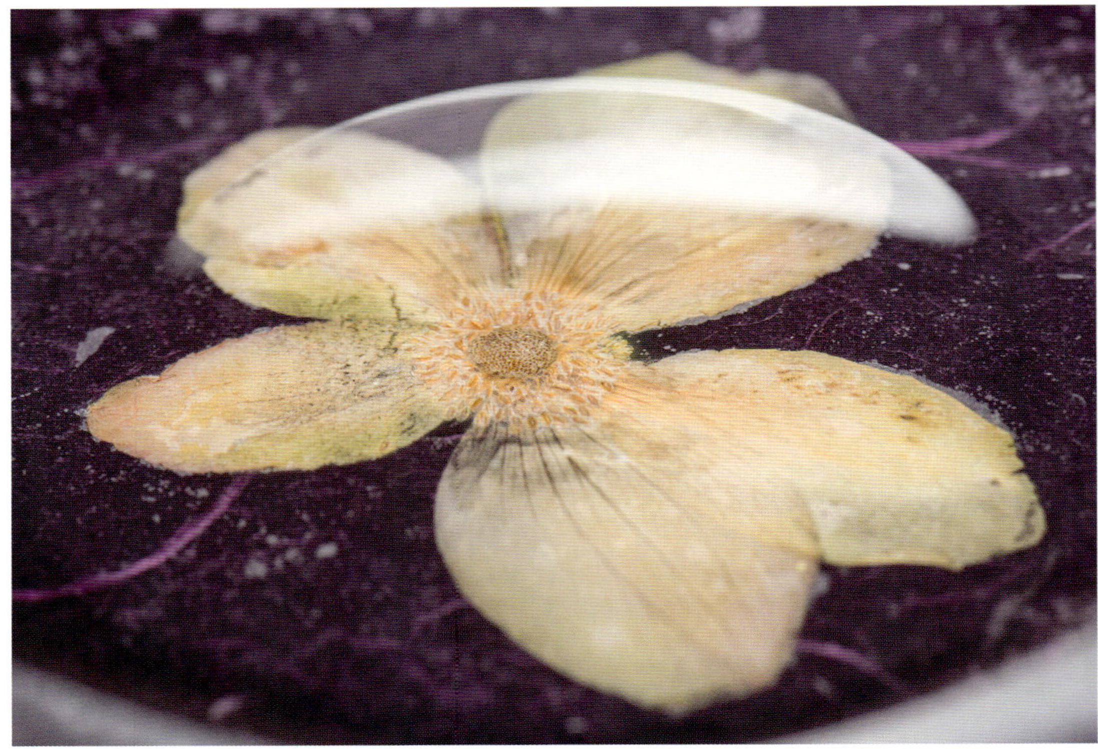

Right: Polarizing filters are incredibly useful when shooting glass subjects that are liable to reflect lighting or even the camera. Without a filter attached (top) this close-up of a glass dish exhibited a strong milky glare, which was caused by the light from a flash. Not only was the glare removed when a polarizing filter was used (bottom), but the underlying colors are more strongly saturated as well.

Focal length: 100mm macro lens

Aperture: f/11

Shutter speed: 1/250 sec.

ISO: 400

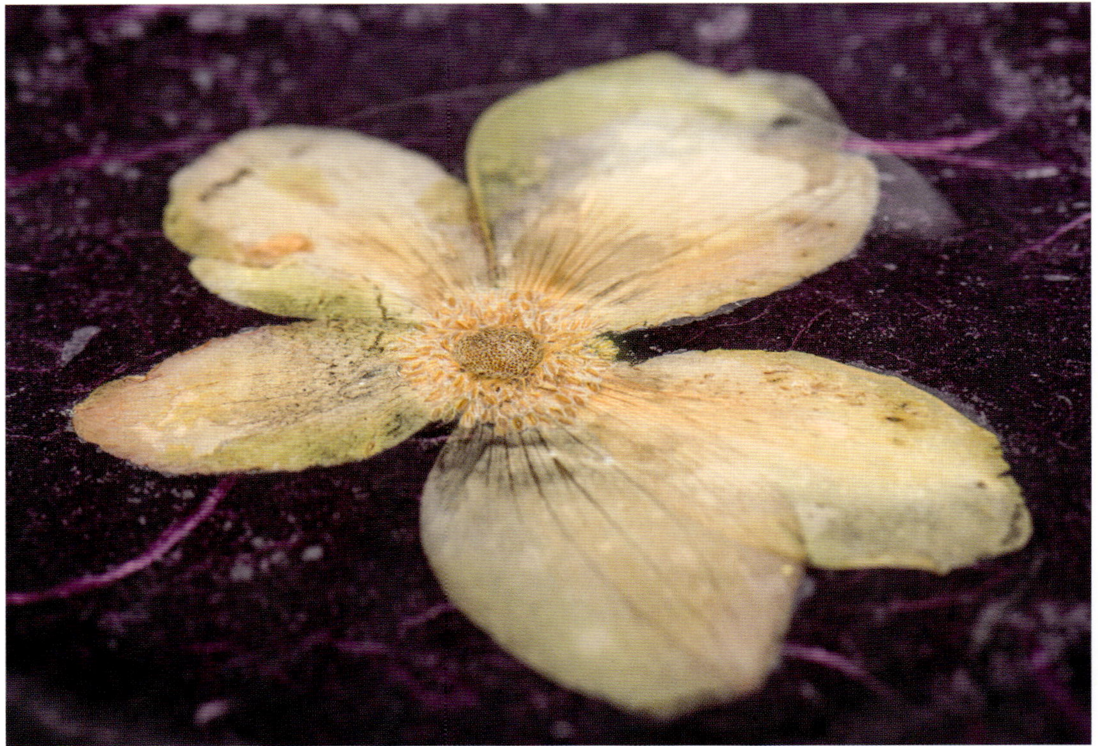

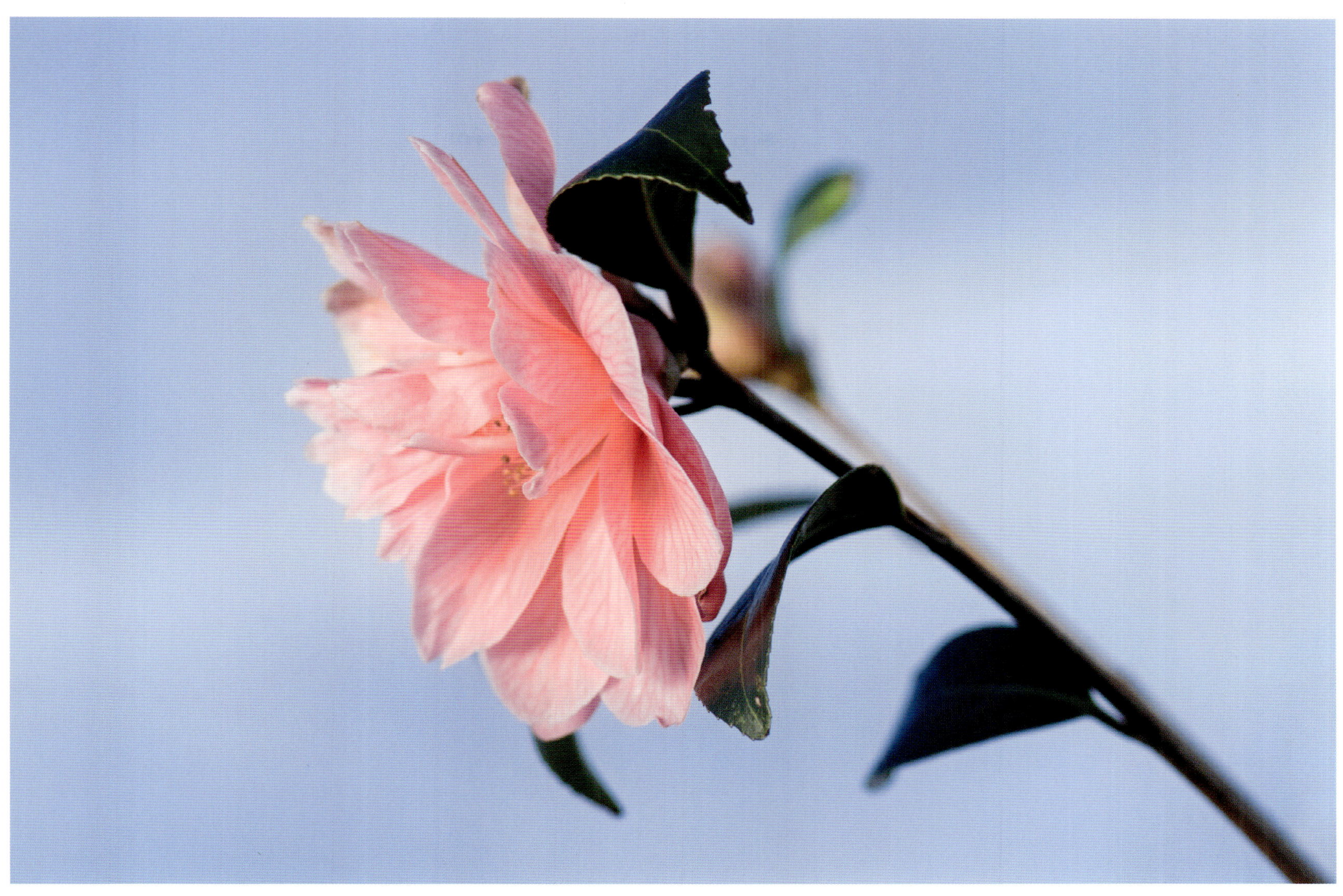

CIRCULAR & LINEAR POLARIZING FILTERS

"Circular" and "linear" describes the type of polarizing filter, not its shape. Circular polarizers are designed for DSLRs that use phase detection autofocus; linear polarizing filters interfere with autofocusing and should not be used.

Above: The second effect of a polarizing filter is to deepen a blue sky at 90° to the sun. This is generally less useful for macro photography unless you are shooting looking up at your subject with the sky as a background.

Focal length: 100mm macro lens

Aperture: f/3.5

Shutter speed: 1/10 sec.

ISO: 100

Miscellaneous Accessories

There are many pieces of equipment that, while not essential, will make macro photography easier and more enjoyable. Some of this equipment is easily found or can be created by modifying household objects. Other pieces of equipment are more specialized and may therefore carry a high price tag.

Flashlight

Shooting in low light or in shadow can cause a camera's AF system to struggle (or make it difficult for you to see your subject clearly through the viewfinder when focusing manually). Pointing the light beam from a flashlight temporarily onto your subject will provide the illumination the AF system needs (you would then need to lock focus, remove the light and meter before shooting). Flashlights can also be used as a source of illumination during an exposure: if the exposure is long enough you can use a flashlight to "paint with light," as outlined on page 121.

Make-Up Mirror

Small, handheld mirrors make excellent reflectors that can be used to bounce light underneath small subjects such as fungi. It is also possible to shoot the reflection of a subject that's otherwise inaccessible to a camera, although the silvered surface of a standard mirror is usually behind a glass substrate, which can cause a slight double reflection when using this technique. A mirror with the silvered surface above the substrate is ideal, but is more expensive and is more prone to scratching than a standard mirror.

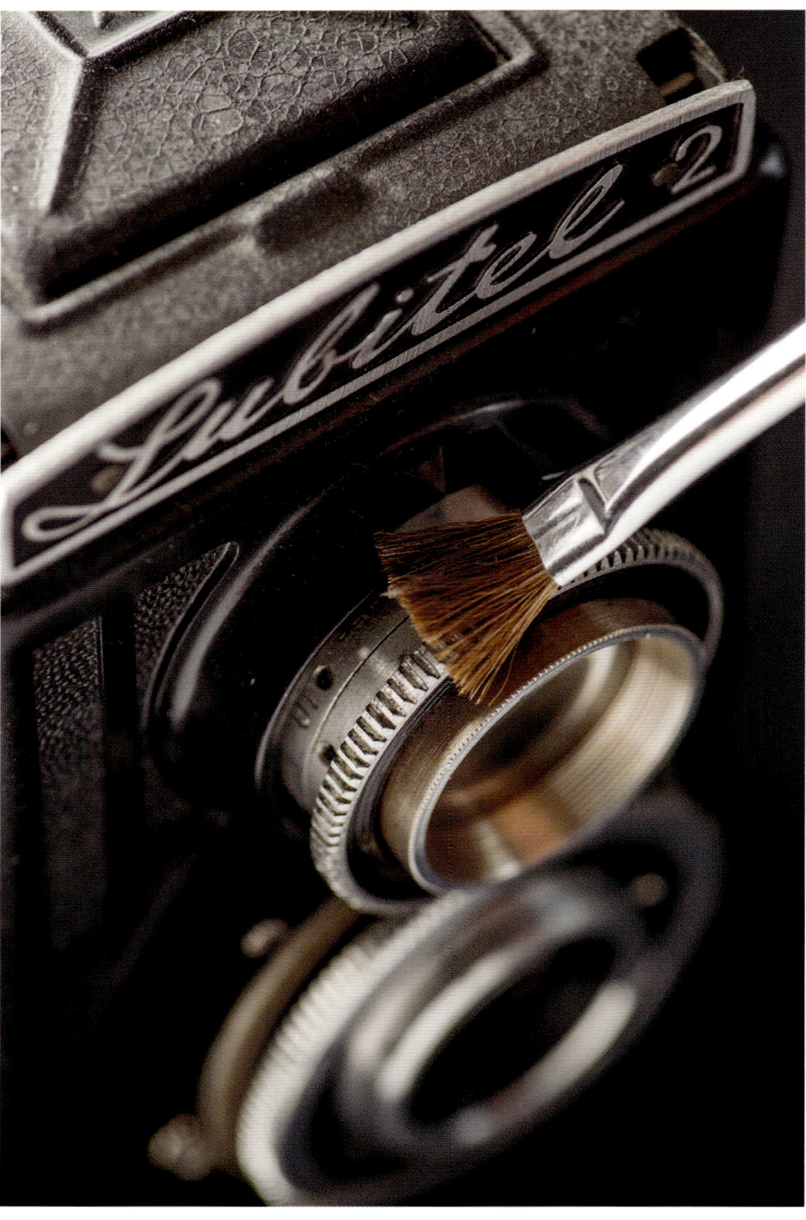

Left: As you'll see later in the book, dust is a big problem when shooting macro subjects. Soft paintbrushes can be used to quickly clean the surface of your subject.

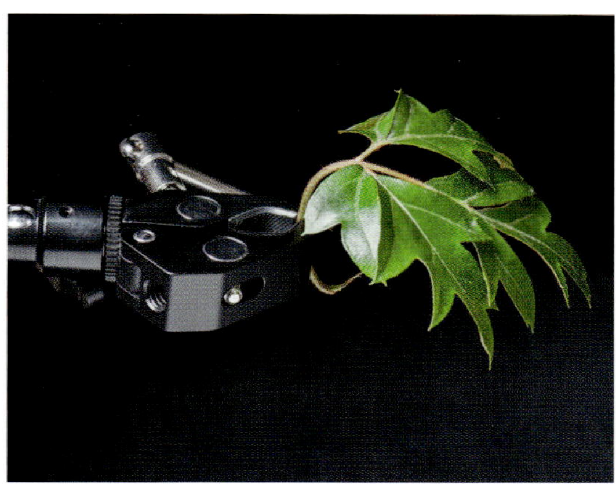

Clamps & Pins

Clamps and pins can be useful for holding a subject in place, especially when you are shooting something delicate that's easily blown away. When shooting delicate subjects, close the clamp sufficiently to hold your subject, without crushing it.

Clamps can also be used to position equipment such as reflectors or a temporary background.

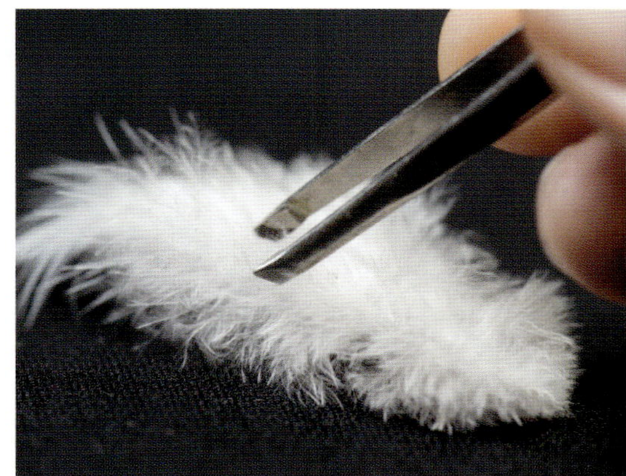

Tweezers

Fine-nosed tweezers are very useful for positioning delicate subjects and minimizing the potential for disturbing their surroundings.

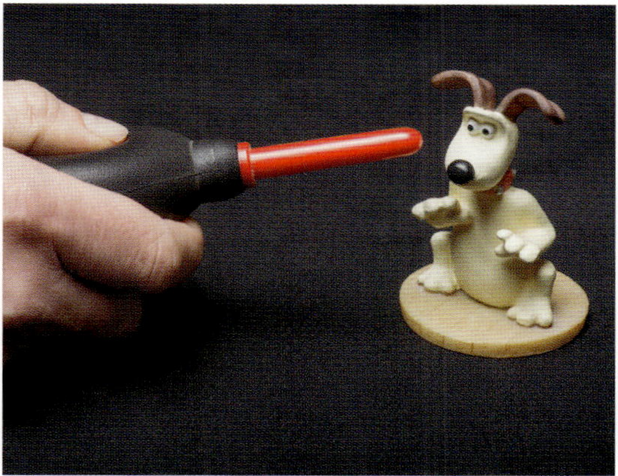

Blower Brush

Blower brushes are useful for removing light dust from your subjects before shooting. Blower brushes designed for photographic use can also be used to gently blow dust from camera sensors when they are cleaned manually.

Adhesive Tape

Adhesive tape can be used to secure your subject and/or equipment. "Gaffer" tape is useful for securing larger items, while low-tack decorator's tape is a better option when it comes to taping down delicate subjects that may otherwise tear or be destroyed when the tape is removed.

Angled Viewfinders

An angled viewfinder is a DSLR-only accessory that fits to the camera's optical viewfinder, making it easier to compose through the viewfinder when the camera is close to the ground. Some models also feature an option to magnify the image to make manual focusing easier. Angled viewfinders are arguably less relevant if your camera features a tilting LCD screen as this can be used to compose by switching to Live View.

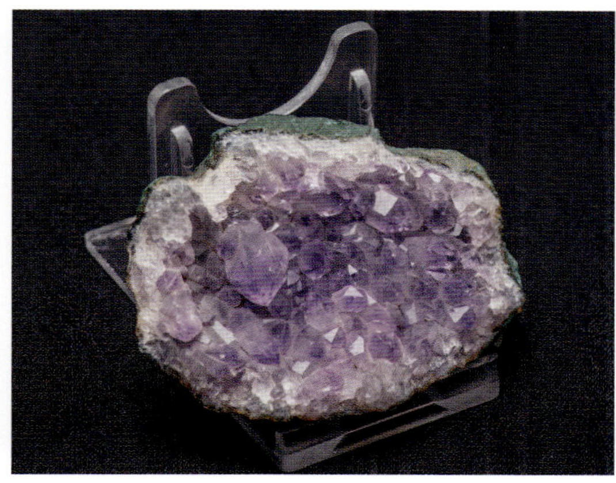

Blocks & Stands

Small blocks—both hard and soft—are useful tools that can help support a subject. Hard blocks are better suited to more robust macro subjects. Children's blocks that can be fixed together are ideal, as they allow you to quickly build support where necessary and are easily disassembled afterward.

Soft blocks made of sponge or polystyrene can be shaped easily, either by cutting or compressing. This type of support is better suited to more delicate subjects such as plants. Sticky putty or modeling clay can also be used as a temporary soft support and can be molded to suit the subject.

Jewelry and craft stores are a good source of adjustable stands that can be adapted to hold a variety of macro subjects.

Fishing Line

Occasionally, you will find a macro subject that needs to be surreptitiously supported. Transparent fishing line will allow you to support your subject from above and is more easily cloned out during postproduction than wire or string.

Chapter 2

Lenses

In order to shoot close-up or macro images you need to either modify a standard lens or fit a true macro lens to your camera. There are many, many different macro lenses and lens accessories to choose from, which can make for a difficult buying decision—it can be very expensive if you make a mistake!

Thankfully, changes to the specifications of macro lenses and accessories are very infrequent—they do happen, but not with the same regularity as other lenses. This makes it very easy to find online reviews for virtually every lens or accessory ever produced. However, there is a lot of "white noise" on the Internet, so you need to find and take note of reputable review websites written by experienced photographers.

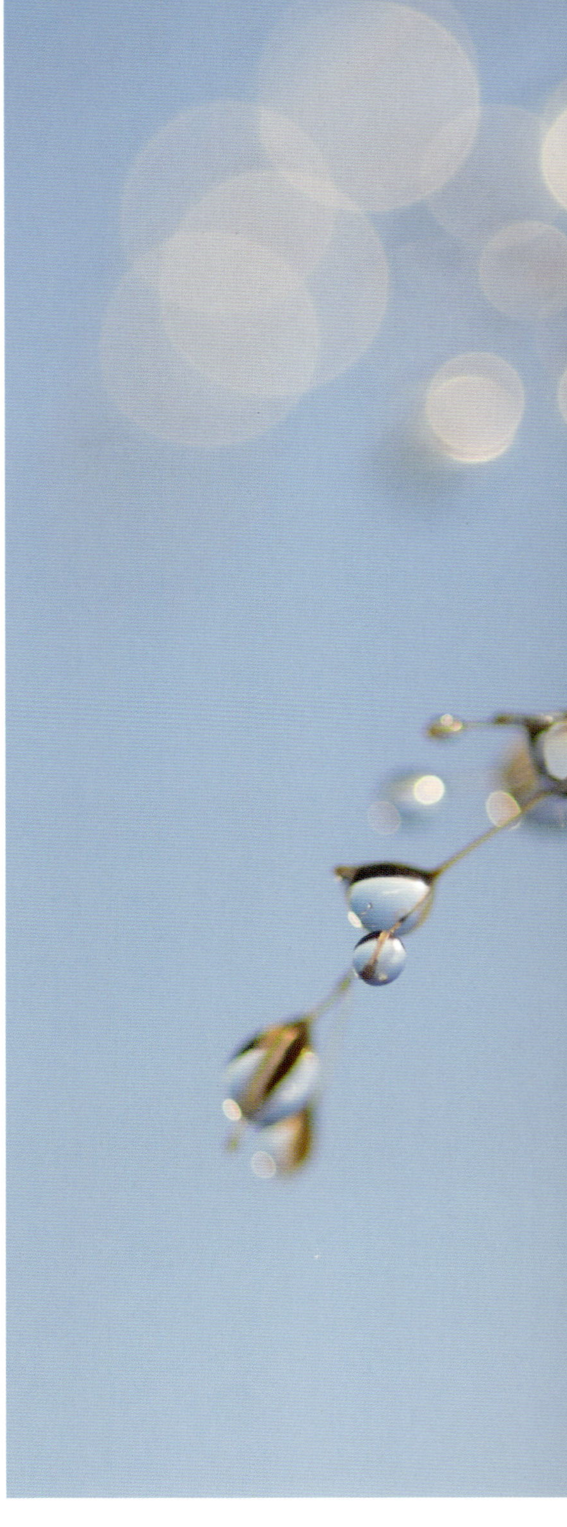

Right: One aspect of macro photography that can be frustrating is the lack of depth of field, particularly at large apertures. However, this can be used creatively to limit sharpness to a specific area of an image. For this shot, with a large aperture set, I focused precisely on one drop of water. The bright out-of-focus highlights at the top left of the image were caused by sunlight reflecting on droplets of water higher up the plant.

Focal length: 100mm

Aperture: f/4.5

Shutter speed: 1/1600

ISO: 400

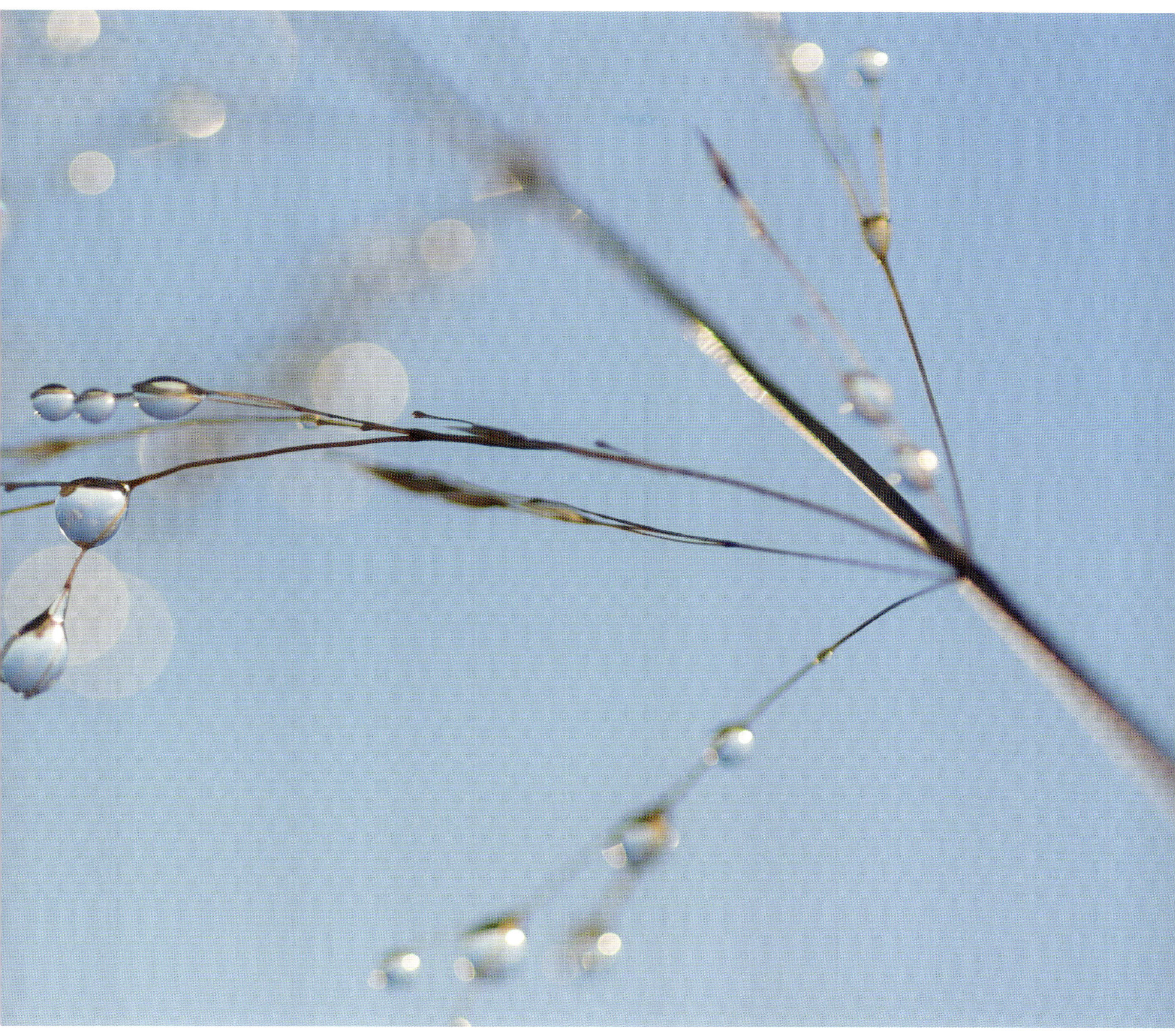

Basic Lens Concepts

Close-Up Vs. Macro

The terms close-up and macro are often used interchangeably, but technically there is a very precise difference between the two. A true macro image is one where the image of the subject projected by the lens onto the camera's sensor is life-size or larger. So, if the subject were ½in (12.5mm) wide, the image projected onto the sensor would also be ½in (12.5mm) wide.

The macro capabilities of a lens are commonly shown as a reproduction ratio. A life-size image projected onto a sensor is said to have a reproduction ratio of 1:1, twice life-size is 2:1 (1in (25mm) in the example above), and so on.

A non-macro lens cannot project a life-sized image onto the sensor, so the reproduction ratio would be 1:2 for a half life-sized image, 1:4 for a quarter life-sized image, and so on.

Magnification

To confuse matters, not all lens manufacturers use a reproduction ratio to define the macro capabilities of its lenses; some manufacturers use a magnification figure instead. This makes it slightly more difficult to quickly compare one lens with another, although it is relatively straightforward to convert a reproduction ratio into a magnification figure and vice versa.

A true macro lens has a magnification of 1x or higher, whereas a non-macro lens has a magnification figure lower than 1x (shown as a decimal fraction, such as 0.25x for quarter life-size, for example). If the magnification figure of a lens is 1 or higher then the reproduction ratio is shown as *magnification figure:1* (a 2x magnification would therefore be 2:1).

If the magnification figure is lower than 1, then divide 1 by the magnification figure and place the result on the right side of the reproduction ratio. For example, if the magnification factor is 0.25x, divide 1 by 0.25x. This gives 4, so in this case the reproduction ratio would be 1:4.

To convert a reproduction ratio into a magnification figure simply divide the number on the left side of the ratio by the number on the right (2:1 would give a magnification figure of 2x and 1:2 would give a magnification figure of 0.5x).

Right: Although shot with a macro lens, this is not a true macro image in the strictest sense of the word. The foreground leaf was approximately 2in (5cm) long, which is far larger than the sensor inside the camera.

Focal length: 100mm macro lens

Aperture: f/5

Shutter speed: 1/6 sec.

ISO: 200

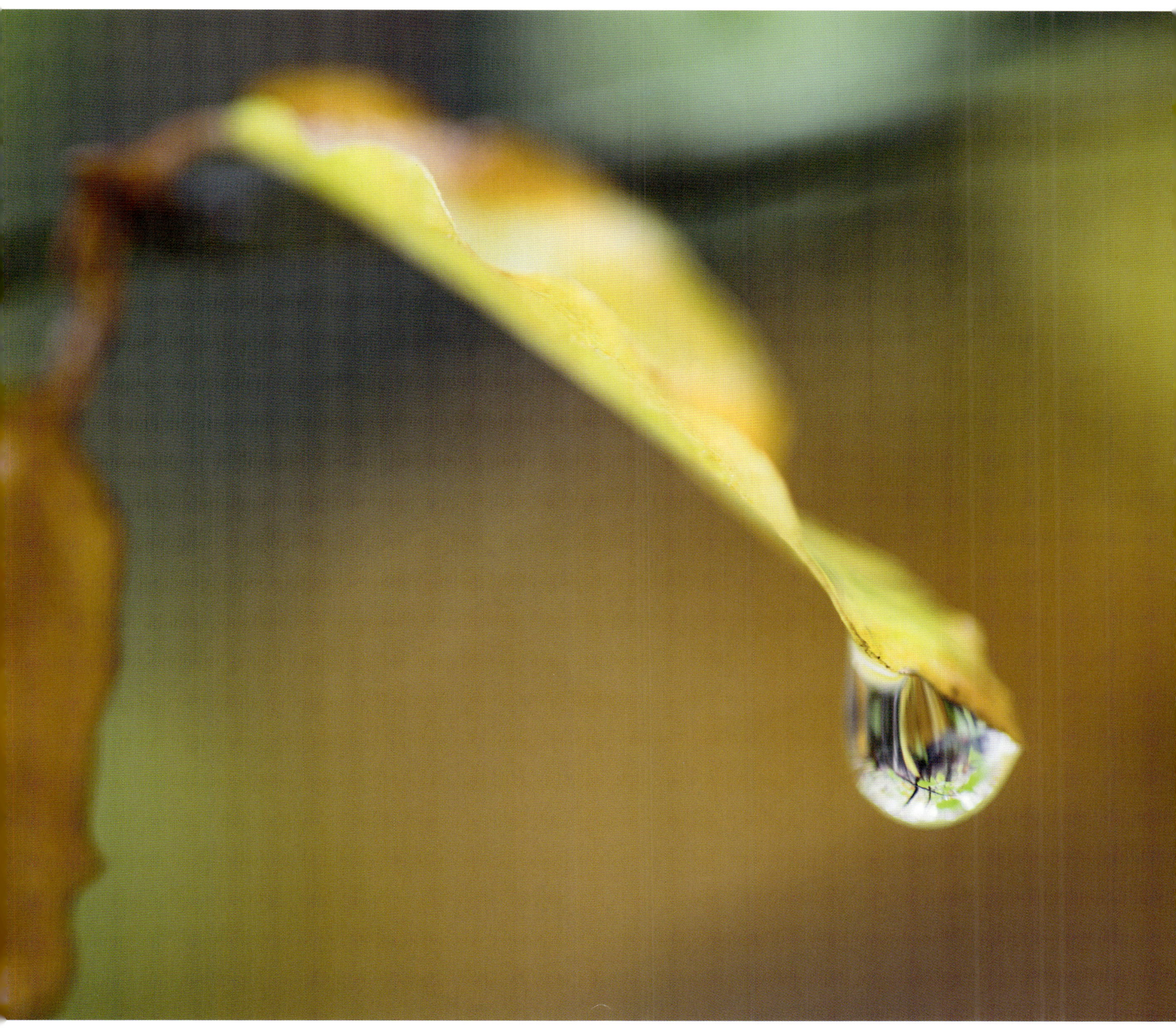

Focal Length

Lenses are needed to focus light onto a camera's sensor. When a lens is focused at infinity (∞), parallel rays converge to form a sharp image on the focal plane. This is where the camera's sensor is placed and is often indicated on the body of the camera with a ⊖ symbol. The focal length of a lens is the physical measurement—in millimeters—from the optical center of the lens to the focal plane.

In conjunction with the size of the sensor inside the camera, the focal length of a lens determines the angle of view of the lens. The shorter the focal length of the lens, the wider the angle of view; short focal length lenses are often referred to as wide-angle lenses for this reason. Short focal length lenses also reduce magnification and appear to exaggerate space, making elements in a scene seem smaller and further apart.

The longer the focal length of a lens, the narrower the angle of view and the greater the magnification of the image. This appears to make elements in a scene closer together relative to each other and larger in the image frame.

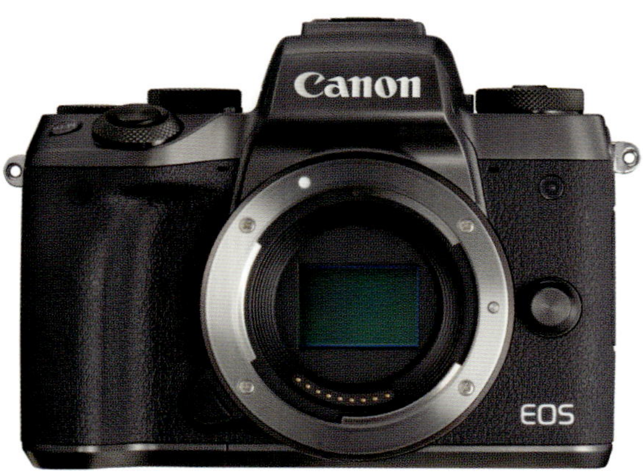

Below: The most common sensor size used in DSLRs and mirrorless cameras is APS-C, as it offers a good compromise between image quality and cost.
© Canon

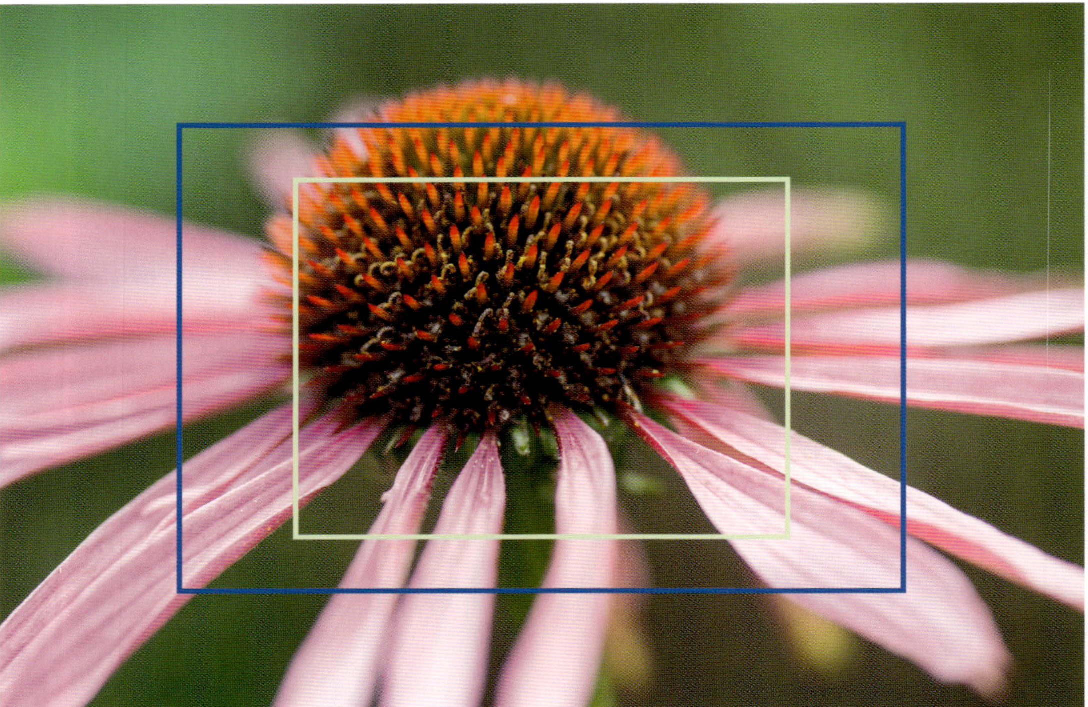

Sensor Size

The size of the sensor is the second factor that affects the angle of view of a lens at a particular focal length. There are three sensor sizes commonly used in system cameras: full frame (36 x 24mm); APS-C (around 24 x 16mm); and Micro Four Thirds (17.3 x 13mm). If you were to fit a lens designed for a full-frame camera onto a Micro Four Thirds camera, the angle of view would be far narrower, leading to an apparent increase in focal length.

However, it is not that the focal length has changed (this is a fixed measurement of distance), but simply that the image projected by the lens has effectively been cropped by the smaller sensor. The degree of cropping is known as the "crop factor," which is used to compare the angle of view of a lens fitted to a full-frame camera and the angle of view of the lens when fitted to a camera with a smaller sensor.

Above: Using a camera with a smaller sensor does not increase the magnification of the lens, so a true macro lens will create a 1:1 image no matter what camera it is attached to. What does change is the angle of view; how much or how little of the subject is captured. This image was shot using a full-frame camera and a 100mm macro lens. If the same lens had been fitted to an APS-C camera, only the area within the blue box would have been captured. On a Micro Four Thirds camera the angle of view would have been restricted to the yellow box.

Focal length: 100mm macro lens

Aperture: f/5

Shutter speed: 1/250 sec.

ISO: 400

ANGLE OF VIEW

Angle of view is measured in degrees (°) and describes the extent of a scene projected by the lens onto the camera's sensor. Angle of view can be used to describe the horizontal, vertical, or diagonal coverage, but it is usually the diagonal coverage that is shown unless noted otherwise.

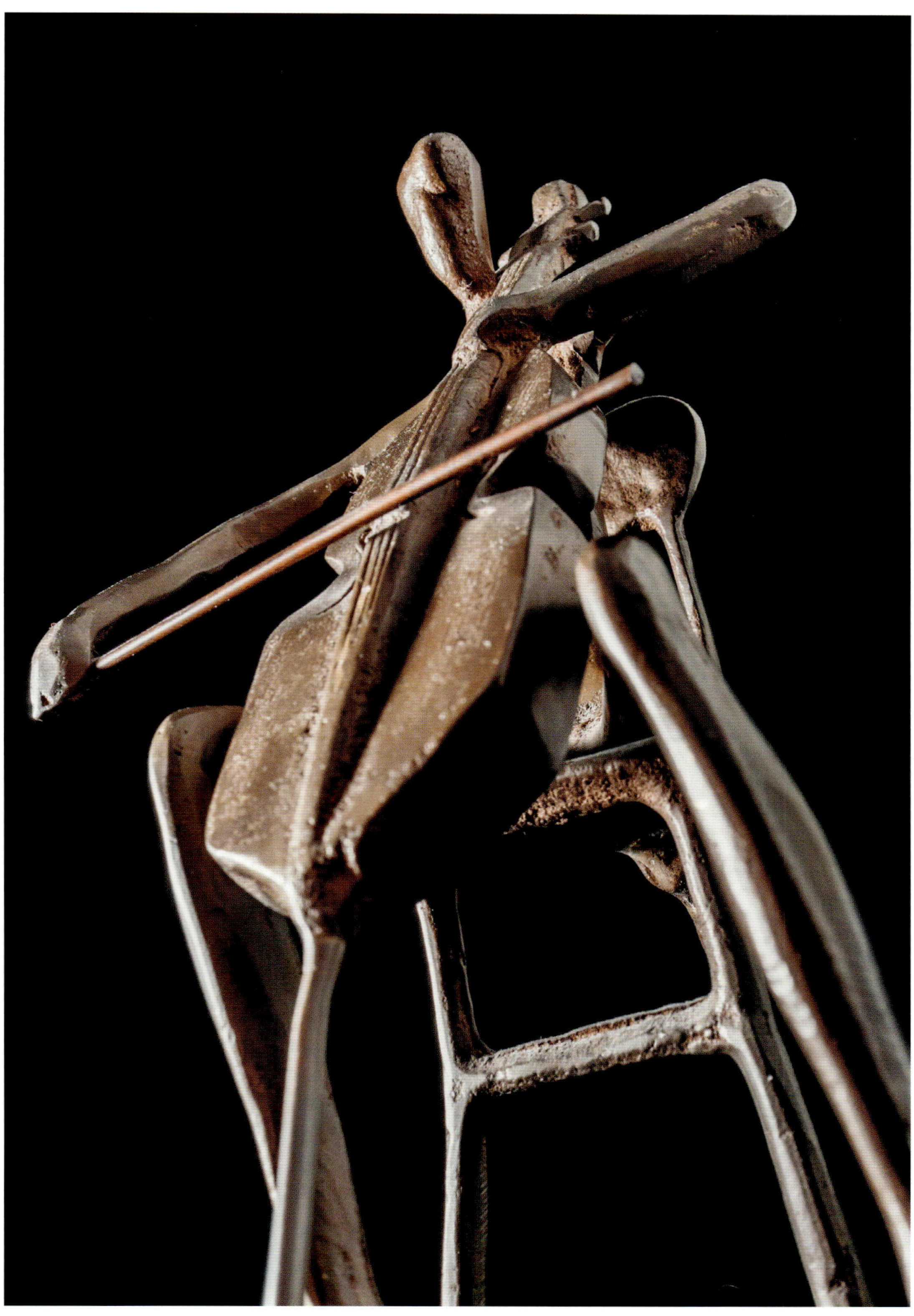

Perspective

In photography, perspective describes the spatial relationships of the various elements in an image. This includes factors such as the apparent distance of the elements from one another and their relative sizes. It is a commonly held belief that altering the focal length of the lens changes the perspective of an image, but this is not quite true.

Perspective is only altered by moving the position of the camera relative to the scene being photographed. For example, if you wanted to match the framing of a subject when swapping between a shorter focal length and a longer one, you would need to move further back from the subject. It is this movement—not the change in the focal length—that alters the perspective.

As a result of the shooting distance, longer focal length lenses generally appear to produce a flatter perspective: space is more compressed, with elements in the image appearing closer together and their relative sizes less exaggerated. As a very general rule, a flatter perspective is more esthetically pleasing and more flattering to the subject. However, like most rules it is there to be broken if it results in a stronger image.

Left: Wide-angle lenses often have a close minimum focus distance, particularly on compact cameras. However, shooting so close with a wide-angle lens results in a very distorted perspective and can also lead to your subject being knocked by the lens.

Focal length: 35mm

Aperture: f/22

Shutter speed: 1/250 sec.

ISO: 400

Working Distance

The working distance of a lens is the distance from the subject to the front element of the lens. This is not the same as the minimum focusing distance, which is the distance from the subject to the focal plane inside the camera (where either the sensor or film is located). The working distance of a lens is usually irrelevant when it is used to shoot "normal" subjects such as landscapes, but it has important consequences when shooting macro images.

The longer the focal length of a macro lens, the greater the working distance will be. This determines how easily a subject can be successfully illuminated or whether a subject is likely to be disturbed or knocked: the greater the working distance, the easier it is to add lights or fit a lens hood or filters. When shooting subjects such as insects, a less intrusive approach is usually required, so longer focal length lenses are preferable. However, the longer the focal length of a macro lens, the heavier and more expensive it will be. A short working distance is therefore a necessary compromise when using shorter focal length macro lenses.

CALCULATING WORKING DISTANCE

Lens manufacturers generally specify the minimum focusing distance of a lens, but not the working distance. However, it is possible to calculate the working distance at a 1:1 reproduction ratio if you have a few other pieces of information: the physical length of the lens when set to the desired focal length (if it is a zoom lens) and the flange distance of your camera system.

To calculate the working distance simply add the physical length of the lens to the flange distance and then subtract the result from the stated minimum focusing distance.

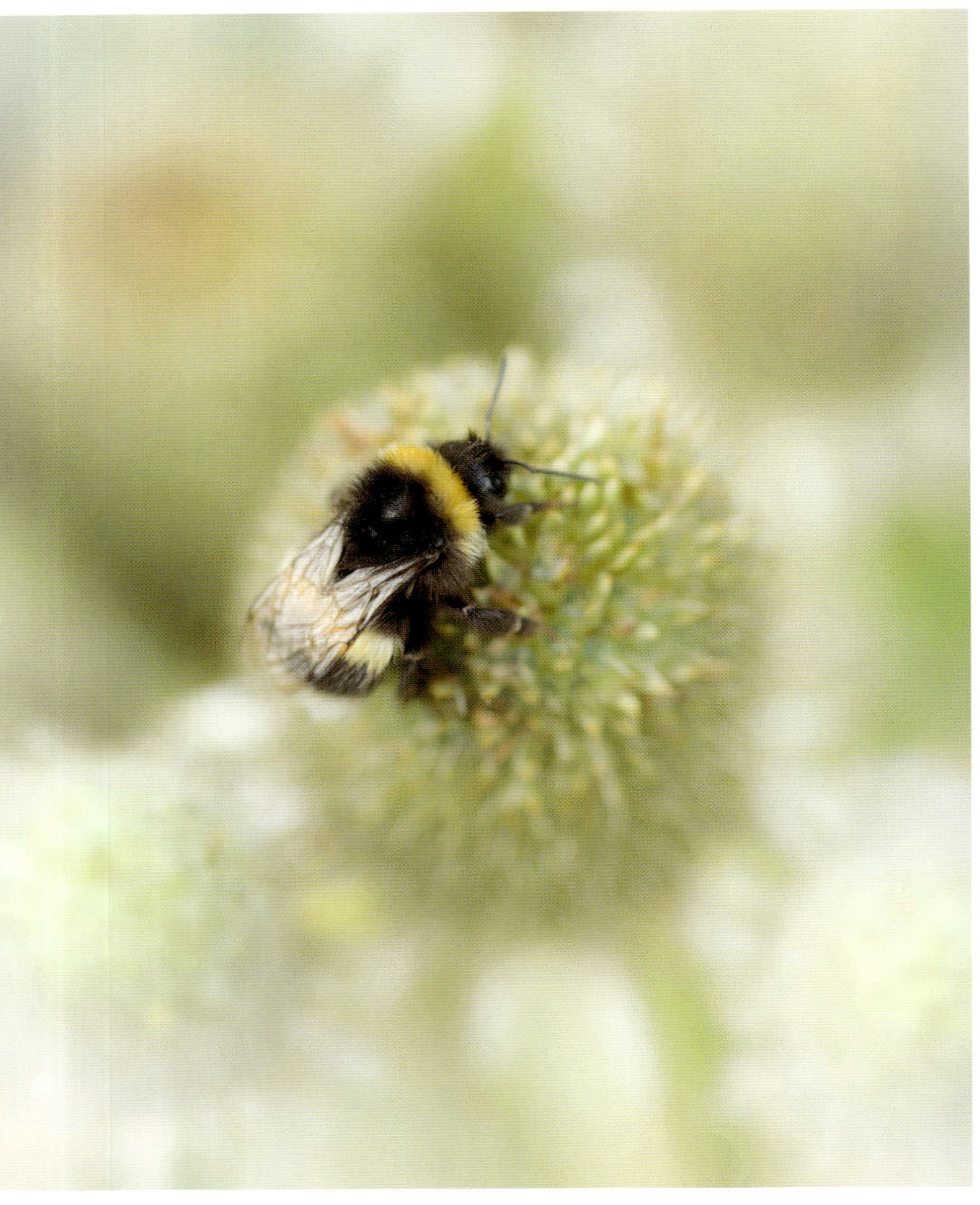

Above: A longer working distance makes it less likely that you'll disturb skittish subjects such as insects.

Focal length: 100mm macro lens

Aperture: f/7.1

Shutter speed: 1/200 sec.

ISO: 400

Primes & Zooms

There are two types of lens. The first has a single, fixed focal length and is known as a prime lens. The other covers a range of focal lengths and is referred to as a zoom lens. Zoom lenses are incredibly useful, as they allow you to fine tune the composition of an image merely by turning the zoom ring. A single zoom lens can also replace a number of different primes, making life far more convenient in the process, and it reduces the risk that you will have the wrong lens fitted to your camera at the wrong moment (an all too common occurrence if you only work with prime lenses).

As versatile as zoom lenses are, true macro lenses are invariably primes. This means that you have to work harder to create a pleasing composition (moving the camera or using adjustment rails), but the advantage of prime lenses—and this is true of macro lenses—is that they typically have large maximum apertures. This can make it easier to focus both manually and automatically, thanks to a brighter viewfinder image and more light for the camera's AF system.

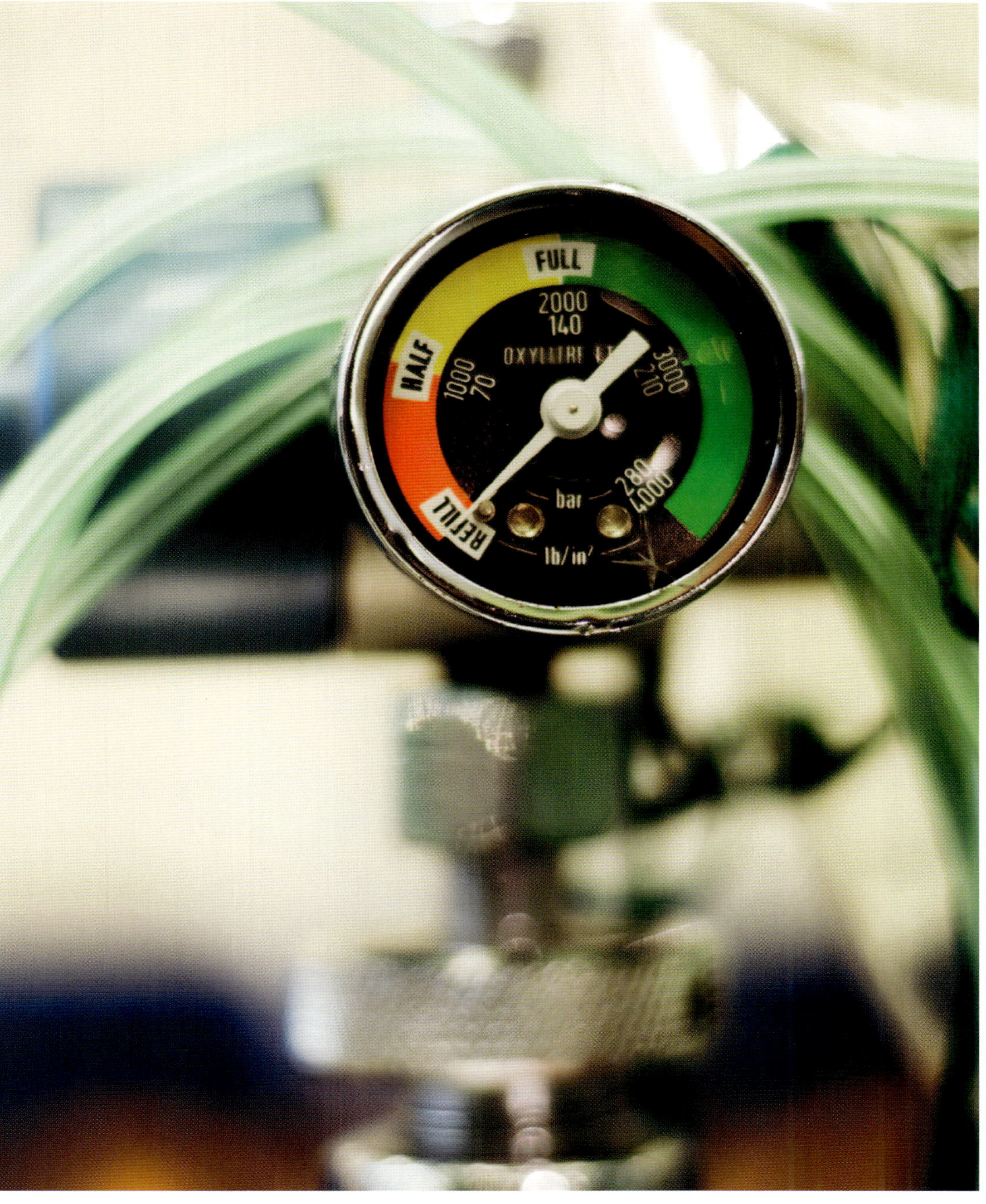

Above: A good zoom lens is worth its weight in gold when shooting in a more spontaneous style. A fast zoom is even better, particularly when you cannot use a tripod.

Focal length: 50mm

Aperture: f/2.8

Shutter speed: 1/15 sec.

ISO: 250

Close-Up Lenses

An alternative to a dedicated macro lens is a close-up lens. This is a simple supplementary lens that screws directly to the filter thread of a "regular" camera lens. Unlike accessories such as reversing rings or extension tubes, close-up lenses can be used to add close-focusing capability to virtually any camera (ideally there should be a filter thread on the lens, but—with care—it is possible to hold a close-up lens temporarily in place if there is no filter thread).

Close-up lenses are sold in different strengths, which are defined by a diopter value: the higher the diopter value, the stronger the lens and the greater the magnification. A close-up lens with a diopter of +1 is relatively weak and will only provide modest magnification. At the opposite end of the scale, a +12 diopter lens is the strongest close-up lens generally available and can be used to achieve 1:1 magnification on lenses with a focal length of 70mm or higher.

Close-up lenses are a good first step into shooting close-up and macro images. They do not affect exposure or AF, so your camera will behave as normal. They are also far cheaper than dedicated macro lenses and can be conveniently kept in a pocket or camera bag to instantly add close-focusing capability to a lens.

As well as being used singly, close-up lenses can be stacked together to increase the degree of magnification. However, this will result in a noticeable drop in image quality, particularly around the edges of the image.

Close-up lenses can also exacerbate the optical failings of a camera lens (such as chromatic aberration). For this reason it is generally preferable to fit them to prime lenses rather than zooms. In any case, to achieve the best possible image quality when using close-up lenses, the aperture of the camera lens needs to be set 3–4-stops smaller than maximum.

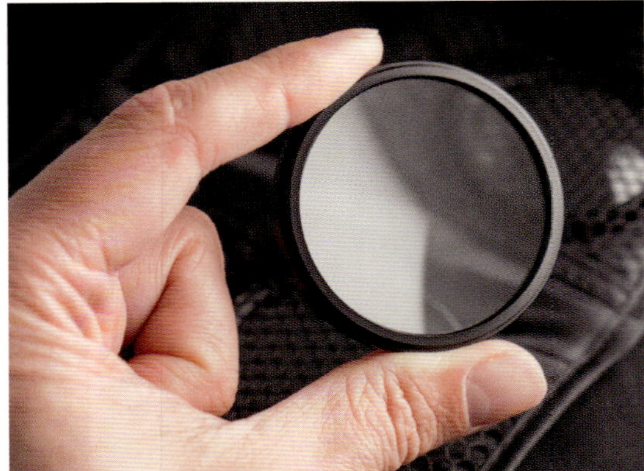

Above: Close-up lenses are available with different filter thread sizes, so choose one that fits the lens you most want to use it with. To fit a close-up lens to lenses with different filter thread sizes you would need to use either a step-up ring or a step-down ring. The latter option is not recommended, though, as this can cause vignetting around the edges of the image.

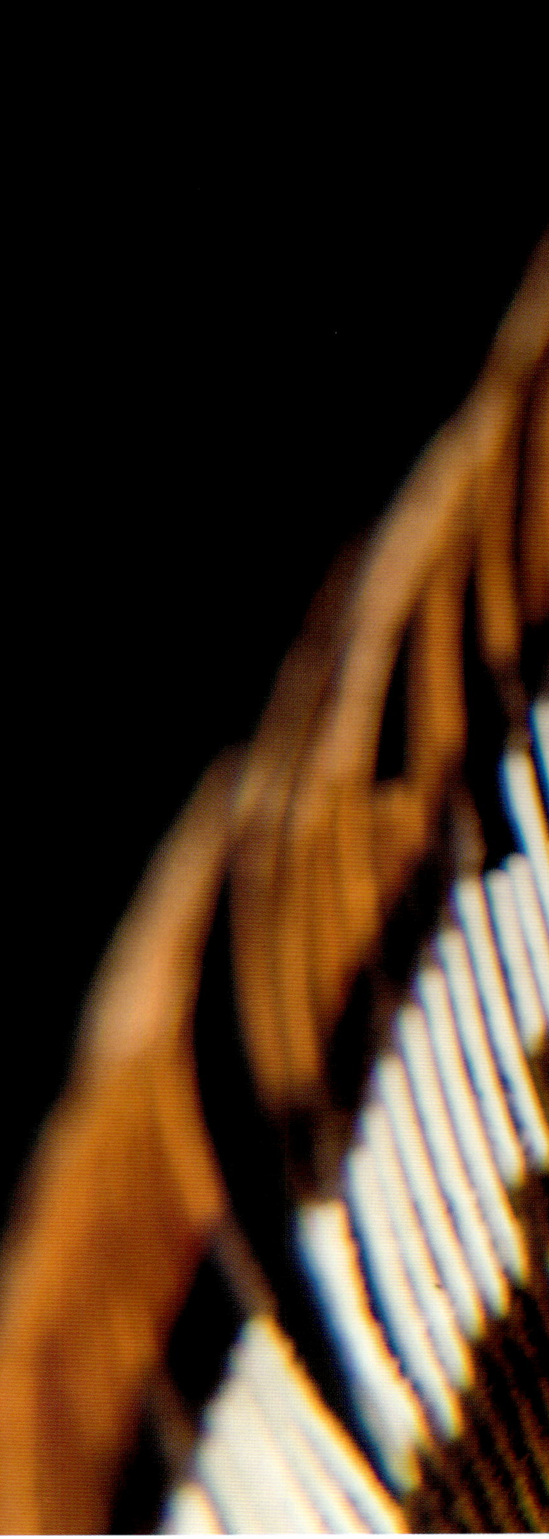

Right: Close-up lenses allow extremely close focusing with standard lenses: this pheasant feather was only ¾in (2cm) wide. However, there are downsides to close-up lenses. Low cost lenses often only deliver mediocre image quality—softness, chromatic aberration, and distortion are common problems. More expensive close-up lenses are described as "achromatic," which shows the lens has been designed to minimize the amount of chromatic aberration.

Focal length: 50mm lens + 10x close-up lens

Aperture: f/29

Shutter speed: 3 sec.

ISO: 100

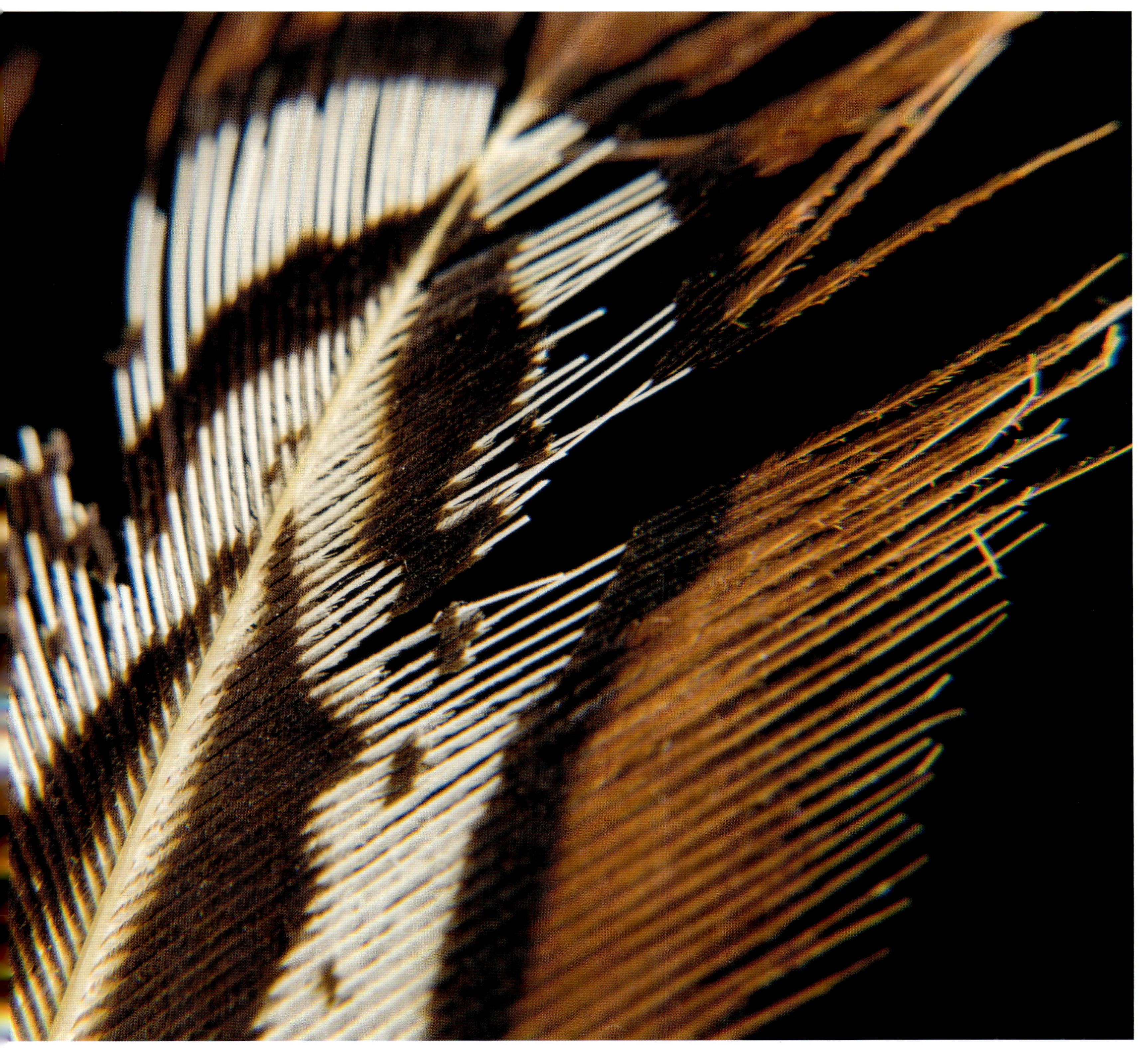

Reversing Rings

A reversing ring is a simple metal adaptor that lets you fit a lens backward on a camera. Although this may sound slightly eccentric, reversing rings can turn normal lenses into very respectable macro lenses. The shorter the focal length of the lens you use, the greater the magnification possible. Generally lenses in the focal length range of 28–50mm work well reversed, with prime lenses more suitable than zooms.

On one side of the reversing ring is the camera mount fitting. The other side is a male thread that screws onto the filter thread of the lens you want to reverse. When you buy a reversing ring you therefore need to buy one that has the correct lens mount for your camera and the correct thread size for the lens you will be using. If you want to use two or more lenses (and they have different filter thread sizes) you will either need to invest in multiple reversing rings or use step-up or step-down adaptor rings to modify a single ring.

One big advantage of reversing rings is that they are simple and light, which means they are easily stored in the pocket of a camera bag.

However, as there is no electronic connection carried through a reversing ring, neither focus nor aperture can be set using the camera's control dials. Although this may seem like a drawback it can actually be beneficial. For example, it means that you can use any lens, including old and obsolescent lenses that can be bought relatively cheaply secondhand. This makes reversing rings one of the most cost-effective ways to start shooting high-quality macro imagery—the key is using a manual focus lens with a manual aperture.

Reversing a lens has a number of other disadvantages compared to shooting with a dedicated macro lens. Although the magnification will be high with a reversing ring, the working distance will be inconveniently short. Reversed lenses are also prone to flare from strong lighting, making the use of backlighting more difficult (and using lens hoods and filters isn't easy due to the reversal of the lens).

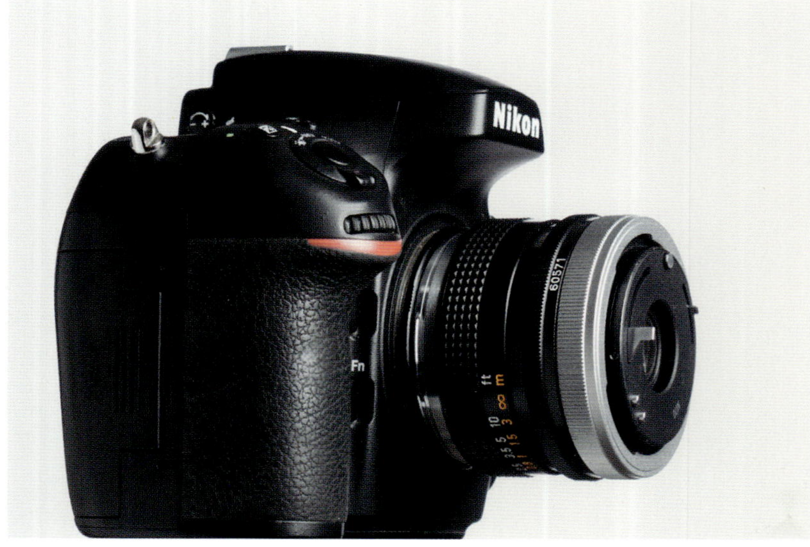

Left: Old Minolta MD and Canon FD lenses are ideal for fitting to a reversing ring, as they are both manual focus designs with an aperture ring. They are also readily available from dealers and through online websites such as eBay.

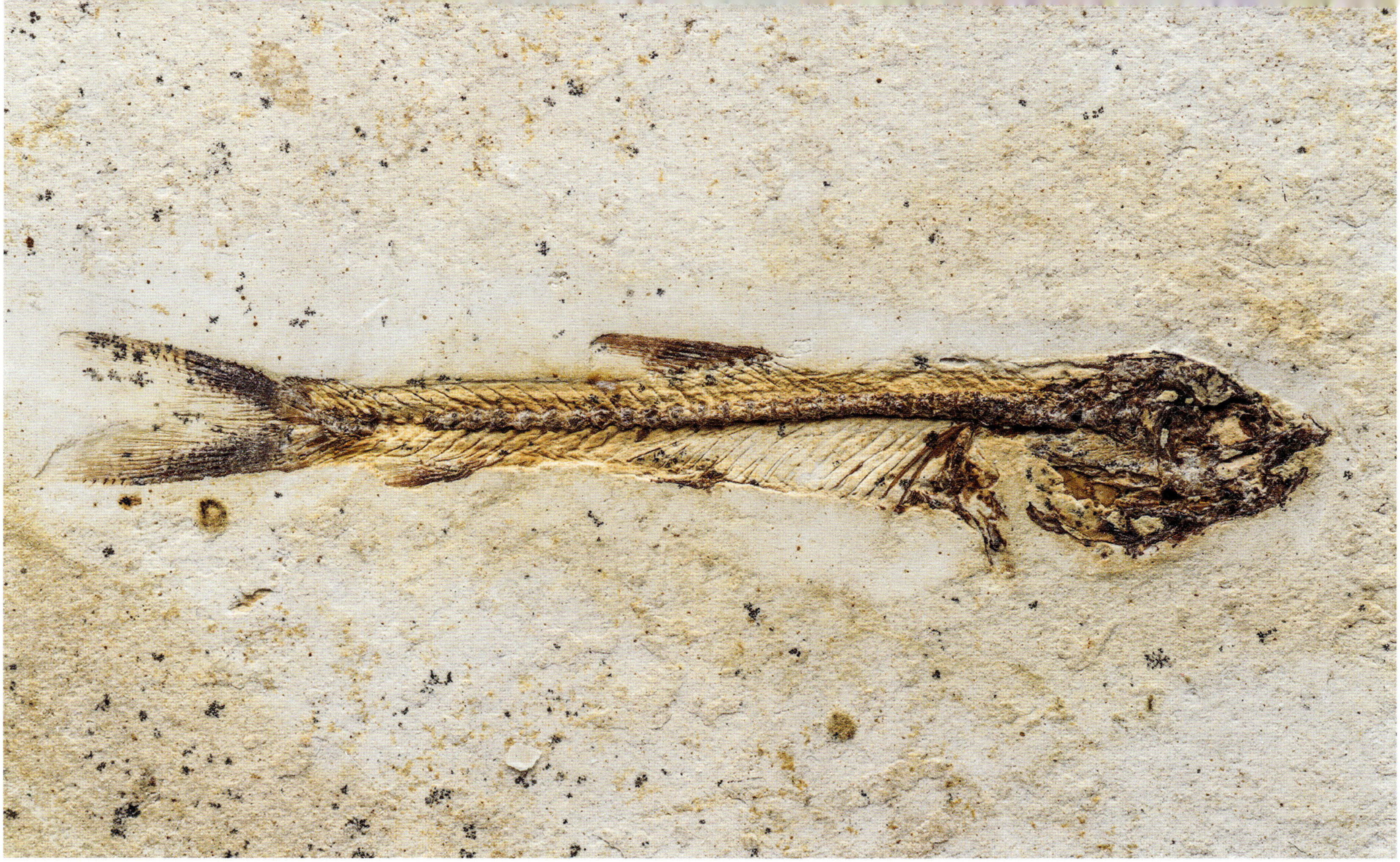

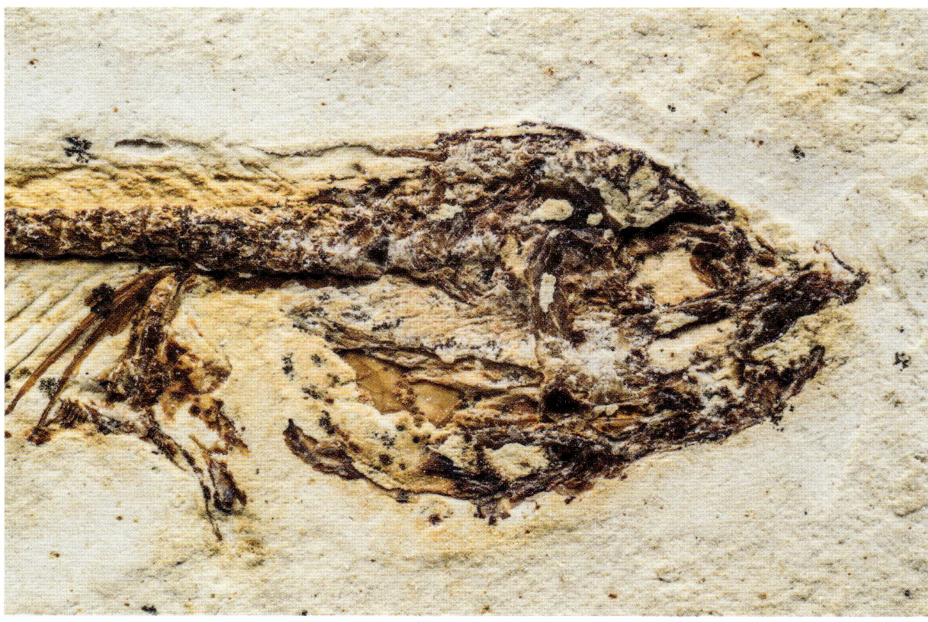

Above: This photograph of a tiny fossil fish was shot with a conventional macro lens at just less than 1:1 magnification. The working distance with lens was approximately 6¼in (16cm).

Focal length: 100mm macro lens

Aperture: f/11

Shutter speed: 1/8 sec.

ISO: 100

Left: By switching to a reversed 28mm lens the magnification could be increased considerably, but the working distance was reduced to just 1½in (4cm). Because of the increase in magnification the shutter speed needed to be extended from 1/8 sec. to 2 seconds.

Focal length: 28mm lens reversed

Aperture: f/11

Shutter speed: 2 sec.

ISO: 100

Coupling Rings

A coupling ring is superficially similar to a reversing ring, but instead of a lens mount, both sides of the ring feature a male filter thread. This allows you to join two lenses together using their respective filter threads. As with reversing rings, you need to choose your coupling ring carefully to match the lenses you want to join. Coupling rings can also be used on compact and bridge cameras providing the camera lens has a filter thread. However, care should be taken that the attached lens isn't so heavy that it damages the camera's own lens.

Using A Coupling Ring

The lens at the front should be set to its maximum aperture (older manual lenses are again ideal for this reason), while the aperture of the lens attached to the camera should be set to achieve the desired depth of field. As this lens is fitted directly to the camera, aperture control will still be available (AF will still be available too, although the lens may struggle to achieve focus if the subject is insufficiently illuminated.)

One problem that can occur when using a coupling ring is heavy vignetting around the edges of the image. Generally, the greater the difference in the focal length of the lenses used and the smaller the aperture of the main lens, the heavier the vignetting will be. Cropping an image in postproduction is one possible solution; another option is to use a relatively large aperture in combination with focus stacking to achieve the required depth of field (see pages 124–125).

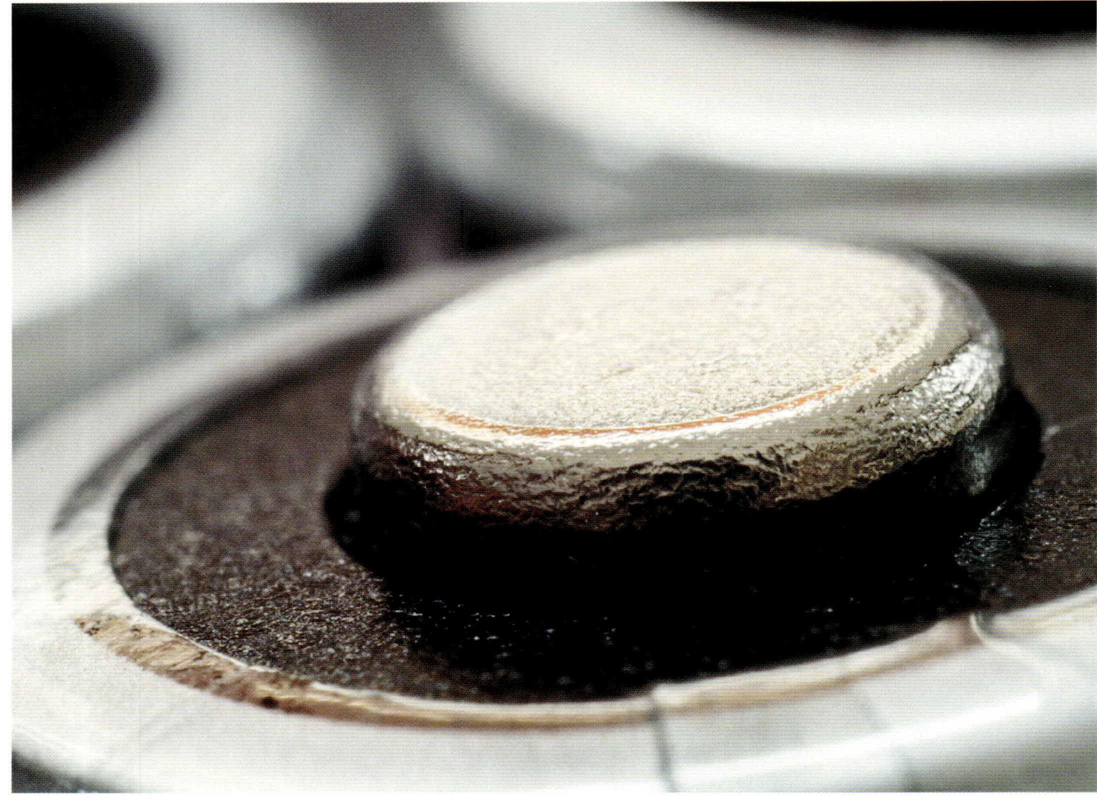

Above: The magnification possible by combining two lenses with a coupling ring is calculated by dividing the focal length of the longer lens by the focal length of the shorter lens. For example, a 100mm lens coupled with a 50mm lens will deliver a 2:1 reproduction ratio (x2 magnification). In all instances the longer focal length lens should be fitted directly to the camera, with the shorter focal length attached using the coupling ring.

Focal length: Coupled 100mm and 50mm

Aperture: f/16

Shutter speed: 6 sec.

ISO: 200

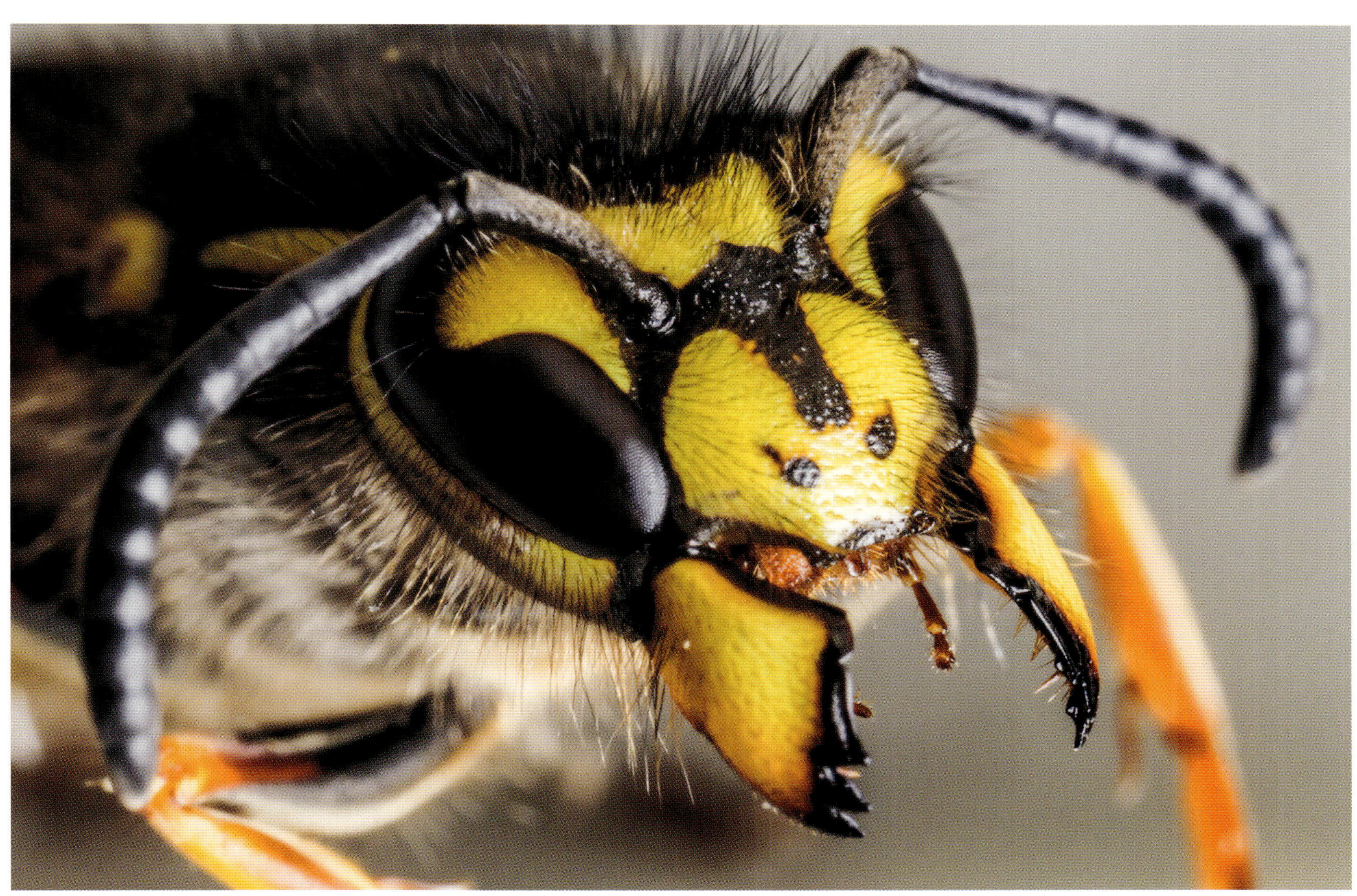

Above: The better the optical quality of the two lenses you "couple," the better the results will be. This image was shot by combining 135mm and 50mm prime lenses. The image quality is more than acceptable, even when compared to a dedicated macro lens.

Focal length: Coupled 135mm and 50mm

Aperture: f/16

Shutter speed: 1/250 sec.

ISO: 500

Extension Tubes

An extension tube is a hollow metal or plastic tube that fits between a camera and a lens. As there are no extra glass elements inside the tube it is ultimately the lens that determines image quality. For this reason, using extension tubes with a prime lens is generally more suitable than with a zoom.

Extension tubes shift the focus range of the lens to allow it to focus more closely than normal, and this is what increases image magnification. However, one of the downsides to using extension tubes is that the lens can no longer be focused at infinity. This makes using extension tubes a far less spontaneous affair than using a true macro lens, which can usually focus through a far wider range (including ∞).

Extension tubes are often sold in sets of three that can be used separately or combined in different ways to vary the degree of magnification. Typically the tubes supplied are 12mm, 20mm, and 36mm in length, producing 68mm of extension in total. To shoot an image with a 1:1 magnification the length of extension should equal (as closely as possible) the focal length of the lens used.

So, for example, to shoot at 1:1 with a 50mm lens you would combine the 12 and 36mm tubes, resulting in 48mm of extension. Extra sets of extension tubes can be stacked together to allow the use of lenses with a focal length longer than 68mm, but this isn't ideal—it is both unwieldy and can place a strain on the lens mount of the camera or extension tubes.

To achieve a magnification factor greater than 1:1 it is easier to use shorter focal length lenses. However, this results in a reduced working distance, which can make lighting your subject problematic (this is less of a problem if your subject is backlit, but top lighting a subject is often virtually impossible). One advantage that extension tubes have over reversing and coupling rings is that the lens filter thread is still available, so—if there's space between the lens and the subject—it's possible to use a ring light.

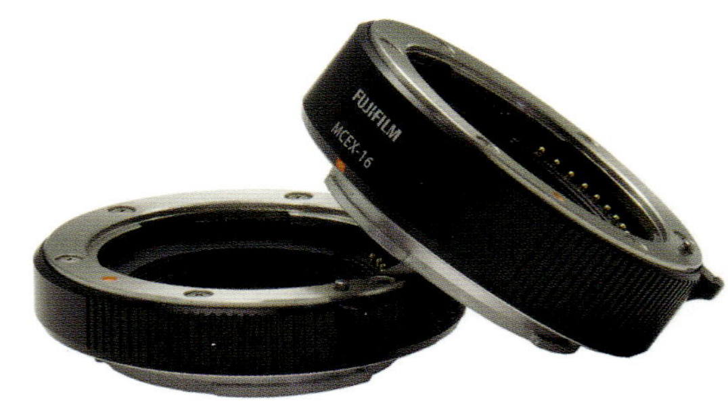

Above: The electronic connections on the inside of Fujifilm's MCEX-11 and MCEX-16 macro extension tubes allow AF and in-camera metering to be retained.
© Fujifilm

Below: This Kenko extension tube set provides 68mm of extension in total or 12mm, 20mm, and 36mm extension when the tubes are used individually.
© Kenko

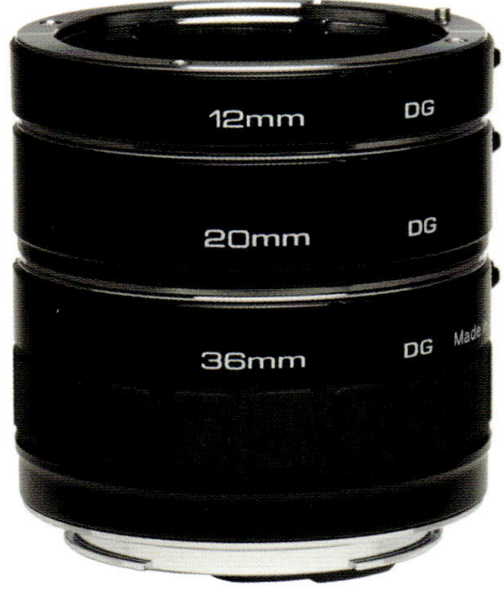

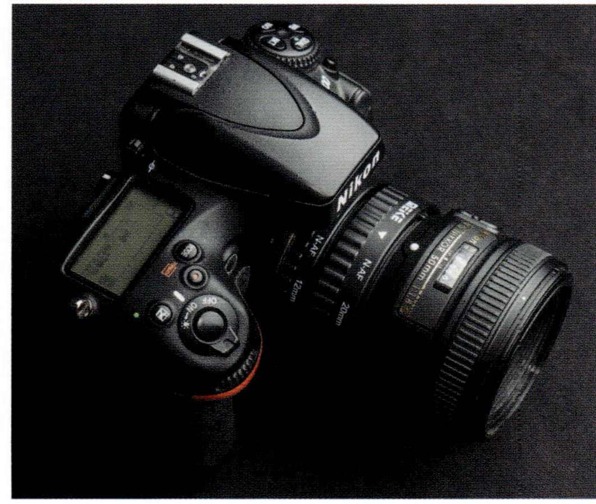

Left: Extension tubes increase the distance between the lens and camera sensor (or film), which allows the lens to focus more closely.

LIGHT LOSS

When you use extension tubes you'll immediately notice how much darker the viewfinder—or grainier the LCD image—is compared to normal. There is always light loss when an image is magnified, and the greater the magnification, the greater the light loss will be. This is another good reason to use a prime lens with extension tubes, as prime lenses typically have a larger maximum aperture.

Connection

There are essentially two different types of extension tubes. Cheaper extension tubes typically do not maintain an electronic connection between the lens and the camera, whereas more expensive extension tubes usually do (this type is often referred to as "auto extension tubes").

The latter option is generally preferable, as you can use your camera's AF system to set focus. Maintaining an electronic connection also lets you set the required aperture using your camera's control dials—something that would be difficult to do otherwise. Another advantage to extension tubes with an electronic connection is that both the focal length of the lens and the selected aperture will be recorded in the image's EXIF metadata.

FOCAL LENGTH	EXTENSION TUBE LENGTH						
	12MM	**20MM**	**32MM**	**36MM**	**48MM**	**56MM**	**68MM**
12MM	1:1	1.6:1	2.6:1	3:1	4:1	4.6:1	5.6:1
18MM	0.6:1	1:1	1.8:1	2:1	2.7:1	3.1:1	3.8:1
24MM	0.5:1	0.8:1	1.3:1	1.5:1	2:1	2.3:1	2.8:1
28MM	0.4:1	0.7:1	1.14:1	1.3:1	1.7:1	2:1	2.4:1
35MM	0.3:1	0.6:1	0.9:1	1:1	1.4:1	1.6:1	1.9:1
50MM	0.2:1	0.4:1	0.6:1	0.7:1	1:1	1.12:1	1.36:1

Above: This grid shows the magnification factors possible when using a variety of different focal length and extension tube combinations.

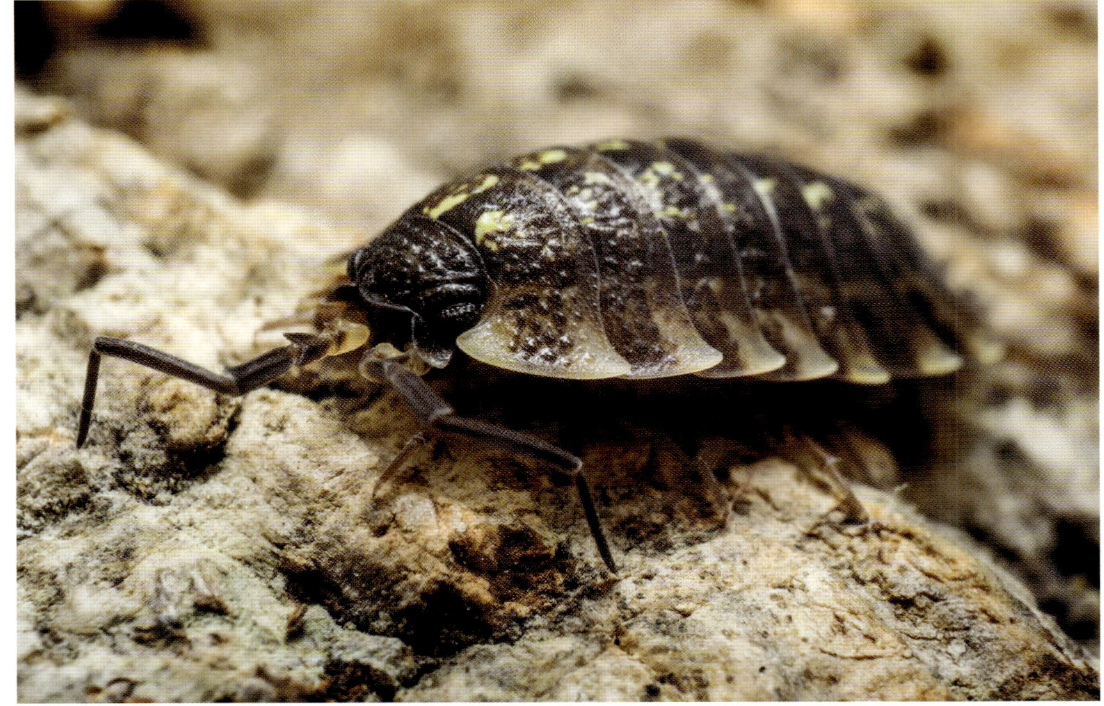

Left: It's possible to use multiple extension tubes with reversing rings and also with macro lenses. Using any of these combinations will increase the range of subjects you can shoot, although you will run into certain limitations. These include a dim viewfinder, which will make it harder to focus and compose, and longer exposure times due to the increase in magnification. This image of a household woodlouse was shot with extension tubes and a macro lens.

Focal length: 100mm macro lens (with 20mm extension tube)

Aperture: f/2.8

Shutter speed: 1/250 sec.

ISO: 400

Bellows

Bellows are essentially extension rings that can be varied in length. Light-tight bellows fit between the lens and your camera and can then be expanded or compressed along a rail to smoothly and accurately adjust the lens-to-camera distance. This means that the degree of magnification can be controlled in a way that is not possible with extension tubes.

However, the complexity of bellows makes them far heavier and more awkward to use than extension tubes, so it is difficult to shoot successfully without mounting the bellows/camera combination on a heavy tripod. Bellows also lose out to extension tubes as the electronic connection between the camera and lens is lost.

Bellows can be bought to fit popular camera systems such as Canon's EOS or Nikon's F mount standard. This means you can fit lenses you already own directly to the bellows. A more universal option is bellows that use the M42 mount. With a suitable lens (ideally in the region of 28–50mm) and an M42 adaptor for your camera it's possible to own a set of bellows that isn't too expensive, but offers excellent macro capability.

Another type of lens that can work well with bellows is an enlarger lens. As these lenses were designed originally for printing from negatives, they tend to be exhibit good edge-to-edge sharpness, are relatively free from curvilinear distortion, and because they are no longer in such high demand, used examples are generally inexpensive.

Most enlarger lenses use a 39mm thread, requiring an M39 adaptor to fit them to modern cameras, but as they have no internal focusing mechanism they are only really suitable for use with bellows (or a separate helicoid focusing adaptor). Another drawback is their often-limited range of small aperture settings, which can force you to use techniques such as focus stacking to achieve sufficient depth of field.

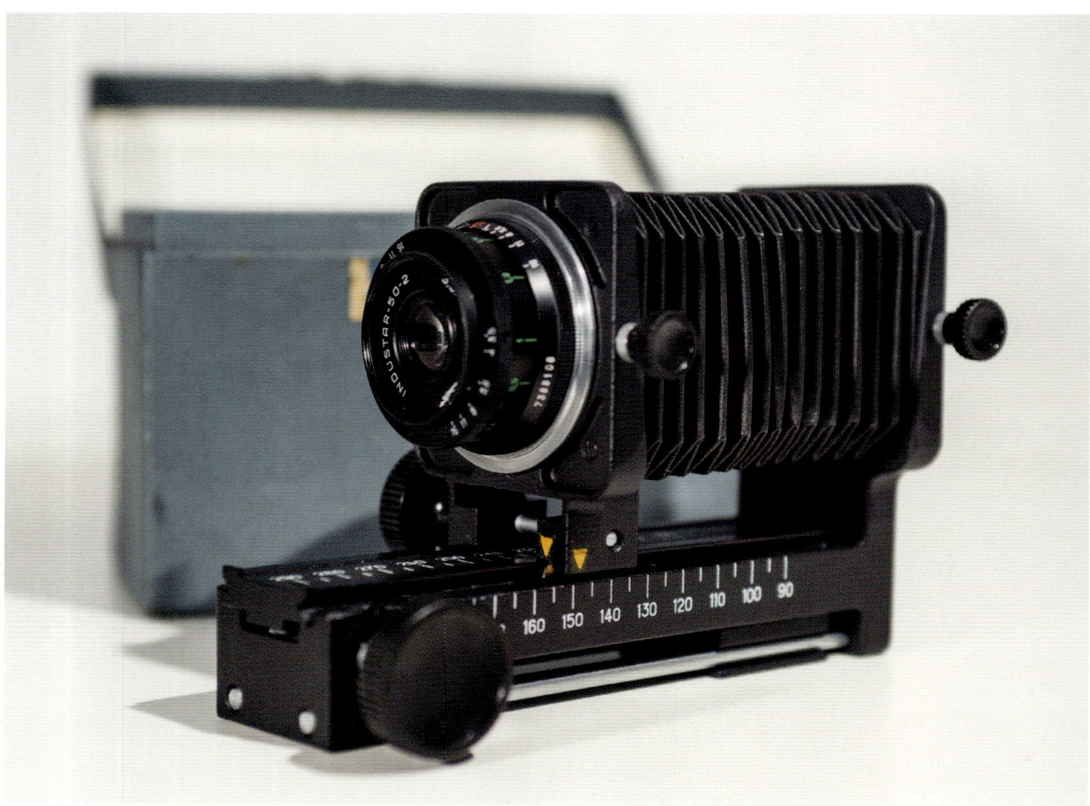

Above: Buying a used set of Soviet-era bellows can be an affordable way to try out shooting with bellows. This type of bellows will typically be M42 fit, so won't be immediately compatible with modern camera systems unless you use an adaptor.

M42 MOUNT

The M42 lens mount was first used in 1938, with lenses continuing to be manufactured all the way through to the 1980s—because of the longevity of the lens mount there are many used M42 lenses available. M42 lenses use a screw thread, which is less convenient to fit or remove than today's bayonet-fitting lenses, but this is less of an issue if the lens is fitted permanently to a set of bellows. All M42 lenses are manual focus and feature an aperture ring, so you can control exposure in a way not possible when a modern electronically controlled lens is fitted to a set of bellows.

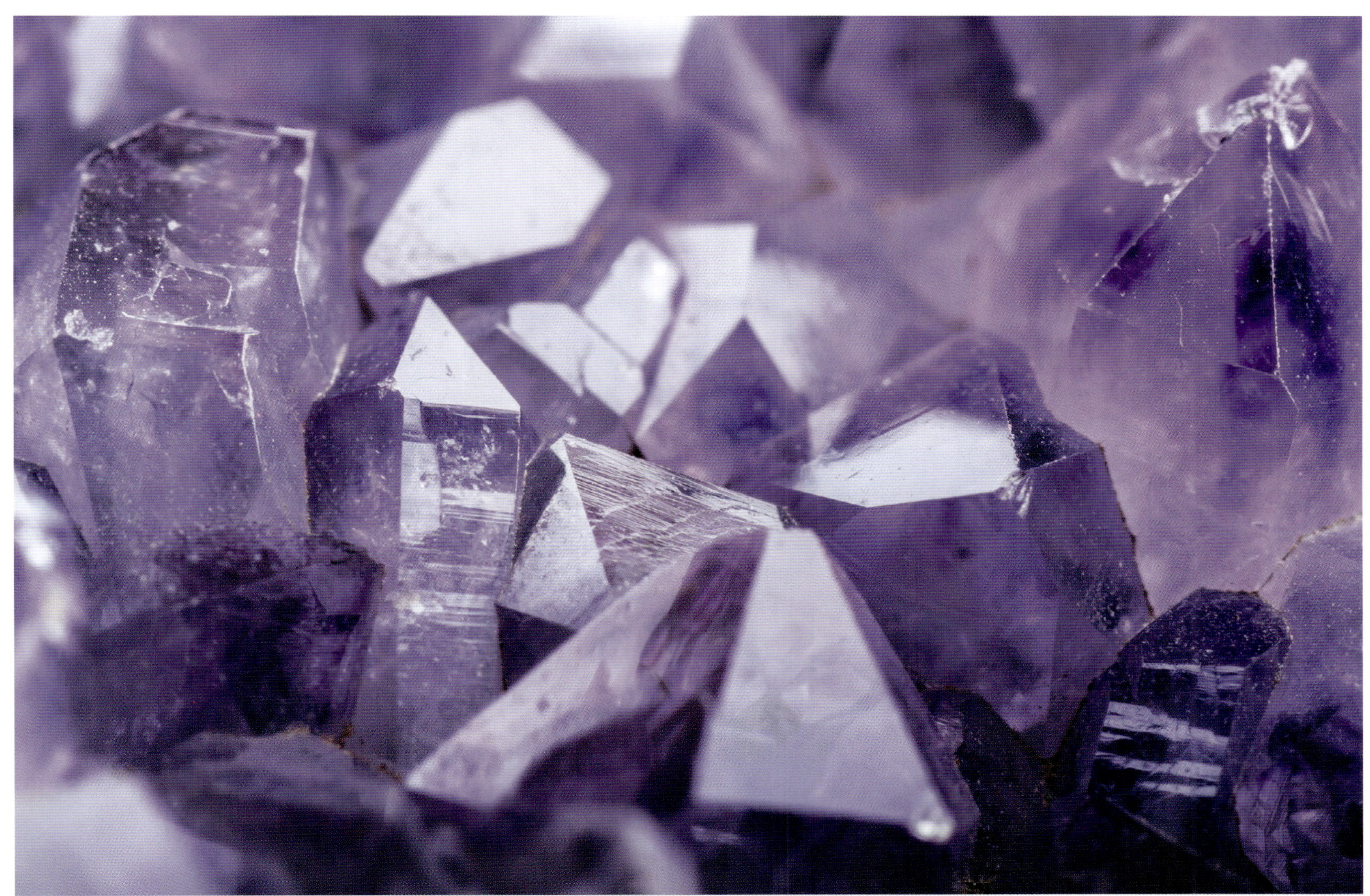

Above: One of the difficulties when using bellows is keeping everything steady during an exposure, especially if you are using a heavy lens with cheaper, less sturdy bellows—slippage of the bellows during an exposure can result in soft images. Using off-camera flash at your camera's maximum sync speed reduces this risk by keeping the exposure time as brief as possible.

Focal length: 100mm macro lens (with bellows)

Aperture: f/16

Shutter speed: 1/250 sec.

ISO: 800

General Lenses

Kit Lenses

System cameras are often sold with a kit zoom lens. This is usually a lens with a reasonable focal length range, generally from wide-angle to short telephoto. Kit lenses tend not be the best lenses in a manufacturer's range, but they are a useful first lens when you're starting out in photography.

In terms of macro, however, they're usually far from ideal. This is because kit lenses (and other cheaper zooms) tend to have relatively small maximum apertures that often vary as you adjust the zoom. This makes focusing through a viewfinder more difficult and makes the Live View display grainier, particularly in low light. Minimum focusing distance and magnification also tends to be compromised. Finally, the flaws in the optics of a kit lens can be all too apparent when the lens is combined with accessories such as close-up lenses or extension tubes.

FLOATING ELEMENTS

Non-macro lenses tend to be weaker optically when set to the minimum focusing distance compared to the infinity (∞) position. This weakness is seen in the form of increased chromatic aberration (see page 54) and significant field curvature resulting in reduced edge sharpness (see page 55).

To combat these problems, an increasing number of lenses are being designed with floating elements. Usually, lenses move a single group of lens elements as focus is adjusted, but floating elements are adjusted independently of the main group to maintain image quality at minimum focusing distances.

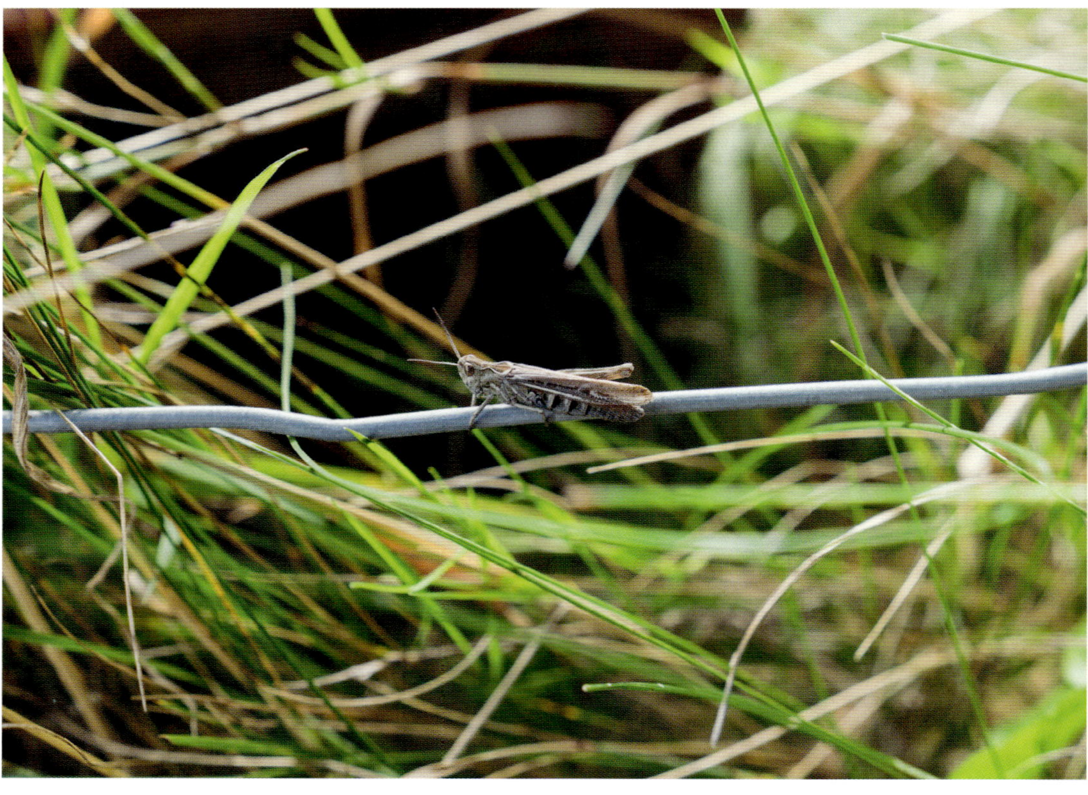

Prime Lenses

Most true macro lenses are prime lenses, but not all prime lenses have macro capabilities. As with kit lenses, non-macro prime lenses are typically compromised in terms of minimum focusing distance and magnification, but they are a far better option than kit lenses when combined with macro-enhancing accessories. This is partially because they tend to have larger maximum apertures, which makes focusing easier. It is also because they are generally superior in an optical sense, which means there are fewer quality compromises when they are combined with accessories such as extension tubes.

Above: This image was shot at the minimum focusing distance and maximum zoom of a camera's kit lens. I would have preferred to fill the frame with the subject, but this was the best that the lens could manage.

Focal length: 35mm

Aperture: f/5.6

Shutter speed: 1/30 sec.

ISO: 200

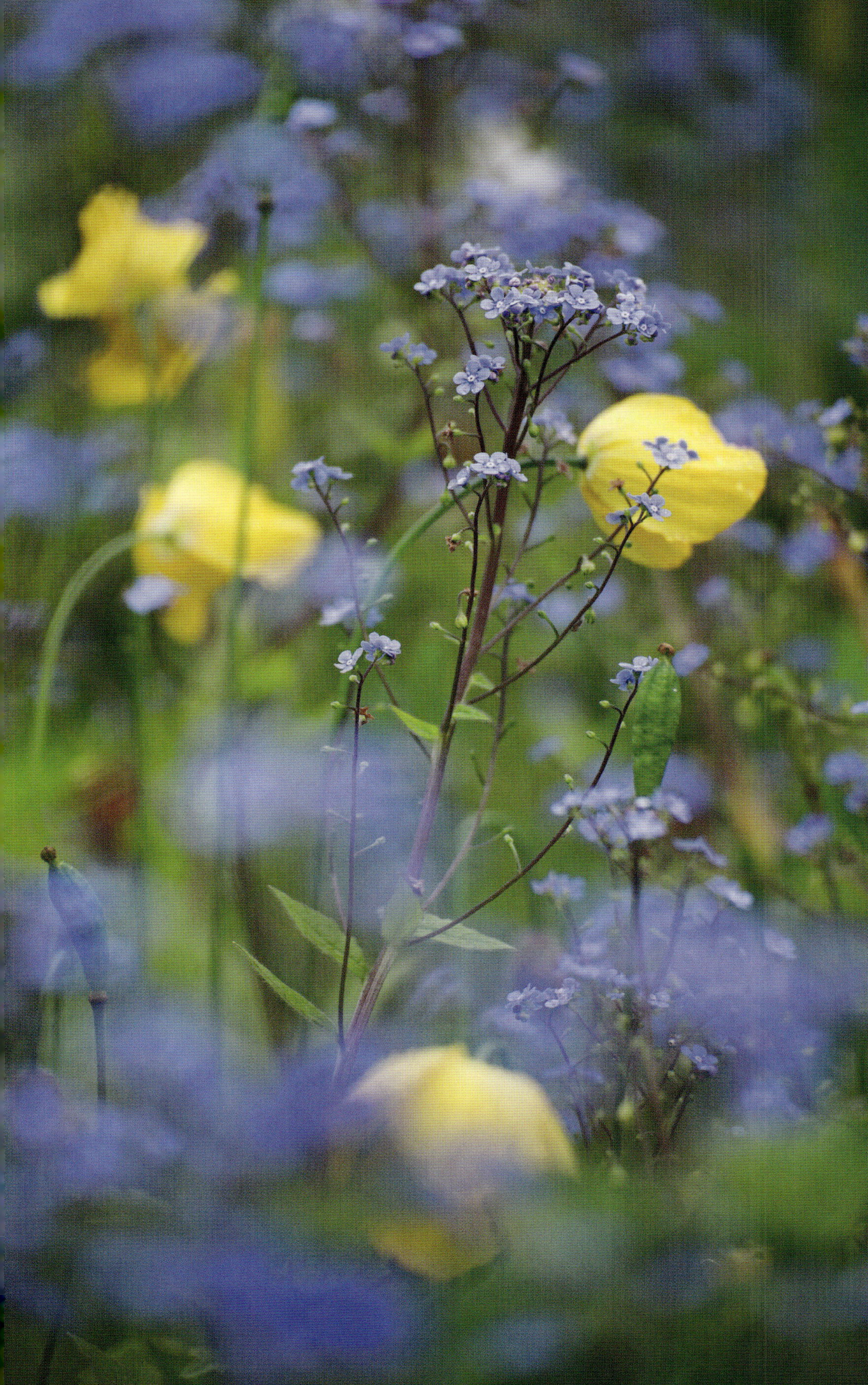

Zoom Lenses

There are many different types of zoom lens available, ranging from wide angle to telephoto. Telephoto zooms are the most useful for close-up shooting and, to a lesser extent, macro.

The drawback—particularly with older lens designs—is the often-lengthy minimum focusing distance. Telephoto zooms are designed to allow you to focus on distant subjects, magnifying their size and making them larger in the frame, rather than close focusing.

Extension tubes can be used to reduce the focusing distance, but infinity (∞) focusing will be lost. However, even with this drawback, telephoto zooms are still a useful addition to a lens collection.

Left: One drawback to telephoto zooms—particularly the less expensive consumer-oriented type—is their relatively small maximum aperture. This can have an impact on focusing speed and accuracy (particularly in low light) and the ability to use techniques such as differential focusing.

Focal length: 160mm

Aperture: f/4.8

Shutter speed: 1/250 sec.

ISO: 400

MACRO SETTING

Some telephoto zooms offer a "Macro" setting, but this is usually not true macro. It may be a 1:2 or even 1:3 reproduction ratio.

Macro Lenses

For the ultimate in image quality and ease of use there is nothing better than a true macro lens. There are two ways to fit a macro lens to a camera: either directly using the standard lens mount, or when shooting with a mirrorless camera, via a lens adaptor. The latter option lets you fit a wide variety of lenses, albeit with some (or complete) loss of automation. True macro lenses typically offer—with a few exceptions—a maximum aperture of f/2.8.

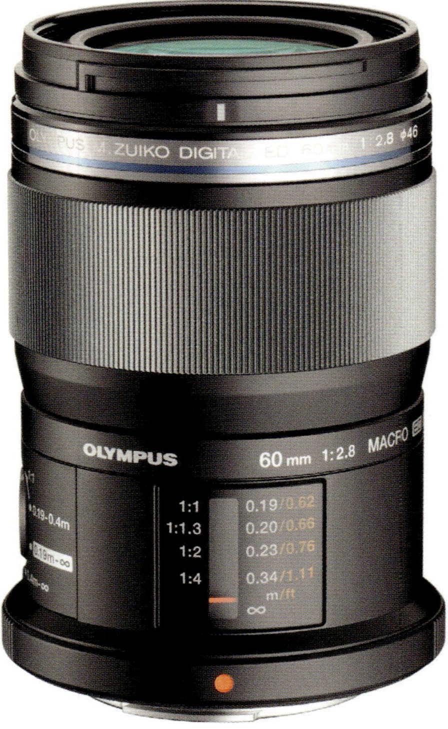

Above: An Olympus 60mm f/2.8 Macro M.ZUIKO Digital ED Micro lens, designed for the Micro Four Thirds system.
© Olympus

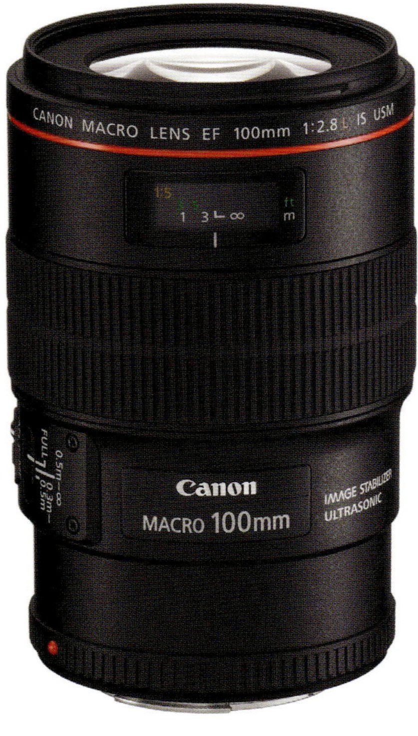

Above: Canon's EF 100mm f/2.8L Macro IS USM is its latest 100mm macro lens featuring Image Stabilization.
© Canon

Proprietary Macro Lenses

All camera manufacturers produce a range of lenses to fit their particular camera system (referred to as proprietary, first-party, or brand lenses), and virtually every proprietary lens range features at least one macro lens.

Buying a proprietary lens has a number of advantages. For a start, you are guaranteed that the lens will be compatible with future camera bodies produced by the manufacturer (third-party lens manufacturers have been caught out when camera manufacturers change how their AF works,

for example). Profiles for proprietary lenses are also typically built-into (or can be easily added to) camera menu systems, enabling any slight aberrations, such as vignetting, to be "dialed out" in camera.

The main disadvantage is that the price of proprietary lenses is typically higher than a comparable third-party alternative. Third-party lens manufacturers will often offer wider and quirkier macro options as well.

MANUFACTURER	LENS SPECIFICATION	COMMENTS
CANON (EOS)	EF-S 60mm f/2.8 USM Macro	APS-C only
	MP-E 65mm f/2.8 1–5x Macro Lens	Manual focus lens offering 1x to 5x magnification; very limited use other than as a macro lens
	EF 100mm f/2.8 USM Macro	Relatively old 100mm macro lens; still on sale, but largely superseded by newer L-series lens
	EF 100mm f/2.8L Macro IS USM	Features Image Stabilization
	EF 180mm f/3.5 L USM Macro	Canon's longest focal length true macro lens
	EF-M 28mm f/3.5 Macro IS STM	For Canon's M-system cameras only; features a built-in LED ring light
NIKON (F-MOUNT)	40mm f/2.8 G AF-S DX Micro	DX (APS-C) only
	60mm f/2.8 D AF Micro	Older D-series lens with aperture ring
	60mm f/2.8 G AF-S ED Micro	Newer G-series lens without aperture ring
	85mm f/3.5 G ED AF-S VR DX Micro	DX (APS-C) only. Features VR (Vibration Reduction; Nikon's lens-based image stabilization system)
	105mm f/2.8 G AF-S VR IF ED Micro	Features VR
	200mm f/4 AF Micro Nikkor	Older D-series lens with aperture ring
PENTAX (K-MOUNT)	50mm f/2.8 SMC D FA Macro	–
	100mm f/2.8 SMC D-FA WR Macro	Features weather-resistant (WR) sealing
SONY (A-MOUNT)	30mm f/2.8 SAM DT Macro	APS-C only
	50mm f/2.8 D Macro AF	Features rounded aperture blades for improved bokeh
	100mm f/2.8 D Macro Lens	–
SONY (E-MOUNT)	30mm f/3.5 Macro	APS-C only
	50mm f/2.8 FE Macro	–
	90mm f/2.8 FE Macro G OSS	Features OSS (Optical Steady Shot—Sony's image stabilization system)
PANASONIC (MICRO FOUR THIRDS)	30mm f/2.8 Macro LUMIX G ASPH MEGA OIS	Features OIS (Optical Image Stabilization)
	45mm f/2.8 Macro Leica D Vario-Elmar	Features OIS
OLYMPUS (MICRO FOUR THIRDS)	60mm f/2.8 Macro M.ZUIKO Digital ED Micro	–
FUJIFILM (X-MOUNT)	60mm f/2.4 R	0.5x magnification maximum

Third-Party Macro Lenses

Lenses produced by third-party manufacturers are a viable alternative to those produced by the camera manufacturers themselves. The three major third-party lens manufacturers are Sigma, Tamron, and (to a slightly lesser extent) Tokina.

All three brands produce a macro lens in the region of 100mm, which in terms of focal length is arguably the sweet spot for macro lenses: not too expensive, too large, or too heavy, while still allowing a reasonable working distance from your subject. Sigma and Tamron also offer longer macro lenses that fill in useful gaps in lens systems, such as Sony's A-mount.

A recent trend has been the appearance of manual-focus-only lenses that have often been developed and produced through successful crowdfunding campaigns. These lenses are niche products (the lack of AF rules them out for many people), but they can fill gaps that are not exploited by the larger manufacturers. Notable producers of these lenses include Laowa/Venus Optics, Nanoha, and Samyang (also known as Rokinon in some territories). These lenses are typically available through specialist dealers, direct from the manufacturer, or via Internet auction websites such as eBay.

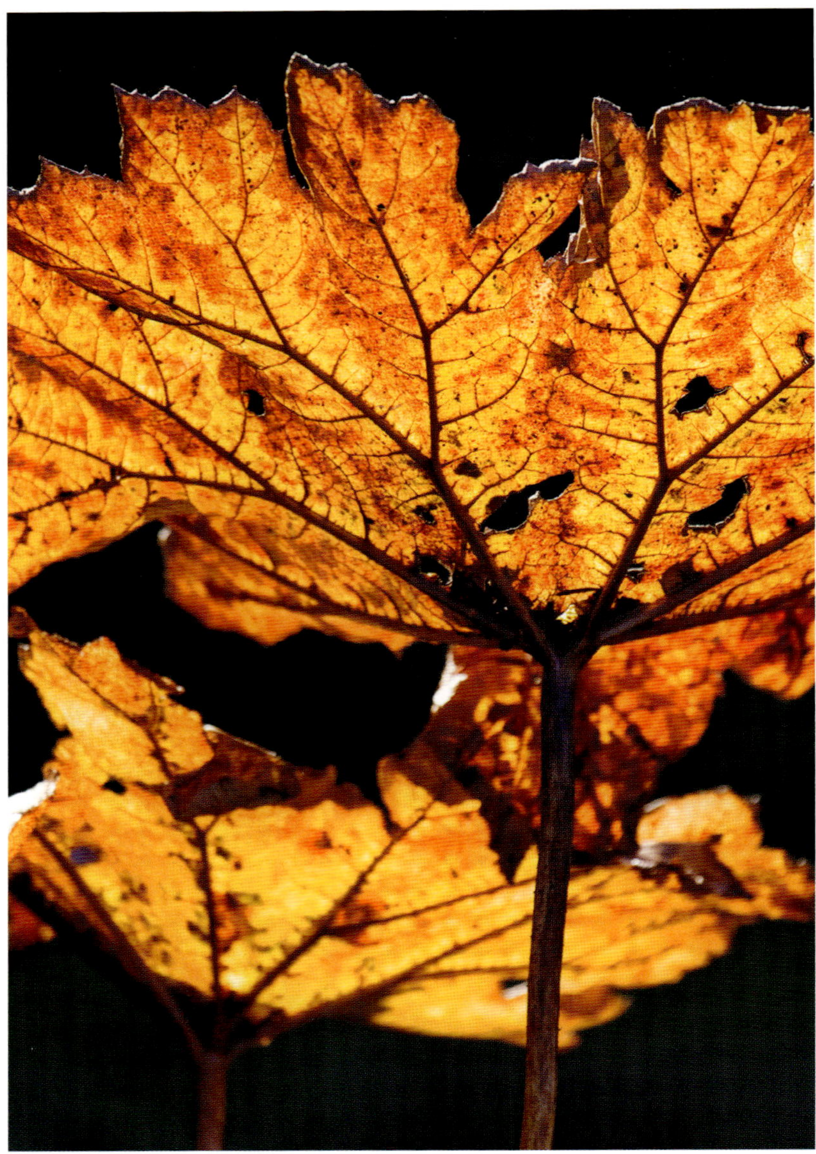

Above: A lens hood is a useful accessory, no matter what type of imagery you create. Lens hoods reduce the risk of lens flare when a point light source—such as the sun— is just outside the image area. This typically occurs when shooting side-lit or backlit subjects. Not all lenses are supplied with a lens hood, so it's worth factoring in the cost of one when buying a new lens.

Focal length: 200mm

Aperture: f/4.5

Shutter speed: 1/200 sec.

ISO: 100

MANUFACTURER	LENS SPECIFICATION	COMMENTS	FITTING
SIGMA	105mm f/2.8 APO EX DG OS HSM	Features OS (Optical Stabilization)	CE / N / SA / SI
	150mm f/2.8 EX DG OS HSM	Features OS	CE / N / SA / SI
	180mm f/2.8 EX DG OS HSM	Features OS	CE / N / SA / SI
TAMRON	60mm f/2 Di II LD SP AF	APS-C only	CE / N / SA
	90mm SP f/2.8 SP Di	–	CE / N / P / SA
	90mm SP f/2.8 SP USD Di VC	Features VC (Vibration Control)	CE / N / SA
	90mm SP f/2.8 SP USD Di VC	New version of 90mm lens above; features VC	CE / N / SA
	180mm f/3.5 SP Di	Built-in tripod collar	CE / N / SA
TOKINA	100mm f/2.8 AT-X	Features clutch control AF/MF	CE / N
SAMYANG/ROKINON	100mm f/2.8 ED UMC MACRO	Manual focus only	CE / CM / N / P / SA / SE / F
LAOWA/VENUS OPTICS	15mm f/4	Manual focus only; ±6mm shift	CE / N / P / SA / SE
	60mm f/2.8 2:1	Manual focus only; 2:1 reproduction ratio	CE / N / P / SA
NANOHA	5x lens	Manual focus only; features removable LED lighting	SE / M

FITTING KEY CE=Canon EOS EF   CM=Canon EOS M   N=Nikon   P=Pentax   SA=Sony A-mount   SE=Sony E-mount   M=Micro Four Thirds   F=Fujifilm   SI=Sigma

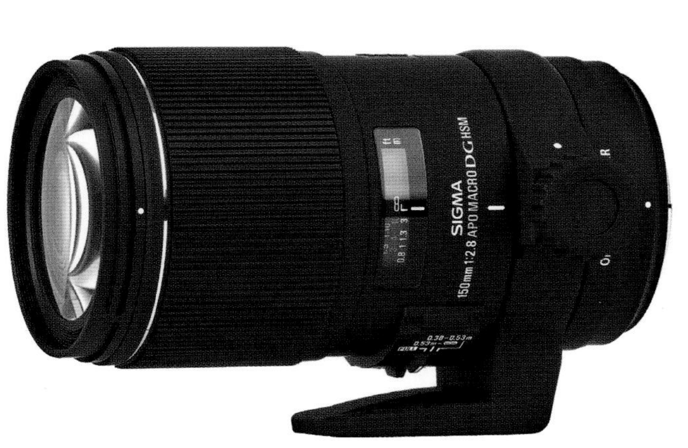

Left: Sigma's 150mm f/2.8 EX DG OS HSM with built-in tripod collar.

© Sigma

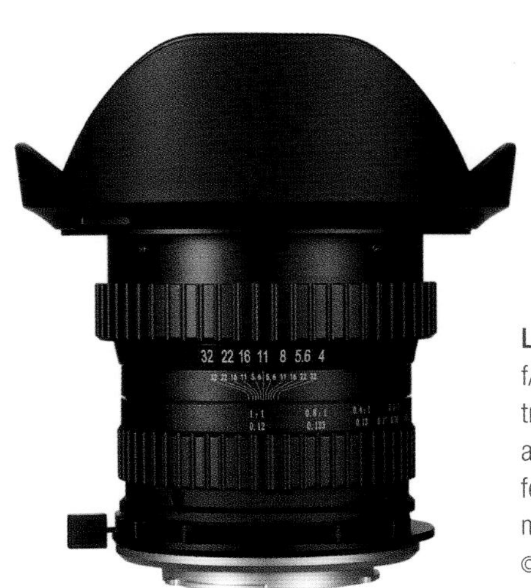

Left: Laowa's 15mm f/4 Macro is the widest true macro lens currently available. Another unique feature is its ±6mm shift mechanism.

© Laowa

Common Lens Problems

There's no such thing as a perfect lens—all lenses suffer from certain optical problems to one degree or another. The most highly regarded lenses are those that suffer least from these various problems. Generally this is reflected in the price, although lens technology is improving constantly and these improvements are being applied to cheaper lenses too.

Shooting macro often means using lenses at the edge of their performance, where problems are most apparent. Optically, lenses are generally at their peak performance when set to the mid-range of apertures (f/5.6–f/11). The optical performance of a lens at—or close—to maximum and minimum aperture is often significantly reduced. Fortunately, some of these optical problems can be mitigated or even removed entirely either in-camera or in postproduction using a lens profile.

Chromatic Aberration

The effects of chromatic aberration are seen as color fringing, which is most visible along high-contrast edges. There are two types of chromatic aberration: axial and transverse.

Axial chromatic aberration is seen across the entire image when a lens is set to maximum aperture, but its effects are reduced and largely eliminated as the lens is stopped down.

Conversely, transverse chromatic aberration is only seen at the periphery of images and is not reduced as the lens is stopped down.

Of the two types, it is easier to correct transverse chromatic aberration, which can be done either in-camera using a lens correction setting or during postproduction. Axial chromatic aberration cannot be corrected in-camera and requires relatively advanced postproduction lens-correction tools.

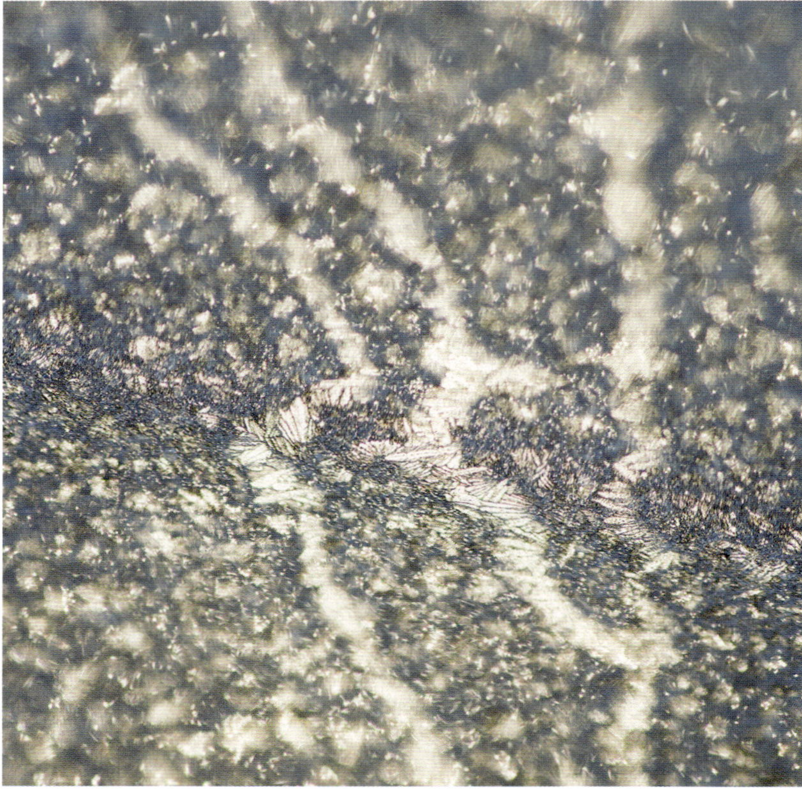

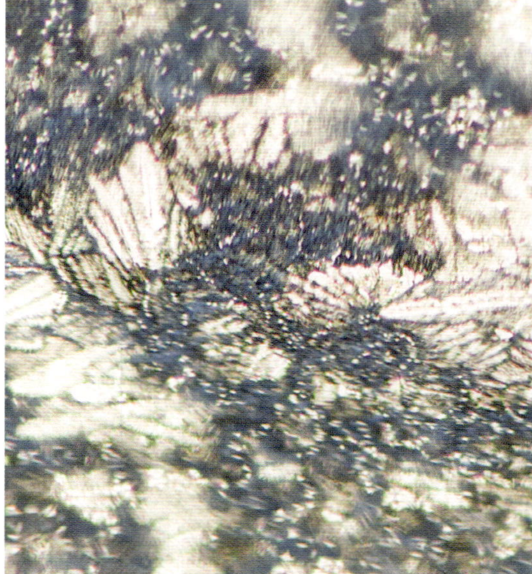

Left: Axial chromatic aberration is often quite pronounced when shooting with fast prime lenses at wider apertures. Here the chromatic aberration is seen as a green and magenta "fringe" around the ice crystals on this frost-covered window.

Focal length: 100mm macro lens

Aperture: f/4

Shutter speed: 1/3200 sec.

ISO: 800

LENS PROFILES

Many of the optical problems of a lens, such as chromatic aberration and vignetting, can be measured. This allows software developers such as Adobe to produce lens profiles for their image-editing software. When applied, these profiles automatically make the adjustments necessary to correct the optical problems of lenses. The drawback to lens profiles is that typically it is only current and popular lenses (and cameras) that are covered; older or more esoteric lenses generally do not have appropriate profiles available.

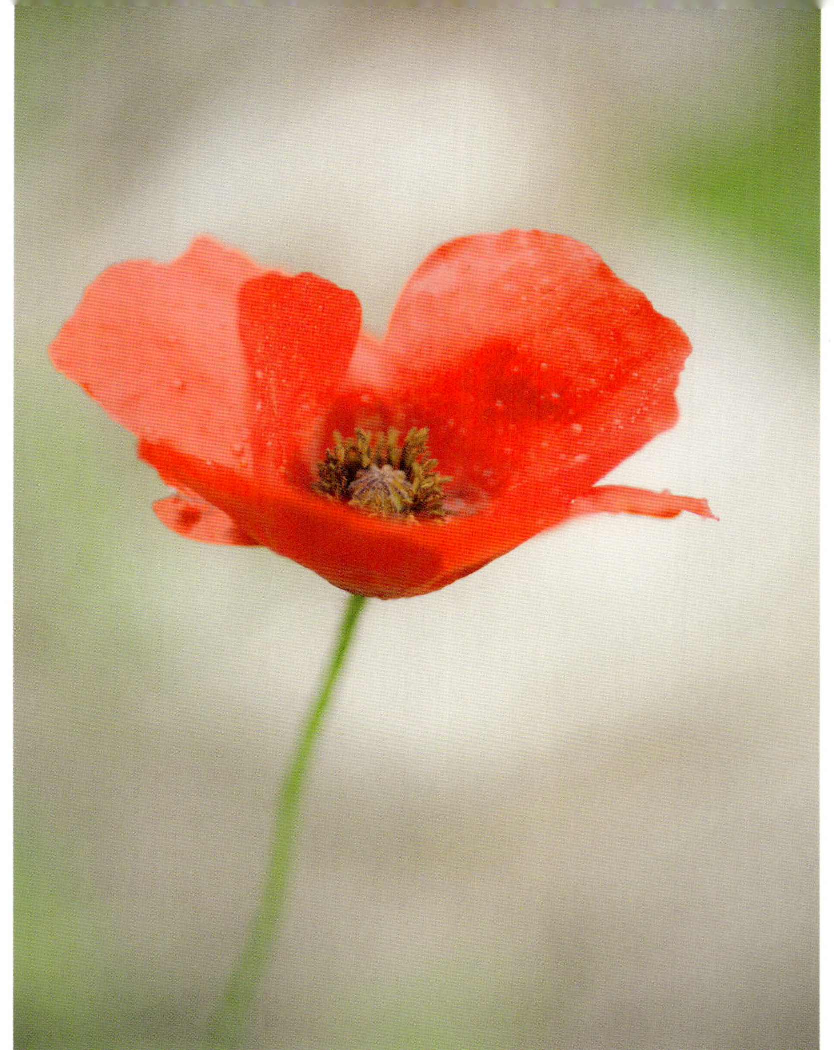

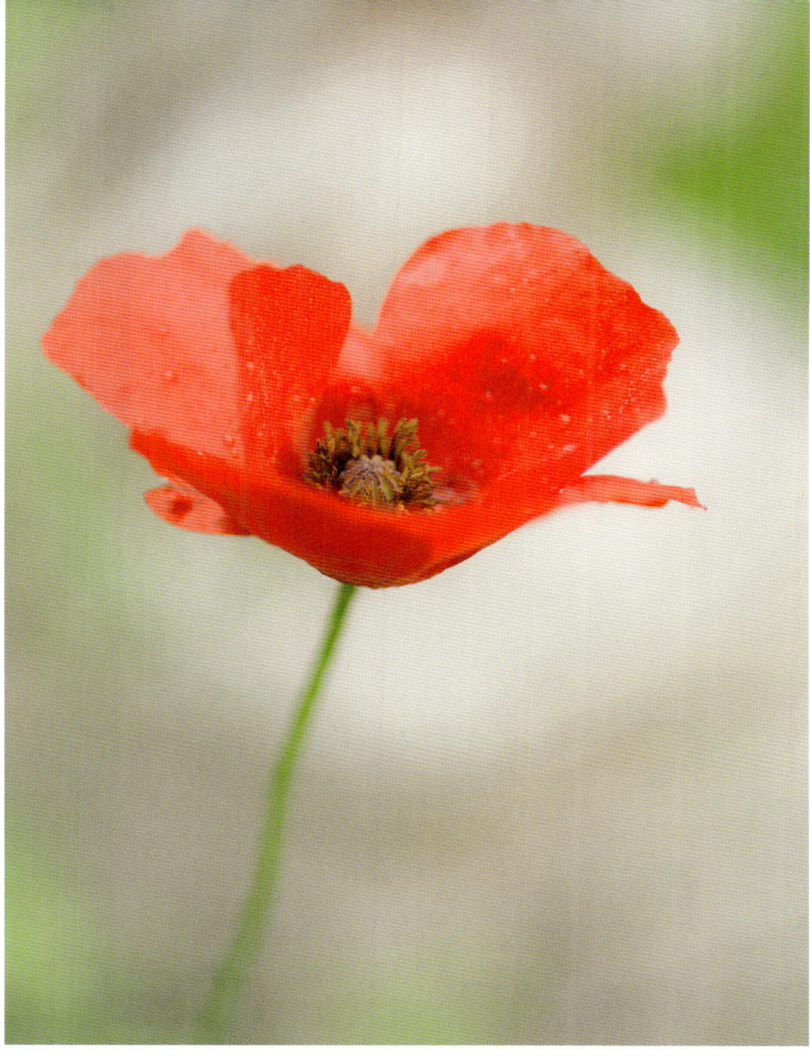

Vignetting

Lenses can also suffer from vignetting when used at or close to maximum aperture. This is seen as a darkening of the edges of an image relative to the center. As with axial chromatic aberration, the degree of vignetting decreases as the lens is stopped down, and when a lens is set to a mid-range aperture, vignetting will no longer be visible. Vignetting is a relatively easy problem to solve either in-camera or during postproduction, but correcting vignetting in images shot using a high ISO can increase the level of image noise in the corrected areas.

Corner Sharpness & Contrast

Another problem that affects lenses when they are used at or close to maximum aperture is a reduction in sharpness and contrast at the corners of the frame. Often, the lens needs to be stopped down to a mid-range aperture before edge sharpness and contrast is even close to equalling the center.

For certain subjects—particularly those placed centrally—edge softness is something that may be an acceptable compromise when the need for a fast shutter speed requires the use of a large aperture. However, if edge-to-edge sharpness is required then stopping down 2–3 stops from a lens' maximum aperture is generally necessary.

Above: When lens correction is applied will depend on what file format you choose. If you select JPEG, it is best to activate lens correction on your camera's menu before shooting (where available). However, if you shoot Raw, lens correction should be applied after shooting. This was the case for this image when noticeable vignetting (above left) was removed (above right) using the editing software's Lens Correction tool.

Focal length: 100mm macro lens

Aperture: f/3.8

Shutter speed: 1/500 sec.

ISO: 400

Diffraction

Many lens problems occur when a lens is used at or close to maximum aperture. However, diffraction is a problem that is seen only when a lens is used at or close to its minimum aperture. The main visual effect is an overall softening across the image. This makes macro images particularly prone to the effects of diffraction, as it is often necessary to use small aperture settings in order to maximize depth of field. One way of mitigating the effects of diffraction is to combine the use of a mid-range aperture with focus stacking (see pages 124–125).

Diffraction is the result of the random scattering of rays of light by the edges of the aperture blades. This causes the rays of light to diverge—or diffract—so they are out of phase with each other by the time they reach the camera's sensor. This reduces the resolution of the resulting image. The size of a sensor and its pixel density has an effect on the size of the aperture at which the effects of diffraction start to become apparent: the smaller the sensor, or the more dense the pixel resolution of the sensor, the greater the risk of diffraction at even relatively moderate apertures. It is partly for this reason that the lenses in compact cameras (with their tiny sensors) are often limited to apertures of f/8–f/11.

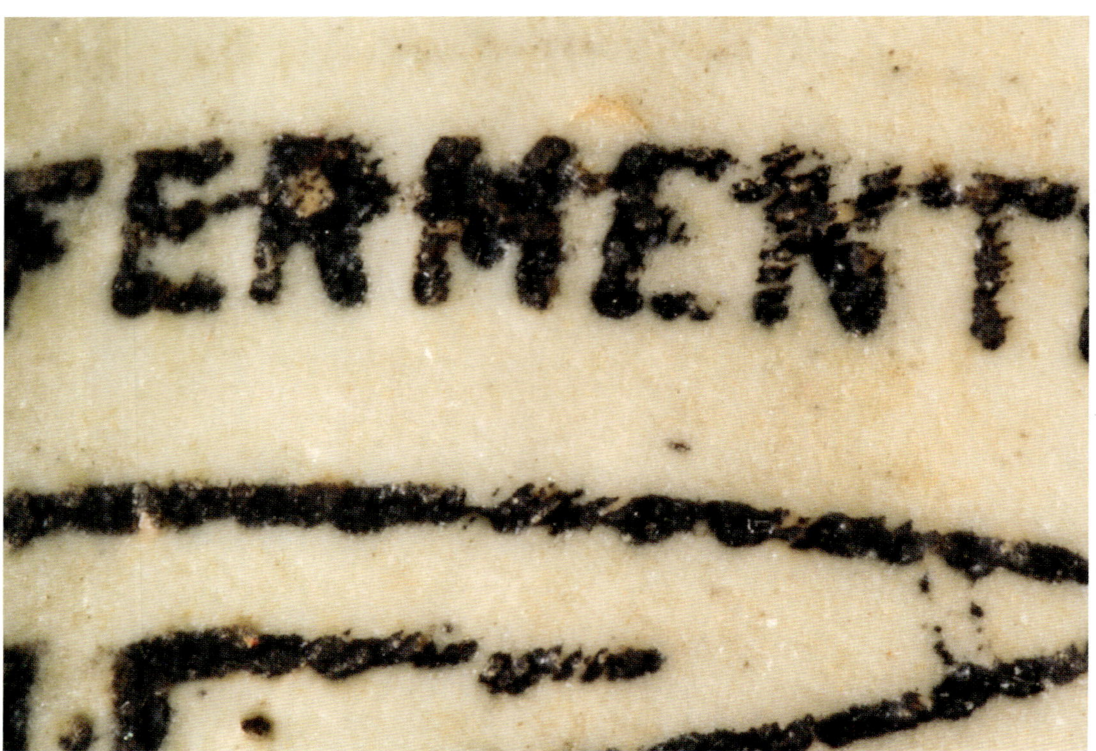

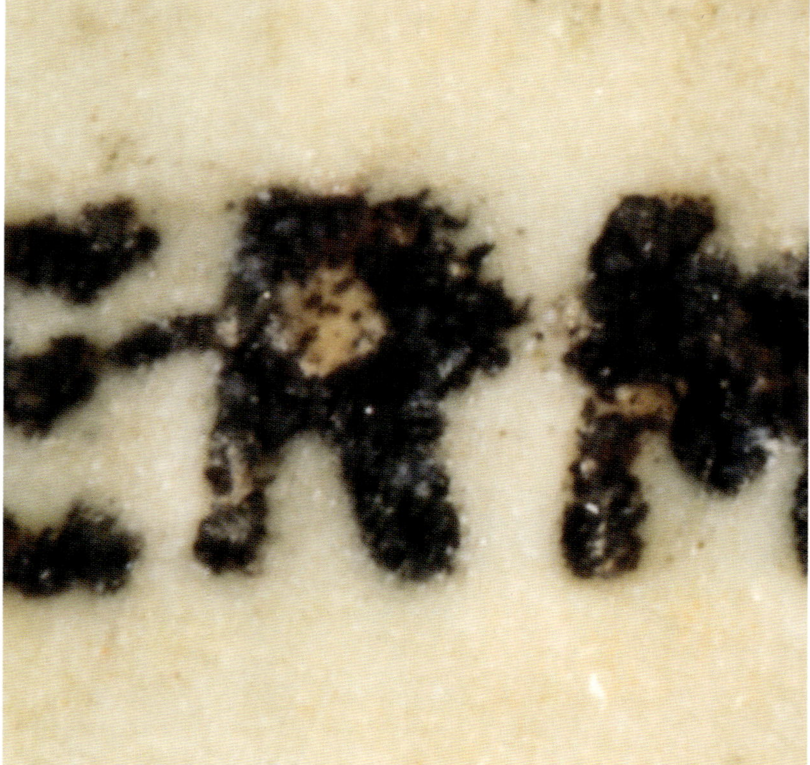

Right: Shot at f/32, diffraction has robbed this shot of an Edwardian clay pot of sharpness, despite the fact that the depth of field is at its maximum.

Focal length: 100mm macro lens

Aperture: f/32

Shutter speed: 25 sec.

ISO: 100

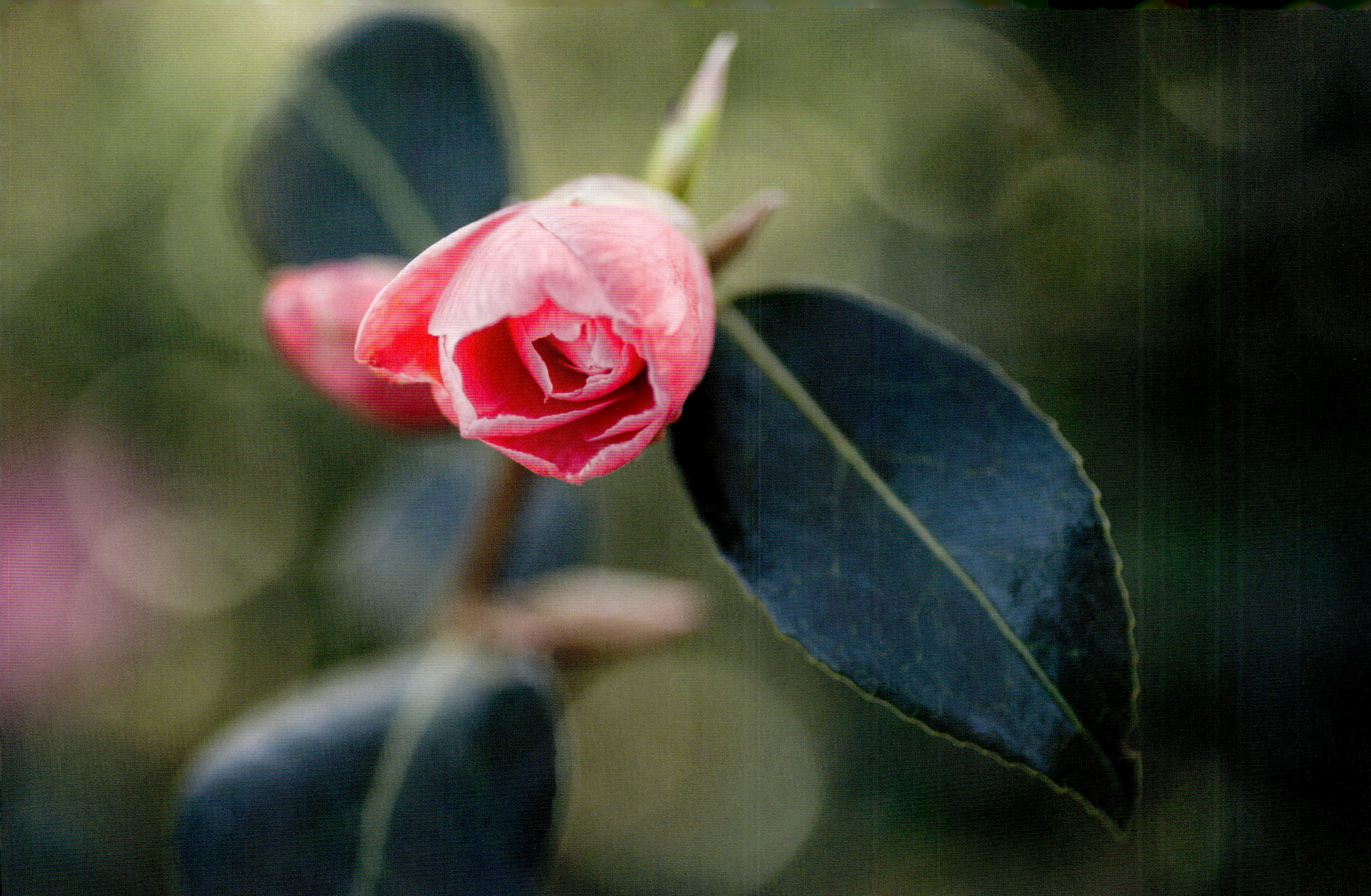

Bokeh

Although not a lens problem as such, the Japanese word "bokeh" refers to the esthetic quality of the out-of-focus areas in an image. A lens is said to either have "good" or "bad" bokeh. A lens with "good" bokeh will have smooth, creamy out-of-focus areas and specular highlights will appear round and have soft edges. "Bad" bokeh is seen as rougher out-of-focus areas with specular highlights that appear asymmetrical and polygonal with a harder edge. (Highlights are also said to look "nervous" and take on an onion-like appearance with distinctive bands of varying brightness visible across the highlight areas.)

Above: Bokeh is more easily assessed when shooting with longer focal lenses at or close to maximum aperture. Fast, long focal length prime lenses typically produce more esthetically pleasing bokeh than slower zoom lenses.

Focal length: 160mm

Aperture: f/3.5

Shutter speed: 1/160 sec.

ISO: 200

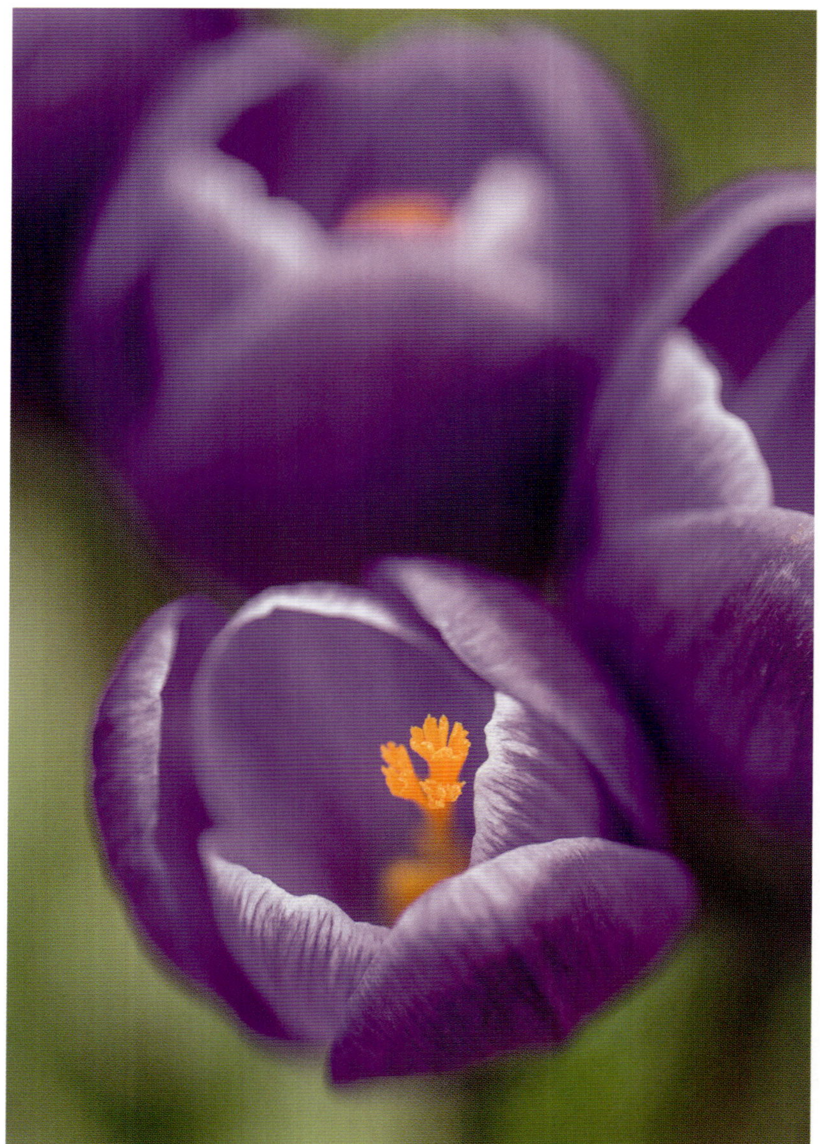

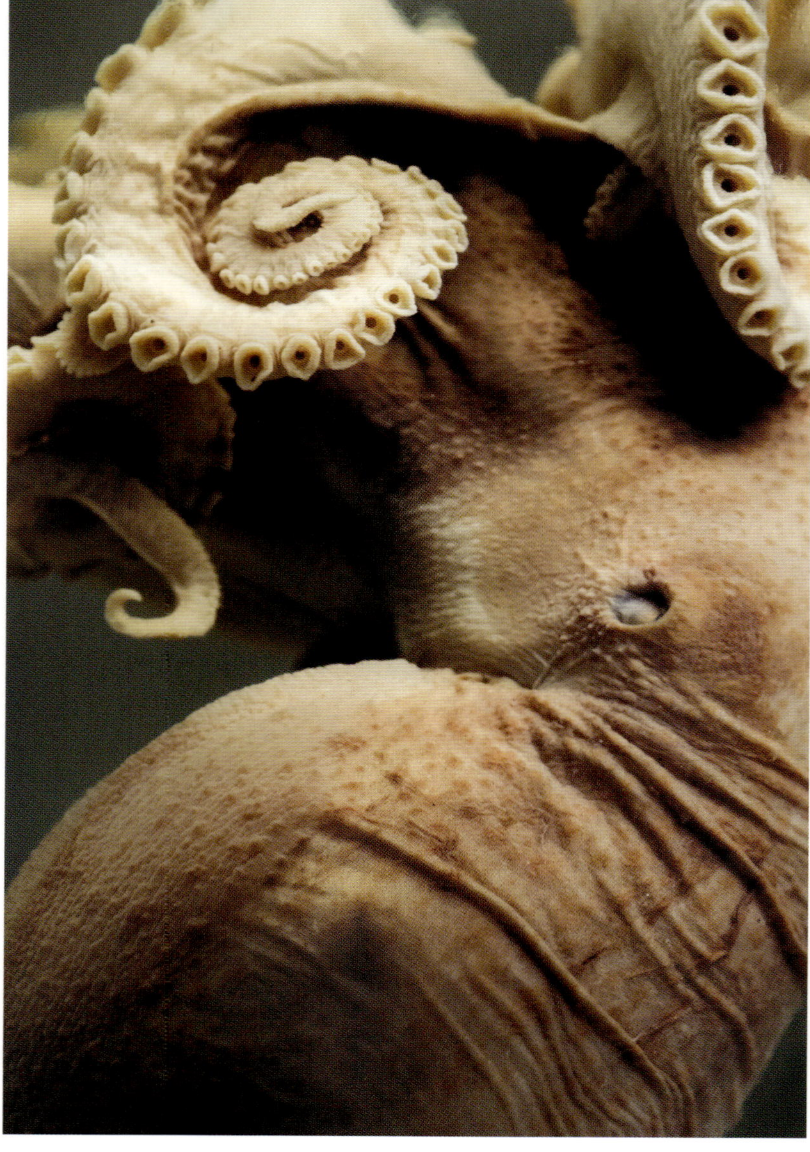

Above: My macro lens of choice is a 100mm lens. This focal length provides a good balance of size, weight, and working distance. It is also a fast, f/2.8 lens, which makes it easy to create soft, out-of-focus images with a very narrow depth of field. This is ideal when shooting organic subjects such as these crocuses.

Focal length: 100mm macro lens

Aperture: f/4.8

Shutter speed: 1/250 sec.

ISO: 400

Above: The 100mm lens I use is designed for use on full-frame cameras, but this doesn't mean that it can't be used on APS-C cameras and even mirrorless cameras via an adaptor. Used on a Micro Four Thirds camera—as with this shot—the apparent focal length increases to 200mm, which makes it easier to exclude unwanted details in a scene. This was necessary for this shot of an octopus on display in a specimen jar in a museum display case.

Focal length: 100mm macro lens

Aperture: f/5.6

Shutter speed: 1/5sec.

ISO: 400

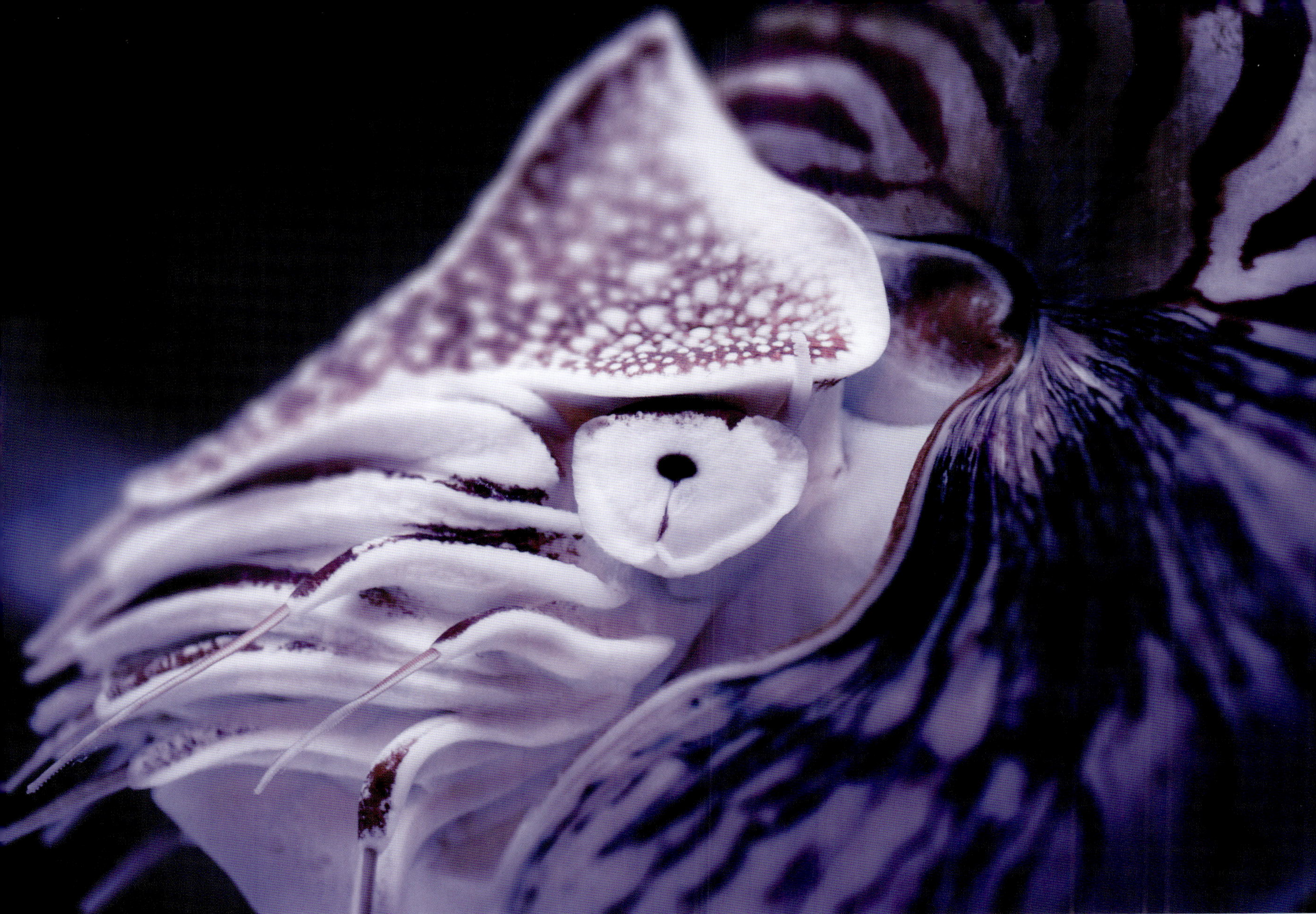

Above: If you shoot through glass it is best to press the lens gently against the glass to avoid reflections—such as when shooting subjects such as this nautilus in an aquarium. This is when shorter focal length macro lenses come into their own, as they allow you to frame more expansively and show more of your subject.

Focal length: 50mm macro lens

Aperture: f/3.5

Shutter speed: 1/60 sec.

ISO: 3200

Profile: Chris Gatcum

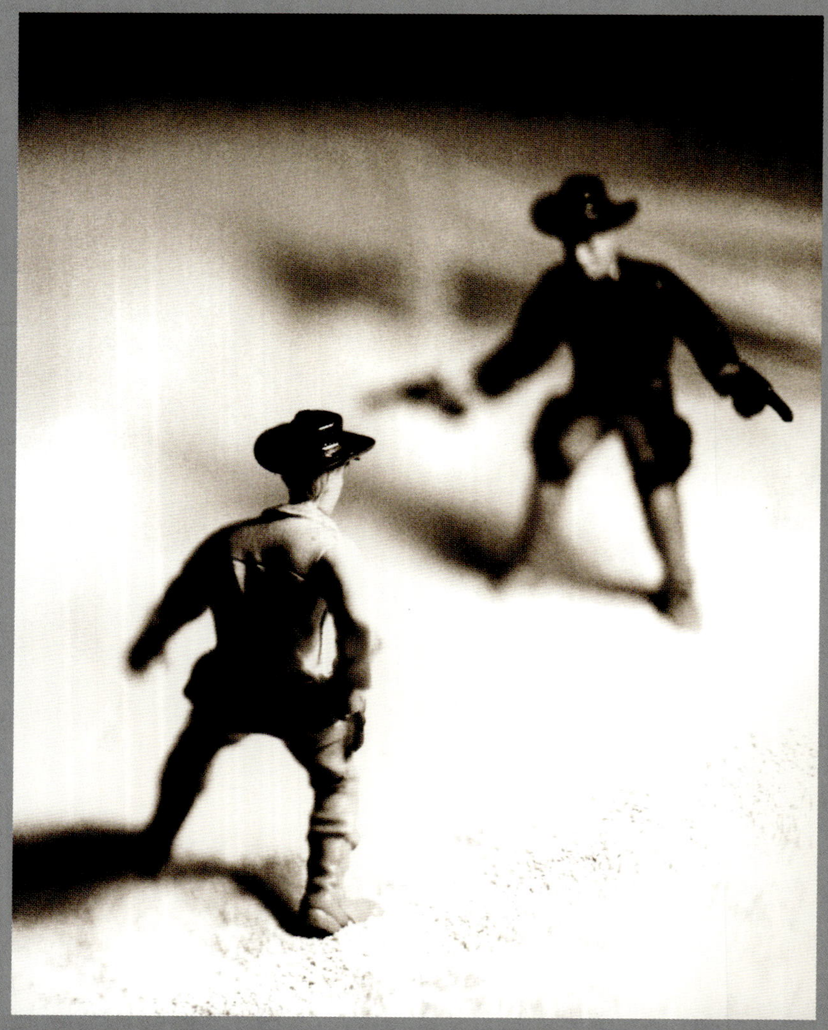

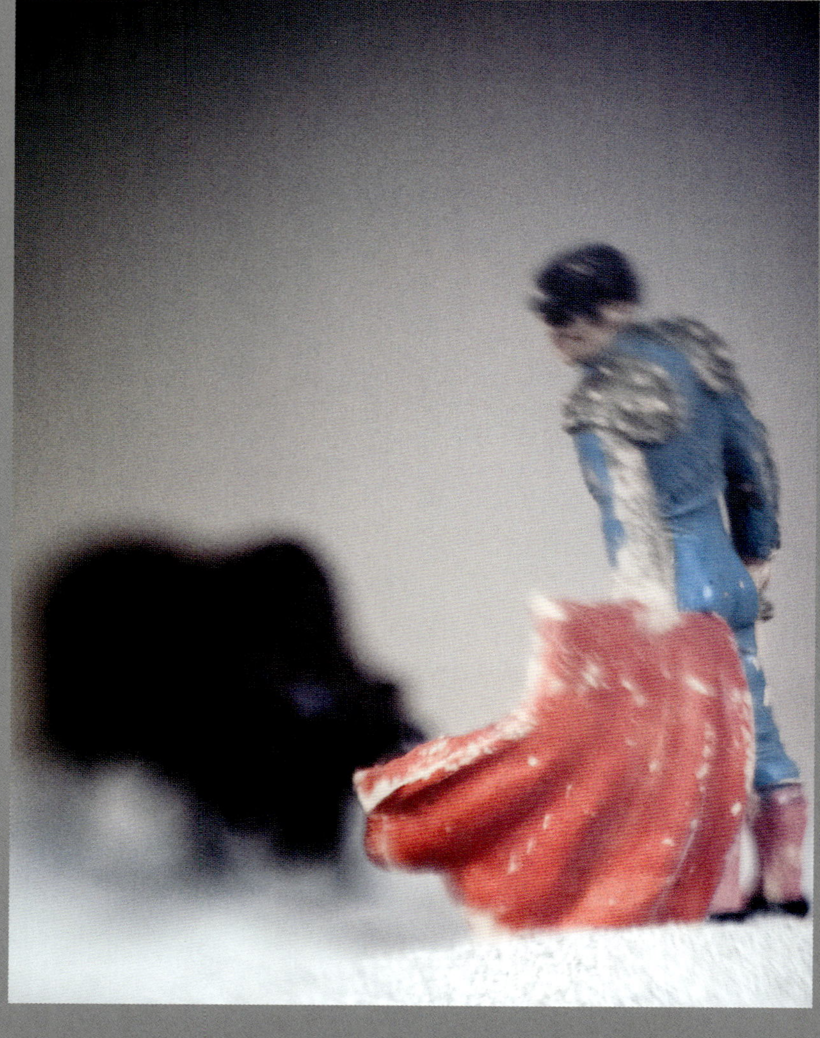

BIOGRAPHY

Chris Gatcum is a photographer and author specializing in practical photography books. His career has seen him work as a set builder and magazine journalist, and he now exists as a freelance photographer, writer, and editor.

www.cgphoto.co.uk

Q) What is your specialty?
A) Playing with toys and trying to legitimize it by setting up a camera! At college I encountered the work of David Levinthal, James Casebere, and Sandy Skoglund, and was blown away by their unique visions and the "fun" that appeared to be behind the creation of their work. Prior to that my exposure to photography had consisted of the "mainstream" images that appeared in magazines and books—smiling models, clean landscapes, and an unhealthy dose of the rule of thirds!

Q) What is it about your specialty that fascinates you?
A) Creating narratives from mass-produced inanimate objects. On their own, these figures are simply plastic or metal shapes, but in front of the lens with a few simple props or lighting they can start to develop their own character and tell a story.

Q) What equipment do you regularly use?
A) Pretty much anything and everything goes when I'm shooting macro! For "straight" shots I'll use a

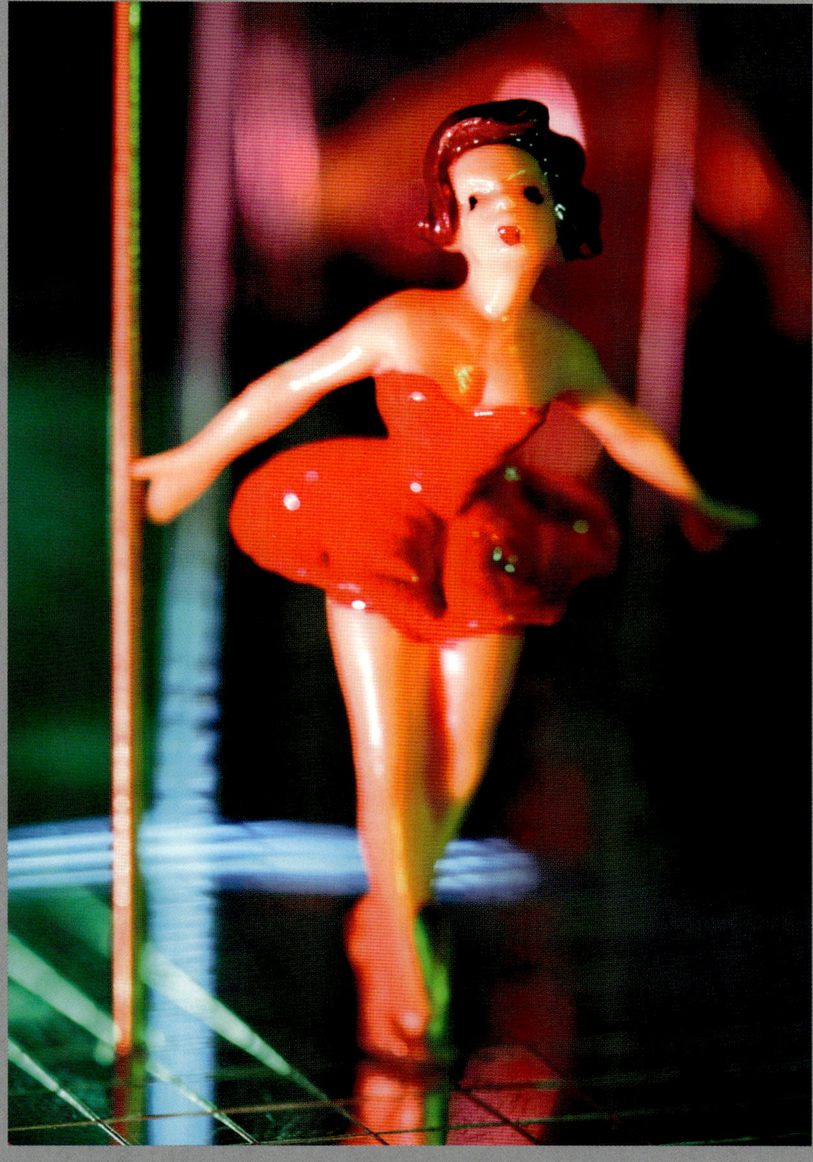

Opposite page, left:

Shot on 5x4in instant
Polaroid film (Type 55);
exposure unrecorded.

Opposite page, right:

Focal length: Modified 50mm prime
lens (freelensed image)
Aperture: f/4
Shutter speed: 1/250 sec.
ISO: 800

Left:

Focal length: 100mm macro lens
Aperture: f/5.6
Shutter speed: 1/3 sec.
ISO: 100

60mm macro lens on an APS-C format Nikon DSLR (giving me a 90mm equivalent focal length), with extension tubes if I want to get closer. However, that tends to be the exception rather than the norm and I'll more often reach for an "alternative" option, such as multiple close-up lenses for a "low-fi" twist; a set of M42 mount bellows fitted with a vintage medium-format enlarger lens that's about half a century old; or a modified 50mm Olympus Zuiko lens that I'll just hold in front of the sensor to shoot "freelens" images (such as the matador, opposite).

I'm also not adverse to shooting film, especially large format. In fact, the last camera I bought was a 5x4 Cambo. Using such a tactile—and relatively primitive—camera offers a different experience to digital and that's usually reflected in the images.

Q) How do you prepare your subjects?
A) I tend to use shallow depth of field, so I find I can get away with keeping things simple. I often don't need highly detailed backgrounds because they'll either not be seen, or thrown so far out of focus that they're unrecognizable. When a background is needed, I'll use low-res prints (to "suggest" the sky or a distant cityscape, for example), or use model trees or fences.

Q) How do you light your subjects?
A) My lighting kit includes tungsten, flash, and LED lights, but the light I return to again and again is a humble Anglepoise. It might not be a "proper" photographic lamp, but for small-scale still-life work I don't always want or need a large, powerful light source. I can fit the Angelpoise with a daylight-balanced bulb if I want to mix it with daylight, or use it with incandescent or even fluorescent bulbs if I need to. I can also position it very precisely. With some simple card reflectors or small mirrors it's easy to create a small "studio" setup.

Q) How important is postproduction to you?
A) It depends on the shot, but I find that I work most heavily on digitally originated images, rather than those that start their life on film. It's a lot easier to "play" with a Raw file and change things around, whereas starting with a scan from film is a lot like starting with a JPEG. I also find digital images inherently more transient—until they're printed they only exist as computer code, whereas you always have a tangible starting point with film.

Q) What is your top macro shooting tip?
A) It's easy to fall into the trap of thinking you need the latest gear to take great shots, but you can't buy your way to better pictures. What's more important is that you understand the basics of exposure, focus, lighting, and composition—and those are all things you can learn with the simplest kit.

Chapter 3

Basic Technique

Close-up and macro photography involves the same basic level of photographic knowledge as other genres, such as how to correctly expose and focus an image. The difference is that there is less room to maneuver in terms of technique. Close-up and macro photography is less forgiving of sloppy photographic practices, so what you might "get away with" elsewhere may no longer be enough when exploring the macro world. In this chapter the basic techniques of photography are covered, as are the refinements to these techniques necessary when shooting macro.

Right: One difference that is immediately apparent when shooting macro is the lack of depth of field. This impacts how and where you focus in order to maximize sharpness in the desired areas of images.

Focal length: 100mm macro lens

Aperture: f/5.6

Shutter speed: 1/640 sec.

ISO: 400

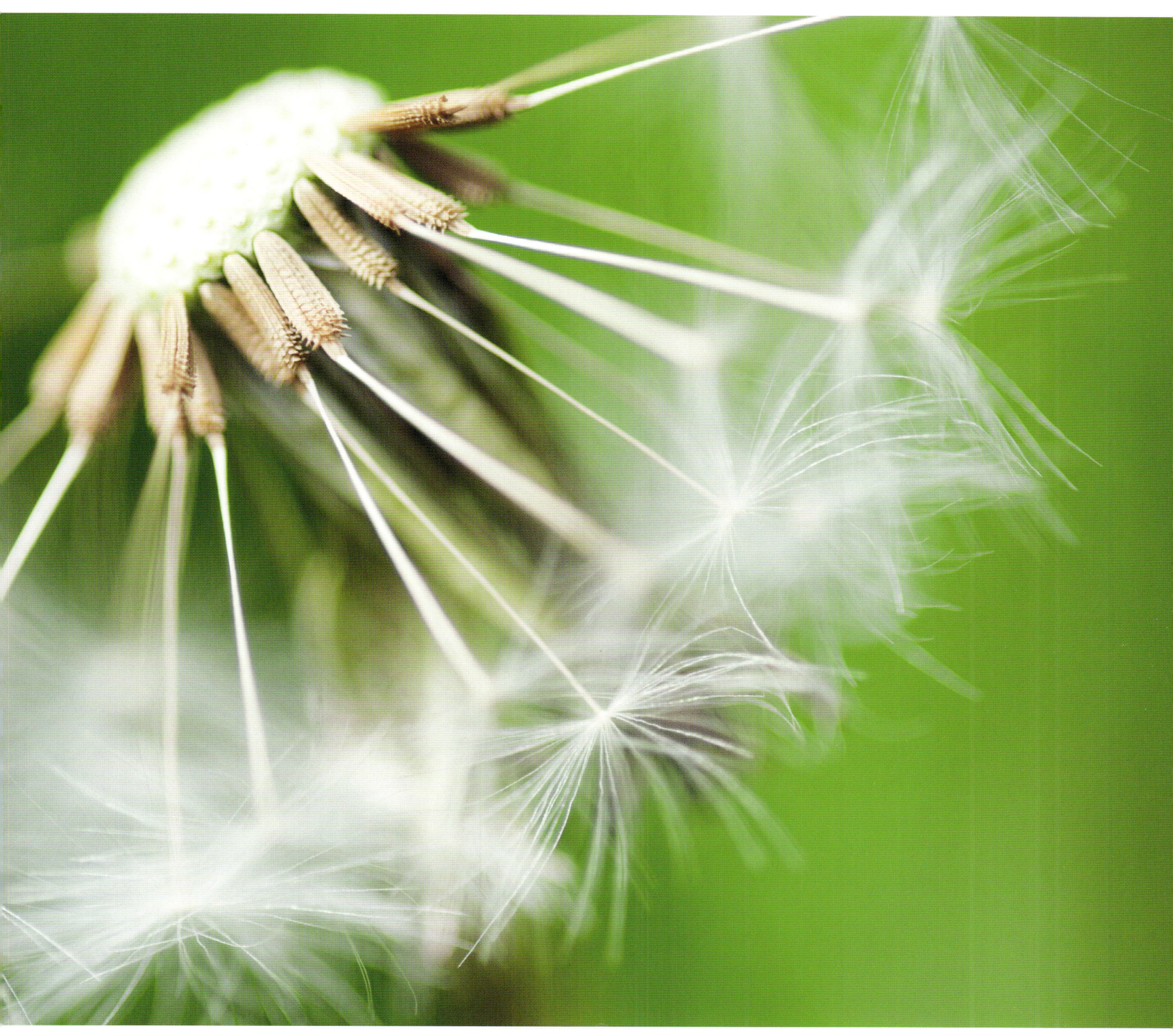

Establishing A Workflow

Between an idea and the final image is the execution. Macro photography often requires you to solve a number of problems before a successful image can be created. A lot of these problems are purely practical and can be encountered frequently: once you can solve these problems consistently, your macro shooting will become more efficient and rewarding, with fewer wasted shots taking up space on your memory card.

Making notes as you shoot is a good habit to acquire. It's not necessary to record exposure details and compatible lenses, as this information is stored in the metadata of the image. However, if you shoot using non-standard lenses (or are using a reversed lens, bellows, and so on) and/or non-TTL flash or other lighting, then making notes will remind you of how a particular problem was solved. Using notes and metadata will also help you to establish a workflow that allows you to shoot more effectively and successfully.

SENSOR CLEANING

Sensor dust-removal systems work well with loose, dry dust. However, they are less efficient when it comes to wet "dust" particles, such as pollen, and do not work at all with oil or water stains on a sensor. This sort of dirt will need to be removed manually using a wet-cleaning system, which typically involves gently wiping the exposed sensor with a swab moistened with an alcohol or detergent-based cleaning fluid. This is a procedure that needs to be done with care, as it is all too easy to scratch a sensor, but it's a skill worth learning, as it is another useful postproduction time saver.

File Types

There are two types of still-image file commonly recorded by cameras: JPEG and Raw. JPEG is a "finished" file that has been processed by the camera and can be used immediately once it has been downloaded to a computer. Raw files are not processed by the camera, so need to be imported into postproduction software, adjusted, and then exported as a more useful JPEG or TIFF file.

This makes JPEGs far more convenient, but convenience comes at a price. Settings such as white balance, color saturation, and contrast are "baked" into the JPEG. Although it is possible to tweak a JPEG during postproduction to change them, image quality suffers if too many adjustments, or overly heavy changes are made.

By comparison, a Raw file can be thought of as a "packet" that includes all the image data captured by the camera at the time of exposure. You can more freely adjust settings such as white balance and picture parameters without any noticeable loss of quality—the processing changes only get "baked" into the file when you output it. This also means you can go back to the Raw file and re-edit and re-output it at any point, again without loss of quality.

Therefore, the first thing to decide with your shooting workflow is what file type to shoot. Raw is highly recommended for the freedom it allows in how you interpret an image in postproduction.

Dust

There are two problems caused by dust that should be tackled before you shoot. If you are using a camera with an interchangeable lens the first problem is dust landing on the camera's sensor. Shooting macro images often means using a small aperture to achieve sufficient depth of field—smaller than you would generally use for more conventional photographic subjects. However, by increasing the depth of field you also increase the sharpness and visibility of any sensor dust, which will be seen as dark circular blobs that are particularly noticeable in areas of light, even tone in an image.

To combat this, most modern system cameras feature a dust-removal system. When activated, the optical low-pass filter in front of the sensor is vibrated, which literally shakes the dust from the sensor. Dust-removal can usually be set to run automatically when the camera is first switched on and then when it is switched off again. When shooting macro images, it is also worth manually running the cleaning cycle just before exposure.

The second problem is the dust (and other matter such as hair) that settles on your subject. This is often not noticeable to the naked eye, and as system cameras typically hold the aperture open at maximum until the moment of exposure, you may not notice dust when you compose the shot. However, it will be readily apparent after you've taken your photograph.

The simplest way to remove dust from a subject is to either use a blower to blow dust away, or wipe a soft paintbrush over your subject. Which method is preferable will be largely down to the delicacy (or otherwise) of the subject.

In both instances, dust can be cloned out of shots later in postproduction. However, this can be time consuming: it often takes far longer than the time it takes to clean both your camera's sensor and the subject.

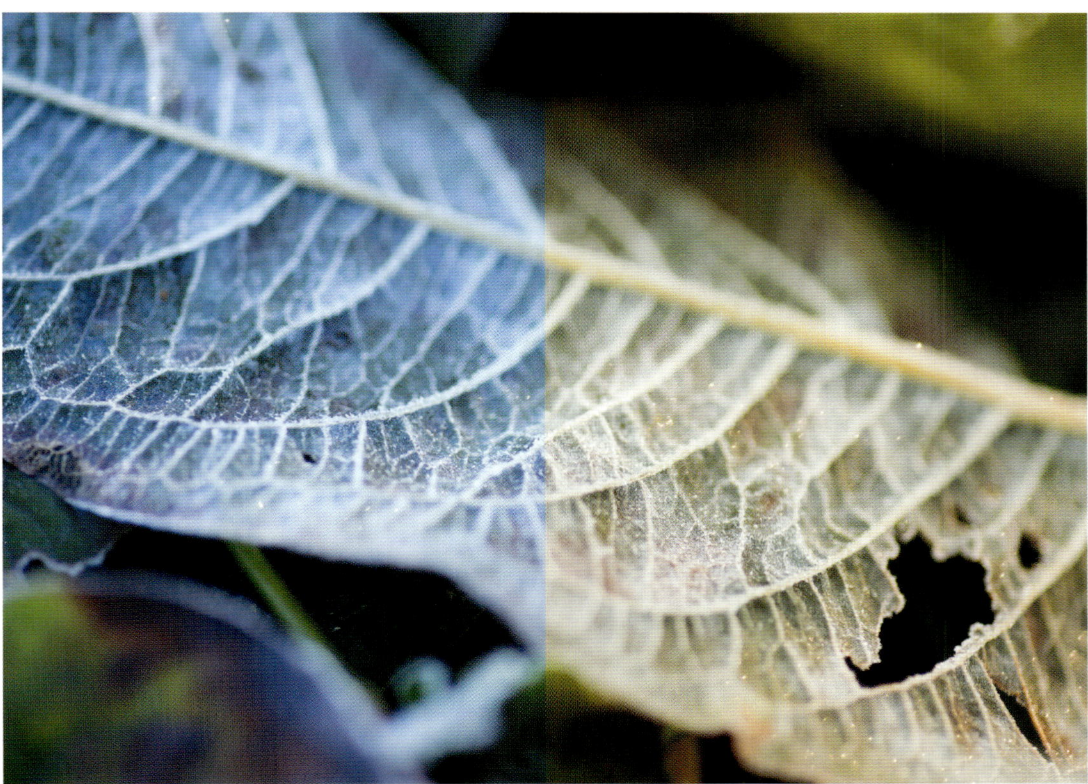

Left: Raw files are the closest a photographer gets to a blank canvas. They can be re-worked over and over again without loss of quality, allowing you to revisit your images if or when your tastes change. This includes altering aspects of an image such as white balance, so you can retain the color bias of the light that illuminated your subject (far left) or remove the bias (left).

Focal length: 100mm macro lens

Aperture: f/3.8

Shutter speed: 1/100 sec.

ISO: 800

Below left & below: Dust and hair is particularly noticeable on high-gloss surfaces, such as this DVD. Care must be taken when cleaning surfaces with a cloth, though, as you can make matters worse if you drop fibers onto your subject.

Focal length: 100mm macro lens

Aperture: f/18

Shutter speed: 1.6 sec.

ISO: 100

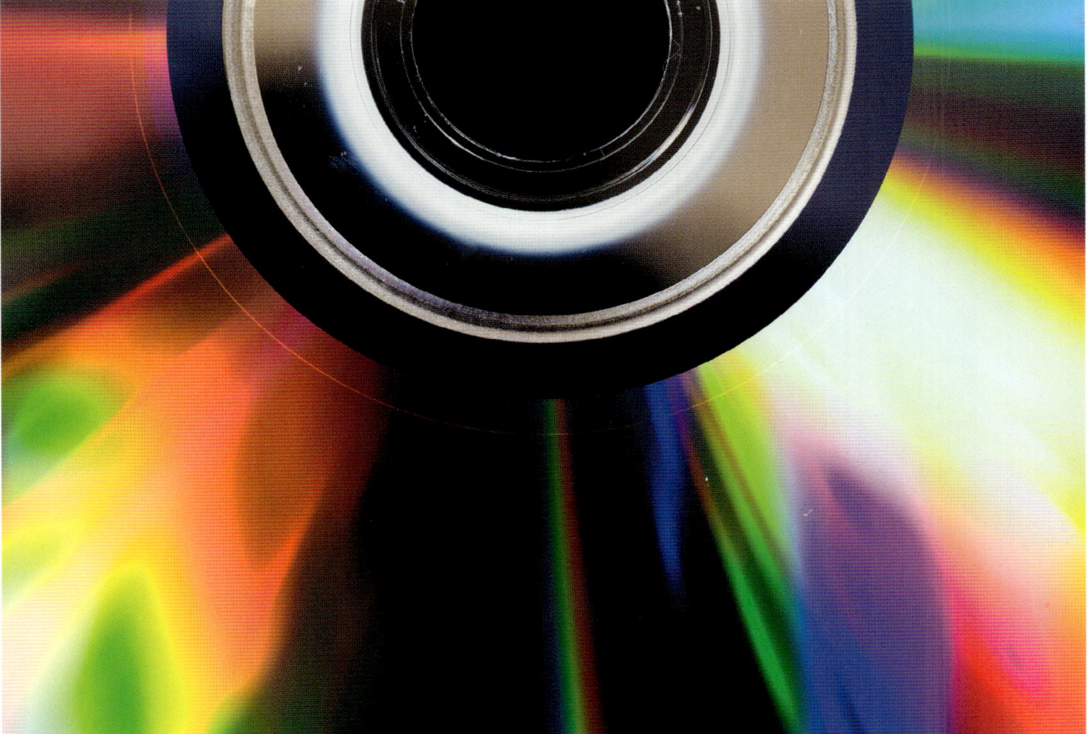

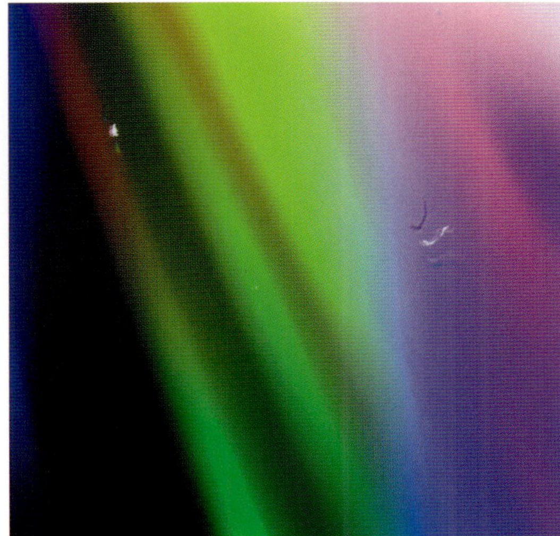

Exposure Modes

Modern cameras feature a range of exposure modes, from fully automatic, which allows virtually no control over exposure, through to manual exposure, which gives you total control over your camera. In theory, you can use any exposure mode when shooting close-up or macro photographs, but taking at least partial control over your exposures is highly recommended.

Fully Automatic

"Full Auto" (or variations of the term) is a mode that typically allows no control over exposure, so the camera selects the shutter speed, aperture, and ISO that will be used. There is also little or no control over other aspects of shooting, such as how and where the camera focuses, making it of limited use for serious macro photography.

Macro

Most consumer DSLRs and mirrorless cameras (as well as compact cameras) have a number of "scene modes" that are designed to optimize the camera's settings when shooting under specific conditions. These modes will typically include a Macro (or Close-Up) mode.

In this mode, shutter speed is typically prioritized over aperture to reduce the risk of camera shake, but like Full Auto there are limitations on how much—if any—influence you have over the exposure. As a result, it is only just better than Fully Automatic.

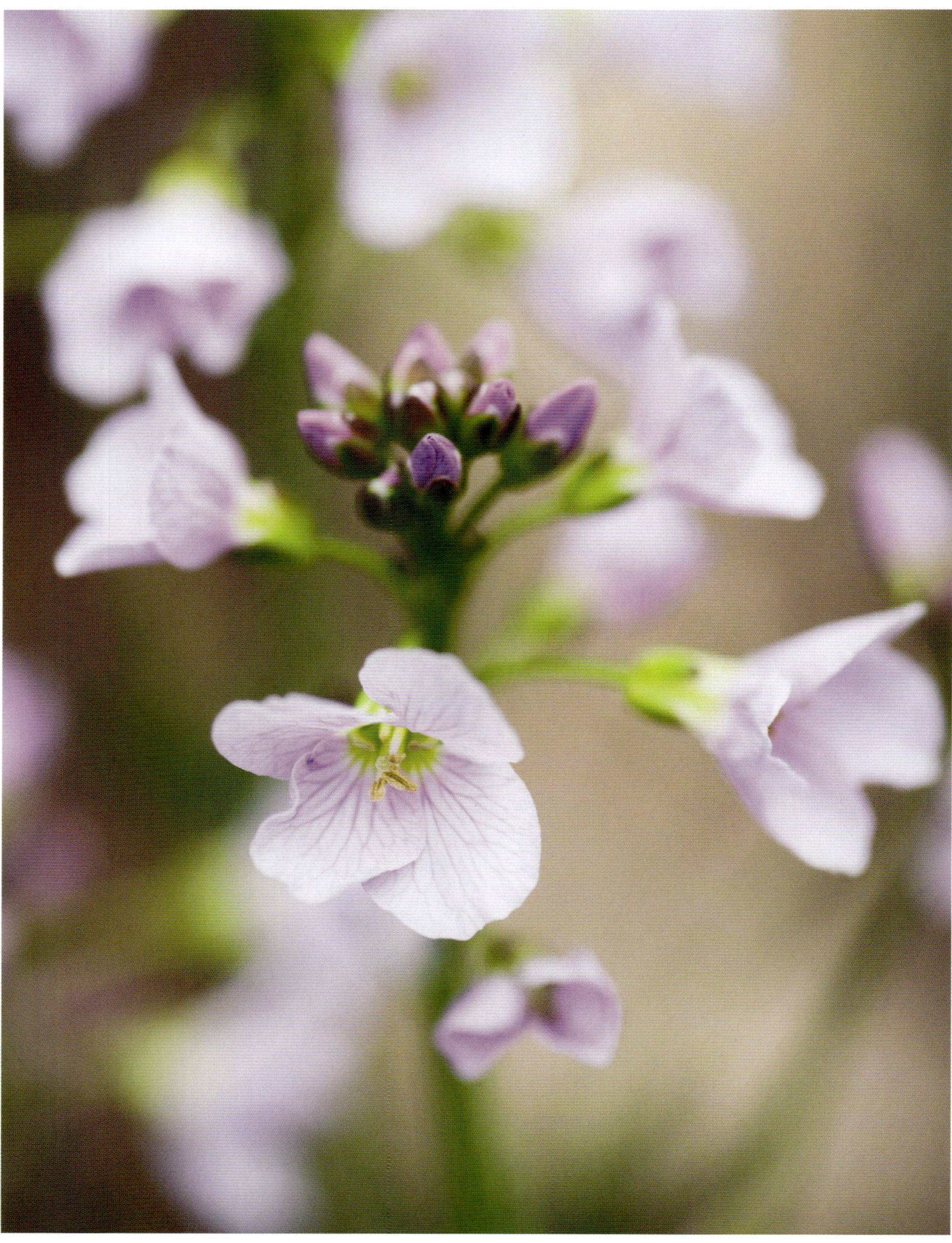

Right: For macro photography, Aperture Priority is arguably the most important of the exposure modes. It allows you to control depth of field, with the safety net of semi-automated exposure.

Focal length: 100mm macro lens

Aperture: f/5.6

Shutter speed: 1/500 sec.

ISO: 400

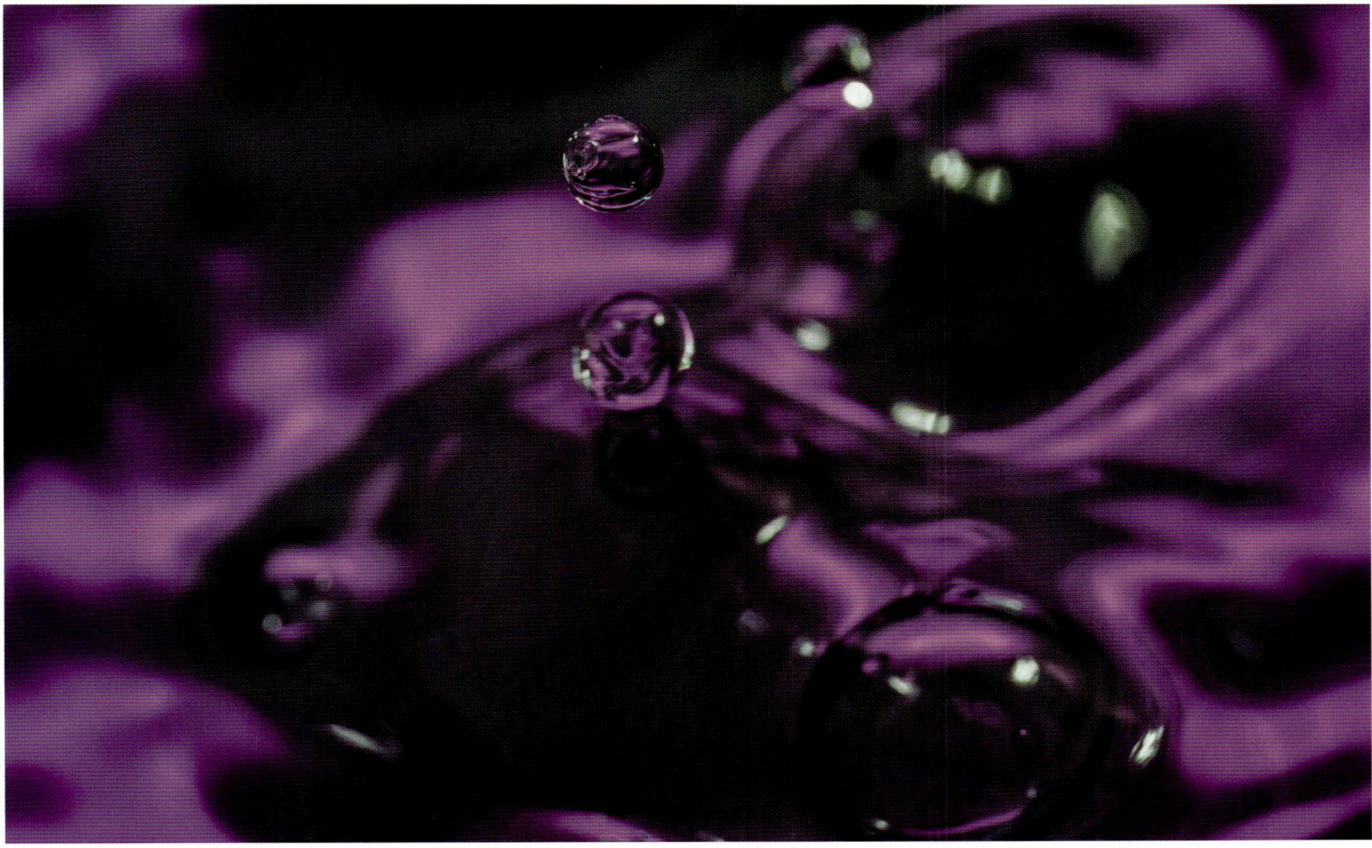

Program (P)

Program mode automates exposure control, but unlike Full Auto it still lets you alter the camera settings. The initial shutter speed and aperture combination selected by the camera can be shifted to a different combination if required. Settings such as ISO, white balance, and focusing modes can also be adjusted. Program is a useful half-way point between Full Auto and modes such as Aperture Priority and Manual.

Shutter Priority (S/Tv)

Shutter Priority is a semi-automatic exposure mode where you select the shutter speed and the camera sets the aperture required to achieve the correct exposure. Shutter Priority is useful when you need to set a precise shutter speed to achieve a particular effect.

Aperture Priority (A/Av)

Aperture Priority is also a semi-automatic exposure mode, but here you set the aperture, with the camera automatically setting the appropriate shutter speed.

For most close-up and macro photography this is a more useful mode than Shutter Priority, as the aperture controls the depth of field in an image. As you will see later in this chapter, controlling depth of field is crucial when it comes to creating satisfyingly sharp macro images.

Manual (M)

Manual mode hands all responsibility for the exposure to you, so you have to set the shutter speed and aperture yourself to create a correctly exposed image (guided either by the exposure meter in the camera or a handheld meter).

It is often necessary to shoot in Manual exposure mode when using a non-standard lens, such as a lens mounted via a reversing ring or bellows; in this instance the aperture would be set via the lens' aperture ring and the shutter speed set manually via the camera.

Bulb (B)

Bulb mode is used when the required shutter speed is greater than the longest setting that can be selected on the camera (this is typically 30 sec., although some cameras allow shutter speeds of 60 sec.). In Bulb mode, the shutter is held open by keeping the shutter-release button pressed down or locking the shutter open with a remote release; the exposure ends when the shutter-release button is released.

Bulb is necessary in very low light—either due to the ambient lighting conditions or through the use of filtration, when low ISOs are used, and when a small aperture has been selected.

Exposure Metering

There are two types of exposure meter: incident and reflective. The difference between the two is that incident metering measures the light falling onto a scene using a handheld exposure meter, whereas reflective metering—the type built-into cameras—measures the light reflected by the scene. It is a subtle but significant difference.

Reflective metering makes the assumption that a scene is an averagely reflective midtone (that is, it reflects approximately 18% of the light that falls on it when all of the tones are balanced out). Generally this is a reasonable assumption, but scenes that are not averagely reflective can cause exposure errors to occur: scenes that are darker-than-average can cause overexposure, while lighter-than-average scenes will lead to underexposure. In both cases this is due to the metering system attempting to average the scene out to a midtone.

Incident exposure meters do not suffer from this problem. The reflective properties of a scene do not affect the reading as the meter only measures the intensity of the light falling on the scene.

Used correctly, this makes incident meters highly accurate, but they are not ideal for macro work for a number of reasons. The first is the working distance of a lens may make it difficult to physically bring the meter close to the subject. The magnification of the lens also has an effect on exposure that would not be accounted for by a handheld exposure meter. Filters that affect exposure (such as ND filters) are also not accounted for by an incident exposure reading.

In the latter two instances the exposure would need to be adjusted manually to ensure correct exposure, but using a camera's reflective metering system would automatically take any light loss into account. Despite its occasional flaws, this means in-camera metering is generally the better option, particularly when used in conjunction with a histogram to monitor its accuracy (see page 70).

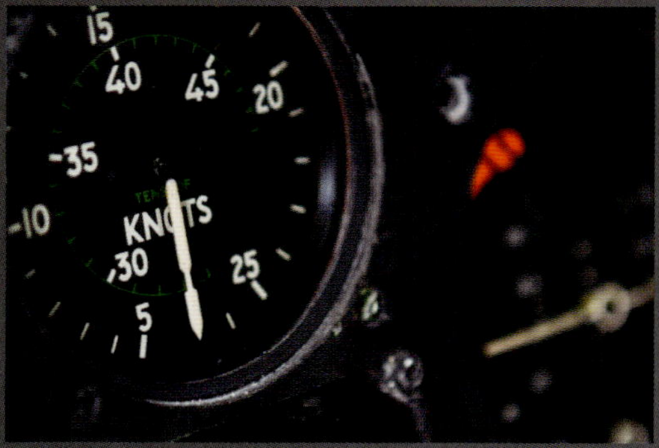

Above: Darker-than-average scene.
Exposure compensation: -1 stop

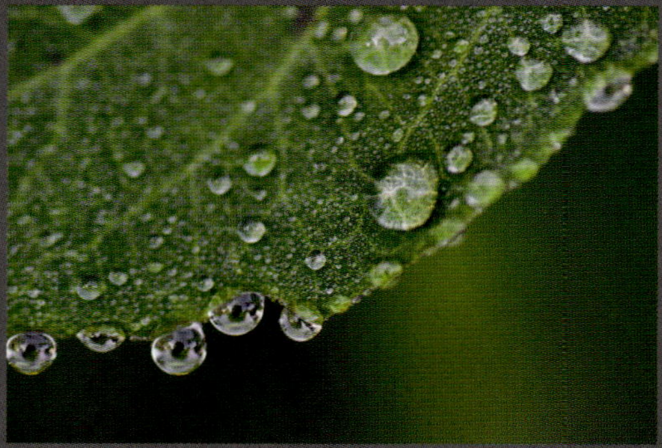

Above: Average scene.
Exposure compensation: 0

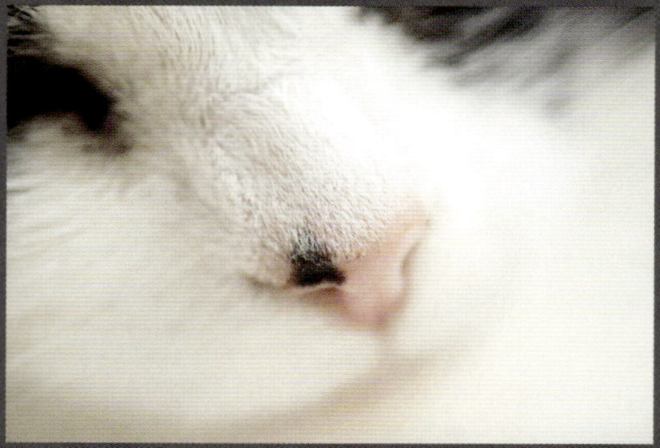

Above: Lighter-than-average scene.
Exposure compensation: +1 stop

Metering Modes

System cameras offer a number of different exposure metering modes that determine how a scene is metered. The modes differ either by how much—or how little—of a scene is metered, or by using different algorithms to assess the metering results to improve accuracy or convenience. Which metering mode you choose therefore has an influence on the final exposure.

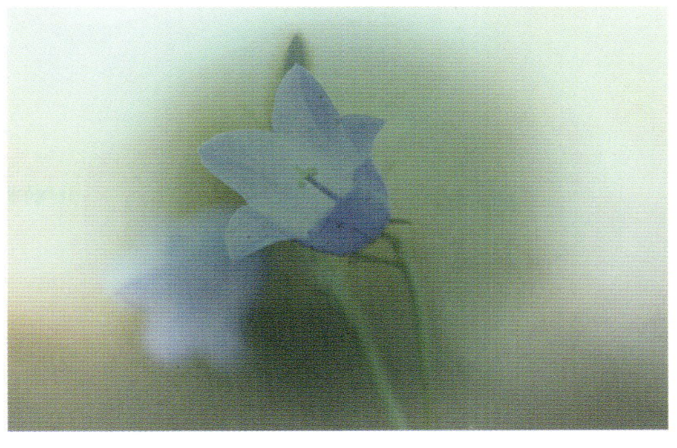

Center-weighted

As the name suggests, the exposure reading is biased toward the center of the scene rather than the periphery (the degree of bias depends on the camera, but is usually around 60%). Center-weighted metering is generally more consistent than Evaluative metering, but it is more likely to be fooled into incorrect exposure in tricky lighting situations.

Evaluative

Also known as Multi-zone, Matrix, or Multi-Pattern metering, depending on the camera brand. Evaluative metering systems divide a scene into a number of different zones or cells. When an exposure reading is made, each of these cells is metered independently. The data from each cell is then analyzed by the camera to look for certain patterns in brightness across the scene. From this, the camera can make an informed guess as to the type of scene being shot and set the exposure accordingly. Data from the cell closest to the focus point is often given higher weighting under the assumption that the lens is focused on the subject.

   This use of data and algorithms to set exposure makes Evaluative metering accurate most of the time. However, it can still be fooled by an overly dark or bright scene. It can also be inconsistent in setting the exposure, particularly if the scene changes slightly between shots or a new focus point is selected.

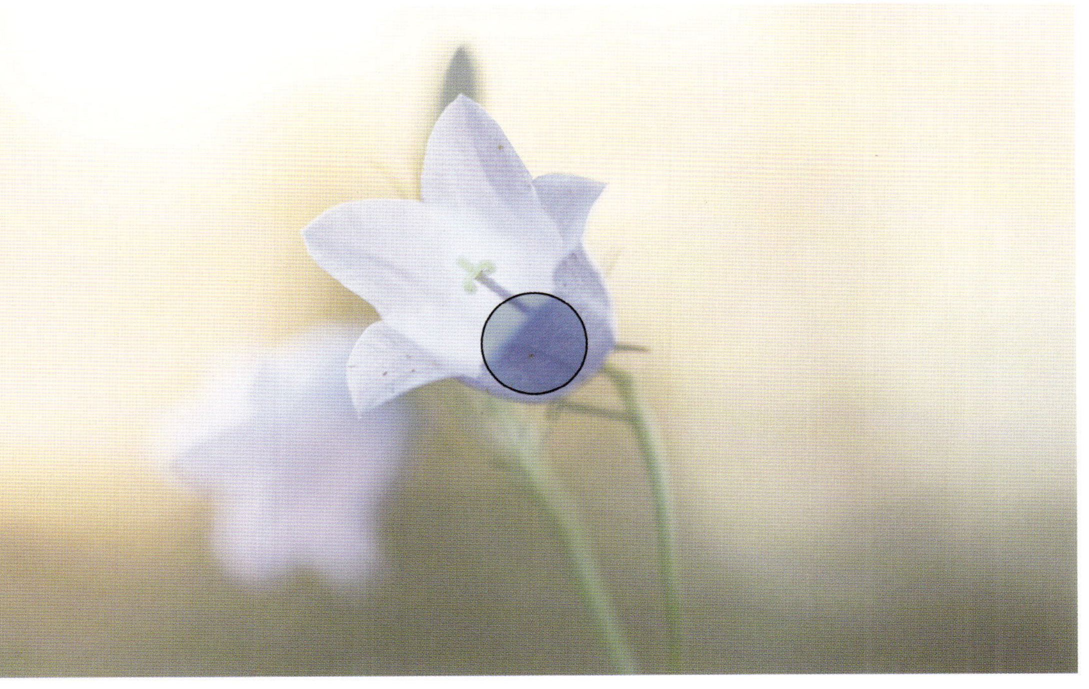

Spot

Spot metering restricts the area being metered to approximately 1–5% of the viewfinder/LCD frame. This area is typically in a marked area at the center of the viewfinder/LCD frame, although some cameras let you tie the metering to the current AF point. The main advantage of spot metering is that you can choose which part of the scene you meter from and set the exposure accordingly. Usually this would be from a midtone in the scene, with the exposure set in Manual mode.

Histograms

A histogram is an invaluable guide to exposure on a digital camera. Essentially it is a graph that shows the tonal range of an image. Along the X-axis are the brightness or luminance values, from pure black (the shadows) at the far left to pure white (the highlights) at the far right, with the tones that correspond to the midtones in the middle. The Y-axis shows the proportional number of pixels that correspond to a particular tone.

The first thing to appreciate is that there is no right or wrong shape to a histogram: the shape is entirely dependent on the tonal range of the image. However, the shape can serve as a warning sign that something is amiss.

One useful sign that the exposure needs to be altered is when either end of the histogram is skewed toward either side of the histogram box. When it is heavily skewed to the left, this is a warning that the image is underexposed (or is correctly exposed if your subject is very dark in color—histograms do need interpreting). A histogram that is heavily skewed to the right is a possible indication of overexposure (or is correctly exposed if your subject is lightly toned).

When a histogram appears to lean against either end of the histogram box then something really is amiss. This is known as "clipping" and indicates that the shadows are pure black with no detail recorded (when the histogram is clipped at the left), or that detail has been lost in the highlights, which are being recorded as pure white (when the histogram is clipping at the right). In both cases exposure adjustments would need to be made to correct the exposure.

Left & below: Once you are familiar with how a histogram works you can start to see which areas of an image correspond to which areas of the histogram. In this image the colored circles correspond to the colored areas in the histogram.

Focal length: 100mm macro lens

Aperture: f/4

Shutter speed: 1/125 sec.

ISO: 100

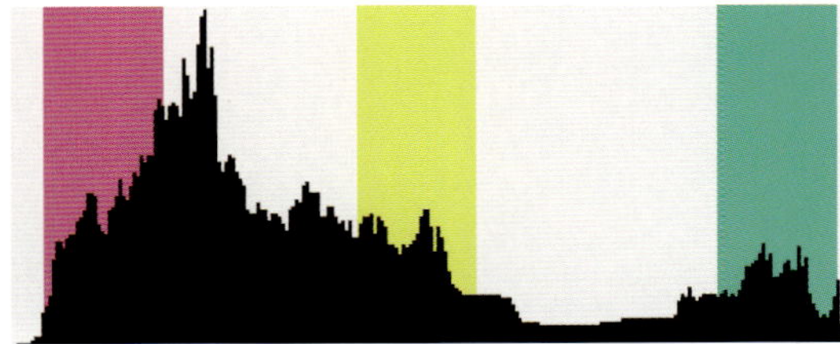

Exposure

Exposure is the art of allowing just the right amount of light to reach a camera's sensor so that an acceptable image is produced. There are two physical controls that let you vary the amount of light reaching the sensor: the shutter speed and the aperture inside the lens. A third exposure control—ISO—sets the amount of light required to make the image to start with.

With each of these controls, the exposure is altered in "stops" (or fractions of a stop). When you adjust the exposure by 1 stop, this means halving or doubling the amount of light captured by the camera (or required by the sensor when adjusting the ISO).

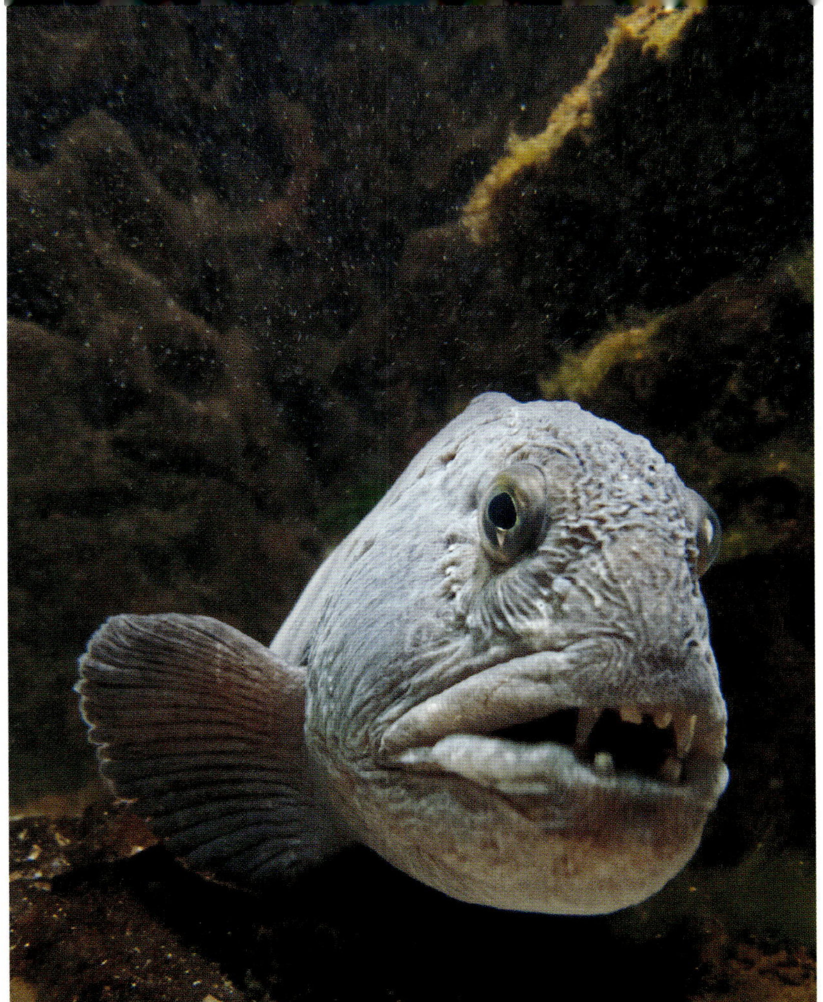

 Knowing the limitations of your camera means you can make informed decisions as you shoot. This image was shot on a compact camera. From experience I know that ISO 400 is the acceptable limit with this camera before noise becomes an issue, whereas the DSLR that I regularly use is virtually noise-free at ISO 400.

Focal length: 6.8mm

Aperture: f/2.8

Shutter speed: 1/15 sec.

ISO: 400

ISO

Changing the ISO setting on a camera effectively alters the sensitivity of the sensor to light (it is actually slightly more complicated than this—adjusting ISO upward amplifies the electronic signal generated by the camera's sensor after exposure, making it appear more sensitive).

At the camera's lowest—or "base"—ISO the sensor is at its least sensitive, so more light is required to make an exposure. This means that a longer shutter speed and/or large aperture are required. Increasing the ISO allows the use of a faster shutter speed and/or smaller aperture, both of which are often necessary when shooting macro imagery.

The downside of high ISO settings is the increase of "noise" in an image, which is seen as pixels with a random brightness or color. There is also a reduction in the dynamic range of the image as ISO increases.

The amount of noise varies between cameras, but the general rule is that cameras with smaller sensors are more prone to the negative effects of higher ISO settings than cameras with larger sensors. Although sensor technology is continually developing—and current sensors are far better than the previous generation—you should always select the camera's "base" ISO to maximize image quality.

Shutter Speed

The shutter speed is the precise amount of time that the camera's shutter mechanism is open, allowing light to reach the sensor and make an image. The shutter speed range available on DSLR and mirrorless cameras is typically 1/4000–30 sec. (plus Bulb). Compact cameras usually do not offer such a wide range of shutter speeds.

The shutter speed you select has an effect on how movement is recorded in an image. Slower shutter speeds blur movement, making the subject soft, and with a sufficiently long shutter speed, almost ethereal. Conversely, faster shutter speeds freeze movement to render your subject in crisp detail. These two aspects of shutter speed are covered in more detail later on.

Shutter speed also affects your ability to handhold a camera successfully during an exposure. The slower the shutter speed and the longer the focal length of a lens, the greater the risk that camera shake will mar an image. Camera shake is seen as an overall softness, with a definite directionality. Macro photography exacerbates the risk of camera shake, as any movement of the camera during an exposure will be magnified as much as the subject itself. Therefore, if you're shooting macro images handheld, use fast shutter speeds whenever possible. The compromise that needs to be made is either to use a larger aperture, which will reduce the depth of field, or increase the ISO, which might increase the appearance of noise in the image.

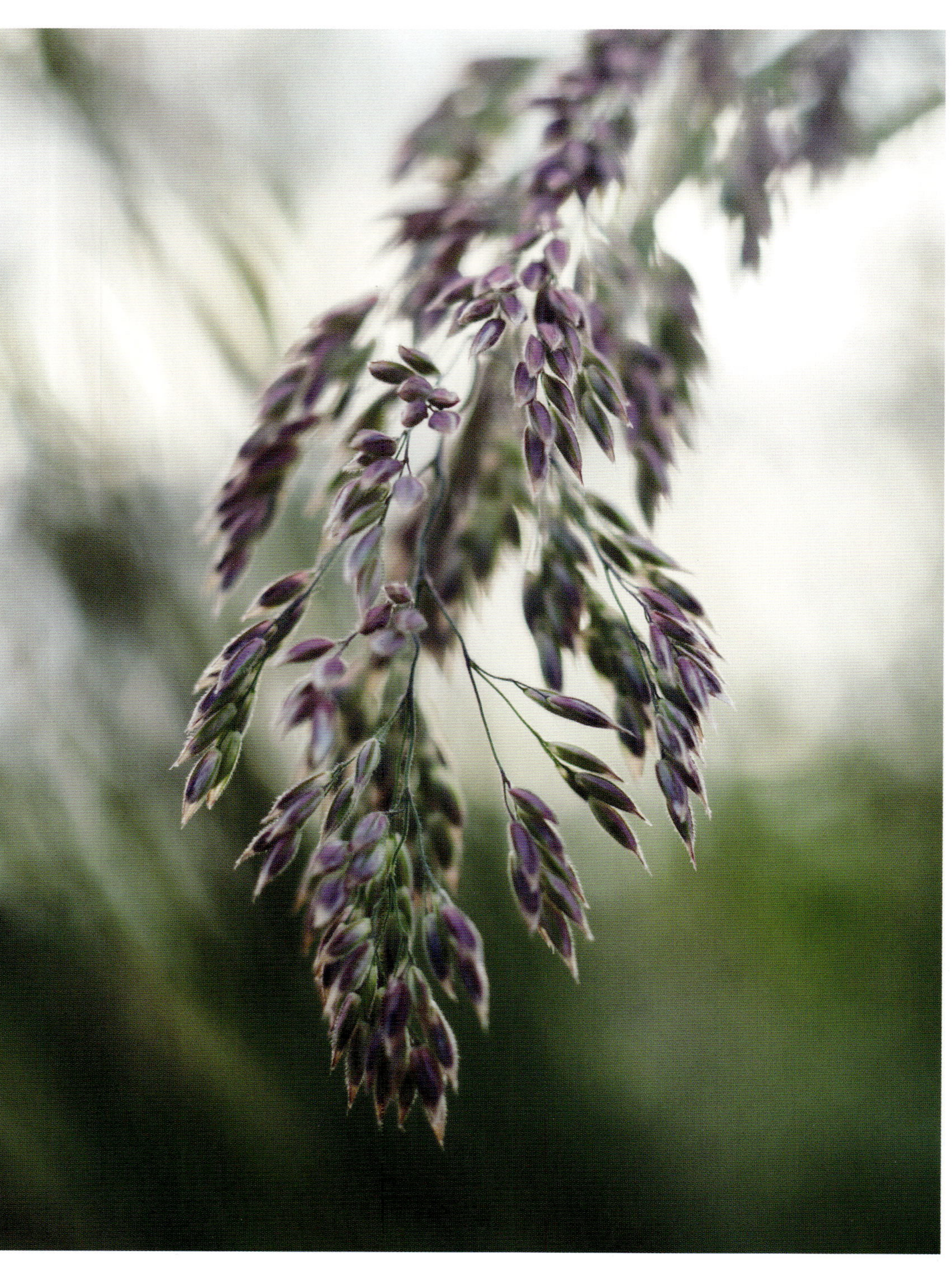

Right: Lightweight subjects—such as this grass head— are easily disturbed by the gentlest of breezes. To shoot this image I prioritized shutter speed over aperture and relied on accurate focusing to ensure the subject was sharp where necessary.

Focal length: 85mm with extension tubes

Aperture: f/2.8

Shutter speed: 1/400 sec.

ISO: 200

Image Stabilization

Image stabilization is a common feature on lenses or cameras, and is designed to reduce the effects of camera shake. There are two types of stabilization technology currently used: lens based and sensor based. As this suggests, lens-based stabilization adjusts optical elements inside the lens to counteract camera shake, whereas sensor-based stabilization moves the image sensor inside the camera to reduce the effects of camera shake.

Both systems typically allow the use of shutter speeds 3-stops slower than would normally cause camera shake, but this is only true when you're shooting non-macro subjects—switch to shooting macro imagery and the effectiveness of the stabilization is often significantly reduced.

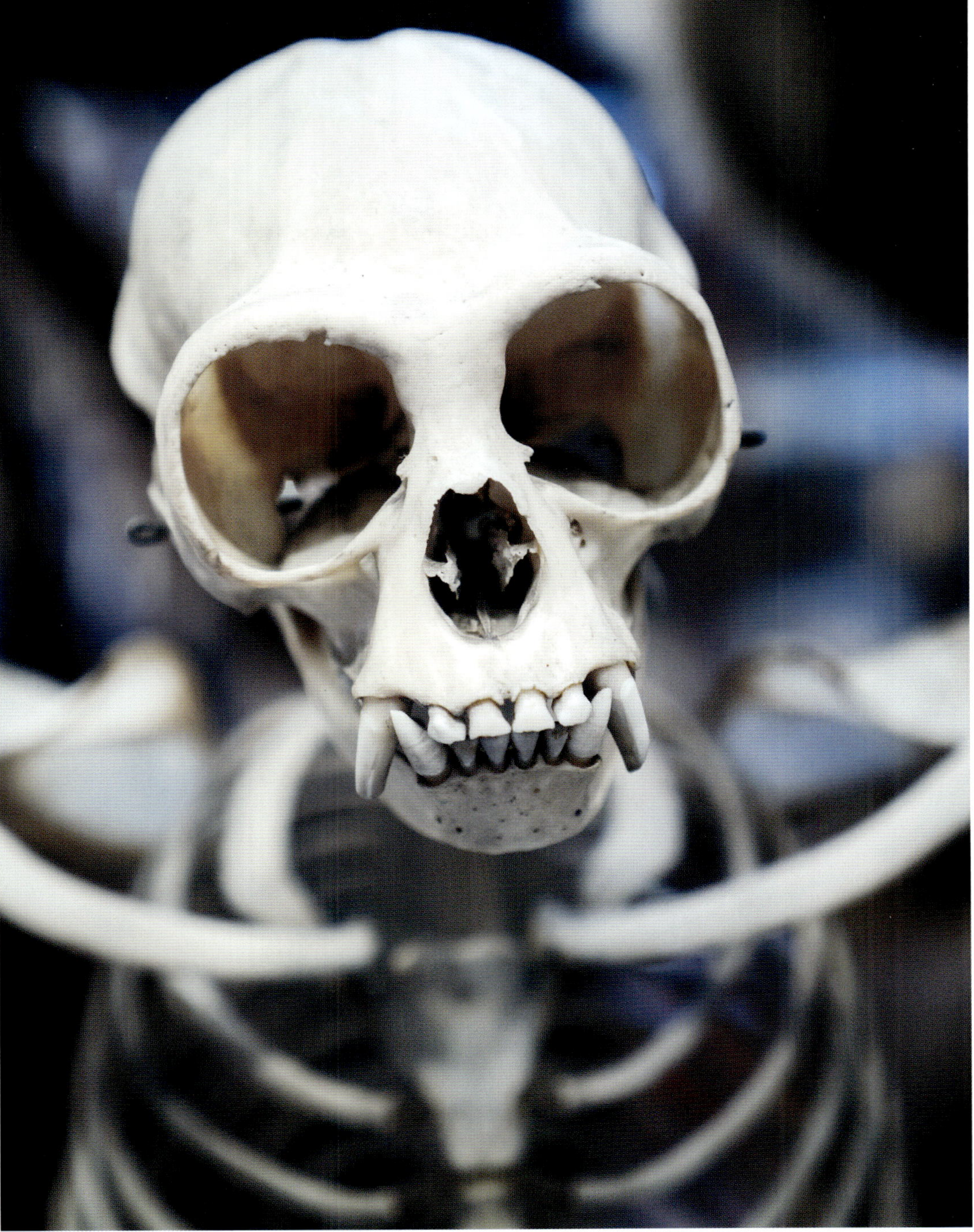

Above: Museums are a good source of interesting subjects, such as this white-handed gibbon skull. If the subject is behind glass, gently press your lens against the glass to stabilize your camera and remove unwanted reflections.

Focal length: 35mm

Aperture: f/2.8

Shutter speed: 0.4 sec.

ISO: 400

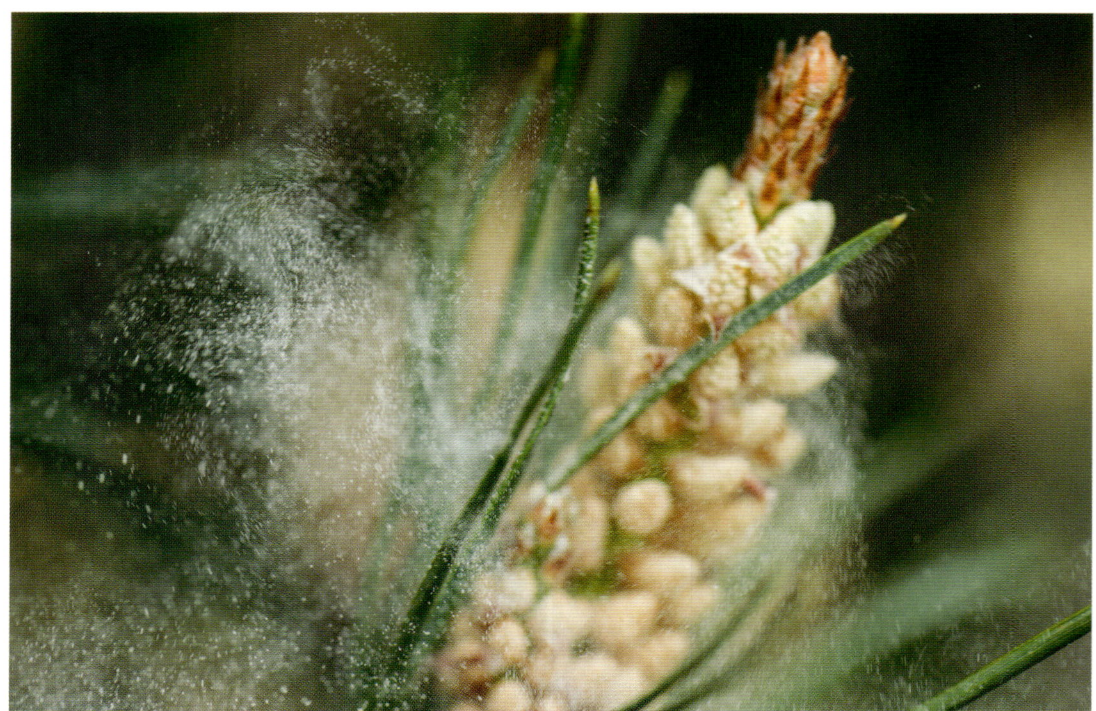

Movement

The shutter speed you use determines how movement is captured in an image. As a general rule, the faster the shutter speed used, the more likely it is that any subject movement will be frozen. However, this also depends on the speed of the subject and its size within the image: slow-moving subjects do not need as fast a shutter speed as subjects that move more quickly, while frame-filling subjects will require a faster shutter speed than a subject that is smaller in the frame if you want to freeze movement.

However, whether you choose to freeze movement is largely an esthetic decision. Although using a slower shutter speed will add blur to a moving subject, this can—slightly ironically—create a greater sense of movement than "freezing" it. If you use a sufficiently long shutter speed your subject will blur completely, losing its shape and texture to create a more abstract interpretation.

Using A Tripod

Shooting close-up or macro photographs with the camera mounted on a tripod is highly recommended. A tripod not only provides a stable platform for the camera, but it also forces you to slow down and thoroughly think through the shooting process from start to finish. Another plus point for tripods is that they allow you to set up a shot—including pre-focusing—and wait until the right moment to shoot. This latter use is especially useful when you're waiting for insects to land on a particular plant or flower.

However, a tripod that is set up incorrectly will be unstable. This is particularly true when you are using a heavy DSLR and large macro lens. To give yourself the best possible platform, the legs of a tripod should be set to their maximum angle of adjustment with the center column as vertical as possible. On flat ground this is relatively easy, but on uneven ground you will need to vary the lengths of the legs. Adjust the angle of the camera using the tripod head and then lock the head as tightly as possible.

During a long exposure try not to move around. Soft ground or even floorboards in a studio can give under your weight and disturb the tripod. If in doubt (particularly if exposure times are in excess of 1 sec.) set the camera to self-timer with a countdown of five seconds or more, and then move several meters away from your camera until the exposure is complete.

Tip

Shutter speed isn't the only option available to freeze movement. The rapid burst of light from a flash can be equally effective, if not more so (see page 122–123 for more details).

Tips

Unless it can be angled at 90º to its default position, a tripod's center column can often stop you getting the camera low to the ground. If the center column can be removed, you may find you can fit it upside down, which will allow you to hang your camera as low to the ground as necessary. It will mean shooting upside down and make looking through a viewfinder difficult, but using Live View will help, particularly if you can swing the LCD to a usable angle.

Use a focus adjustment rail to make minor changes to the camera position rather than the tripod. It is easy to "overshoot" when moving a tripod, especially when shooting at magnifications greater than 1x.

DSLRs often feature a function known as "mirror-lock up," which swings the camera's reflex mirror up and pauses before the shutter opens and the exposure is made. This stops the mirror sending vibrations through the camera that can cause an effect similar to camera shake. However, as you can no longer see through the viewfinder, mirror-lock up is only suitable when using a tripod. Mirror-lock up is not necessary when using Live View.

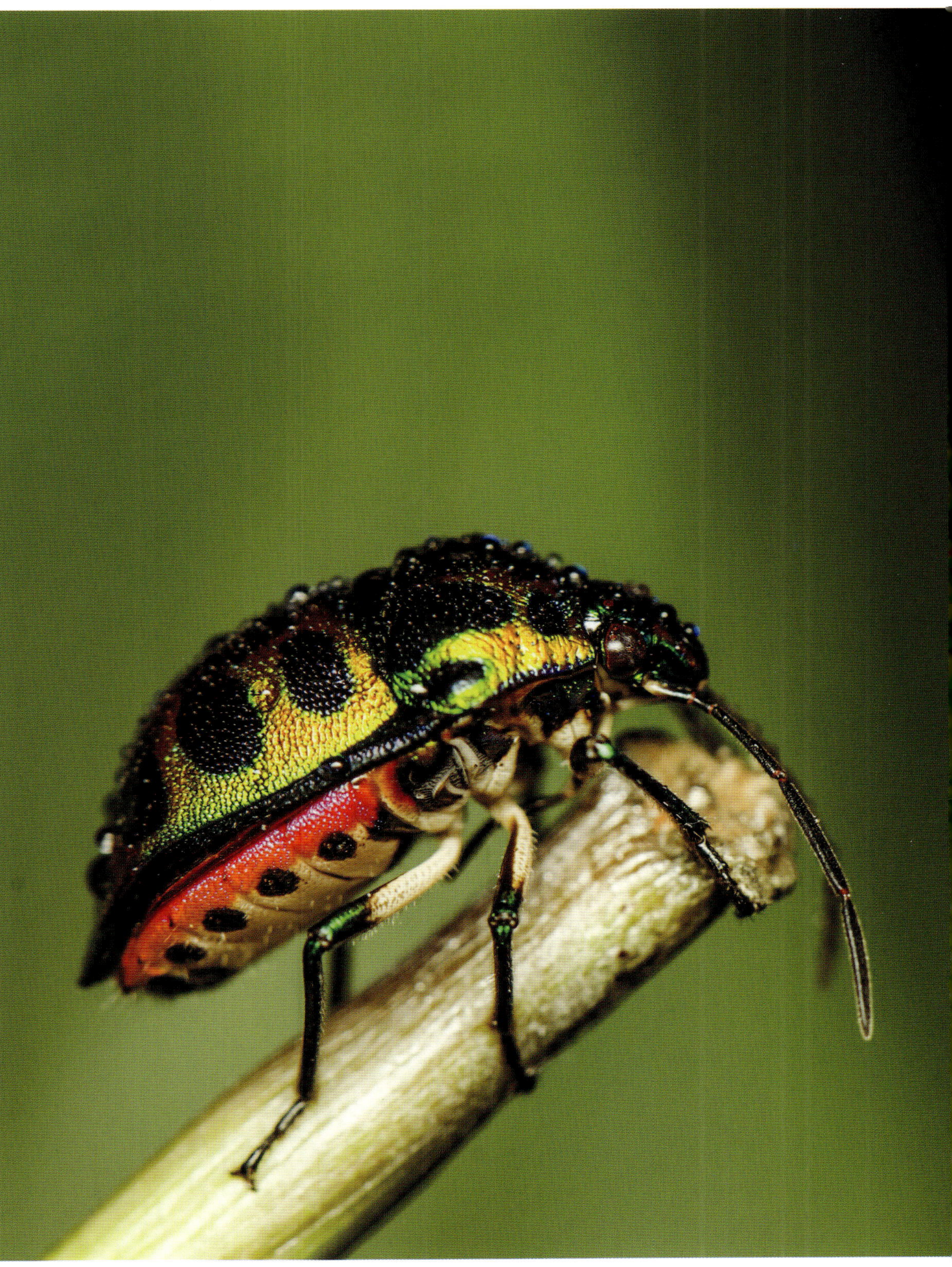

Right: Tripods take time to set up, so are not well suited to subjects that may move before you finish framing your shot. Insects are one such type of subject, unless they are shot early in the morning when they are cold and relatively sluggish, as with this dew-covered jewel bug.

Focal length: 180mm macro lens

Aperture: f/16

Shutter speed: 1/50 sec.

ISO: 400

Handholding A Camera

Although a tripod should be used to minimize the risk of camera shake when shooting macro, this is not always physically possible and sometimes it is necessary to shoot handheld. This is when good shooting discipline will maximize your chances of creating an acceptably sharp image.

If you need to stand to take a shot, tuck your elbows into your chest and support the lens with your left hand. Keep your feet slightly apart and stand as straight as possible. Just before you shoot take a breath, breathe out and then—just before you breathe in again—gently push the shutter-release button down to take the shot.

Whenever possible, find something you can use as a support. Walls or fence posts are useful, as are railings, signposts, and other street furniture. Either support the camera itself or support yourself to keep the camera steady.

Using a beanbag will help you keep your camera steady on virtually any surface and is generally far easier to use than a tripod when shooting at ground level.

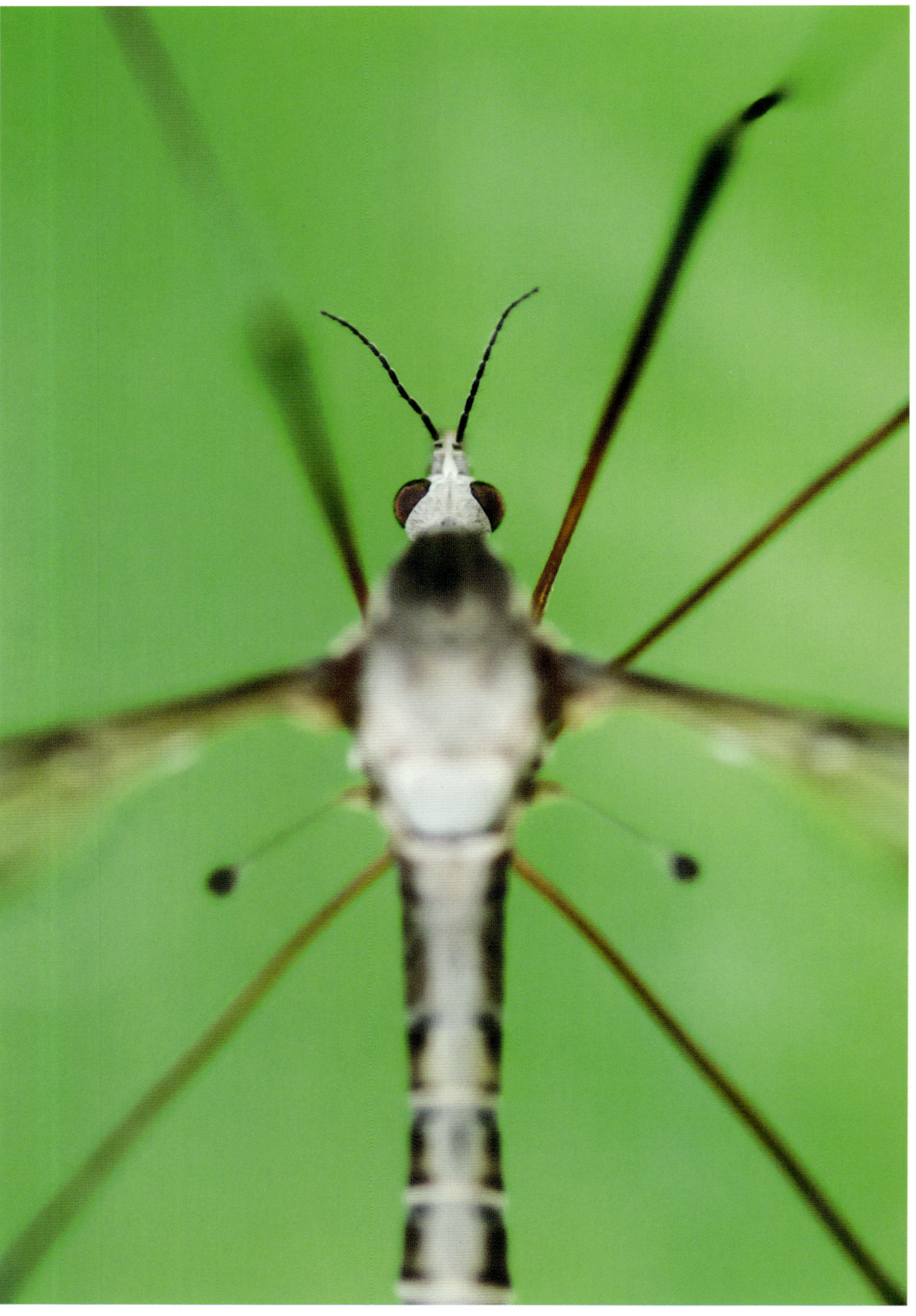

Tips

A traditional way to avoid camera shake is to set the shutter speed so that it is at least *1/focal length* of the (full-frame equivalent) focal length. For example, use a 50mm focal length and the shutter speed should be at least 1/50 sec.

However, this is less useful when shooting close-ups and macro, as slight camera movements are magnified more than when shooting non-close-up subjects. Instead, *1/focal length x 2* is a reasonable guide for close-ups (so 1/100 sec. with a 50mm focal length) and *1/focal length x 3* is safer when shooting close to a 1:1 reproduction ratio (1/150 sec. with a 50mm focal length).

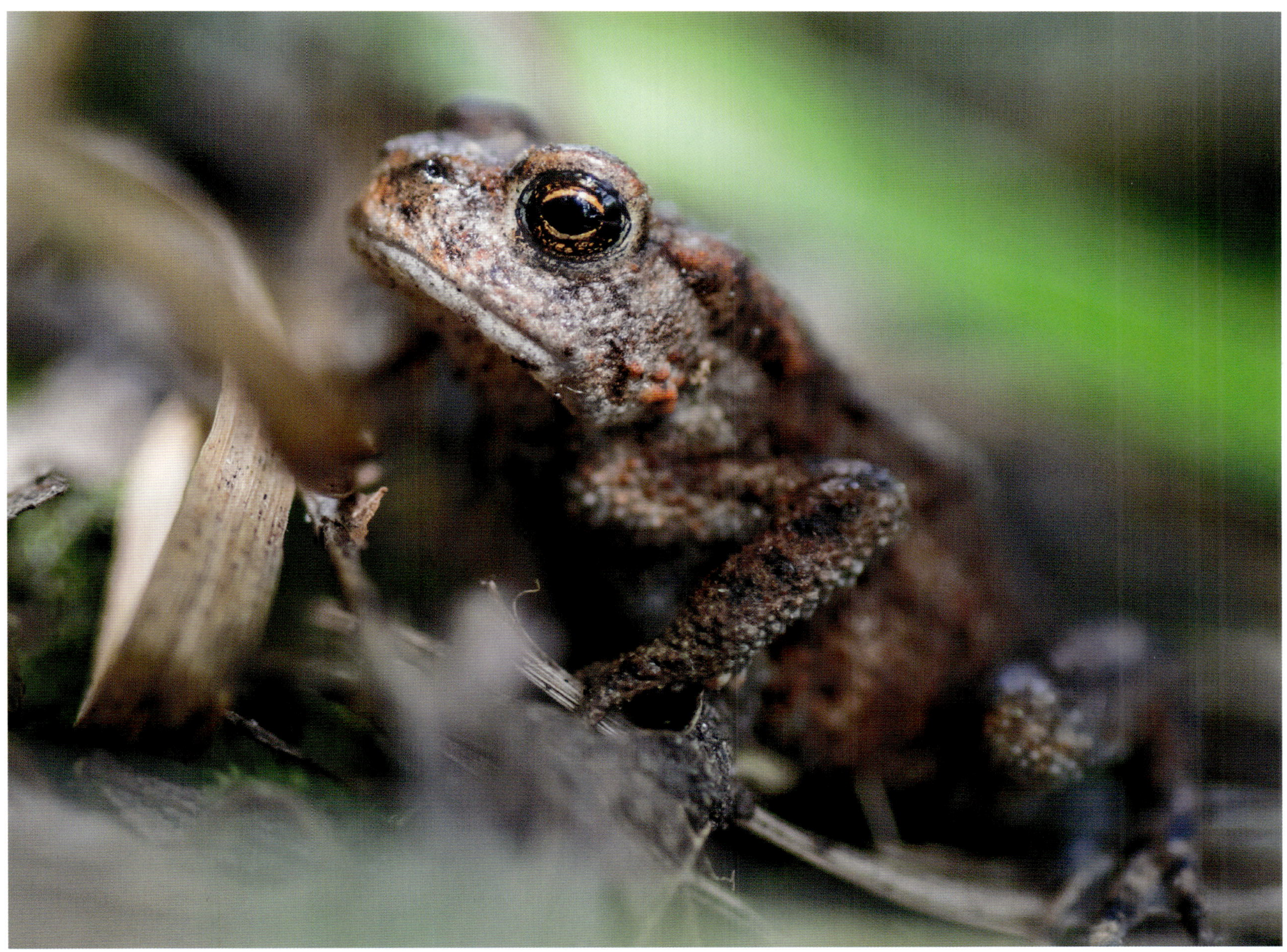

Left: Increasing the ISO allows you to use faster shutter speeds, but this can also increase the level of unwanted noise in an image. Sometimes it is unavoidable, though, especially when shooting in dark woodland with the aperture in the lens stopped down.

Focal length: 100mm macro lens

Aperture: f/5.6

Shutter speed: 1/160 sec.

ISO: 1600

Above: Sometimes your subject will be inconveniently close to the ground, making a tripod difficult to use. When that happens you have little choice but to lie on the ground and shoot at the same level as your subject. Brace your elbows against the ground so you are reasonably stable and you will find you can use relatively long shutter speeds.

Focal length: 100mm macro lens

Aperture: f/5.6

Shutter speed: 1/50 sec.

ISO: 800

Aperture

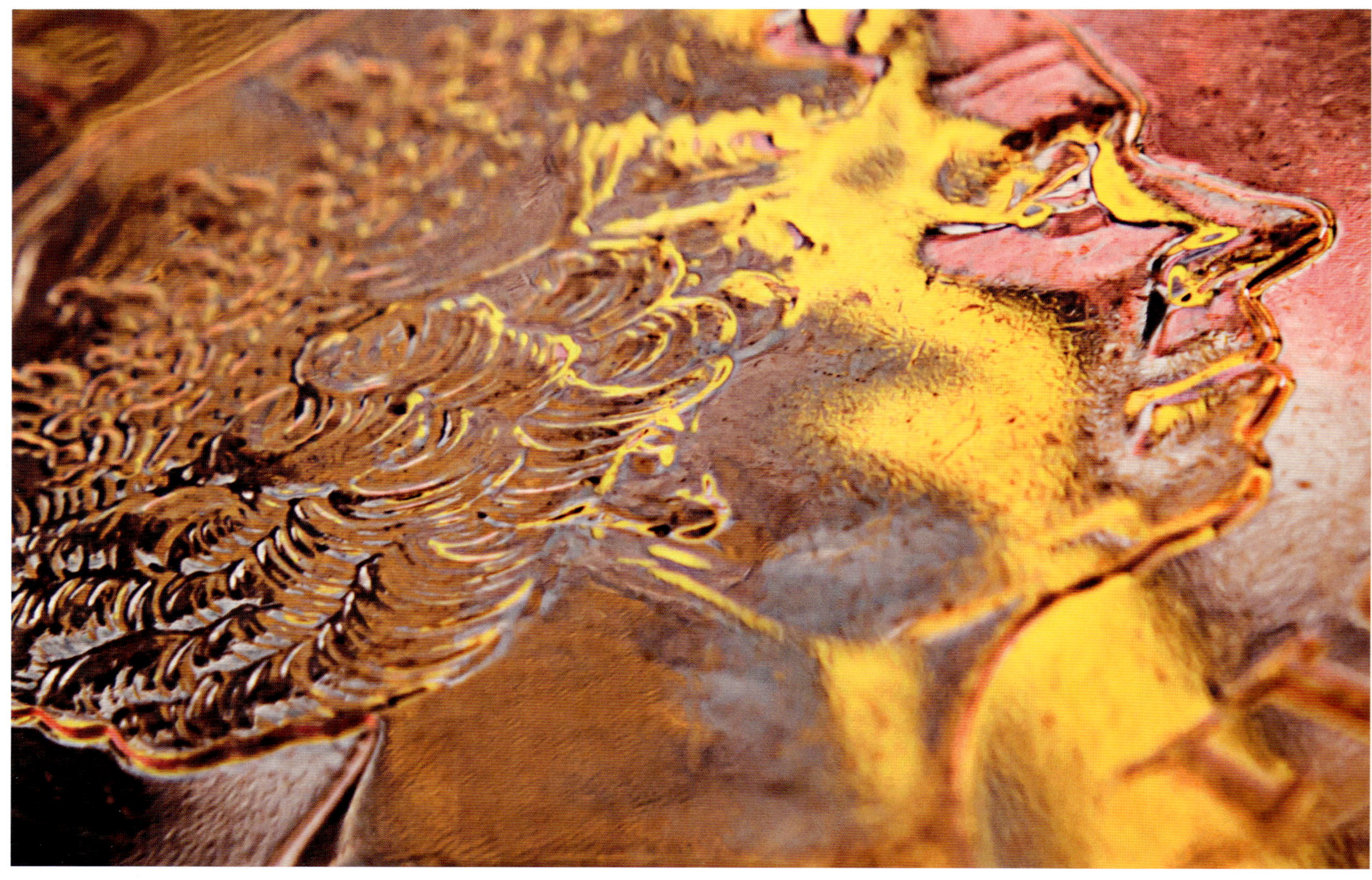

The aperture in a lens is a variable iris, which is adjusted in a series of steps known as "f/stops" (or just "stops"). A typical range of f/stops on a prime macro lens is f/2.8, f/4, f/5.6, f/8, f/11, f/16, f/22, and f/32. The first f-stop in this sequence (f/2.8) is the largest aperture and allows the maximum amount of light through the lens. Each step to the right in this sequence halves the amount of light allowed to pass through the aperture and each jump to the left doubles it.

Every time the aperture is adjusted by 1 stop, either the shutter speed or the ISO needs to be adjusted by 1 stop in the opposite direction to maintain the same level of exposure overall.

Above: Obtaining the desired degree of sharpness in a closeup image is a combination of selecting the right aperture and precise focusing. When composing this shot of a small copper coin I wanted a soft feel with very little sharpness. Shooting using a large aperture (close to maximum for the lens used) and focusing on the eye of the face on the coin ensured that I achieved the effect I was after.

Focal length: 50mm (with 68mm extension tubes)

Aperture: f/4

Shutter speed: 1/10 sec.

ISO: 100

Depth Of Field

The sharpest area in an image is the distance at which the lens is focused, which is known as the point or plane of focus. However, the aperture also has an influence on image sharpness. As the aperture is made smaller, a zone of sharpness known as depth of field extends out from the focus point both away from and back toward the camera. Depth of field does not extend equally in both directions, though—it extends twice as far away from the focus point toward ∞ as it does from the focus point back toward the camera.

Apart from aperture there are two other factors that determine depth of field. The first is the focal length of the lens: the longer the focal length of the lens, the less depth of field is available at a given aperture. The second factor is very relevant for close-up and macro photography: depth of field diminishes the shorter the camera-to-subject distance. It is this second factor that makes it more and more difficult to achieve front-to-back sharpness in close-up images.

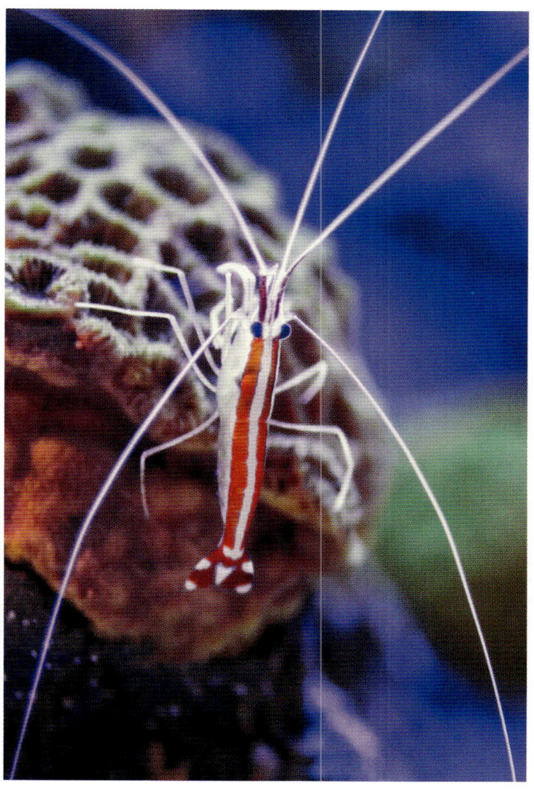

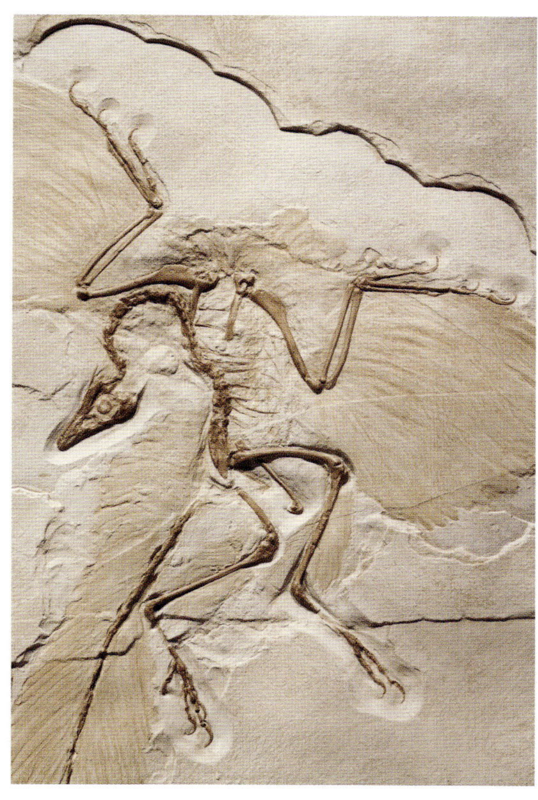

Tip

The smaller the sensor is in a camera, the greater the depth of field will be at any given aperture. One reason for this is subject distance. If you use the same focal length lens—a 100mm lens for example—you would need to stand further back to frame an identical shot with a smaller sensor camera than if the camera had a larger sensor. This increase in the camera-to-subject distance is what increases the depth of field at a given aperture.

Above: The available depth of field diminishes at a given aperture the higher the magnification of the image. Shot at f/3.5, depth of field is extremely shallow in this shot of a shrimp. This lack of depth of field means that focusing needs to be extremely precise, which in this case was a difficult task as the shrimp refused to stay still for long.

Focal length: 100mm macro lens

Aperture: f/3.5

Shutter speed: 1/20 sec.

ISO: 3200

Above: Depth of field is less of an issue when shooting an almost perfectly flat subject. By keeping the camera perfectly parallel to this cast of an archaeopteryx fossil I was able to use an aperture of f/3.5 (necessary as the shot was handheld and I was at the limit of how steady I could keep the camera). However, if the camera had not been parallel to the fossil then a significant part of the shot would have been soft and slightly out of focus.

Focal length: 35mm

Aperture: f/3.5

Shutter speed: 1/2 sec.

ISO: 200

Creative Depth Of Field

Photography is often a compromise between what you would like to achieve and what it is actually possible to achieve. The restrictions of depth of field in macro photography often lead to a number of compromises. It is, for instance, often difficult to achieve front-to-back sharpness through the image even when using a lens' minimum aperture (and even that involves a compromise in image quality—see page 56).

One way around depth of field limitations is to use a technique known as focus stacking (see pages 124–125). Another option is to use a tilt/shift macro lens or bellows with a tilt facility. A lens that tilts allows you to adjust the angle of the focus plane, which is normally parallel to the camera. By dropping the focus plane onto your subject you effectively focus along it; depth of field is still restricted, but by altering the focus plane you push the problem above or below your subject where it is less noticeable. Tilt/shift macro lenses are rare and expensive, though—the Zörk Multi Focus System is one of the few on the market and only offers a 1:2 reproduction ratio.

The alternative to maximum sharpness is to embrace softness. Soft, restricted depth of field imagery has a unique esthetic appeal. By using restricted depth of field you can simplify images to reduce distracting visual clutter and direct a viewer's gaze to the most important area of the image.

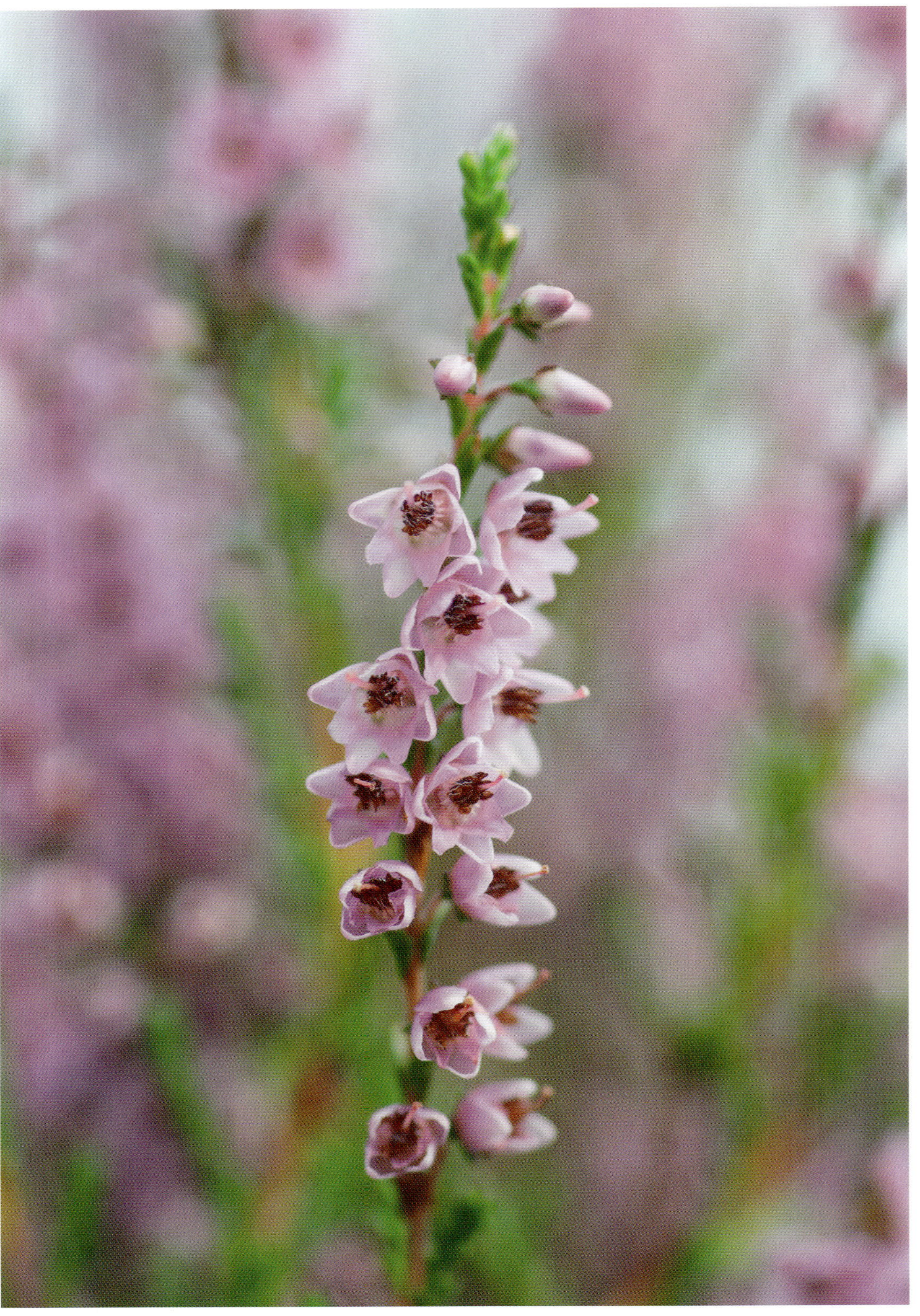

Right: Minimizing depth of field by using a large aperture has the often-useful effect of increasing shutter speed. This image benefited from that effect, with the wind-blown heather flowers requiring a shutter speed of 1/320 sec. to freeze their movement.

Focal length: 100mm macro lens

Aperture: f/6.3

Shutter speed: 1/320 sec.

ISO: 400

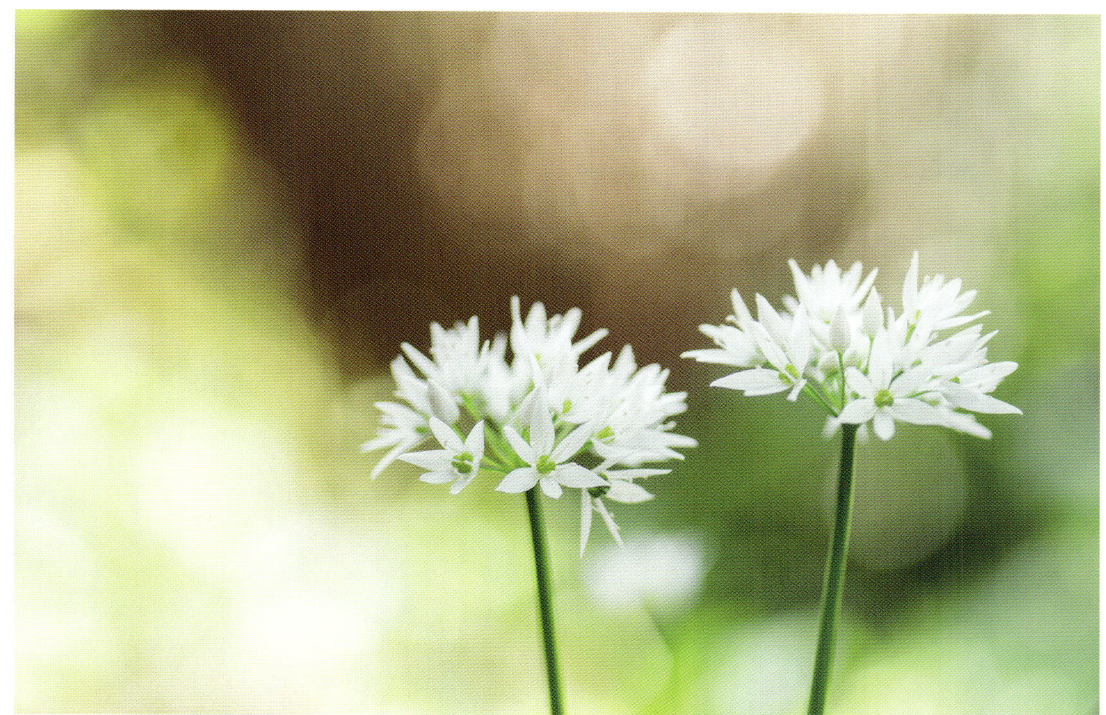

APERTURE RANGE

Camera systems handle the difference between the actual aperture set and the effective aperture in two different ways. Canon cameras show a consistent available aperture range, so a macro lens with an aperture range of f/2.8–f/22 is always an f/2.8–f/22 macro lens regardless of the magnification factor. However, Nikon cameras shift the available aperture range upward depending on the degree of magnification, so an f/2.8–f/22 macro lens changes to an f/5.6–f/45 lens when used at a 1:1 magnification (in other words, Nikon cameras show the effective aperture, rather than the actual aperture).

Light Loss

There is a small, but significant difference between the exposure necessary for a normal-sized subject and a macro subject, even if the two are illuminated equally. If you magnify a scene by increasing the distance between the front lens element and the camera's sensor there is a loss of light; the greater the magnification, the greater the light loss will be. In practical terms this means that exposure will need to be increased or ISO adjusted upward.

This light loss is dealt with automatically when a camera's built-in metering system is used to determine exposure. However, if you're using a handheld light meter, life is suddenly made more complicated, as you need to take account of the degree of light loss due to the magnification of the image and adjust your exposures accordingly. The easiest way to do this is to turn the metered aperture value into an *effective* aperture value and work out the difference in stops between the two.

This is achieved by simply adding 1 to the magnification factor. For example, if the

magnification factor were 2x (or 2:1), then the difference would be 3 stops. So, if the metered aperture is f/8, the *effective* aperture is actually f/22 (f/8 > f/11 > f/16 > f/22). You would set the aperture on the camera to f/8 as originally metered, but the shutter speed or ISO (or both) should be increased by a total of 3 stops to ensure that exposure is correct.

Right: Shot at close to a 1:1 reproduction ratio, the metadata in this image shows an aperture of f/11, even though the aperture ring was set at f/5.6.
Focal length: 100mm macro lens
Aperture: f/11
Shutter speed: 1/5 sec.
ISO: 100

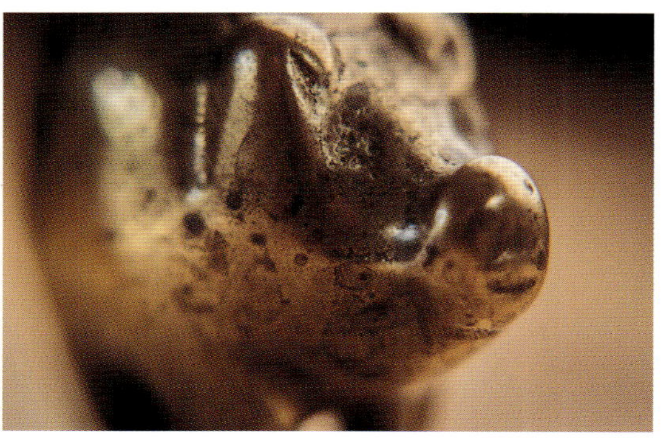

Focusing

Due to depth of field restrictions, accurate focusing is more important in macro photography than when you are shooting non-close-up subjects. This typically means deciding what should be the area of a macro shot that should be critically sharp. Although this will vary from subject to subject, it would typically be the point of maximum visual interest: on an insect this is likely to be an eye, for example. For three-dimensional subjects it is generally a good idea to bias the focus toward the front of the subject, as depth of field is always greater behind the focus point. By focusing forward you maximize the depth of field in the image.

AF Modes

Cameras typically offer a range of autofocus (AF) modes. These determine whether focusing stops once a focus lock has been acquired, or whether AF is continuously updated until the shutter-release button is pressed down fully to take the shot. Like a number of camera functions, the names for these modes vary from manufacturer to manufacturer: AF that stops once focus has been acquired is known as AF-S (Single) or One-Shot AF (or variations on this theme), while continuously updated AF is known as AF-C (Continuous) or AI Servo AF (or similar).

For static macro subjects Single AF is usually preferable. Once focus has been acquired there is no need for the focus distance to change, so you could switch the camera to manual focus or apply focus lock to ensure that focus is permanently set at the correct distance.

Alternatively, for moving subjects it is often better to use Continuous AF, allowing the camera track the subject and adjust focus as necessary.

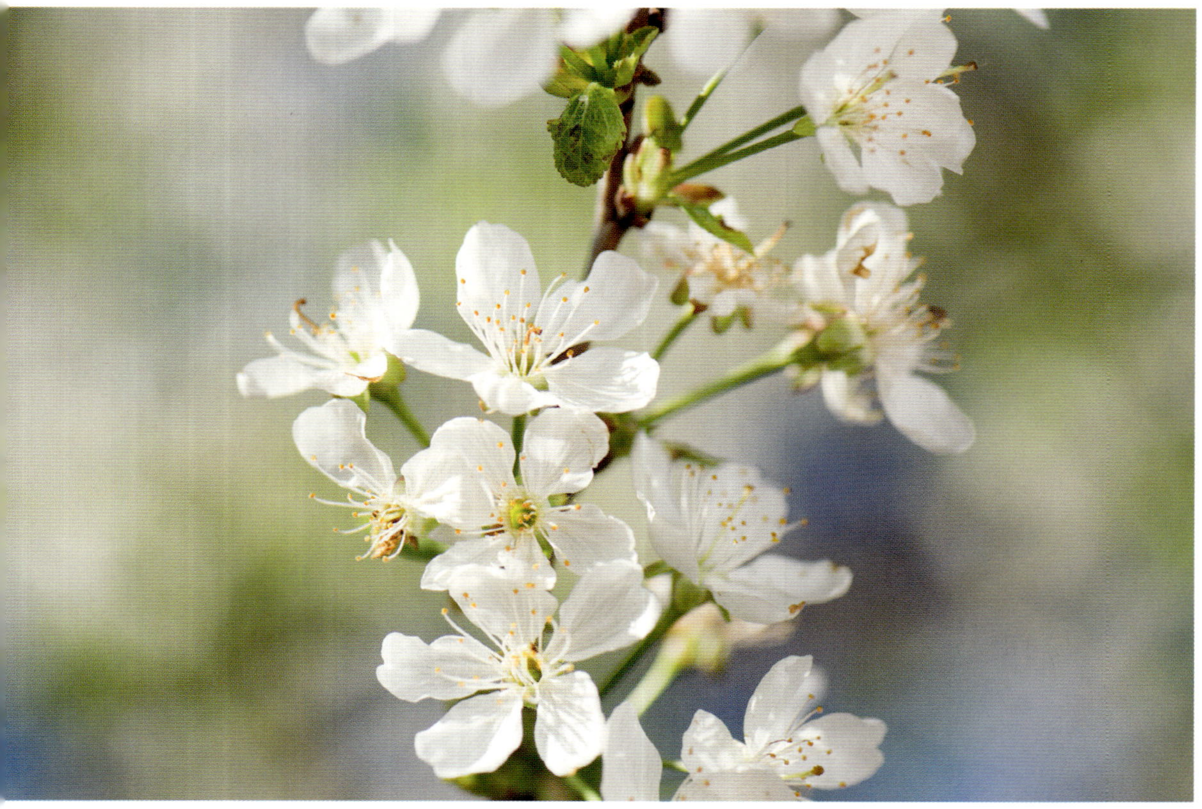

Left: Wind-blown plants can be tricky subjects to shoot. Using Continuous AF lets your camera track the movement and maintain focus. The use of a fast shutter speed for this shot also helped to "freeze" the movement of the flower.

Focal length: 100mm macro lens

Aperture: f/5

Shutter speed: 1/2000 sec.

ISO: 400

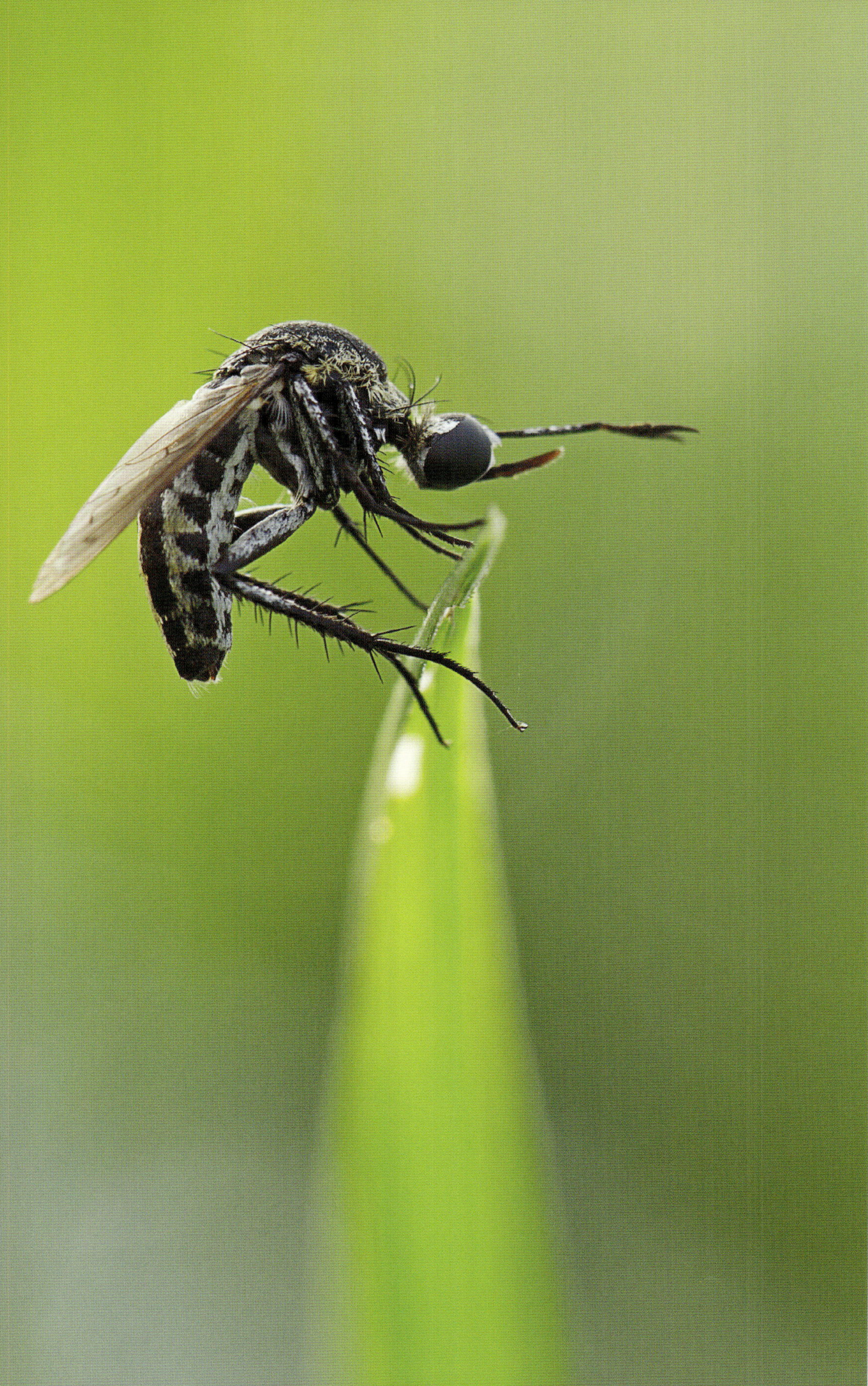

Left: We tend to look straight at the sharpest part of an image and ignore those areas that are unsharp. Using a relatively large aperture to minimize depth of field and focusing precisely means it is possible to guide the viewer of your shot to look exactly where you want them to. In this instance, focus was set on the eye of the robber fly.
Focal length: 180mm macro lens
Aperture: f/8
Shutter speed: 1/250 sec.
ISO: 800

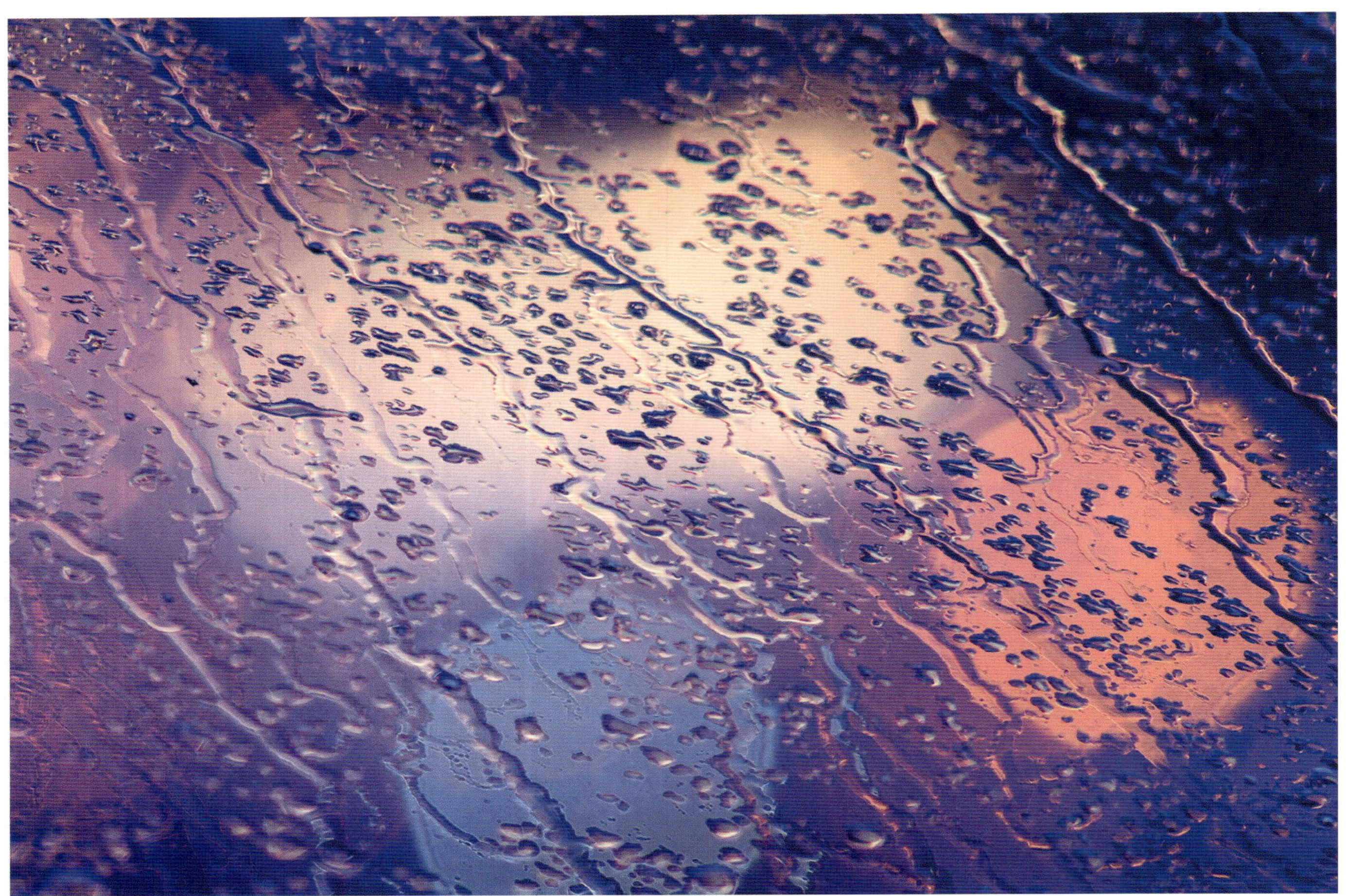

Phase Detection Vs. Contrast Detection

There are two different AF systems used by camera manufacturers: phase detection and contrast detection. Phase detection is used in DSLRs when the optical viewfinder is selected and contrast detection when the camera is switched to Live View. Mirrorless cameras and other types, such as compacts, use contrast detection exclusively (although the distinction is slightly blurred as some camera sensors now also include phase detection technology).

Of the two systems, phase detection AF is extremely quick at acquiring focus. However, this speed is occasionally at the expense of some accuracy. With most other photographic genres any slight focusing inaccuracy is usually masked by depth of field sharpness, but the lack of depth of field when shooting macro reveals any and all focusing issues.

There are two types of error: front focusing, which is when the AF system focuses a lens in front of the intended area, and back focusing, which is when the AF system focuses behind where it should. Some DSLRs allow you to calibrate your lenses to cure these problems (if they exist) and improve accuracy (different lenses will require individual calibration). To calibrate a lens you should use a calibration tool, such as those produced by Datacolor and Reikan, which will help you measure any inaccuracy and apply the required degree of correction.

Contrast detection focusing is far more accurate, but it is also slower than phase detection at acquiring a focus lock (although technology is constantly improving and the speed difference is narrowing). When shooting static subjects with a DSLR, this makes contrast detection via Live View preferable, but for moving subjects phase detection is by far the better option.

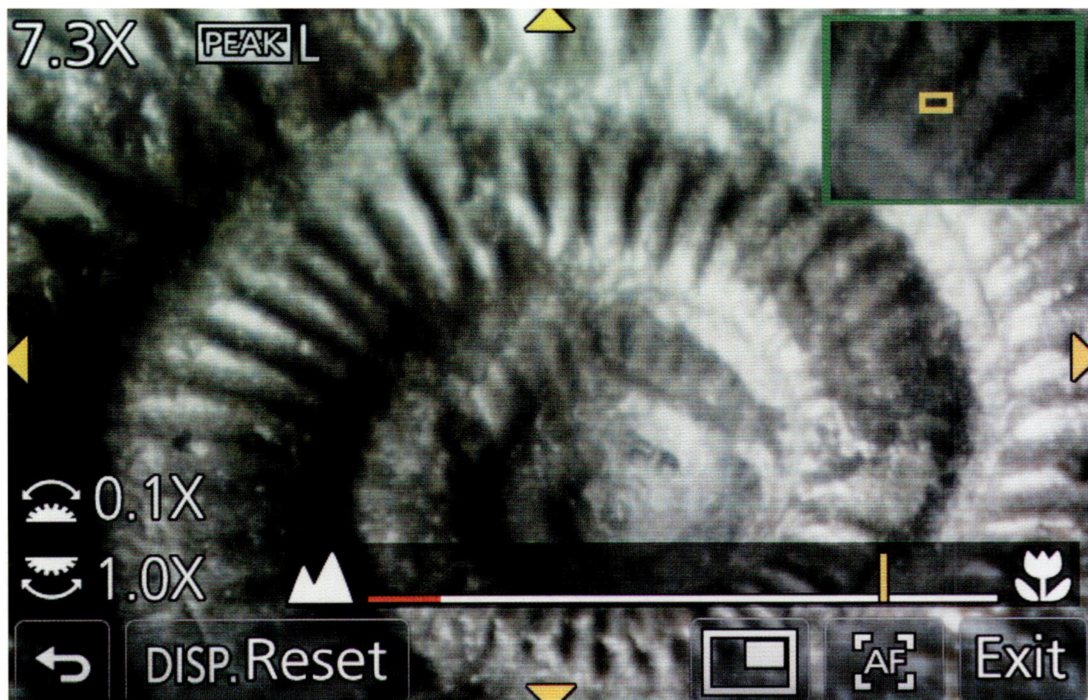

Above: When using an electronic display you can typically zoom into the image in order to check critical focusing. Combined with functions such as focus peaking, this is a very powerful way to ensure sharp imagery.

Manual Focus

Manually focusing a lens when shooting macro—particularly with static subjects—has a lot to recommend it (and is often necessary when using adaptors such as reversing rings). Setting focus manually gives you more control over which areas of an image are sharp, with less restriction than the often-small array of AF points. The downside to manual focusing is that pinpoint accuracy is required, which takes time and practice to achieve reliably. Unfortunately, the optical viewfinders of many DSLRs aren't ideal; they can be dim and hard to read when shooting in low light or when using a lens with a relatively small maximum aperture. Accessories such as angled viewfinders can help a little, as they often magnify the viewfinder image, but this has no effect on viewfinder brightness.

Electronic viewfinders or the LCD in Live View are often a better option when manually focusing. The main advantage is that the image can be magnified, which helps you to see when focus has been achieved. Some cameras, particularly mirrorless models, offer various aids to focusing manually, such as focus peaking. Peaking adds a colored outline around the edges of elements in a scene that are sharp. If choosing a peaking color is an option, it pays to choose a color that is most visible and therefore easiest to see (when shooting a predominantly red scene, for example, choose a contrasting peaking color such as blue).

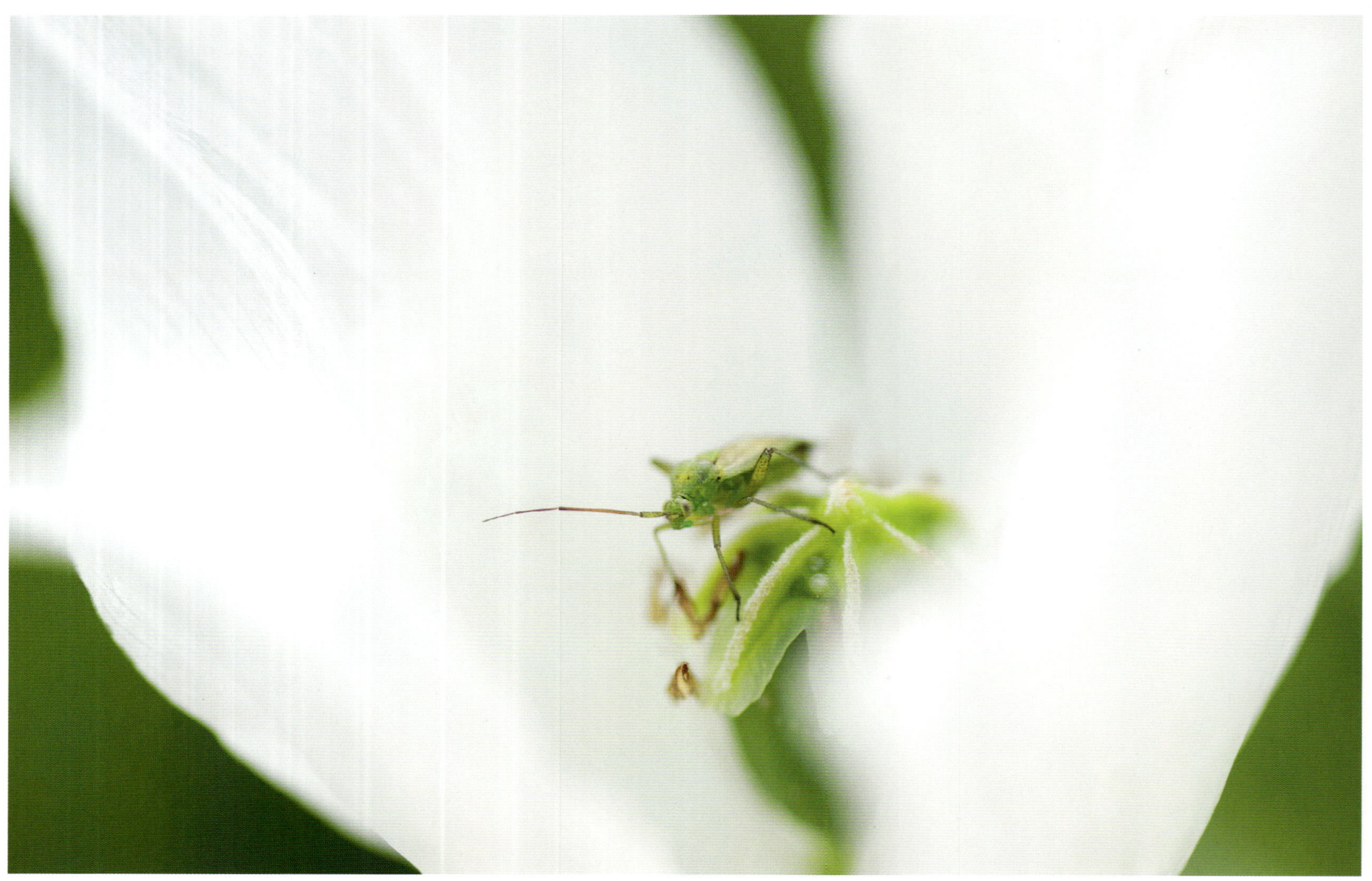

Above: Cameras have an array of AF points that can be used to set focus. For this shot I switched to an AF point mode that allowed me to choose the AF point I wanted to use for focus. I then selected the AF point directly over the insect's head to set the focus.

Focal length: 100mm macro lens

Aperture: f/5.6

Shutter speed: 1/1600 sec.

ISO: 400

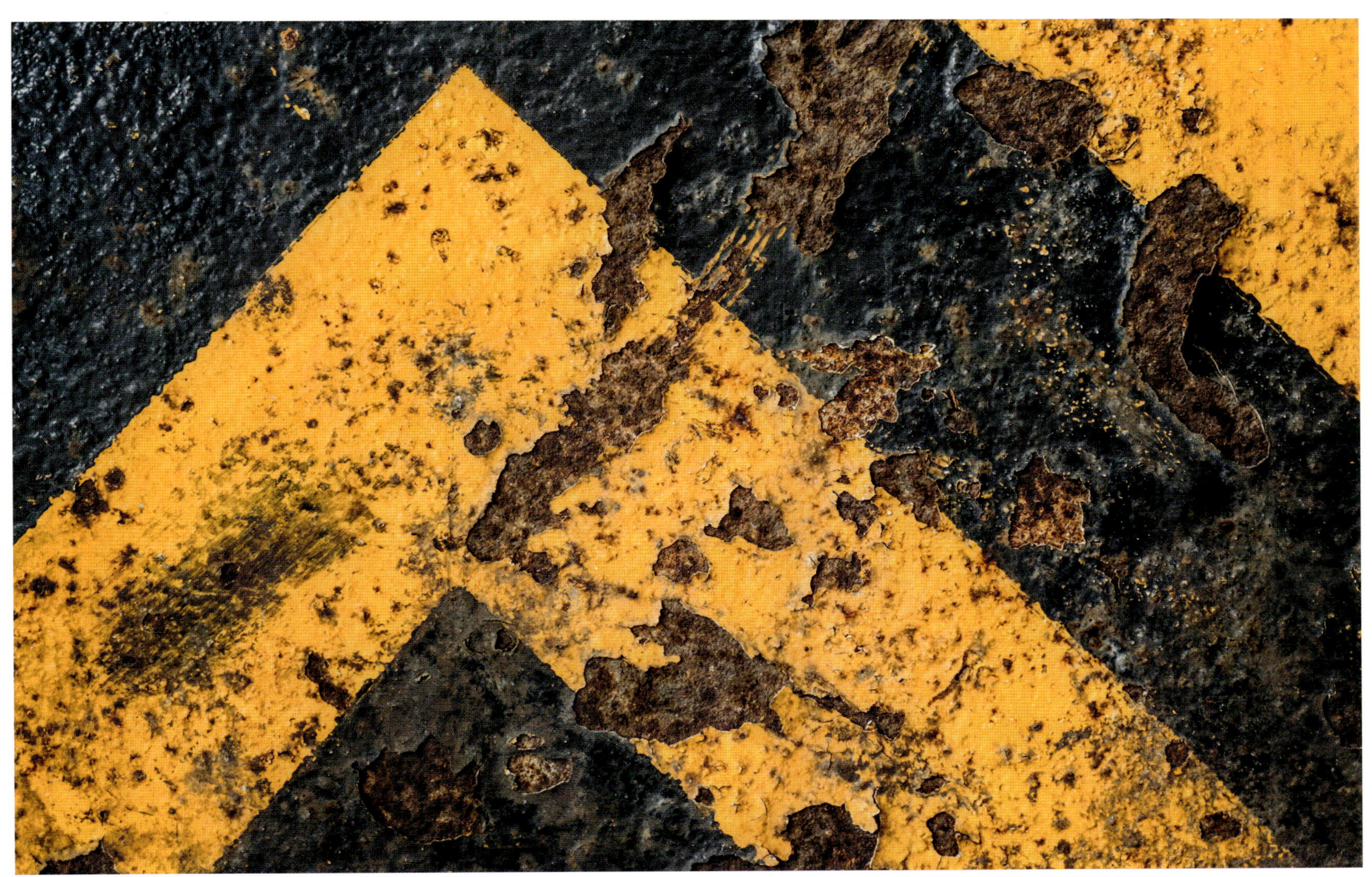

Above: Even this simple "grab" shot of a rusting metal
barrier required some thought about focus and exposure.
The decision process was made trickier as the ambient light
levels were low and I was handholding the camera.

Focal length: 30mm

Aperture: f/2.8

Shutter speed: 1/30 sec.

ISO: 400

Composition

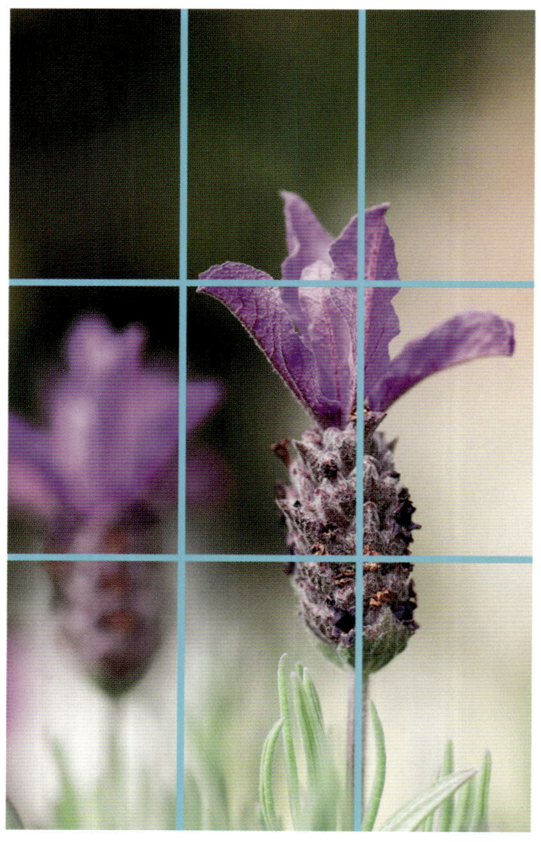

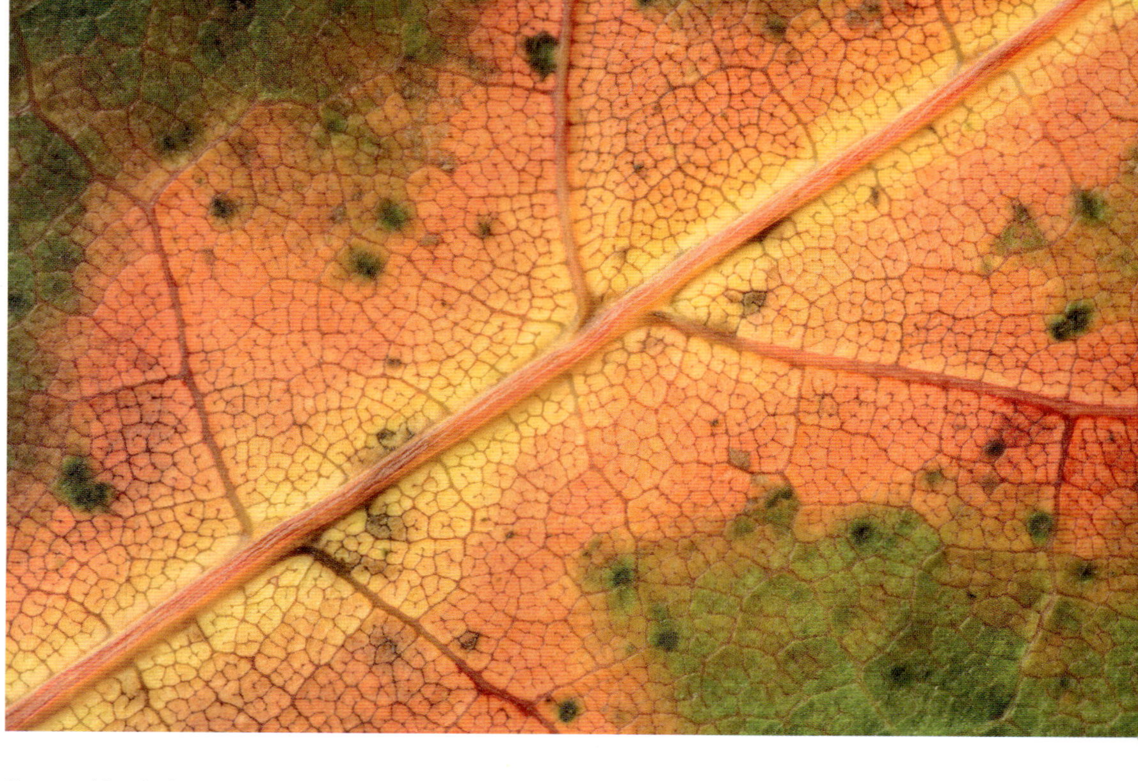

Above: The rule of thirds requires you to imagine an image split into three equal slices both horizontally and vertically, as shown here. The rule suggests that more pleasing compositions occur when an important element in the image space is placed on one of these lines or at the point where two of the lines intersect.

Focal length: 100mm macro lens

Aperture: f/5.6

Shutter speed: 1/500 sec.

ISO: 400

Composition is the art of creating a striking and memorable image through the purposeful arrangement of the various elements in a scene within the image space. There are a number of rules that can be followed when it comes to composing a photograph, and perhaps the one most often cited is the rule of thirds. However, while they are useful as a guide, these rules should not get in the way of intuition when it comes to deciding whether a shot works or not.

There is a lot to be said for keeping images simple, and this often occurs naturally when shooting macro imagery—at a very basic level a limited depth of field tends to simplify images. As the subject is always the most important element of a shot, thought should be given to where it is placed within the image space, and what else should be in the shot and—perhaps more importantly—what should not.

Leaving space around your subject will make a composition feel less cramped and constrained. If your subject is moving, or has implied directionality, leave space in front of it, so it has space to move into. This will emphasize the direction of travel and reduce the impression that the subject is trying to leave the image space.

Left: The orientation of lines in an image is important, as it affects how your images are interpreted. Horizontal lines imply stasis, calmness, and balance. Vertical lines also suggest stasis (less so than horizontal lines), solidity, and strength. Diagonal lines are far more dynamic and suggest movement and depth. There is no right or wrong answer to how you use lines in an image—much will depend on the mood that you want to create.

Focal length: 100mm macro lens

Aperture: f/22

Shutter speed: 2 sec.

ISO: 100

Right: The rule of thirds is a useful guide to how a shot could be composed. However, there is nothing wrong with placing objects centrally if you feel this would produce a stronger composition.

Focal length: 100mm macro lens

Aperture: f/22

Shutter speed: 1/6 sec.

ISO: 100

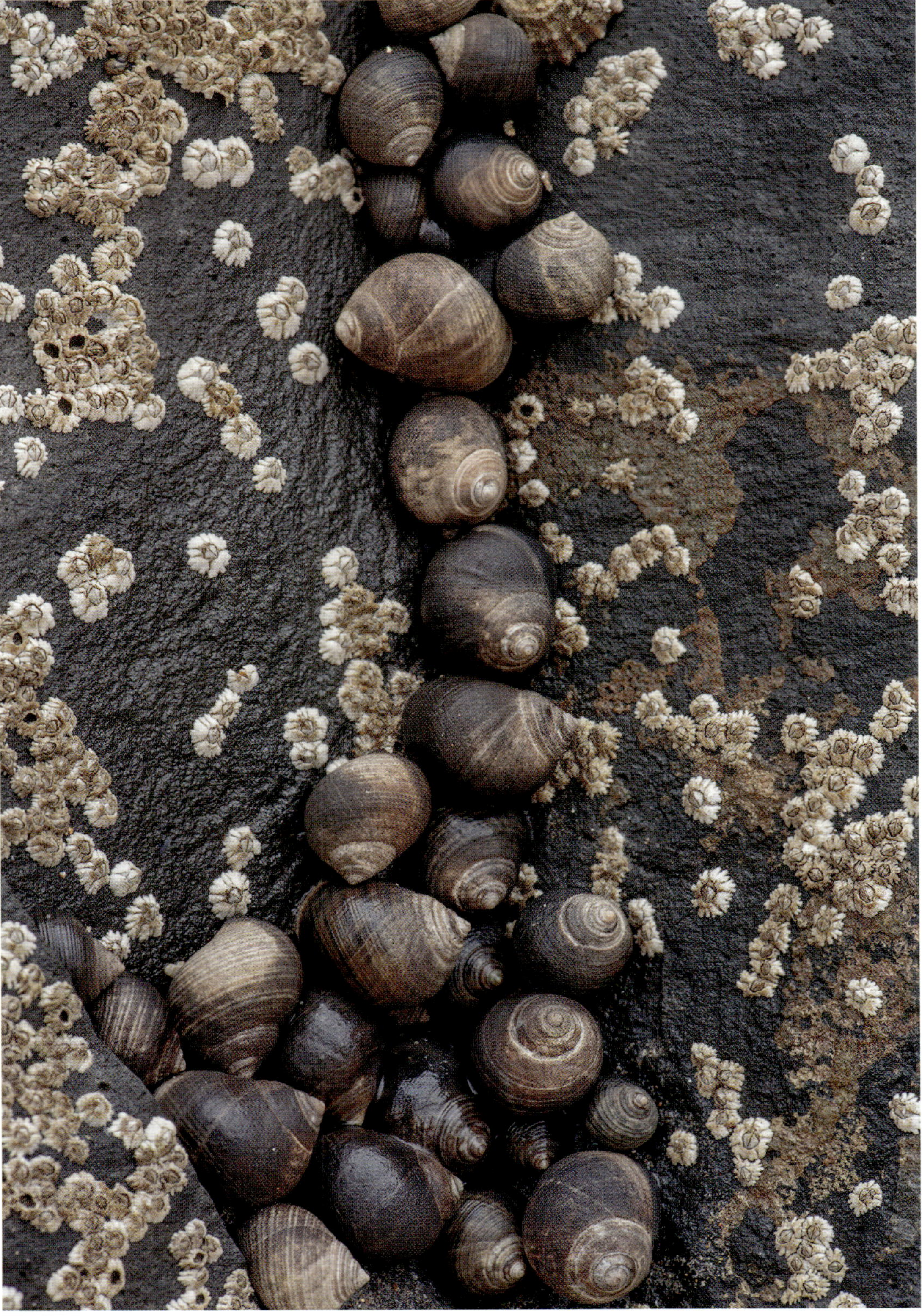

Color

How color is used is an important component of composition. Color has an emotional impact, both positive and negative, and will affect how your images are viewed. There are a number of ways to use color, of which a few are described here. An artist's color wheel is a useful tool when it comes to visualizing these color relationships.

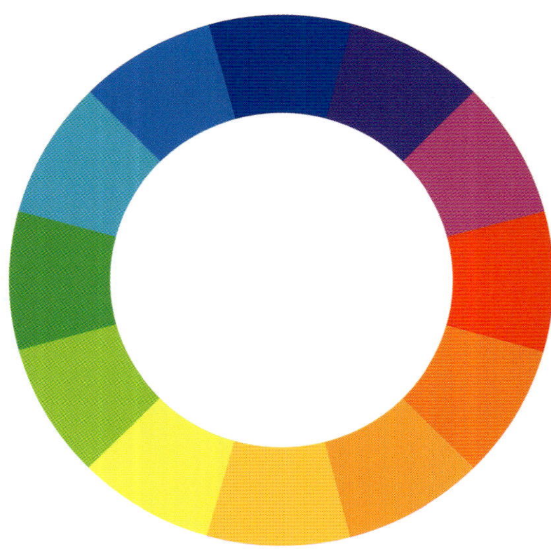

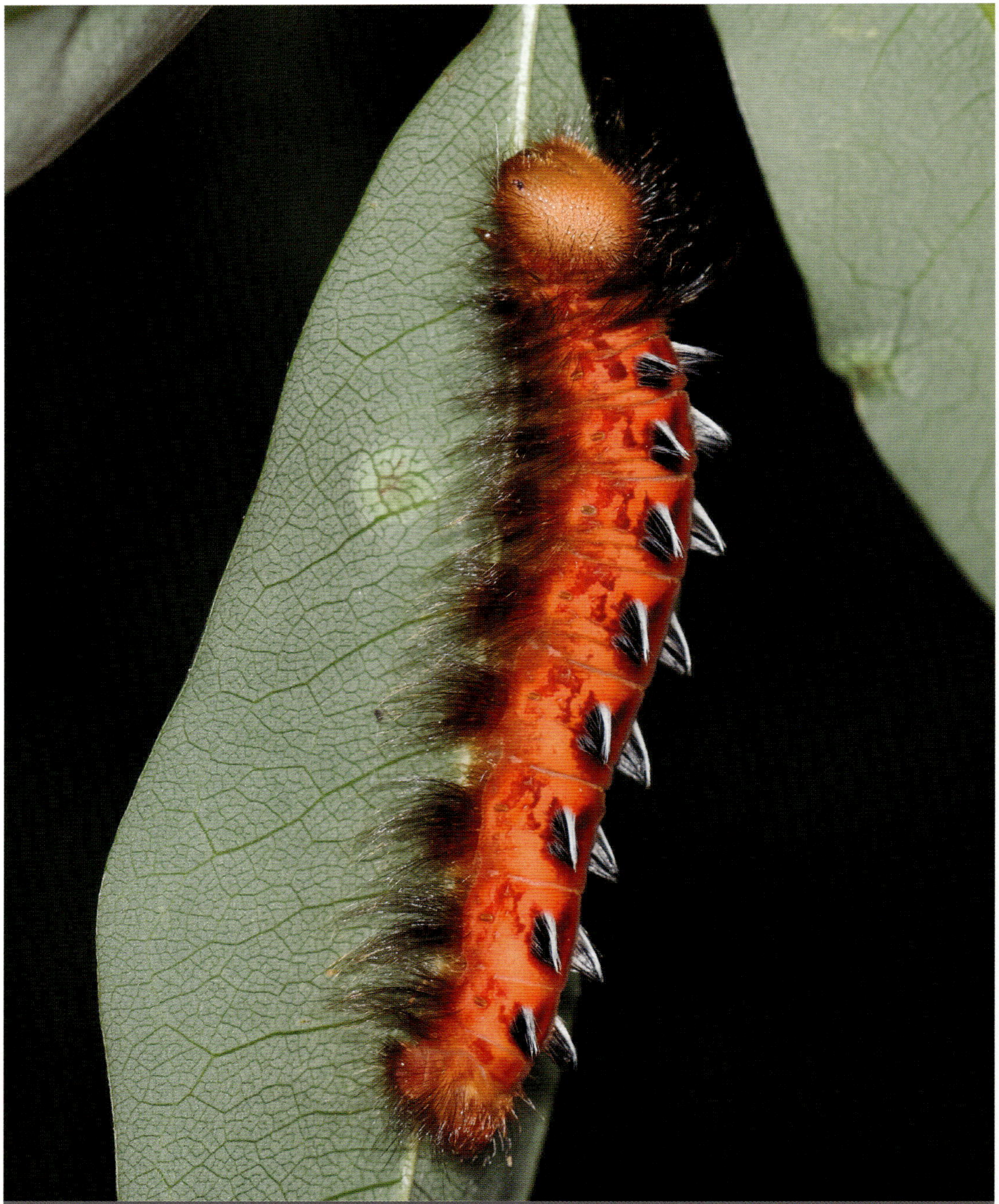

Above: Color wheels have been used by artists for centuries to explore the relationships between various hues.

VISUAL WEIGHT

Visual weight describes how eye-catching an element is within the image space. Elements that are visually "heavy" are more eye-catching than those that are visually less heavy. The color red—the predominant color of this caterpillar—is visually heavy and tends to come forward more in an image than colors such as green and blue.

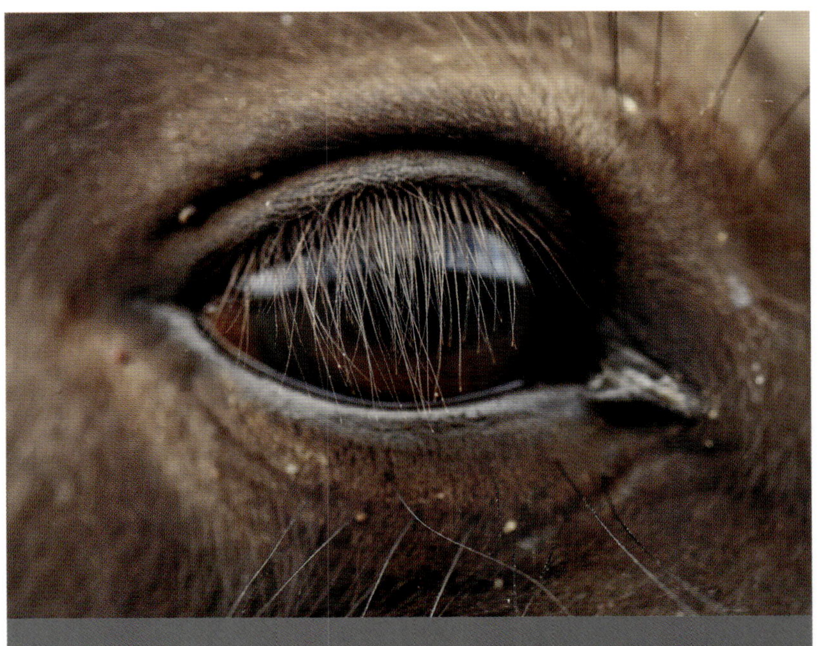

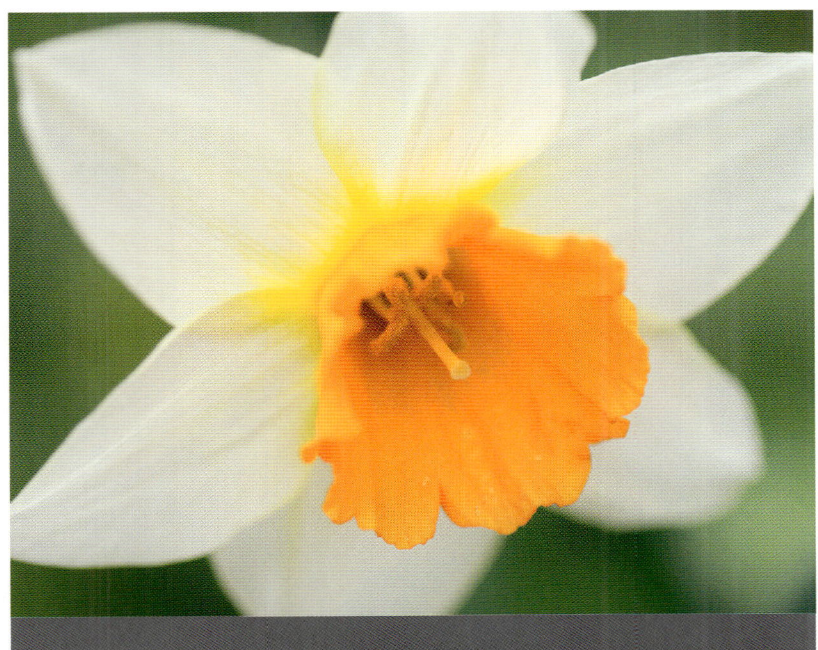

LIMITED COLOR

This is when one color is used throughout an image. The color can be muted or vibrant, but other colors must be excluded or the impact of the image will be lost. Using a single color will typically require subjects with strong forms to provide visual interest.

HARMONIOUS COLORS

These are two or more colors that are neighbors on the color wheel, such as yellow and green. Images with a harmonious color scheme tend to be pleasing, ordered, and calming. However, they can also be visually less engaging than a complementary color scheme.

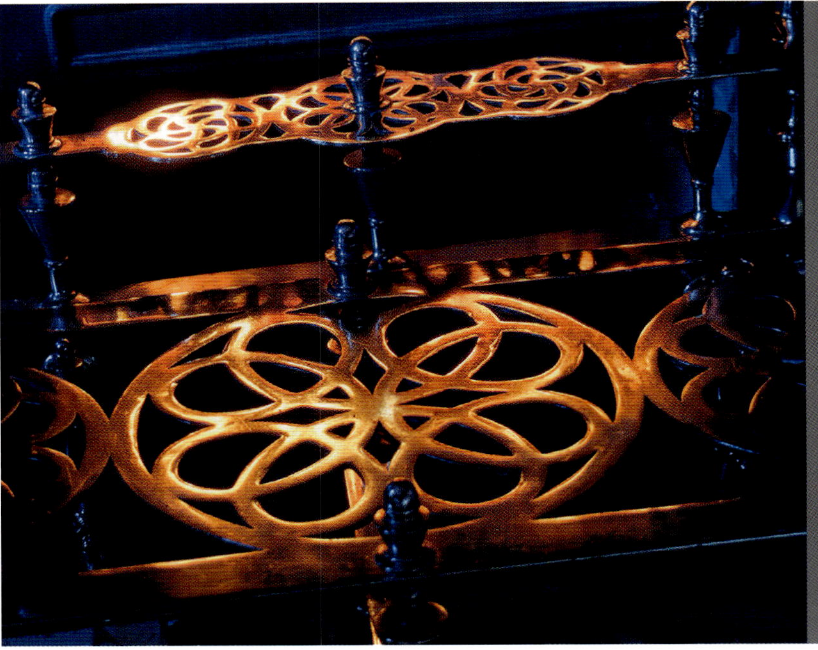

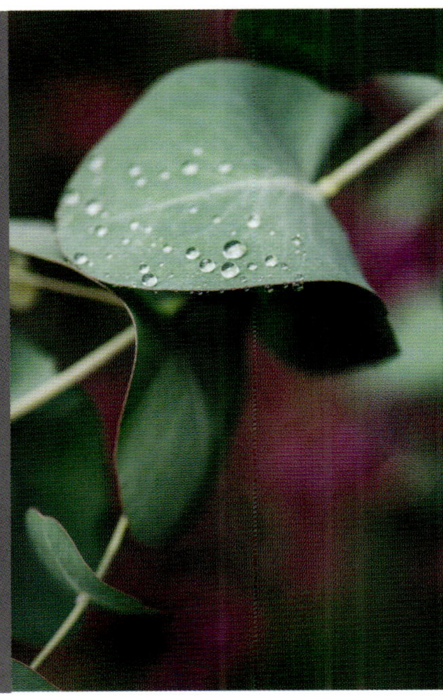

COMPLEMENTARY COLORS

Complementary colors are those that sit opposite each other on a color wheel. Although there is an extreme visual contrast, complementary colors always work well in combination and add visual interest to an image. Perhaps the most common complementary color combination is orange and blue (left). Green and magenta (right) is less commonly seen, but it is equally valid. Its relative rarity perhaps makes it more striking.

Profile: Ross Hoddinott

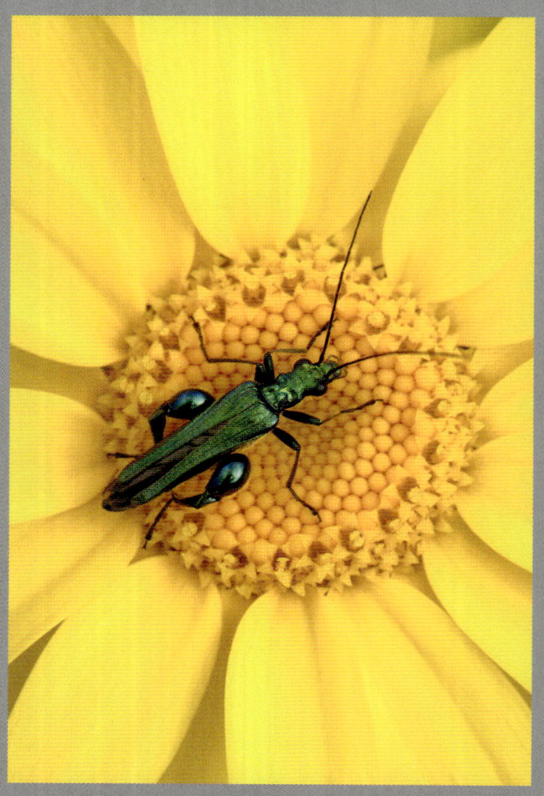

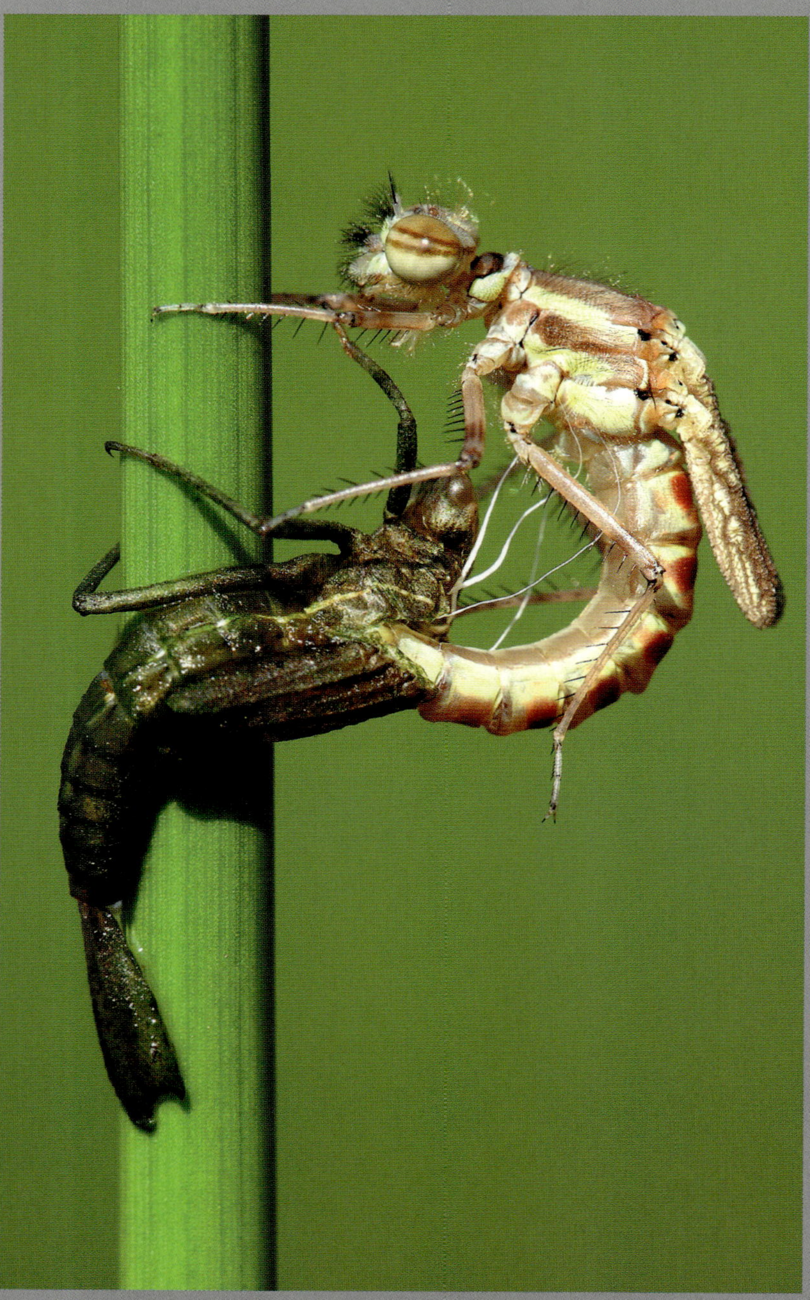

BIOGRAPHY

Ross Hoddinott is one of the UK's leading natural history and landscape photographers. He is the author of seven photography books and a multi award winner. Based in the South West of England, Ross is best known for his intimate close-up images of nature, and for evocative landscape photographs. He is an Ambassador for Nikon and Manfrotto and co-runs Dawn 2 Dusk Photography.

www.rosshoddinott.co.uk

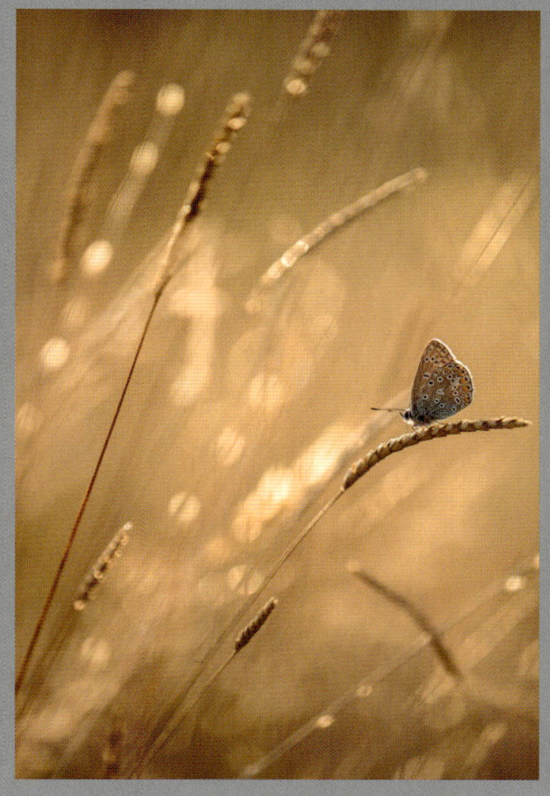

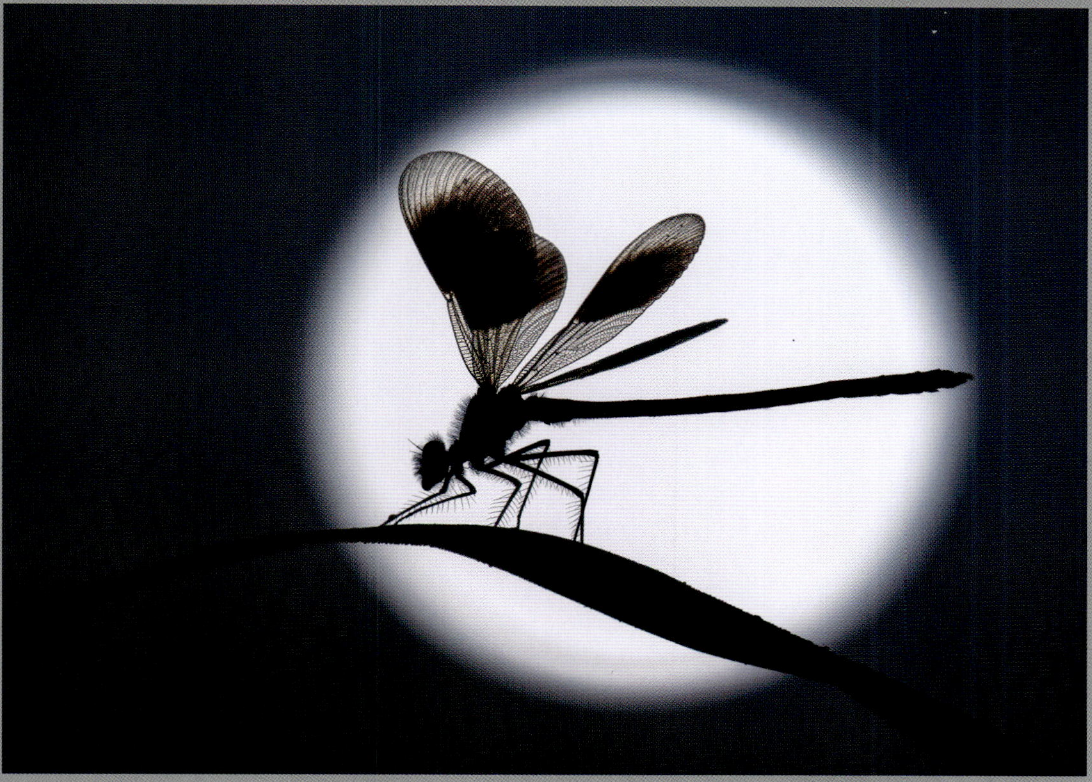

Q) What is it about your specialty that fascinates you?

A) From a young age, I've been fascinated by nature. I love getting close to small things and highlighting detail, beauty, color, shape, and form that is otherwise easily overlooked. In close-up, you can discover, reveal, and capture a whole new world.

Q) What equipment do you regularly use?

A) I've long been a Nikon user and rely on Nikon DSLRs. I use a number of dedicated macro lenses, including the Nikkor 200mm Micro, Nikkor 105mm Micro, and the innovative Laowa 15mm wide-angle macro. I use Gitzo tripod legs and a Manfrotto geared head.

Q) How do you plan a photography session?

A) Sometimes the best images are unplanned and opportunistic. However, for my wildlife work I will often research subjects in order to understand their lifecycle and preferred habitat before planning a shoot. As most of my shots are taken outdoors in situ, the weather plays a key role. I try to wait for still, clear days before visiting reserves.

Q) How do you light your subjects?

A) I much prefer natural light. Although it has limitations, I enjoy its authenticity. I am particularly fond of backlighting, as it highlights a subject's shape and form so beautifully. However, when required I will use reflectors and LED devices to supplement the natural light (I generally don't use flash for my work).

Q) How important is postproduction to you?

A) I shoot Raw, so all my files need a degree of processing, but for me, photography is very much an in-camera skill. I generally dedicate a couple of minutes (per shot) to developing my photographs in Adobe Lightroom.

Q) What is your top tip?

A) Keep it simple! The best close-ups are normally wonderfully simple in their construction. Don't try to cram too much into your shots and keep the emphasis clear.

Chapter 4
Lighting

Light has many different qualities that have an effect on how an image is rendered. A good example of how the quality of light can affect an image is its intensity: an intense light source illuminating a subject will allow the use of faster shutter speeds and smaller apertures without the need to increase the ISO. Another example is color temperature, which affects how neutral in color or not a light source is. A reasonably in-depth knowledge of all the qualities of light is essential to how you plan to shoot an image, as it will determine its impact and esthetic appeal. This chapter is an introduction to the many qualities of light and how they can be used to improve your close-up and macro photography.

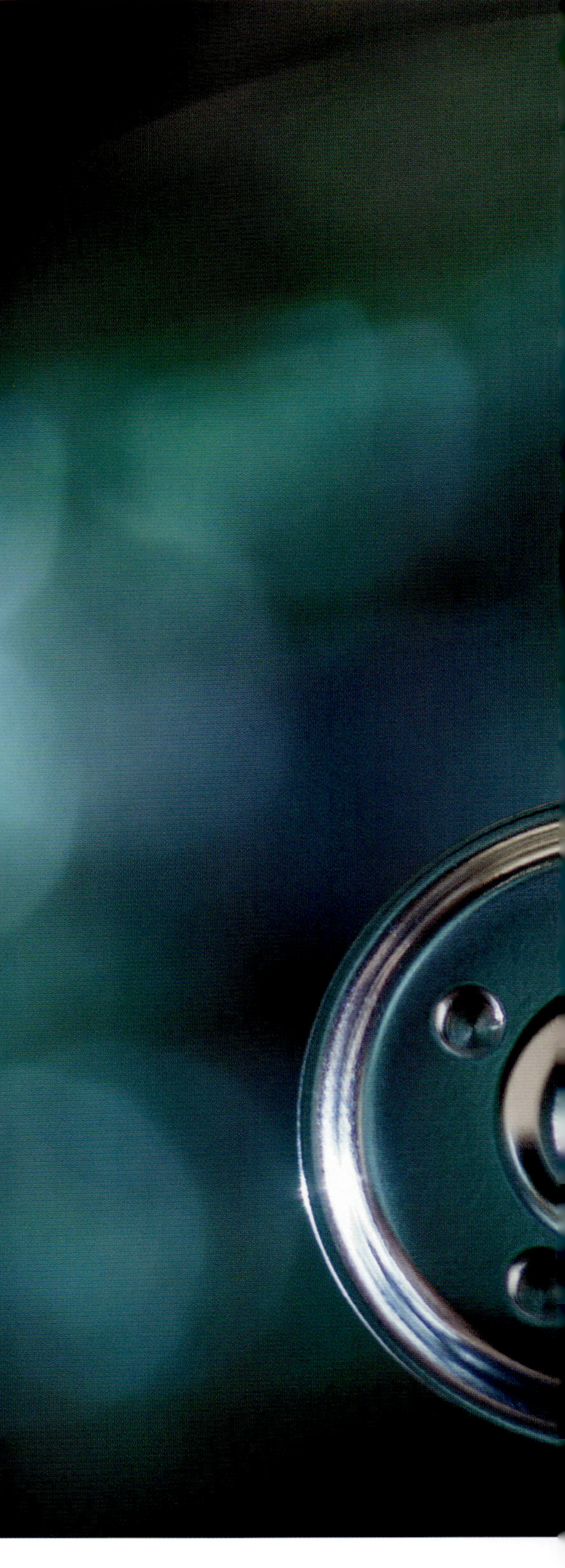

Right: Light can be used to add color where none was before. The green tint on this hard drive platter came from light being reflected from a green surface held directly above it.

Focal length: 100mm macro lens

Aperture: f/8

Shutter speed: 2 sec.

ISO: 100

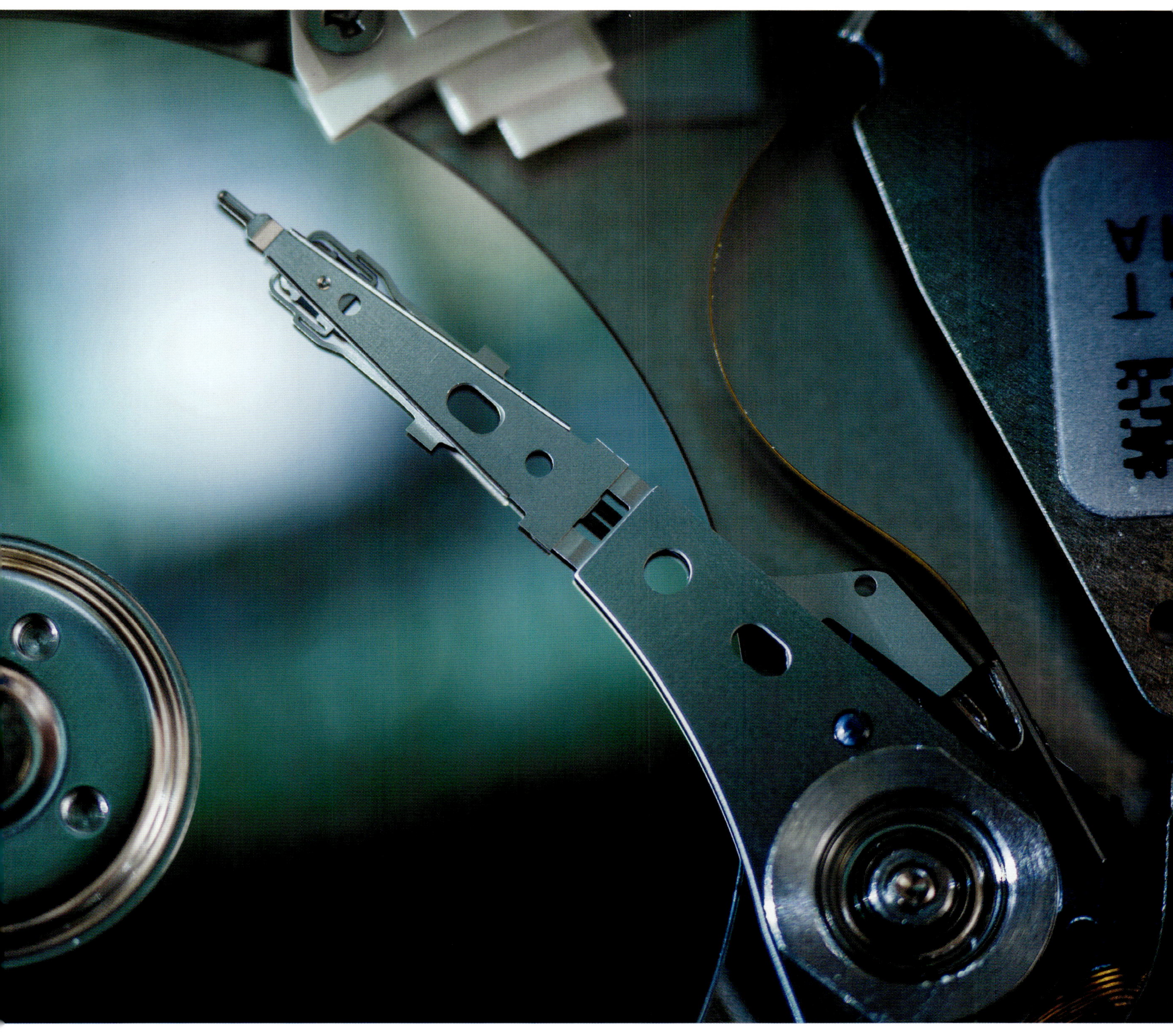

Qualities Of Light

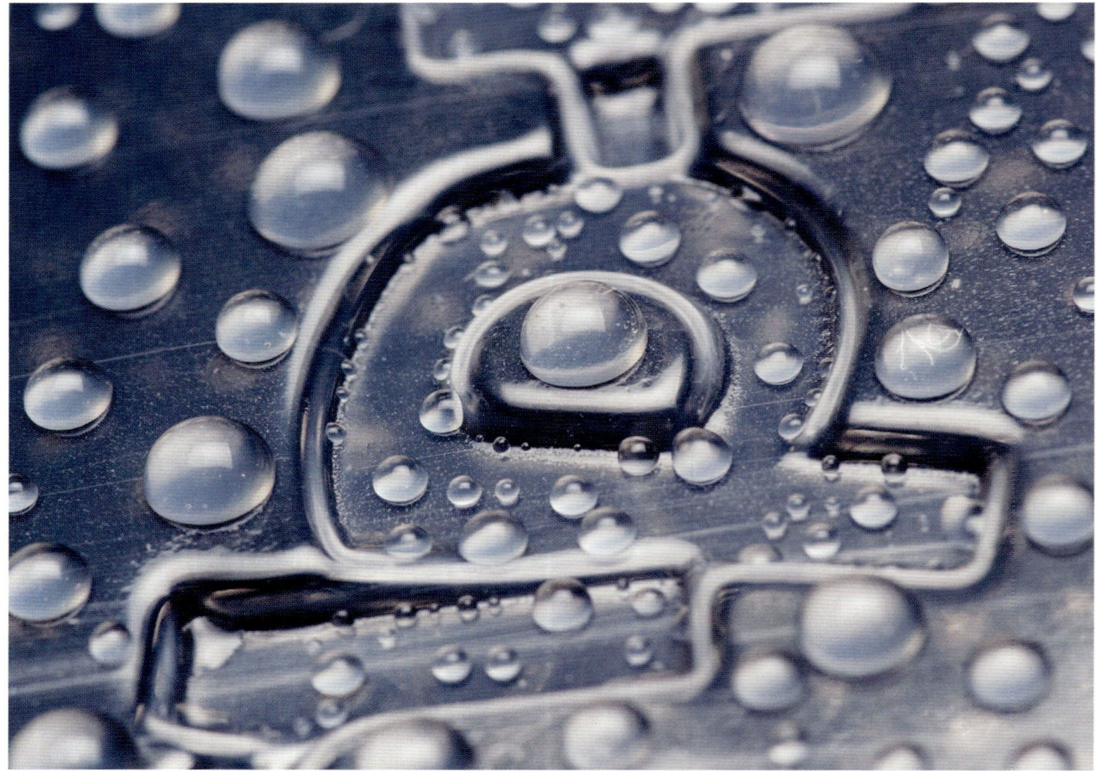

Hardness & Softness

Light can be described as being either "hard" or "soft" (although it is often somewhere between these two extremes). Hard light results in high contrast, with hard-edged shadows and bright highlights that can be intense and pin-sharp on high-gloss surfaces, whereas soft light results in low contrast, with pale shadows and highlights with attenuated edges (in very soft light, shadows and highlights can be all but invisible).

It is the size of the light source relative to the subject that determines whether a light source is hard or soft. A light source that is relatively small in comparison to the subject produces hard light, whereas a light source that is larger than the subject will produce soft light. It is worth noting that the sun, although massive, produces hard light on a cloudless day because it is relatively small in size.

The type of subject you are photographing and the effect or atmosphere you are trying to create should determine whether you opt for hard light or soft light. In general, hard lighting is often a better option for geometric objects and objects with texture, as soft lighting tends to flatten texture and form, making objects appear less three-dimensional. Soft lighting works well with organic subjects and subjects that don't require their form to be as well defined less definition in comparison to other factors, such as color saturation.

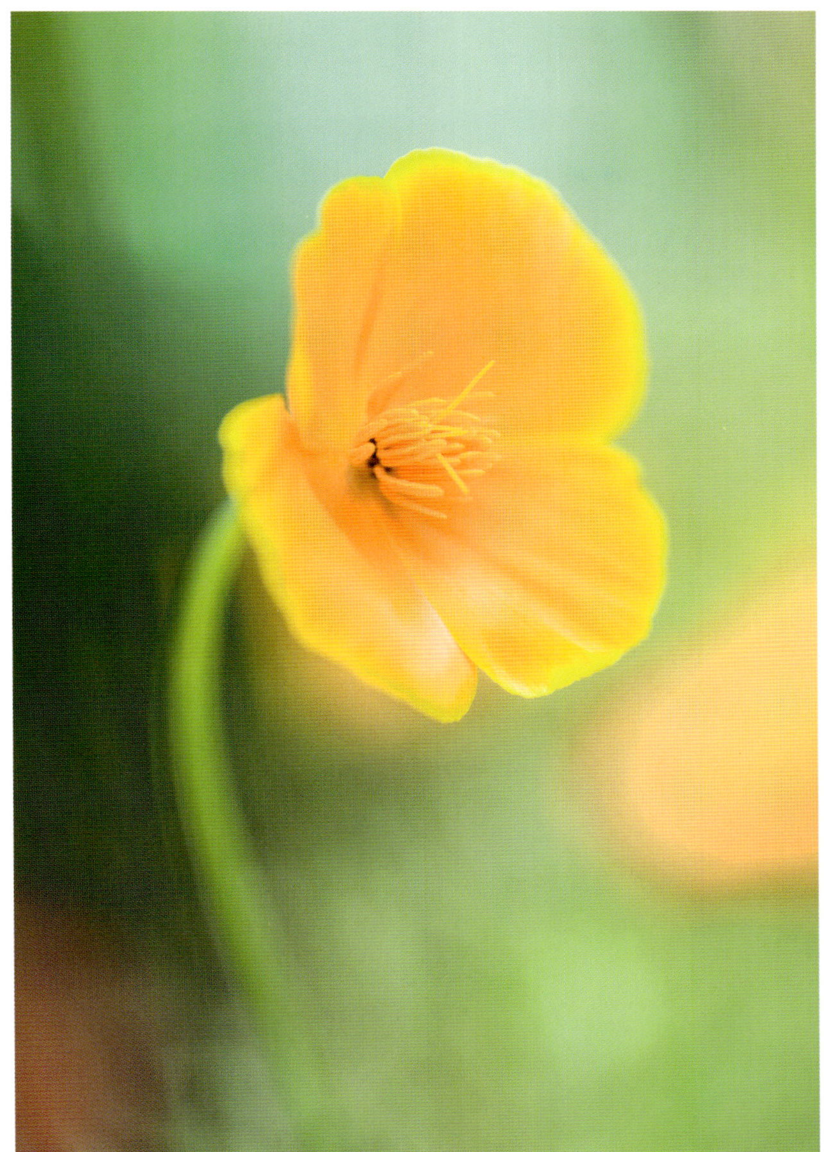

Above: Soft light is ideal for organic subjects such as flowers. Light on an overcast day is soft, and as long as there's no strong breeze it is an excellent time to be out shooting in a garden or meadow. Using a reflector to shade a flower on a sunny day will create the same type of soft light. However, care must be taken so that the entire scene you are shooting is in shadow—the contrast may be too high to record the full tonal range of the scene if there are patches of sunlight in the background.

Focal length: 100mm macro lens

Aperture: f/4.2

Shutter speed: 1/400 sec.

ISO: 400

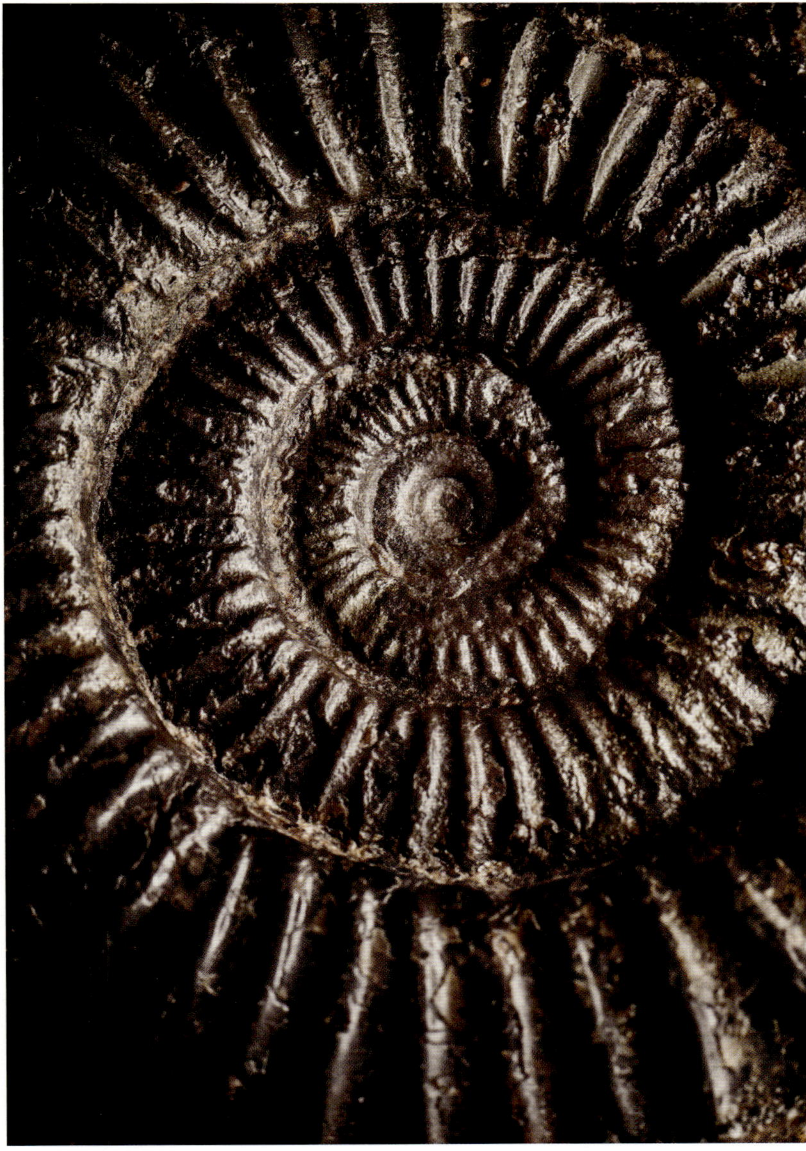

Above: Hard light is better suited to more sculptural subjects, such as this fossil ammonite. To create the hard light in this shot an un-diffused flash was taken off-camera and positioned close to the top of the subject.

Focal length: 100mm macro lens

Aperture: f/18

Shutter speed: 1/250 sec.

ISO: 100

Contrast

Contrast describes how different two comparable qualities are, such as whether a surface is rough or smooth, hard or soft. In terms of lighting, contrast describes the tonal range of a scene.

A high contrast scene occurs when there is an extremely pronounced difference between the relative brightness of the shadows and the highlights with few if any midtones (at maximum contrast, the shadows would be completely black and the highlights entirely white, with no tones in between). High-contrast scenes can be difficult to expose correctly without losing detail in either the shadows or the highlights. In this situation, it is usually best to set the exposure to retain detail in the highlights, as darker shadows are more acceptable than burnt out highlights.

Low-contrast lighting reduces the relative brightness of the shadows and highlights. This makes it much easier to expose an image correctly, but contrast that is too low will result in images that appear flat and two-dimensional. Thankfully, it is easy to boost the contrast cf an image during postproduction to increase impact, but high contrast should be dealt with at the time of shooting (it is difficult to reduce high contrast without a loss of image quality). This can be achieved by adding extra light into the shadow areas using a flash or reflector, or by preventing light from falling on the highlights.

Below: In this example the contrast was adjusted during postproduction. The left side of the image is close to maximum contrast, resulting in near-white highlights, deep black shadows, and very few tones in between. The right side had the contrast lowered, resulting in an image that is close to mid-gray overall.

Focal length: 100mm macro lens

Aperture: f/5

Shutter speed: 1/320 sec.

ISO: 100

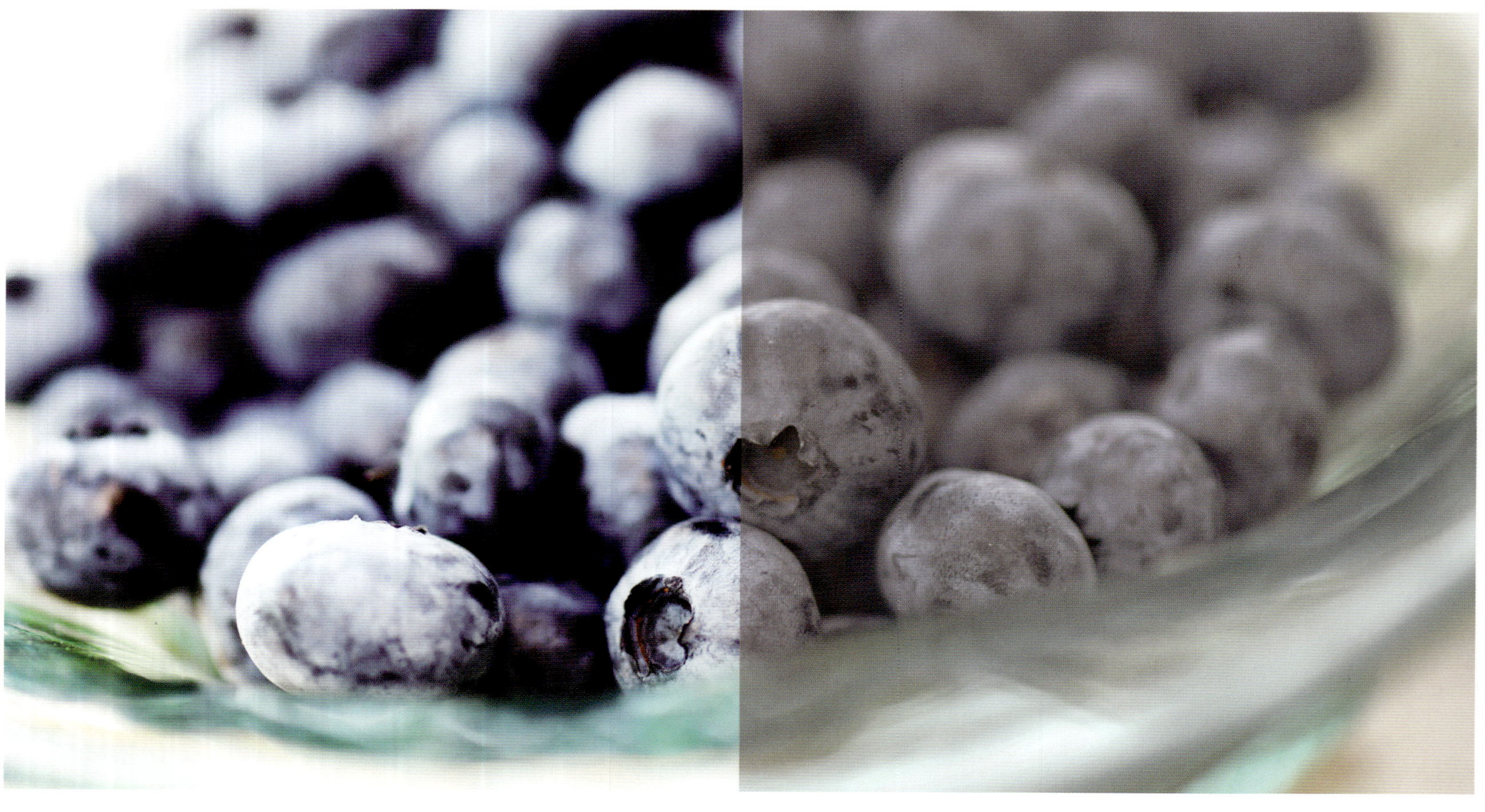

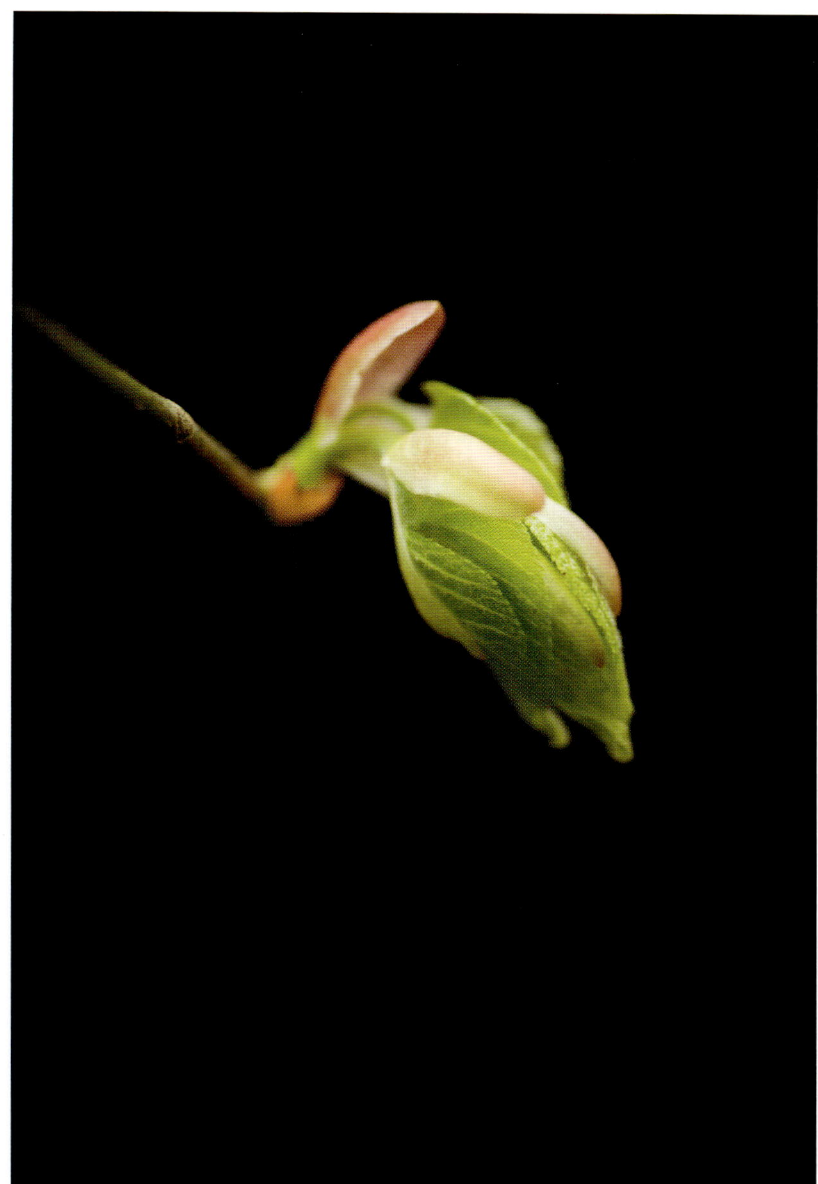

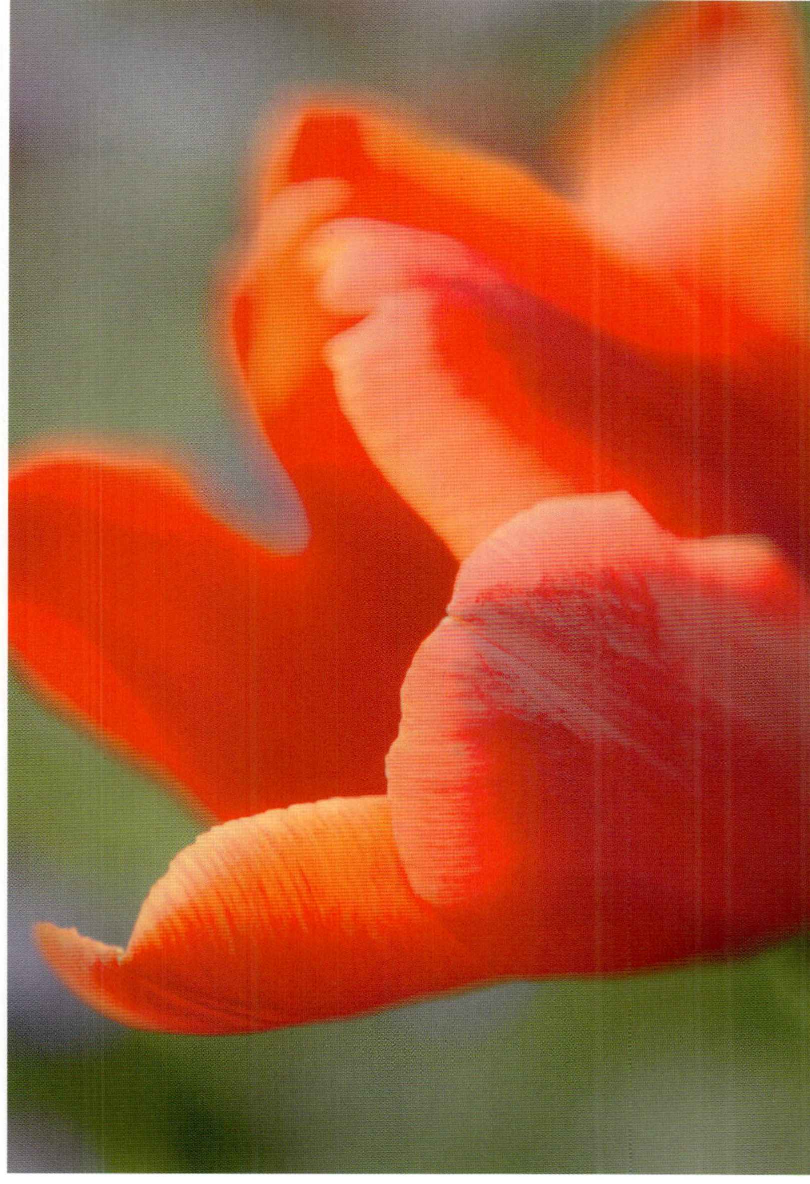

Above: Contrast can be used to add drama to an image. The budding leaves in this shot were softly lit by a slightly overcast sky. However, the background was heavily in shade, which created a useful degree of contrast. To ensure the correct exposure I took a spot-meter reading from the leaves so that the dark background did not influence the exposure.

Focal length: 100mm macro lens

Aperture: f/4.2

Shutter speed: 1/200 sec.

ISO: 800

Above: Contrast is controlled by adjusting how hard or soft your light source is. This close-up of a tulip flower was shot on an overcast day, which resulted in naturally low contrast. To reduce the contrast still further a reflector was used below the flower to even out the illumination.

Focal length: 70mm

Aperture: f/2.8

Shutter speed: 1/125 sec.

ISO: 100

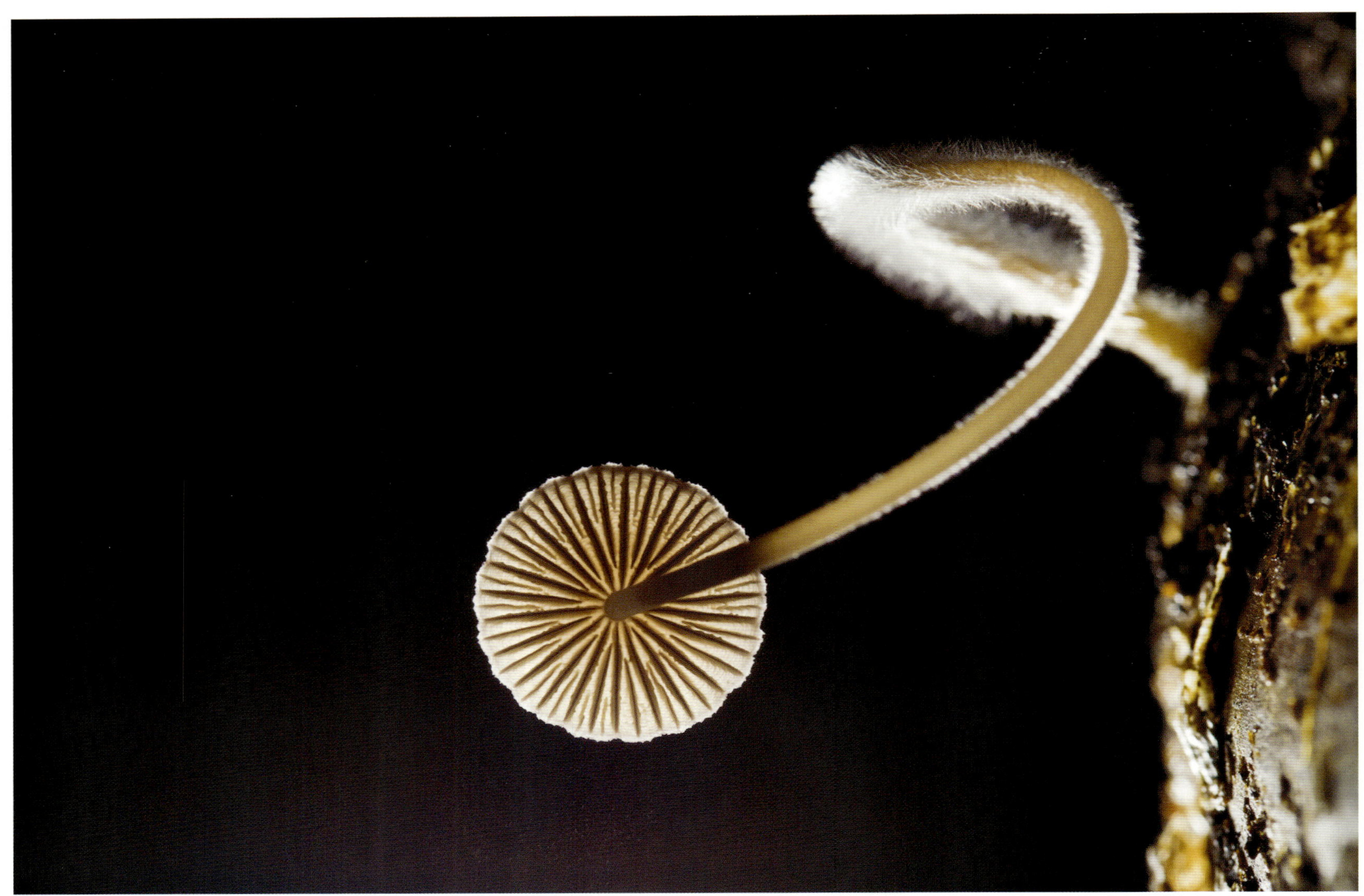

Above: Light can be used to create mood, and two important lighting schemes are low key and high key. Low-key images are comprised mainly of dark tones, with few—if any—lighter tones. Low-key images are created by restricting the light falling onto the subject. This is typically achieved by using a single light, with no ambient light and no extra lighting to fill in the shadows. To shoot this small toadstool I used a single flash.

Focal length: 100mm macro

Aperture: f/8

Shutter speed: 1/200 sec.

ISO: 200

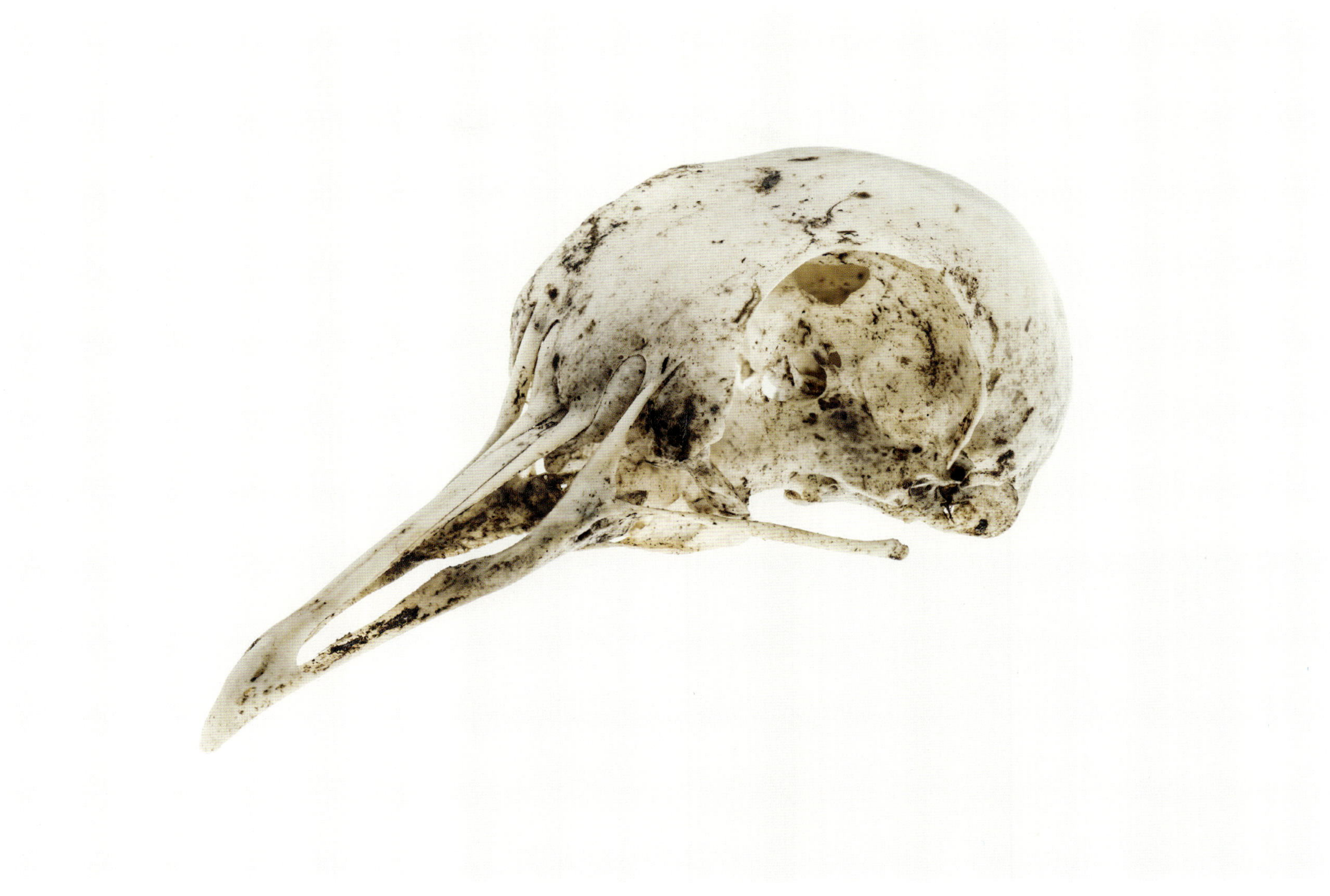

Above: High-key images are the exact opposite to low key: they are biased toward lighter tones with few—if any—darker tones. High-key images are created by adding light into the shadow areas of a scene, either with additional lighting or by using accessories such as reflectors. To create this image I placed the pigeon skull on a lightbox so that it was illuminated from below. A piece of white card was then held above the skull to reflect light back down to even out the lighting.

Focal length: 100mm macro lens

Aperture: f/13 (five images stacked)

Shutter speed: 1/25 sec.

ISO: 100

Lighting Direction

When you are creating a photograph, the directionality of light is described in relation to the position of the light source to the camera. There are three basic lighting direction schemes that photographers regularly use: front, side, and back.

Frontal Lighting

A light that falls onto the subject from just behind or actually from the camera position is known as frontal lighting, which is arguably the least satisfying of the three lighting schemes. Light helps to define the shape and texture of an object in an image, but frontal lighting tends to flatten shape and texture as any shadows are cast behind the subject (and therefore out of sight to the camera).

Frontal lighting also increases the possibility that you or your camera's shadow will appear in the image. The one good thing about frontal light is that it typically illuminates your subject evenly, making metering relatively straightforward. On-camera flash is a frontal light source, as are lens-mounted ring lights.

Side Lighting

Side lighting is more interesting visually. This is light that is positioned approximately 35–100° to the camera either on the left or the right (top and under lighting are variations of side lighting where the lighting is positioned above and below the subject respectively).

Side lighting increases contrast by casting shadows across the image space. This can make metering more difficult, especially when the side lighting is hard and the contrast is high (although contrast can be lowered by adding extra light). The benefit of side lighting is that these shadows (and highlights) define the shape and texture of the subject, increasing the sense that the subject in an image is three-dimensional.

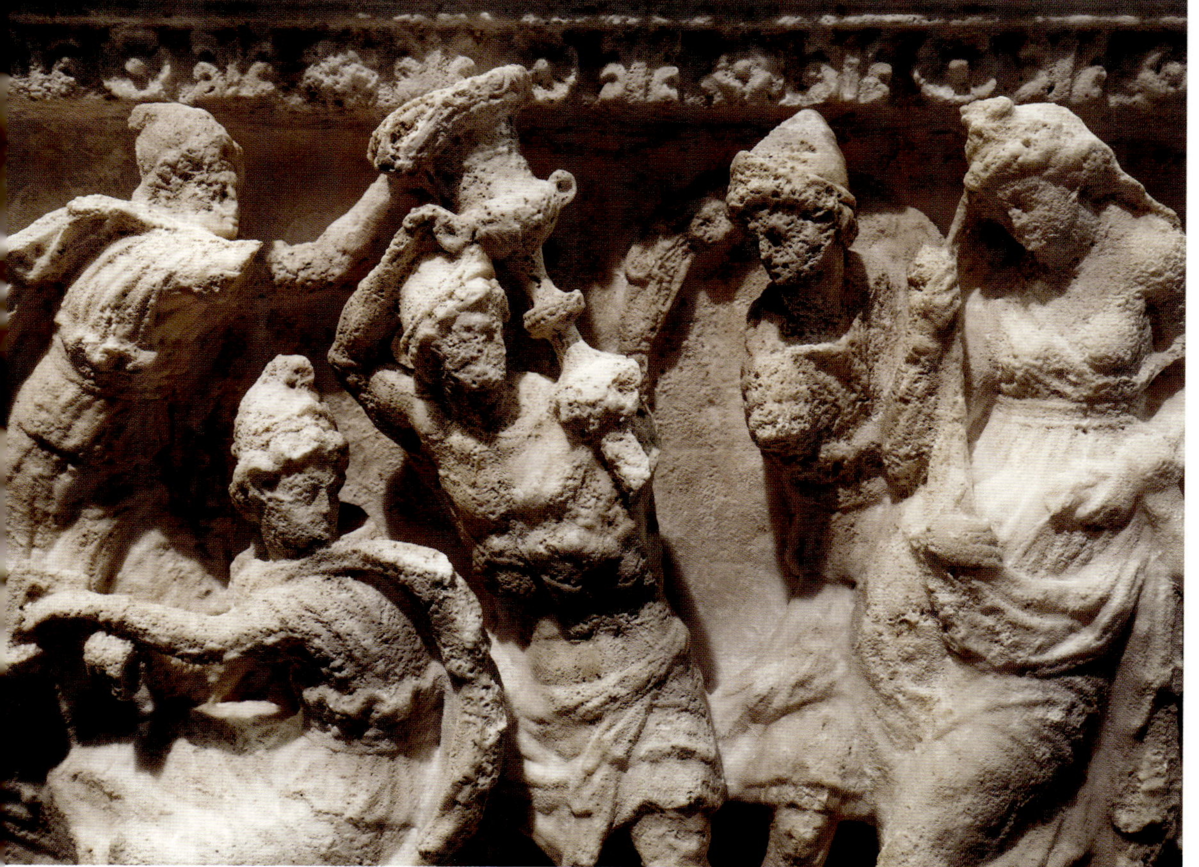

Left: Side lighting reveals the texture and form of a subject. Here, high-placed side lighting has been combined with a hard light source to produce sharply defined shadows; if the light had been soft and frontal the shot would have appeared flat and been more difficult to "read."

Focal length: 40mm

Aperture: f/4

Shutter speed: 1/5 sec.

ISO: 400

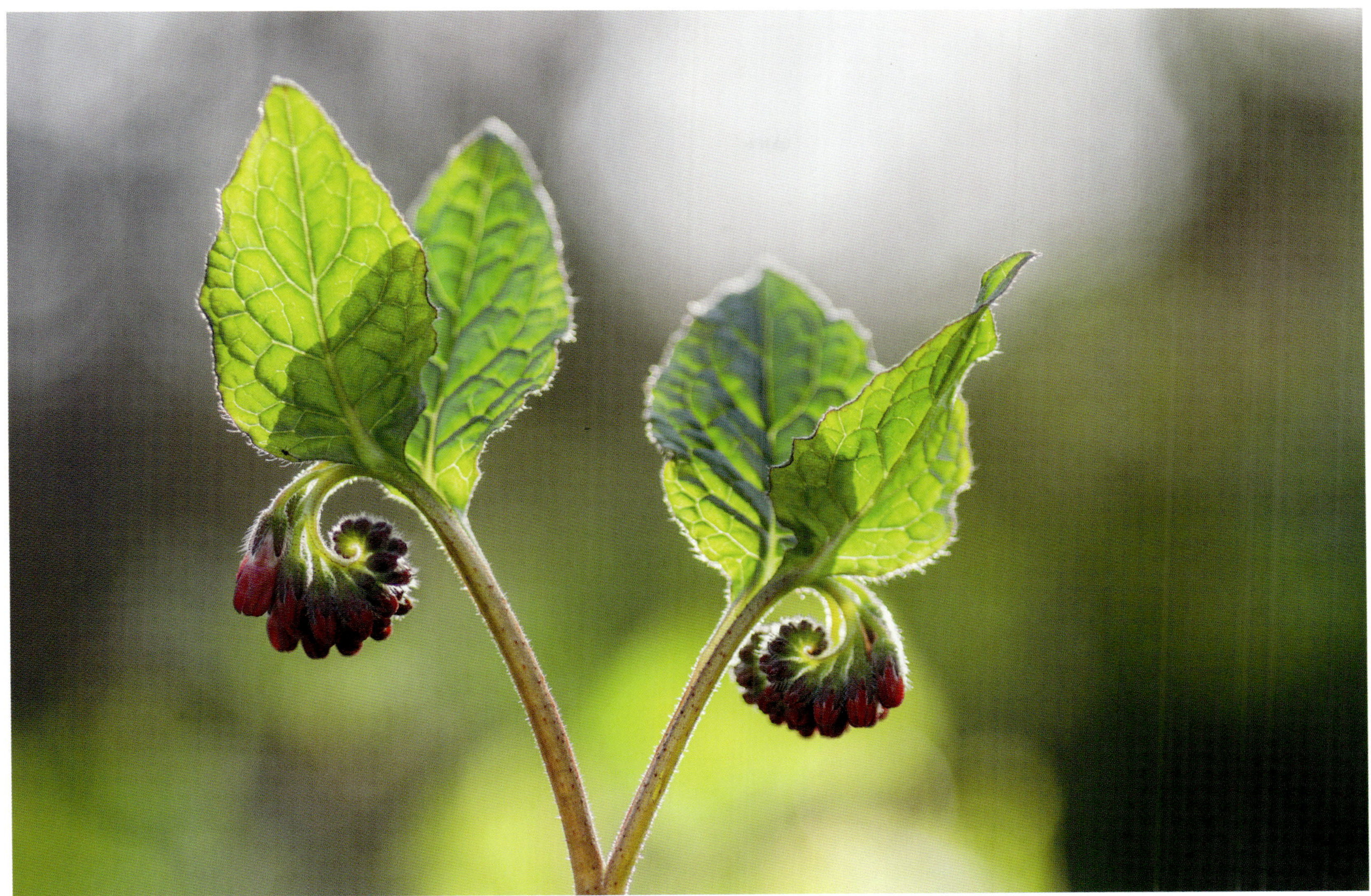

Backlighting

When the light source is in front of the camera, the scene is said to be backlit. Backlighting increases contrast and can cause subjects to be silhouetted, particularly when the light source is within the image space.

Backlighting also has the esthetically pleasing effect of creating rim lighting. This is a thin bright highlight around the edge of the subject that is accentuated by any fine hairs or filaments on the surface of the subject. As contrast is high with backlighting, it is often necessary to use additional lights or reflectors to avoid exposure issues.

Flash

Flash is incredibly useful when shooting macro subjects. Not only are flashes relatively small compared to studio lighting, but they also give off less heat and can be used outdoors, either as the sole source of illumination or as a fill light to reduce contrast. The short duration of flash is also useful when it comes to freezing any movement in your subject, while accessories can be used to modify the quality of the light.

Exposure

Of the two ways you can physically change the exposure on a camera—shutter speed and aperture—only the aperture has an effect on flash exposure. The shutter speed controls the exposure of the ambient light in the areas of the scene not lit by flash, which would typically be the background. One way to control flash exposure is to adjust the size of the aperture, opening the aperture wider to increase the flash exposure or closing it to decrease flash exposure. It's worth noting that the smaller the aperture you use, the shorter the effective range of the flash becomes.

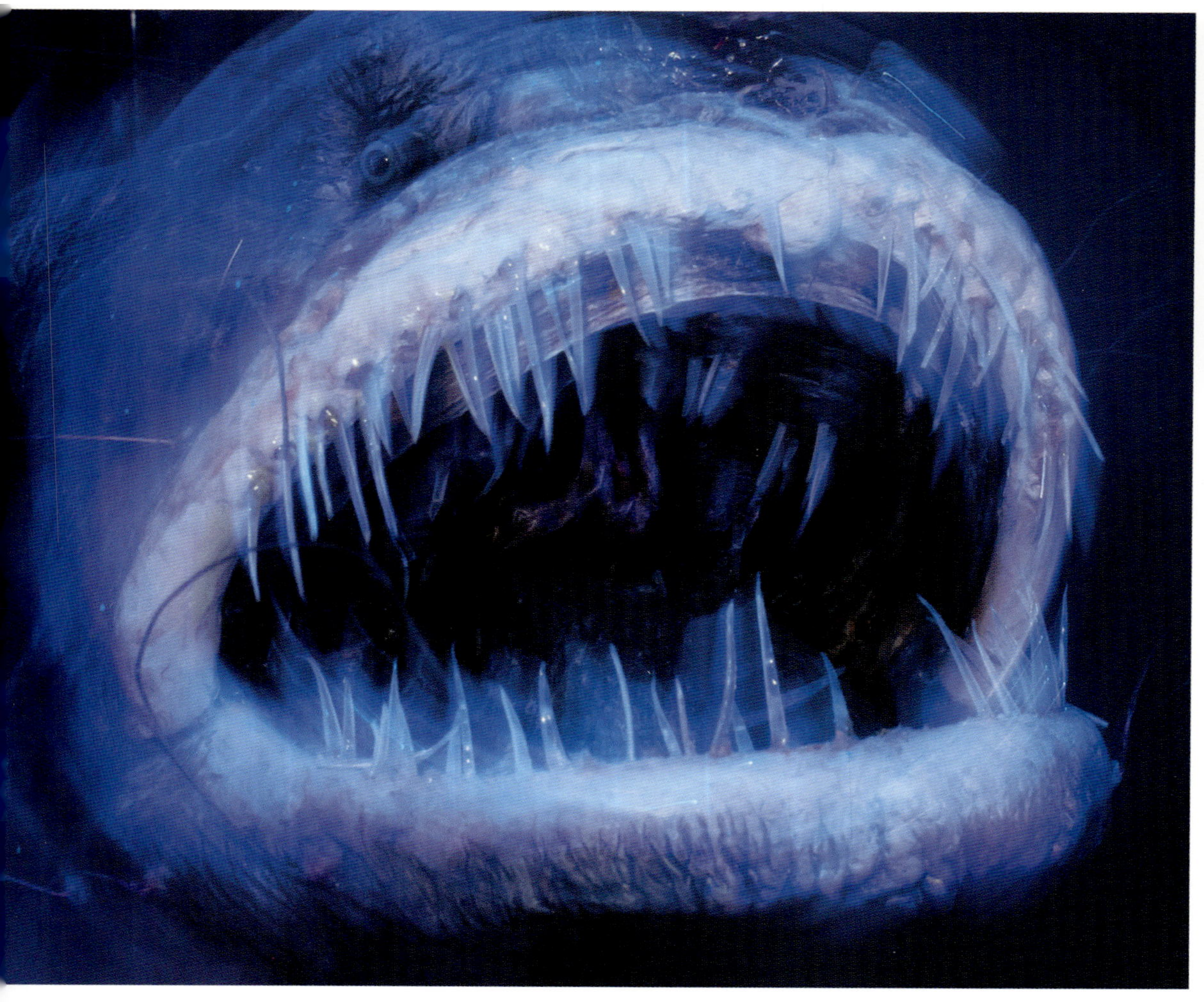

GN & ISO

The GN of a flash increases as ISO is increased. However, doubling the ISO (from ISO 100 to ISO 200, for example) does not double the GN. Instead, the GN increases by 1.4x. It is only when the ISO is quadrupled (from ISO 100 to ISO 400, for example) that the GN is doubled.

Left: Shutter speed has no effect on flash exposure, so using a long shutter speed will only help to expose the areas lit by ambient light. If either the subject or camera moves during the exposure then areas illuminated by the flash will be sharp, while those areas lit by the ambient light will be blurred.

Focal length: 12.1mm

Aperture: f/7.1

Shutter speed: 2.5 sec.

ISO: 200

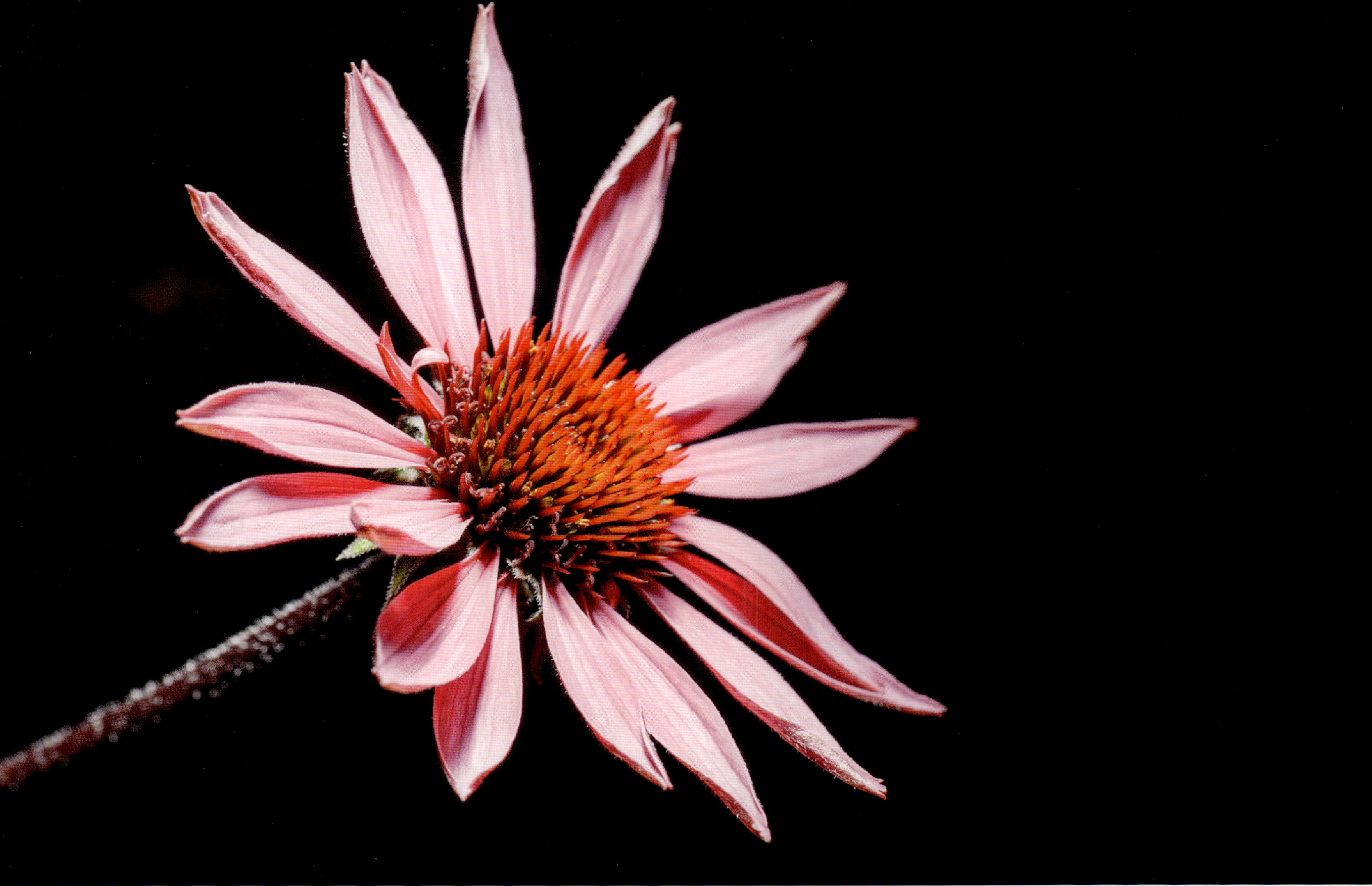

Guide Number

The power of a flash—and therefore its maximum effective range at a particular ISO and aperture setting—is determined by its guide number, or GN. With macro photography, this is often irrelevant, as the flash would usually be relatively close to the subject. However, the effective range can be surprisingly small when you are using a small aperture to maximize depth of field, so it is still useful to be aware of it.

To calculate the effective flash range at a particular aperture you should use the formula *GN/aperture=distance*. To calculate the aperture required when the flash is a certain distance from the subject, the formula *GN/distance=aperture* should be used instead.

There are numerous apps for cellphones and tablets that can solve these formulas for you, but it's worth noting that the effective range of a flash is the distance between the flash and the subject, which may not be the same as the camera-to-subject distance.

Above: In the right conditions, flash can be used to overpower the areas of a scene lit purely by ambient light. For this shot I metered the background to determine the exposure and set the shutter speed to the camera's flash sync speed. After positioning the flash, the aperture and flash power were set so the flower was correctly illuminated and the background was underexposed by 2 stops to hide the fact that it was chaotic and distracting.

Focal length: 100mm macro lens

Aperture: f/16

Shutter speed: 1/250 sec.

ISO: 100

Flash Power

Although the GN determines the maximum effective range of a flash, it does not mean that the flash has to be used at full power every time it is fired. When using flash to illuminate a macro subject it is often necessary to reduce the power of the flash in order to avoid overexposure.

The simplest method is known as through-the-lens (TTL) metering, where the camera takes control of the flash exposure. It does this by firing a pre-flash, which is metered by the camera. The flash power is then adjusted and the flash fired again to make the exposure. Depending on the curtain sync and shutter speed settings, the pre-flash may not be noticed as it almost immediately precedes the main flash. The problem with TTL flash is that it can be fooled by the reflectivity of your subject—a subject with a higher-than-average reflectivity can lead to underexposure, while a subject with a lower-than-average reflectivity can cause overexposure.

Flash exposures can also be set manually, which puts you in full control of the power output of the flash. The power is altered in fractions of the full power output of the flash: ½ power halves the power output of the flash, ¼ power quarters it, and so on. For large-scale subjects the correct power setting is most easily determined by using an exposure meter with a flash setting. The exposure meter is held close to the subject, with the metering dome aimed toward the camera. When a test flash is fired, the meter measures the intensity of the light emitted by the flash that is reaching it and displays the aperture required.

There are two problems with using flash exposure meters when shooting macro subjects. The first is that it can be physically difficult to fit the meter between the flash and the subject (especially if the camera is close to the subject). The second is that flash exposure meters do not automatically take account of light loss due to magnification (see page 81), so extra flash exposure must be factored in. For these reasons it is often easier to make a test exposure, read the resulting histogram, and adjust the flash if necessary before shooting again.

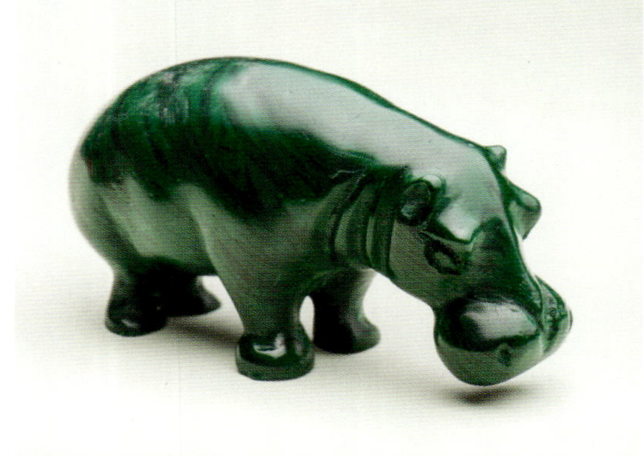

1/1

1/4

1/32

1/128

SYNC SPEED

The maximum shutter speed you can set when using flash with a DSLR or mirrorless camera is known as the sync speed. This varies between camera models, but is typically in the region of 1/150–1/250 sec.

High-end flashes often offer a mode known as high-speed sync (HSS) that allows you to use faster shutter speeds, but the trade-off is that the maximum effective range of the flash is significantly reduced.

Compact cameras and cameras that use leaf shutters do not have a sync speed, so flash can generally be used at any shutter speed.

Above: Altering the flash power has a huge impact on exposure. Here, the flash was set at different power settings, ranging from 1/1 (the correct setting for the subject-to-flash distance) to 1/128. The difference between the settings is obvious.

Focal length: 100mm macro lens

Aperture: f/22

Shutter speed: 1/250 sec.

ISO: 100

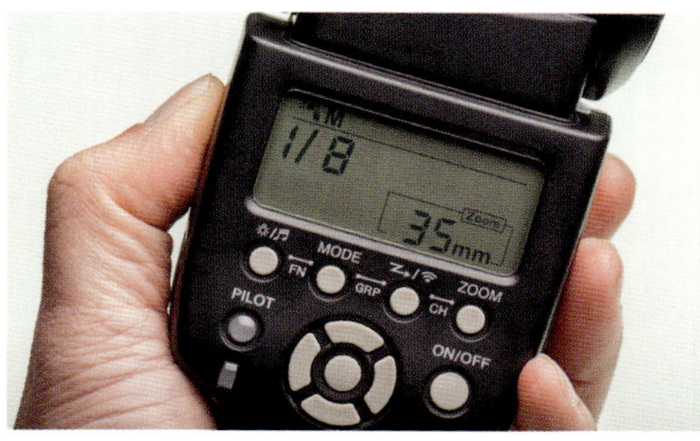

Above: Flash power is typically given as a fraction, displayed on the rear of the flash. This flash has been manually set to 1/8 power.

Right: For this shot, flash was used to reveal detail in smoke rising from a match that had just been extinguished. The flash was placed at 90° to the camera so the smoke was lit from the side. I also set the maximum sync speed and a small aperture to ensure the background was underexposed and to increase contrast.

Focal length: 100mm macro lens

Aperture: f/16

Shutter speed: 1/250 sec.

ISO: 100

CURTAIN SYNC

Focal plane shutters are used in both DSLRs and mirrorless cameras. This type of shutter has two metal curtains. The first curtain opens to allow light to reach the sensor and then the second curtain follows to stop light from reaching the sensor, ending the exposure.

Flash can be set to either 1st curtain sync or 2nd curtain sync. This determines when the flash fires during an exposure. Set to 1st curtain sync, the flash fires when the first curtain begins to move, at the start of the exposure, while 2nd curtain sync fires the flash as the second curtain moves, at the end of the exposure.

If you're shooting static subjects these two settings are largely irrelevant, but shoot a moving subject and you will find that 2nd curtain sync produces the most "natural" results.

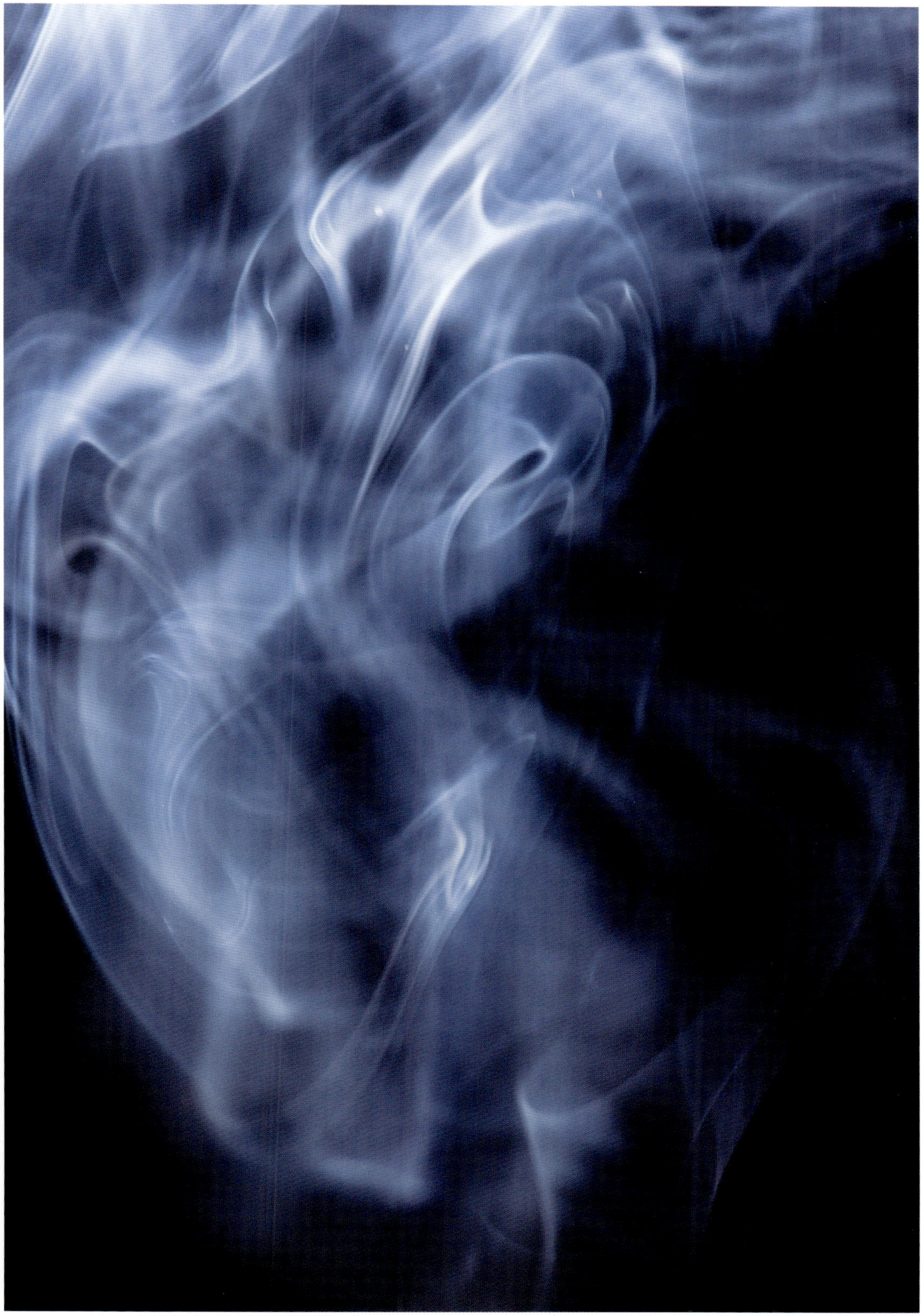

Off-Camera Flash

Using a flash away from the camera will give you greater control over the esthetic qualities of your lighting—the lighting direction in particular. There are a number of ways to take flash off-camera. The simplest is with a TTL cord, with one end connected to the camera's hotshoe and the other to the foot of the flash. Using a TTL cord has the major benefit of maintaining TTL control, so the camera can still control the flash exposure automatically. The drawback to using a TTL cord (or a cord connection via a PC terminal) is that you are limited by the length of the cord. It is also easy to trip over the cord and pull your flash or camera over.

An alternative is wireless flash, and there are two main systems in use. The first is optical triggering, which uses the camera's built-in flash to fire an off-camera flash. Optical triggering often maintains TTL exposure automation (particularly when a camera manufacturer's own brand of flash is used), but it has a limited range—especially outdoors—and the off-camera flash must be able to "see" the camera flash (although in a studio the flash light bouncing off the walls or ceiling will often still trigger an off-camera flash).

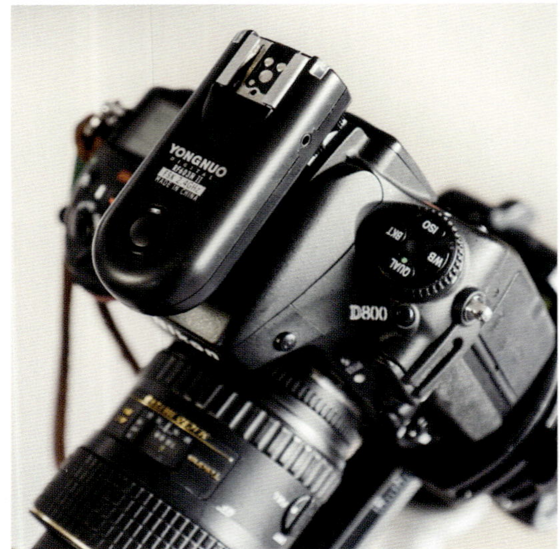

The second option is radio triggering, which uses a small radio transceiver fitted to the camera's hotshoe to fire a compatible off-camera flash. Unlike optical triggering this usually doesn't provide TTL automation, so flash exposures must be set manually, but maintaining "line of sight" between the camera and flash is not necessarily needed.

Tips

When using optical triggering, position the off-camera (slave) flash so that it faces the master flash and then angle the slave's flash head toward your subject. This will help ensure that the slave flash sees the master fire.

When you use two or more flashes, adjust their power independently to vary the degree of illumination on your subject. The greater the power difference between the flashes, the greater the contrast levels of your shot will be.

MASTER & SLAVE

The flash that controls when the off-camera flash fires is known as the "master," while the triggered flash is known as the "slave." Flash systems often allow you to assign a channel to your master and slave: you need to make sure that both channel numbers are the same, but different to the channel numbers of anyone else using optically triggered flashes in the immediate vicinity.

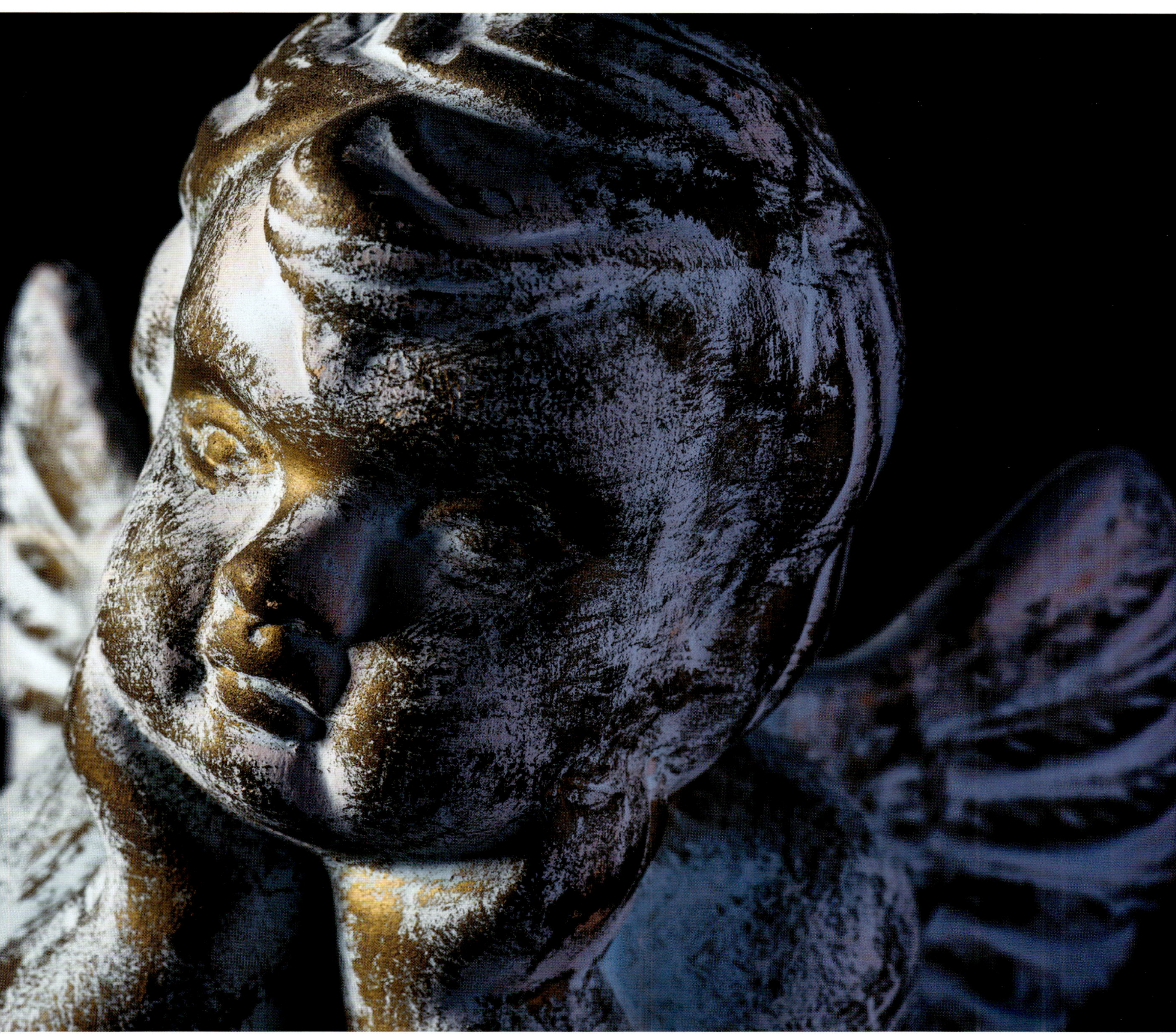

Color Temperature

Visible light is a mix of different wavelengths, extending from red through to violet. "White" light has an equal mix of all these wavelengths and is said to be neutral. However, light is rarely neutral, particularly in nature. Light with an unequal mix of wavelengths will have a color bias. Commonly this bias is either toward the red end of the spectrum or the blue end: red-biased light is said to be "warm," blue-biased light "cool."

The color of light is represented by a color "temperature" that is measured in degrees Kelvin (K). Light is neutral when the color temperature is approximately 5200–5500K. Red-biased light has a lower Kelvin value; blue-biased light a higher one.

The human eye (in combination with the brain) is remarkably adept at compensating for subtle variations in the color temperature of light. However, a camera needs to be told what the temperature is, so any bias is neutralized or—for esthetic reasons—retained. This is done by adjusting a camera's white balance (WB) setting. WB is set either by choosing a preset that matches the type of lighting that illuminates a scene (as shown in the grid below); by setting a specific Kelvin value; or by using Auto WB, which lets the camera determine the WB adjustment needed.

COLOR TEMPERATURE	LIGHTING TYPE	WB PRESET SYMBOL
1800–2000K	*Candlelight*	*N/A*
2500K	*Torchlight*	*N/A*
2800K	*Domestic lighting*	(incandescent symbol)
3000K	*Sunrise/Sunset*	*N/A*
3500K	*Morning/Afternoon sunlight*	*N/A*
5200K	*Midday sunlight*	(daylight/sun symbol)
5500K	*Electronic flash*	(flash symbol)
6000–6500K	*Overcast*	(cloud symbol)
7000–8000K	*Shade*	(shade/house symbol)

Right: These honesty seed heads were in shade, which has a very "cool" color temperature. Shots were taken with the WB set at 4500K, 5500K, 6500K, and 7500K. Technically, the correct WB would be in the region of 6500–7500K. However, I prefer the image that was set at 4500K: the seed heads have an attractive coolness that contrasts with the warmer light in the background.

Focal length: 100mm macro lens

Aperture: f/3.5

Shutter speed: 1/400 sec.

ISO: 400

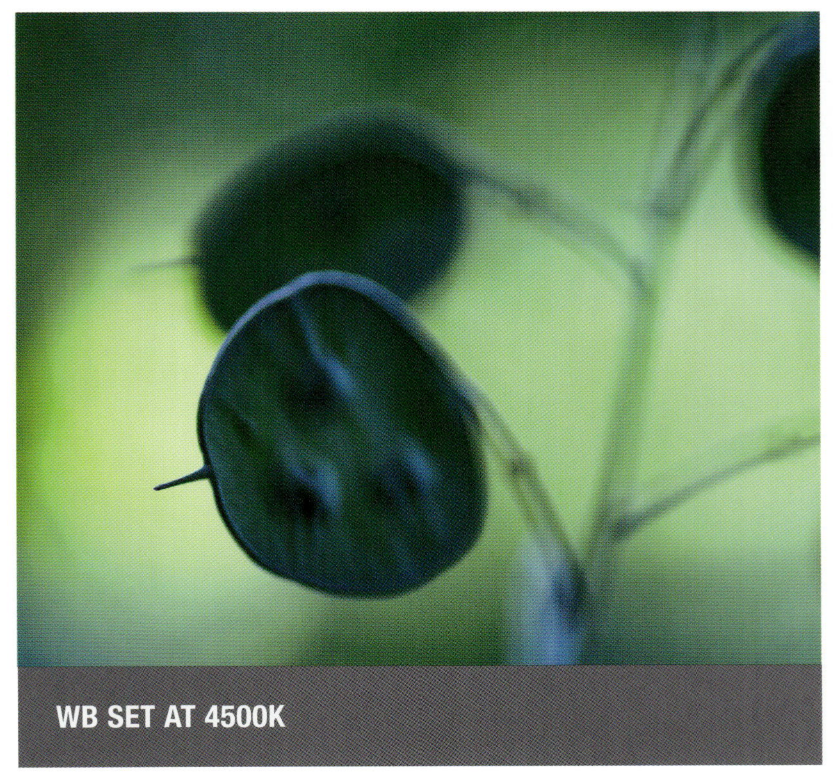
WB SET AT 4500K

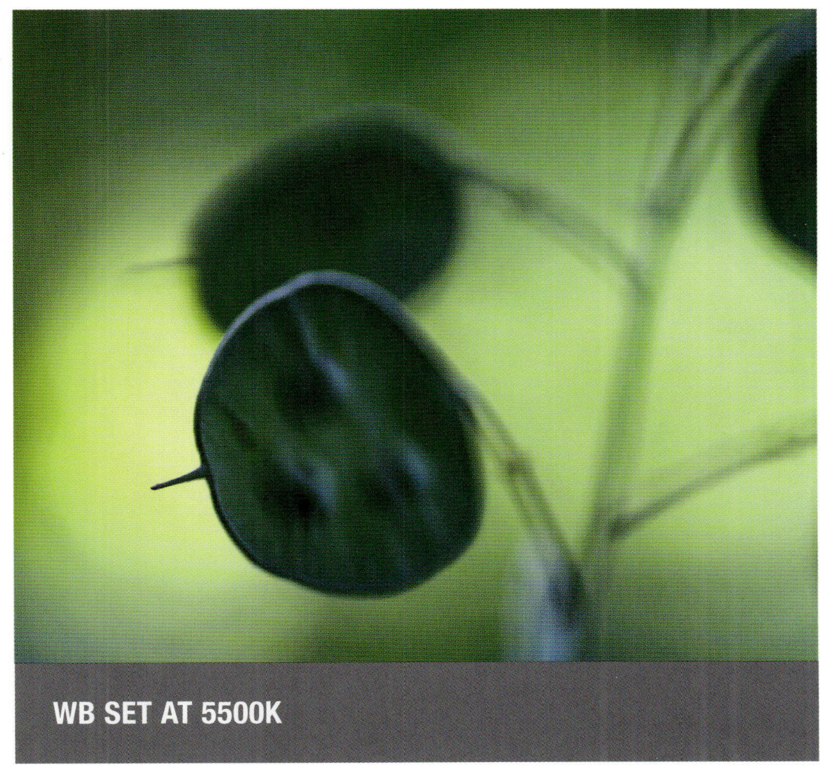
WB SET AT 5500K

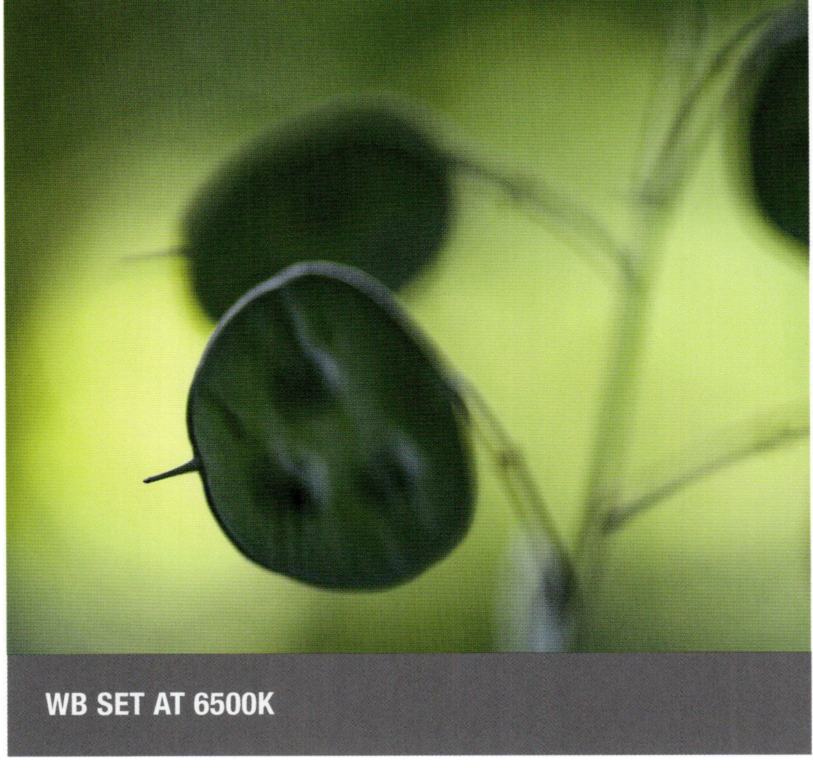
WB SET AT 6500K

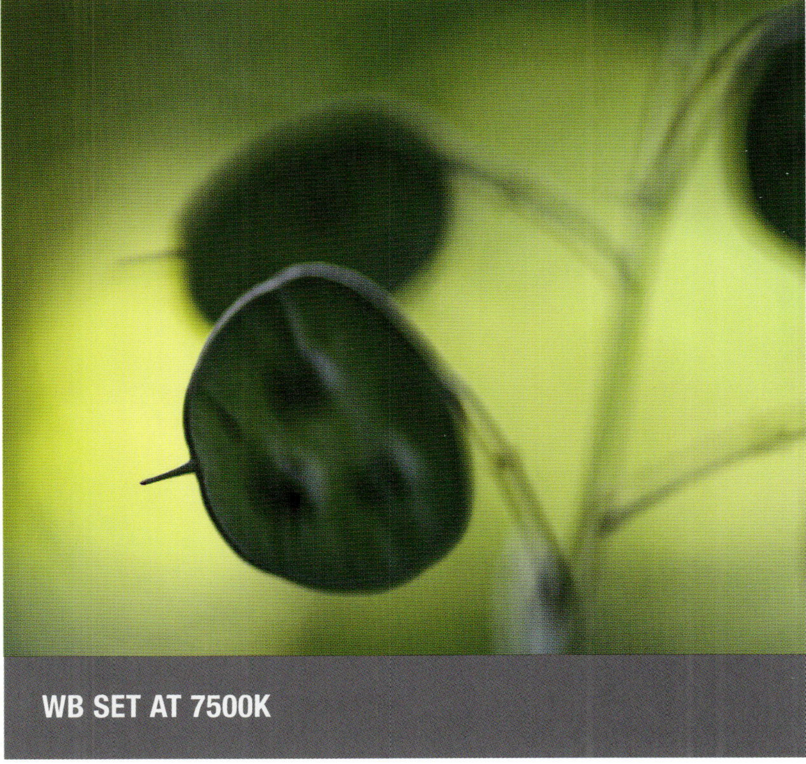
WB SET AT 7500K

Profile: Polina Plotnikova

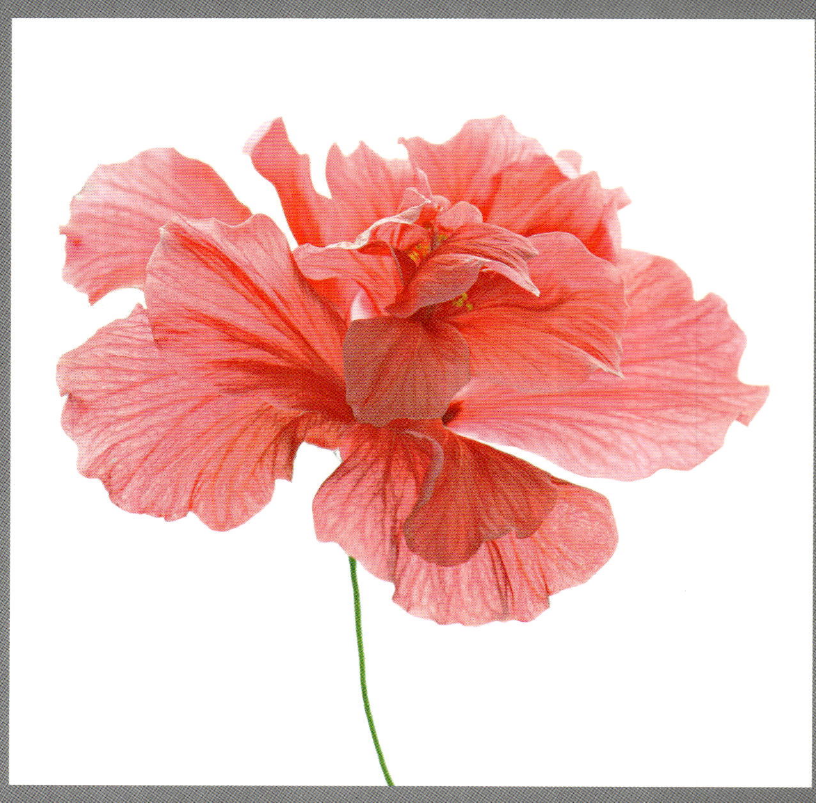

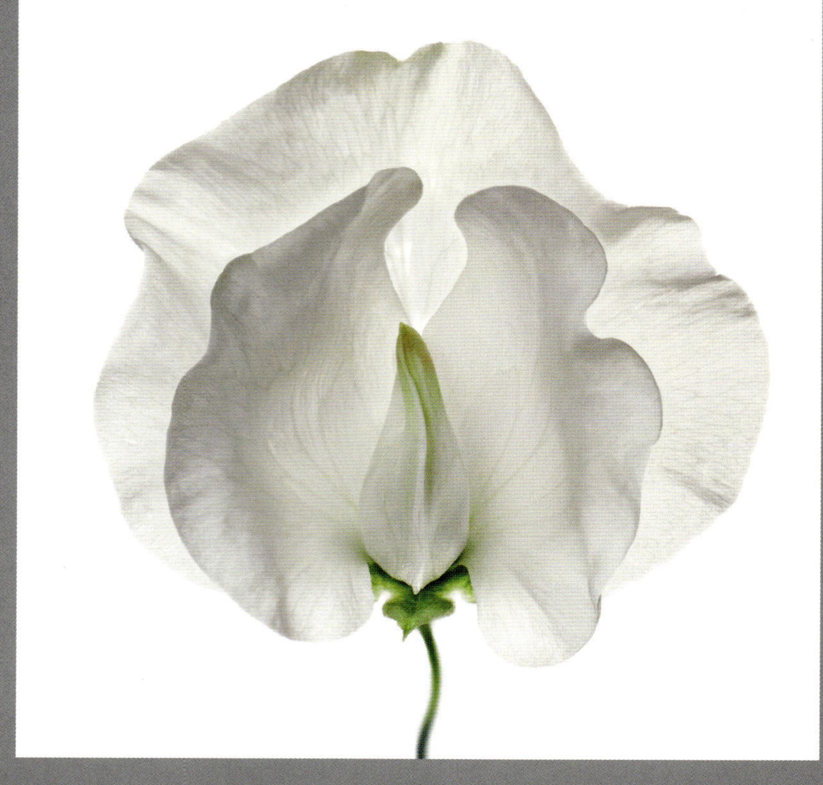

BIOGRAPHY

Polina Plotnikova is a Russian-born, UK-based photographer. Before she started to take pictures herself, she worked in image libraries for over ten years, dealing with great images produced by the most successful commercial and fine-art photographers. She is a member of the Royal Photographic Society (with ARPS distinction) and the current President of Beckenham Photographic Society.

www.polinaplotnikova.com

Q) What is your specialty?

A) One of my favorite subjects is flowers. Having started with what might be referred to as "pretty pictures" of flowers as they are, I then moved away from that and developed an approach whereby I don't just shoot what is in front of me, but rather imagine a picture first, and then work toward getting it onto my photographic canvas. As part of this process, I often take liberties with details of plants such as the position of individual petals and stems. I also use various lighting and postproduction techniques to achieve the result that I am after.

Q) What is it about your specialty that fascinates you?

A) The approach to flower photography that I take is similar to that of a portrait photographer—for every flower and plant that I photograph, I try to find its unique look, study its mood and character, and ultimately unlock the concealed beauty of my models. A successful flower portrait attempts to discover something unique in a flower; something hidden or not necessarily obvious at first sight. Also, a good floral portrait—unlike a purely botanical illustration—should trigger a thought or an emotion in a viewer's mind.

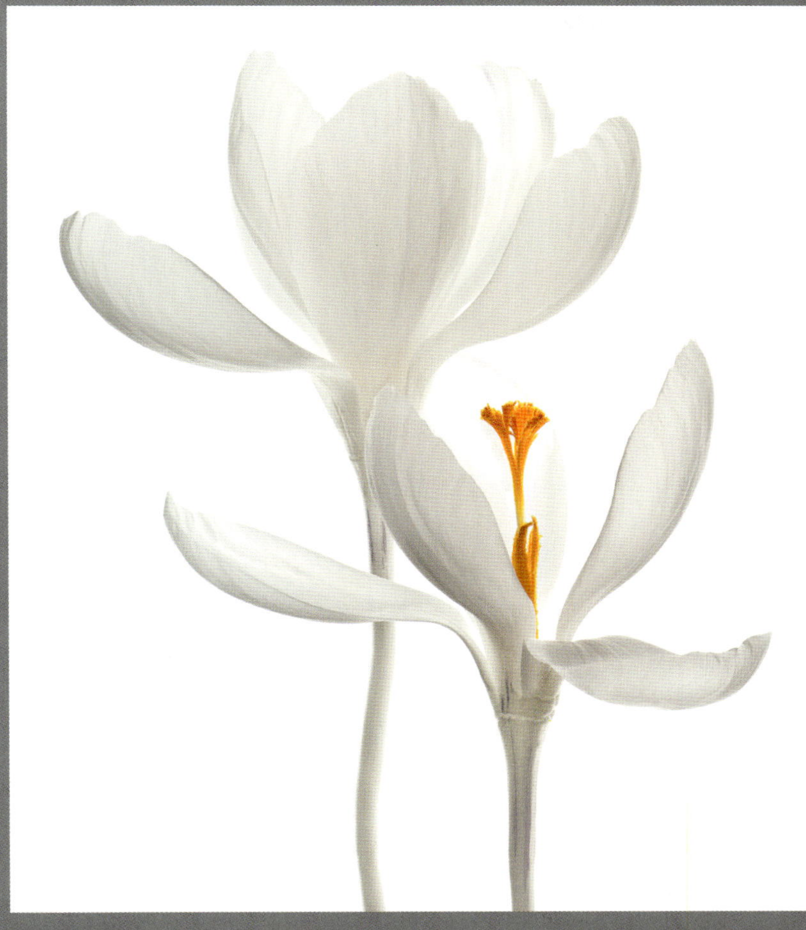

Opposite page, left:

Focal length: 100mm macro lens

Aperture: f/9

Shutter speed: 1/125 sec.

ISO: 100

Opposite page, right:

Focal length: 100mm macro lens

Aperture: f/11

Shutter speed: 1/125 sec.

ISO: 100

Left:

Focal length: 100mm macro lens

Aperture: f/13

Shutter speed: 1/125 sec.

ISO: 100

Q) How do you plan a photography session?

A) My usual approach to creating a new photograph starts with constructing an image in my head— visualizing the overall composition, the flowers I am going to use, the color scheme, the lighting, the background, and so on. It pays to have a good working relationship with your local flower stalls so that you can get what you need to shoot. Sometimes I have to wait until a certain flower can be obtained if it is out of flowering season.

Q) How do you light your subjects?

A) I use both natural and artificial lighting, and with the latter I use both flash and continuous light. The kit I work with consists of two Bowens Gemini 500 flash heads; I use softboxes, an umbrella, grids (such as honeycomb), and filters to create certain light effects. If I shoot with natural light, I use various reflectors and diffusers to modify the light and create shadows or highlights. I need to have full control over my setup and lighting, and the only way I can achieve this is to create all these elements in my studio.

Q) How important is postproduction to you?

A) As much as I love the power of Photoshop, I prefer to get my images as close to my vision in-camera. When it comes to postproduction I usually know in advance what I am going to do with every single shot—whether it is adding a textured layer or cropping to a square format, for example.

Q) What is your top tip?

A) Always get the best flower you can find! Unless you are capturing the beauty of decaying flowers (which I also enjoy), try to shoot "perfect" flowers. One thing that also makes my life easier is Helicon Remote software, which lets me connect my camera to a laptop so I can see the image on screen before I take it.

Studio flower photography is great for a perfectionist—no one fidgets or makes faces, your models don't talk back, and no sudden gust of wind or other quirk of ever-changing weather can spoil your shot. But at the same time, you cannot count on something interesting to "just happen"— it is all up to you; the choices are infinite, and the final result is entirely in your own hands.

Q) What equipment do you regularly use?

A) I shoot with a Canon EOS 5DSr and my favorite lens is the Canon EF 100mm F2.8 L IS USM Macro. I also love working with various Lensbaby optics, including the Velvet 56 and Edge 80. Lensbabys are amazing if you want to unleash your creativity in-camera without any special postproduction tricks.

Chapter 5

Advanced Technique

Once you've mastered the basics of shooting close-up and macro imagery, there are other, more advanced techniques that you can learn. Some of these techniques are not unique to close-up and macro photography, but there are specific issues that need to be thought about carefully. Other techniques—such as photomicrography—are very much in the domain of close-up and macro photography. This chapter covers both types of technique and explores how they can help you master the art of close-up and macro photography.

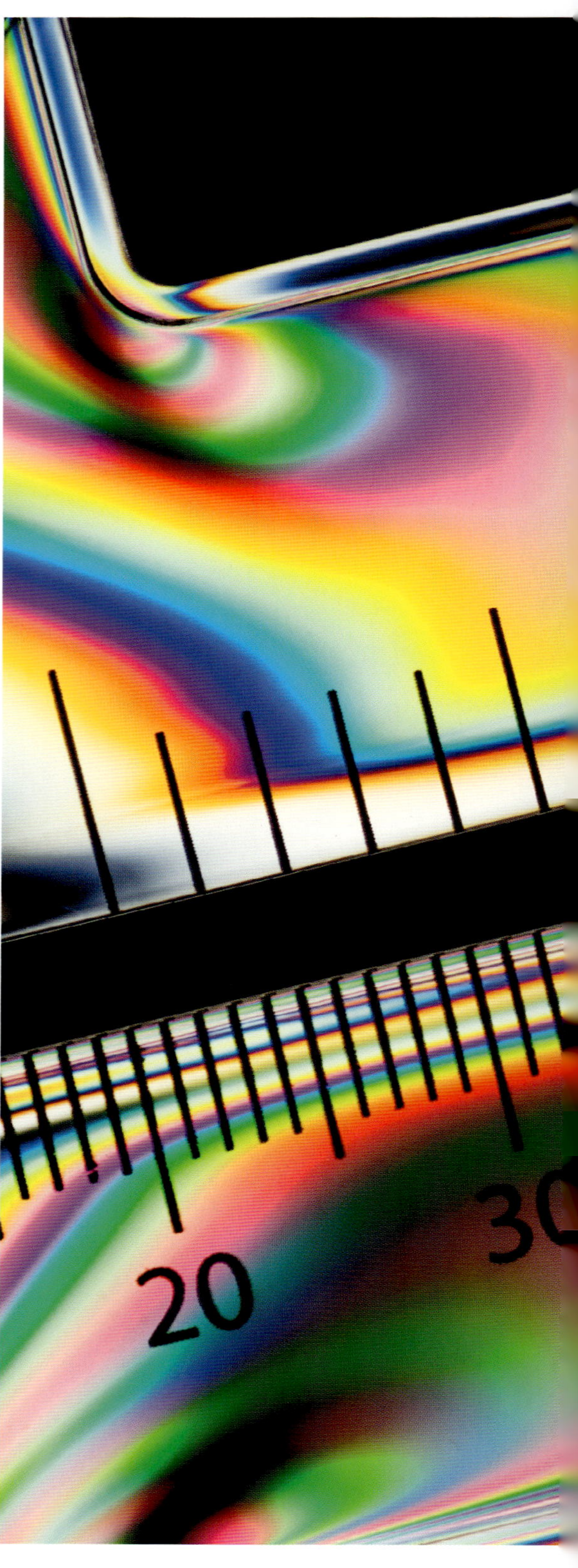

Right: Cross-polarization is a technique that reveals the hidden stress lines in clear plastic objects. Not only is it scientifically interesting, but it also has a surreal, abstract, and colorful beauty.

Focal length: 100mm macro lens

Aperture: f/9

Shutter speed: 1/25 sec.

ISO: 400

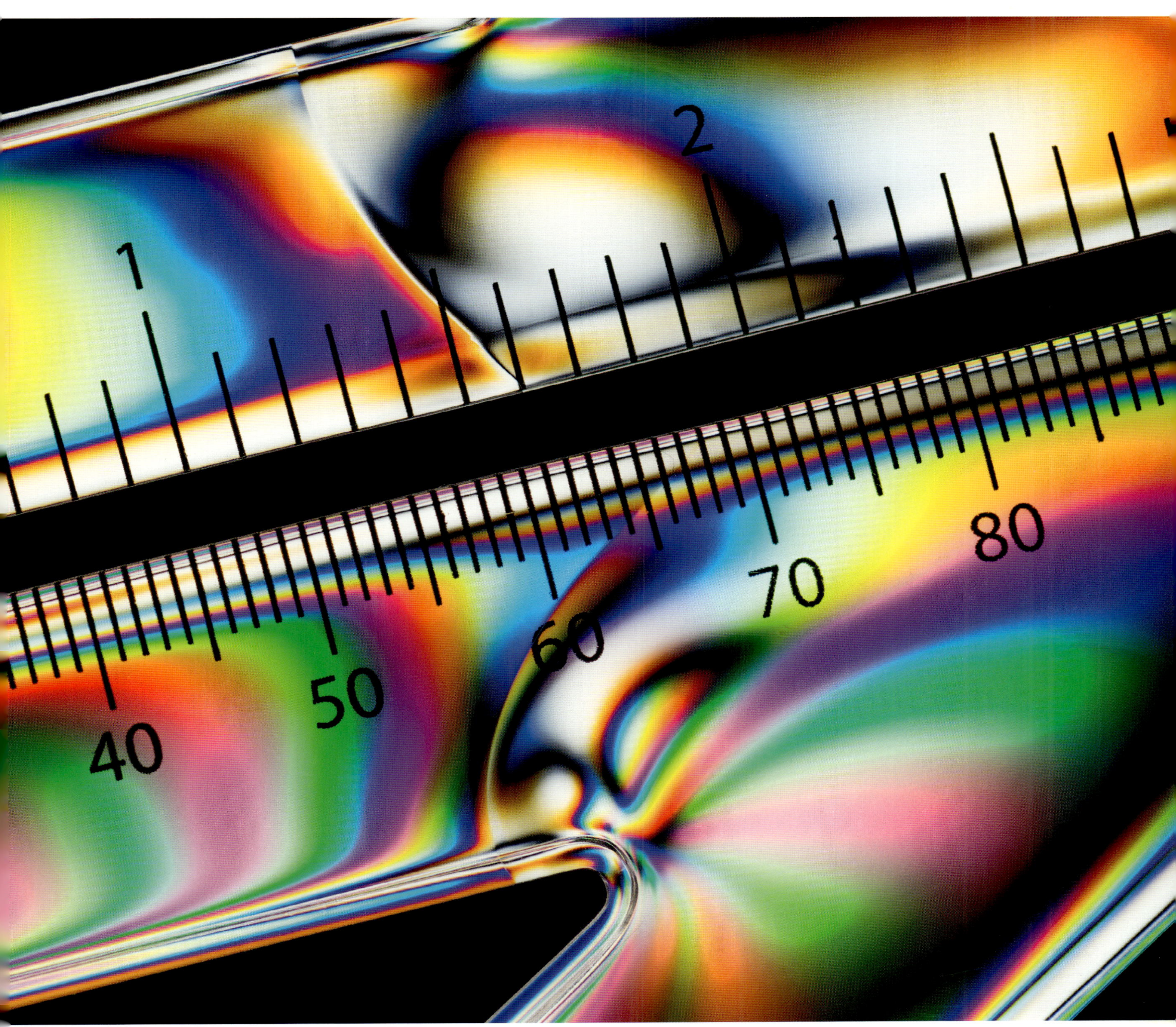

Shooting Outdoors

The one constant about shooting outdoors is that the light changes throughout the day and also with the weather. This means that shooting macro outdoors requires additional planning, as well as a more flexible approach to working in a studio.

Direct Sunlight

The maximum height (or elevation) of the sun at midday and the length of the day vary throughout the year, with less variation near the equator and greater variation at the poles. At local midwinter—December in the northern hemisphere, June in the southern—the length of the days is shorter than the nights and the sun does not rise as high in the sky.

This is reversed at local midsummer (June in the northern hemisphere, December in the southern). At this time of year the nights are shorter than the days and the sun reaches its maximum possible elevation at midday. At the spring and autumn equinoxes, in March and September respectively, the length of the day and night are equal and the elevation of the sun at midday is somewhere between the two extremes of winter and summer.

The height of the sun above the horizon has an effect on the color temperature of sunlight. When the sun is close to the horizon the light is more biased toward red and is therefore warmer in color. The higher the sun is above the horizon, the more neutral in color the light becomes. Winter is often a good time to be shooting outdoors: the ambient temperature may be colder, but the light from the sun stays relatively warm in color throughout the day. The low raking angle of winter sunlight is also attractive, particularly for subjects close to the ground. In summer, the sun acts more like a top light at midday, which tends to flatten texture and cast deep shadows under the subject.

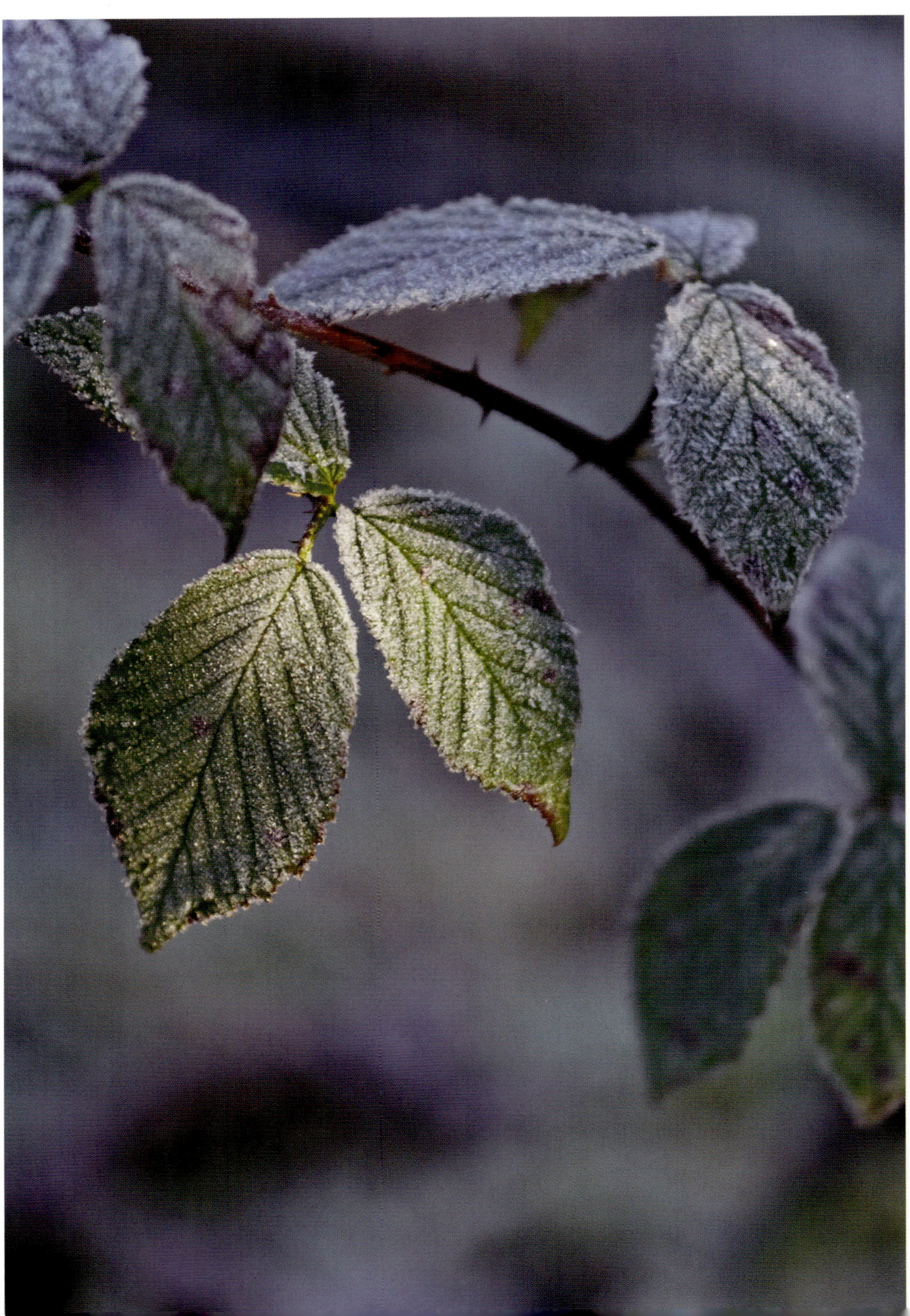

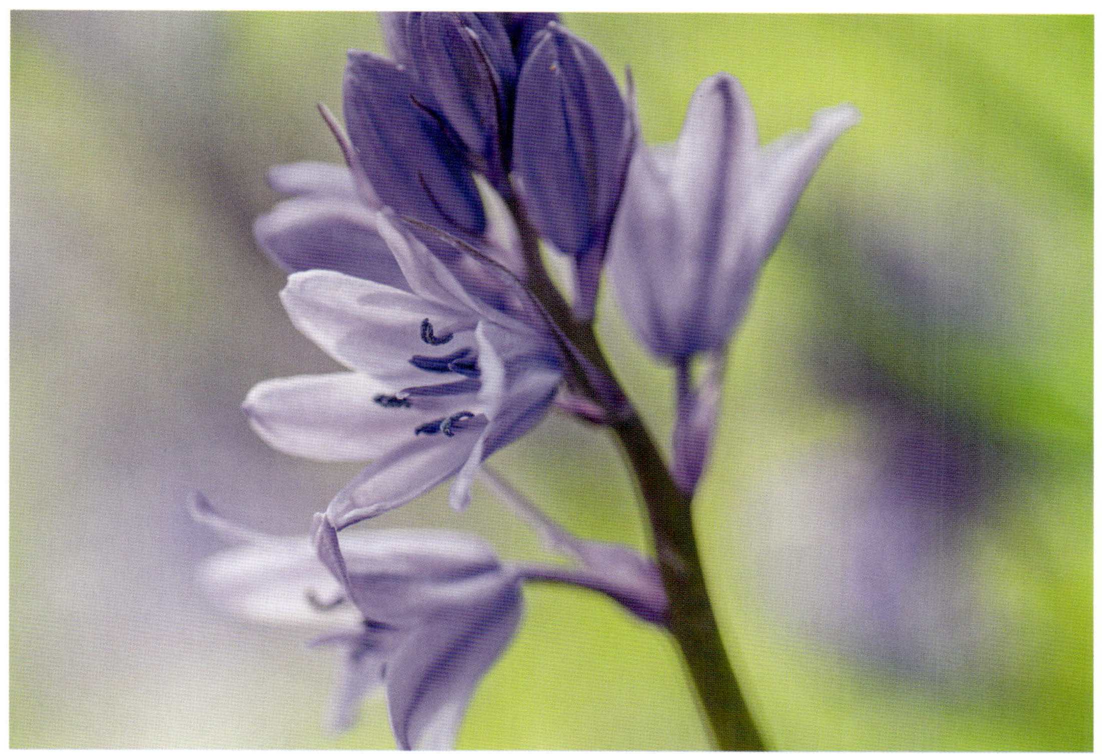

The Cloudy WB setting is generally best left for heavily overcast days. The adjustment to color temperature is (arguably) too strong for lightly overcast days when Daylight WB would be a more pleasing option.

Casting a shadow over your subject with your body or a reflector will help lower contrast. Be sure that the shadow covers the entire area within the image frame to avoid bright hotspots in the image. Set WB to Shade to compensate for the resulting coolness of the image.

Sunlight is lower in contrast just after sunrise and just before sunset. Contrast quickly rises the higher the sun is in the sky.

Use a reflector to bounce light into shadows to reduce contrast.

Above: The lack of contrast on overcast days can lead to relatively flat-looking images. One solution is to shoot subjects that differ in color, shape, or sharpness to their background. The shape and color of this bluebell is visually different to the softer, paler green background.

Focal length: 100mm macro lens

Aperture: f/5.6

Shutter speed: 1/180 sec.

ISO: 200

Left: Warm—in terms of color—winter sunlight on these ice-covered leaves makes an attractive contrast to the blue shadows in the background (the shadows are blue because they are mainly lit from ambient light above, which in this case was clear blue sky).

Focal length: 200mm

Aperture: f/4

Shutter speed: 1/400 sec.

ISO: 400

Overcast Light

Intense sunlight increases contrast, which is not ideal for all subjects. Flowers, for example, typically do not benefit from the bright highlights and deep shadows of direct sunlight. Thin cloud will soften sunlight slightly and this type of light is better suited to delicate subjects. Soft overcast light also helps to increase color saturation by reducing the intensity of highlights or glare on the surface of your subjects.

Thicker cloud softens sunlight still further, as well as lowering light levels. However, there's often a fine balance to be struck when choosing to shoot in overcast conditions. Very soft, almost shadowless light is poor at creating the contrast necessary to help define shape and texture. The lower light levels will also make it more difficult to set a suitably fast shutter speed, which will make it harder to freeze any subject movement.

SUNRISE/SUNSET DIRECTION

The direction that the sun rises and sets also varies throughout the year. At the equinoxes, the sun rises and sets almost due east and due west respectively. In December the sun rises in the south east and sets in the south west, in June the sun rises in the north east and sets in the north west. When planning an early morning or late evening shoot it is useful to know where the sun rises or sets so that you can be confident that your subject will be adequately lit. There are many cellphone apps available that can supply this information, using GPS or other location services to calculate the correct information for your current position.

Shooting In A Studio

Shooting macro subjects in a studio allows greater control and consistency than shooting outdoors. A good photographic studio (whether that's a professional space or one set up in a spare room) should have a number of characteristics.

The first—and most important—is that there should be total control over the light. This means being able to cut out all ambient light if necessary, and to be able to move, direct, and adjust the intensity and contrast of any supplementary lighting that is used. Blackout curtains or blinds at windows are the best solution to control the former, while placing lighting on adjustable stands solves the latter. Ideally, the walls and ceiling of a studio should be either white or a light, neutral gray, which will allow you to bounce light off them and onto the subject; walls that are tinted will alter the color of the light, while darker walls will absorb too much light.

A studio should provide enough space for you to work comfortably and be able to move lights around freely (and, if they are on stands, minimize the risk of knocking them over too). There should also be enough space to be able to set up a reasonably sized table or bench that you can arrange your subjects on and that you can move your camera around and compose without being hindered. Remember also that you need to account for the lens' working distance—a long focal length lens will require a larger working distance than a lens with a shorter focal length, meaning there is the distinct possibility that you cannot step far enough back from your subject to frame it successfully.

If you use multiple light sources, it helps if they are the same color temperature. Mixed lighting can produce a visually striking effect when it's used intentionally, but it will look distinctly odd if it is uncontrolled and accidental. The color temperature of most light sources can be changed by fitting a colored gel over the light, although some light loss will occur and your exposure will need to be adjusted.

Lighting gels can also be used to add a strong color tint to a light. If you have more than one light, this is a very useful way of adding color to an otherwise white background.

Do not dismiss window light as a light source. North-facing windows produce a very soft light, particularly at midday when the sun is in the south.

LIGHT SOURCE TYPE	GEL NAME/NUMBER		CAMERA WB SETTING
Candlelight	–/287		Custom/2000K
Fluorescent	Half plus green/245		Fluorescent
Studio lighting (tungsten)	Quarter CT orange/206		Tungsten/Incandescent
Domestic lighting (tungsten)	Full CT orange/204		Tungsten/Incandescent
Sodium vapor street lighting	Urban sodium/652		Custom WB

Left: If you're mixing flash with a different light source (other than daylight), you may want or need to put a gel on the flash so that its output matches the other light source's color temperature. This grid shows which gel you need to use on the flash to match a range of different lighting types, as well as the WB you should set.

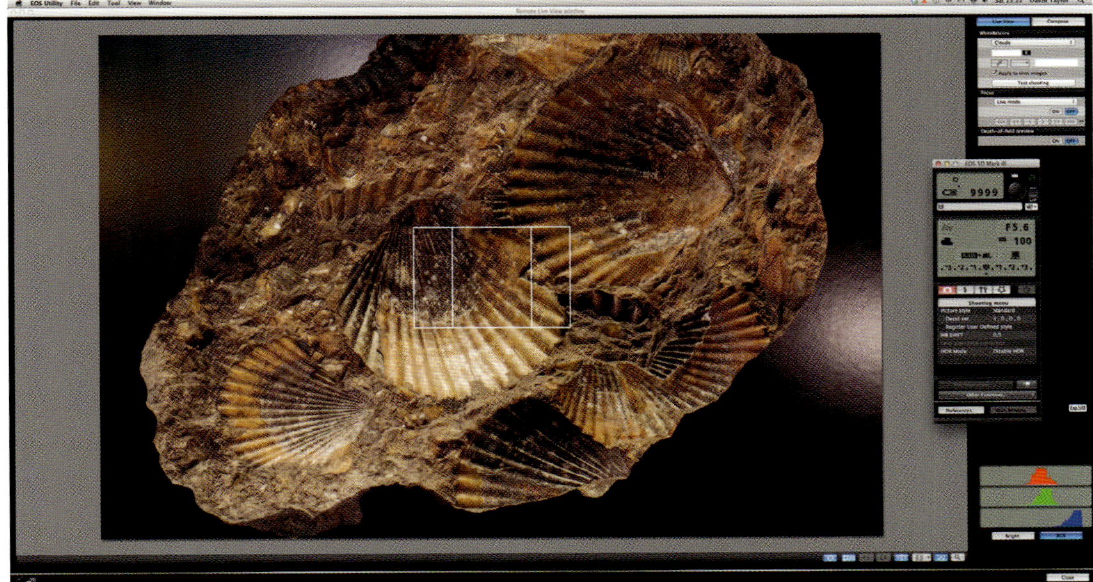

Above: Canon's EOS Utility
software allows Live View
tethered shooting.

Tethered Shooting

Connecting your camera to a PC or tablet—either
by USB cable or wirelessly through a Wi-Fi or
Bluetooth— is a very useful technique for the
macro photographer, especially when working in
a studio. Simple tethering (known as "tethered
capture") allows the instant (or at least reasonably
instant) transmission of images to your PC or
tablet as you shoot, effectively turning your PC
or tablet into a huge memory card. If you're
shooting with other people—an assistant, client,
or family member—this is a great way to get
comments or suggestions as you work, as images
can be viewed on a larger screen than on your
camera's LCD. The level of connectivity depends
on the camera model and you will also need to
install tethering software before you begin.

Some manufacturers—such as Canon—
include this software with their cameras,
while others do not. Some postproduction
software, such as Adobe Lightroom, will also
allow you to capture images directly to the
software, with the added benefit of compatibility
with a wide range of camera models.

"Live View tethering" is more useful still. This
mode transmits a feed from your camera to the
screen of your PC or tablet. With compatible
software you can adjust camera settings such
as exposure and WB from your PC or tablet
and see how the image changes. As with most
Live View displays, you can also zoom into the
image to check critical focusing—again on a
screen far larger than that of your camera.

Cross Polarization

Cross polarization is a technique that reveals the stress points in clear plastic as a rainbow of colors. To create the effect you need two polarizing filters: one fitted to the camera lens and the other covering the light source used to illuminate your subject (polarizing filters designed for lenses tend to be relatively small so a sheet of polarizing gel will be needed for larger light sources).

The light source needs to be aimed toward the camera, so your subject is positioned between the light source and camera, and is directly parallel to both. Then, gently turn the polarizing filter on the camera lens to alter the colors. When the polarizing filter on the camera is at a certain position the background will turn black, which will emphasize the colors on your subject still further.

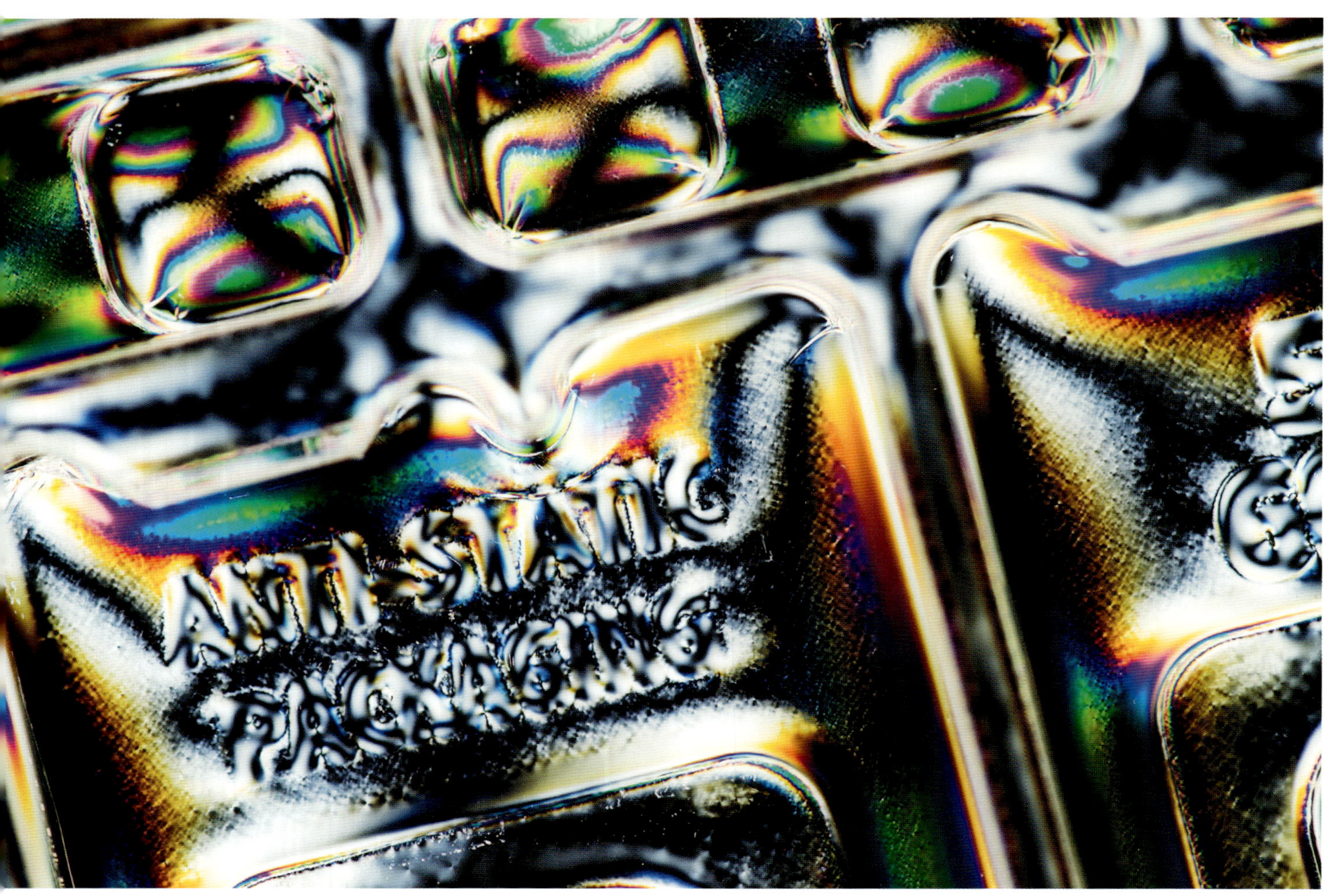

Left: Cross polarization works best with cheap plastic—in fact, the cheaper the plastic, the better the effect! This image was created using the clear plastic tray that a computer memory upgrade came in.

Focal length: 100mm macro lens

Aperture: f/11

Shutter speed: 1/5 sec.

ISO: 100

Right: Mixing different light creates interesting effects. To create this painting-with-light image of a lily, I lit the flower with a daylight-balanced LED torch and added "white" tungsten Christmas lights to the background. Setting the WB to Daylight made the flower neutral in colour but retained the warmth of the Christmas lights.

Focal length: 100mm macro lens

Aperture: f/7.1

Shutter speed: 2 sec.

ISO: 100

Painting With Light

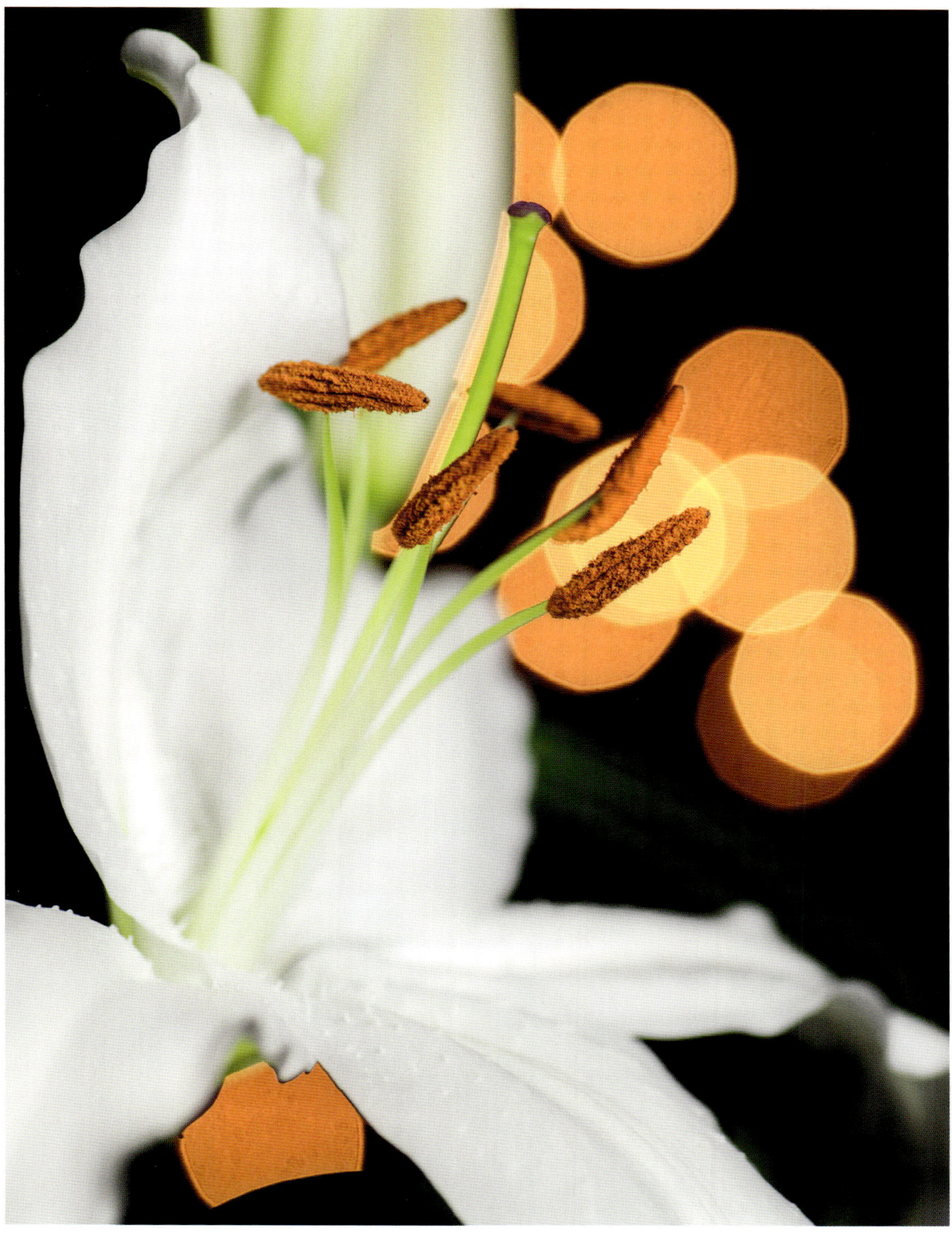

Painting with light is the technique of adding light to an otherwise relatively unlit scene using a flashlight or photographic flash. The idea is that you don't just shine the light directly at the subject, but "paint" with the light by moving it around the subject during the exposure. To give you time to do this the shutter speed should be in the region of 5 sec. or longer.

As you will be shooting in darkness, using autofocus is difficult, so you need to set the focus before you begin to shoot. Shining your flashlight directly at the subject should give you enough light for the AF system to lock onto. Better still is a flash unit's AF assist light, which produces a more intensely focused beam of light. Once the focus has locked on, switch to MF so it won't be adjusted when you fire the shutter.

By its very nature, painting with light is a hit-and-miss technique. You'll need to experiment to figure out what works and what doesn't, and review your images immediately after shooting them. When painting macro subjects with light, you will find that most flashlights and flashes produce a beam of light that is too broad. Restricting the light output with a snoot or mask made of black card will produce a smaller, more focused light. As you paint you also need to be careful not to shine the flashlight directly at the camera as this will result in overexposure and flare.

High-Speed Macro Photography

The need to often use a small aperture to maximize depth of field is not conducive to fast shutter speeds (increasing the ISO is one solution, but image noise can quickly become a limiting factor). This means that shooting fast-moving macro events requires a different approach.

When you reduce the power of a flash, you aren't simply dimming its output in the way you might turn a domestic lamp down. Instead, the power is reduced by shortening the duration of the burst of light emitted by the flash. Each time you halve the power, the duration of the flash is halved: set to full power the burst of light produced by a hotshoe flash is approximately 1/800 sec.; at ½ power the duration is closer to 1/1600 sec.; at ¼ power the duration is 1/3200 sec., and so on.

Although reducing the power of a flash reduces its effective range, it increases the flash's ability to freeze movement. It also has the added bonus of reducing the recycling time of the flash (the time it takes for the flash to fire, recharge, and then be ready to fire again). This means it is possible to use flash in conjunction with continuous shooting to increase the chance that the decisive movement is caught on camera.

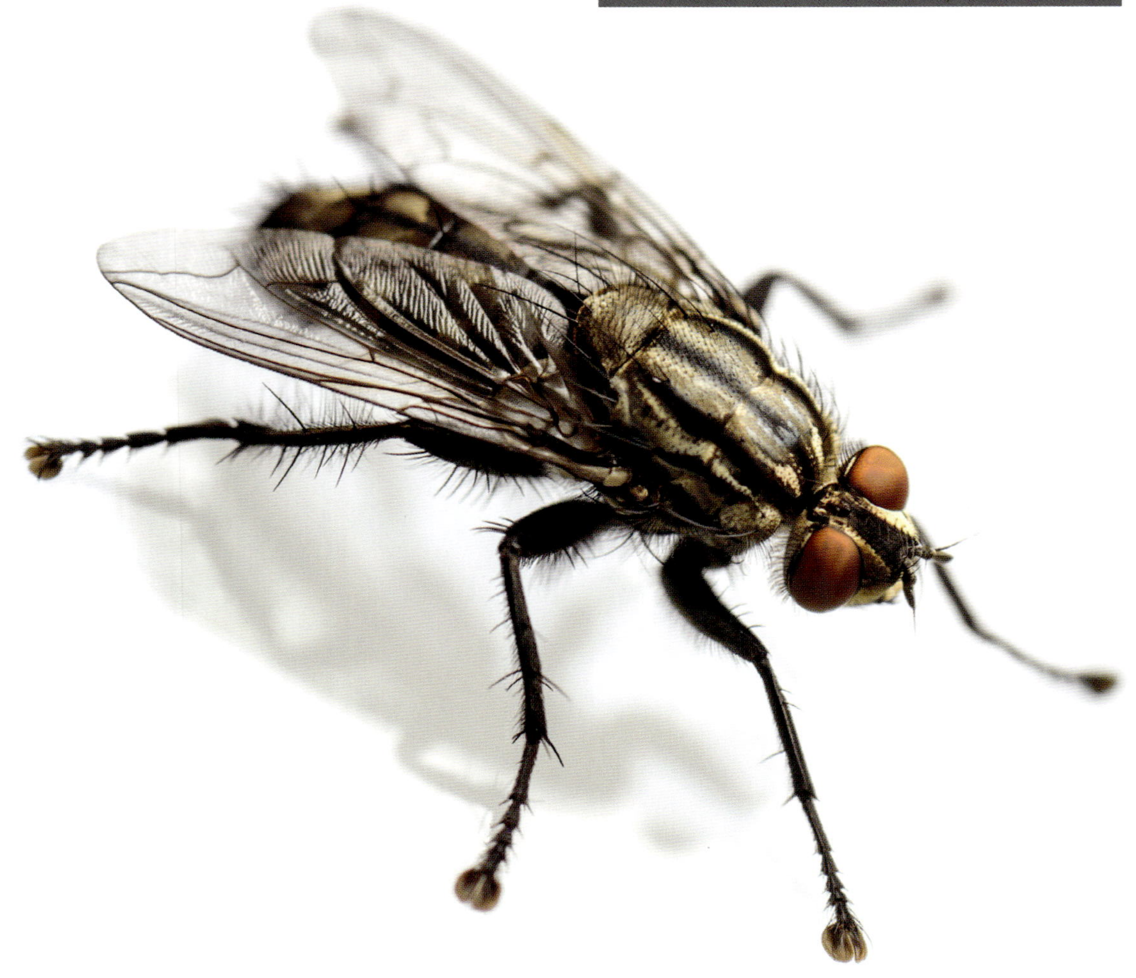

Right: Getting close to a subject invariably means reducing the power of a flash, even when using small apertures to maximize depth of field. This is beneficial when shooting subjects that have the potential to move during an exposure, as the short flash duration reduces the risk of motion blur.

Focal length: 100mm macro lens

Aperture: f/16

Shutter speed: 1/250 sec.

ISO: 200

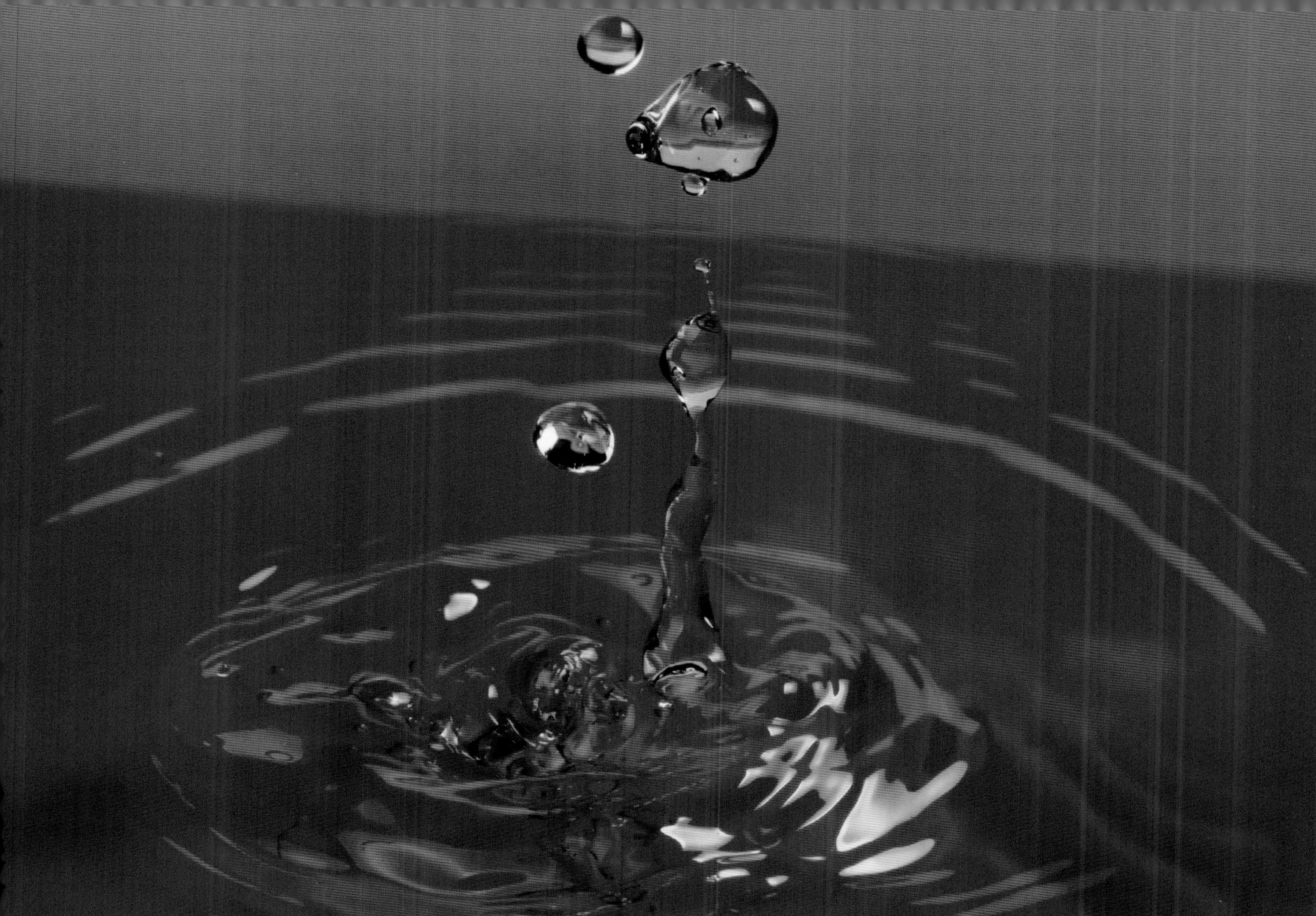

Above: The faster recycling time of a flash used at a fraction of its maximum power allows the use of continuous shooting. This makes shooting less predictable subjects—such as droplets hitting a pool of water—far easier. If you set the shutter speed at the camera's sync speed you can rapidly shoot multiple frames and then select the most pleasing image from the sequence.

Focal length: 100mm macro lens

Aperture: f/22

Shutter speed: 1/250 sec.

ISO: 1600

Focus Stacking

The lack of depth of field that you will encounter when shooting macro imagery can be overcome by using a postproduction technique known as focus stacking. This relies on combining multiple shots of the same subject, each with a slightly different point of focus. When the shots are combined, the sharp area of each frame is used, effectively "extending" the depth of field.

To produce a focus stacked image you first need to shoot a sequence of images of your subject. The first image in the sequence should start with focus set at the front of the subject. You then focus slightly further back and shoot again. The focus is adjusted again and another shot is taken, and so on. You continue to do this until you reach the point on the subject furthest from the camera.

If you have shot your sequence correctly, each part of the subject should be in focus in at least one of the images (how many images you need in the sequence will depend on the size of the subject and the aperture you use). The key is striking the right balance: too few images and the stacking process may not work as intended, but with too many images the processing time can be frustratingly long.

The sequence should then be imported into software that supports focus stacking, such as Adobe Photoshop (used here), or a dedicated program such as HeliconSoft's Helicon Focus or Zerene System's Stacker.

Focus Stacking In Photoshop

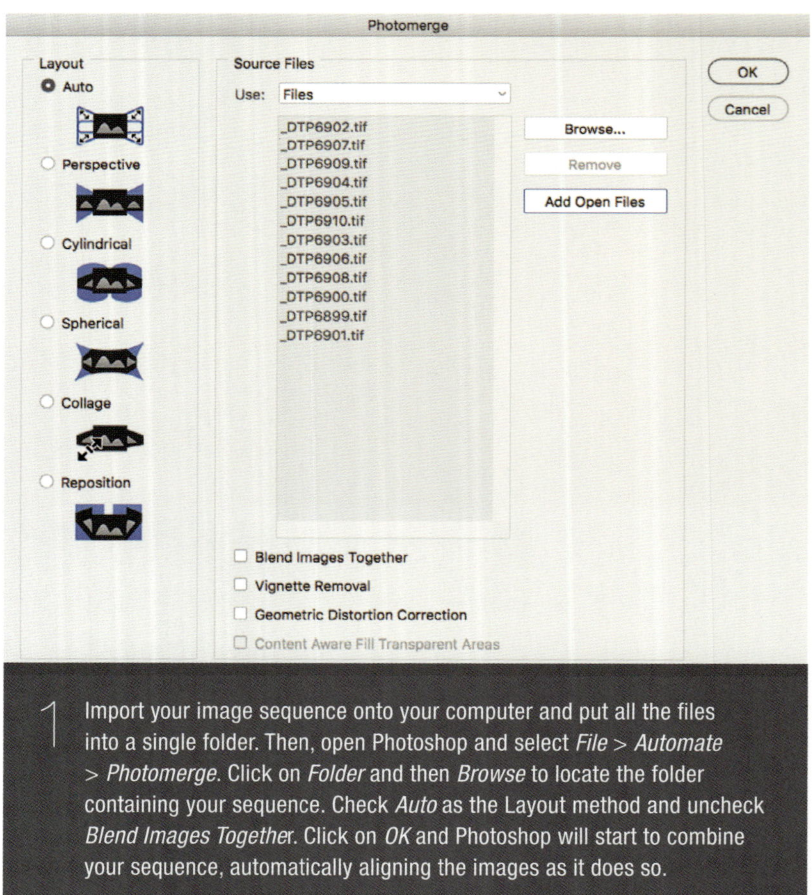

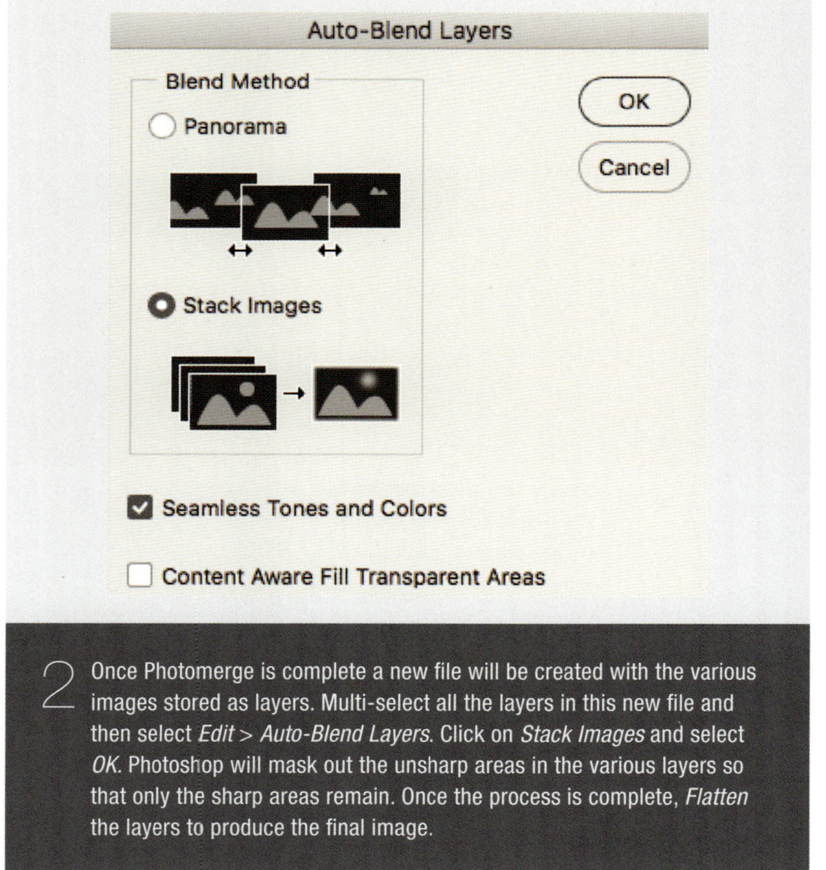

1 Import your image sequence onto your computer and put all the files into a single folder. Then, open Photoshop and select *File > Automate > Photomerge*. Click on *Folder* and then *Browse* to locate the folder containing your sequence. Check *Auto* as the Layout method and uncheck *Blend Images Together*. Click on *OK* and Photoshop will start to combine your sequence, automatically aligning the images as it does so.

2 Once Photomerge is complete a new file will be created with the various images stored as layers. Multi-select all the layers in this new file and then select *Edit > Auto-Blend Layers*. Click on *Stack Images* and select *OK*. Photoshop will mask out the unsharp areas in the various layers so that only the sharp areas remain. Once the process is complete, *Flatten* the layers to produce the final image.

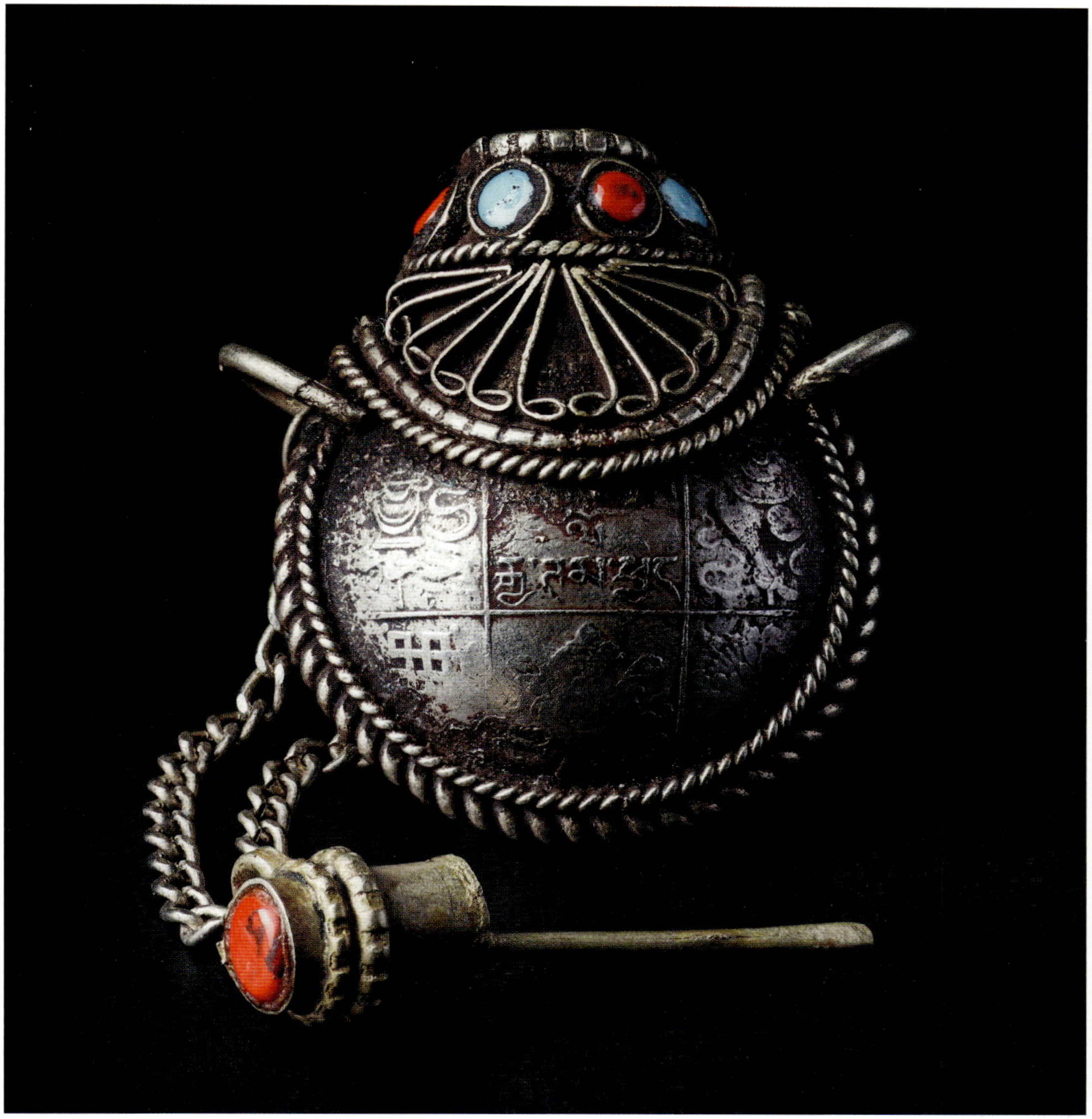

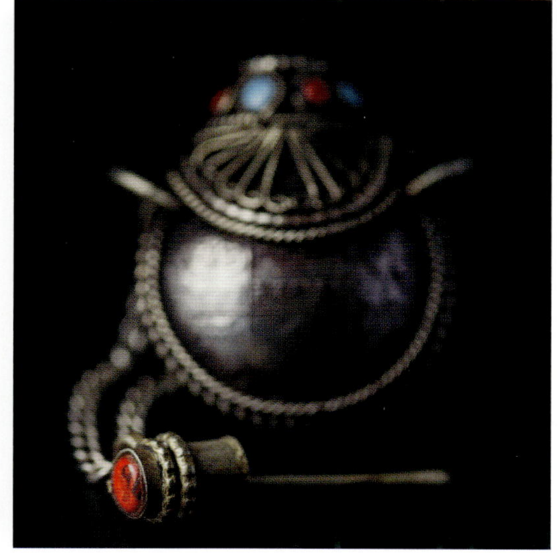

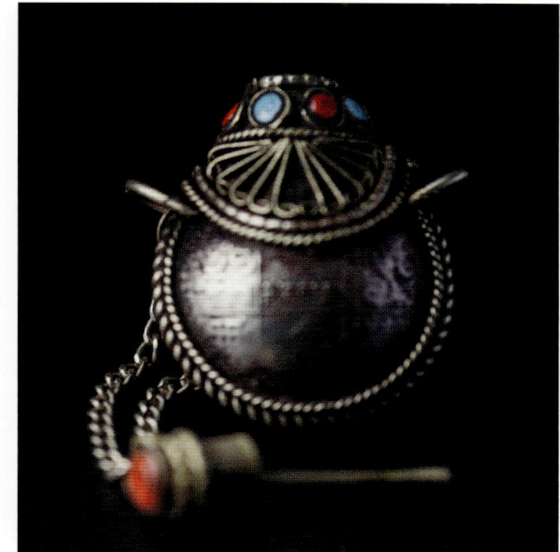

Above: Stacking was necessary to create a completely sharp image of this Nepalese trinket. To create the final stacked image, I shot 12 photographs. For the first in the sequence, I focused on the pin (top right). I progressively moved the focus further away from the camera until, at the end of the sequence, the focus was on the neck of the trinket (above right).

Focal length: 100mm macro lens

Aperture: f/16

Shutter speed: 1/250 sec.

ISO: 100

FOCUS BREATHING

Some lenses change focal length slightly as they are focused, which alters the size of the subject in the image space. This flaw is known as "focus breathing" and is not ideal for focus stacking images. However, when you set the Layout method to *Auto*, Photoshop will automatically resize your images, as well as repositioning them during the alignment process.

Photomicrography

Photomicrography is the use of a microscope to capture images, rather than a regular camera lens. Cameras can be connected to microscopes in a number of different ways and some microscopes now come with a cellphone adaptor that lets you fit your phone directly to the eyepiece. Depending on your phone, this can be the most straightforward way to produce high-quality images.

Life becomes more complicated when you try to connect a system camera to a microscope: ideally you need a microscope that allows you to remove the eyepiece or that has a supplementary eyepiece tube designed for the attachment of cameras.

There are two types of adaptor that can be fitted to system cameras, both of which replace the camera's lens so you can fit the camera to the eyepiece tube of the microscope (once the eyepiece lens has been removed). The simplest type has no optical components. As the image produced by the objective lens of a microscope is relatively large compared to most cameras' sensors, this means that only a small section of the subject can be adequately captured with this type of adaptor. The image from the microscope's objective lens can also be very dark—particularly when using higher magnifications—which requires long shutter speeds.

More complex adaptors—known as reduction lenses—feature optical components that alter the size of the image produced by the objective lens to better fit the angle of view of the camera. Reduction lenses have the added benefit of increasing the amount of light reaching the camera's sensor, allowing faster shutter speeds to be used.

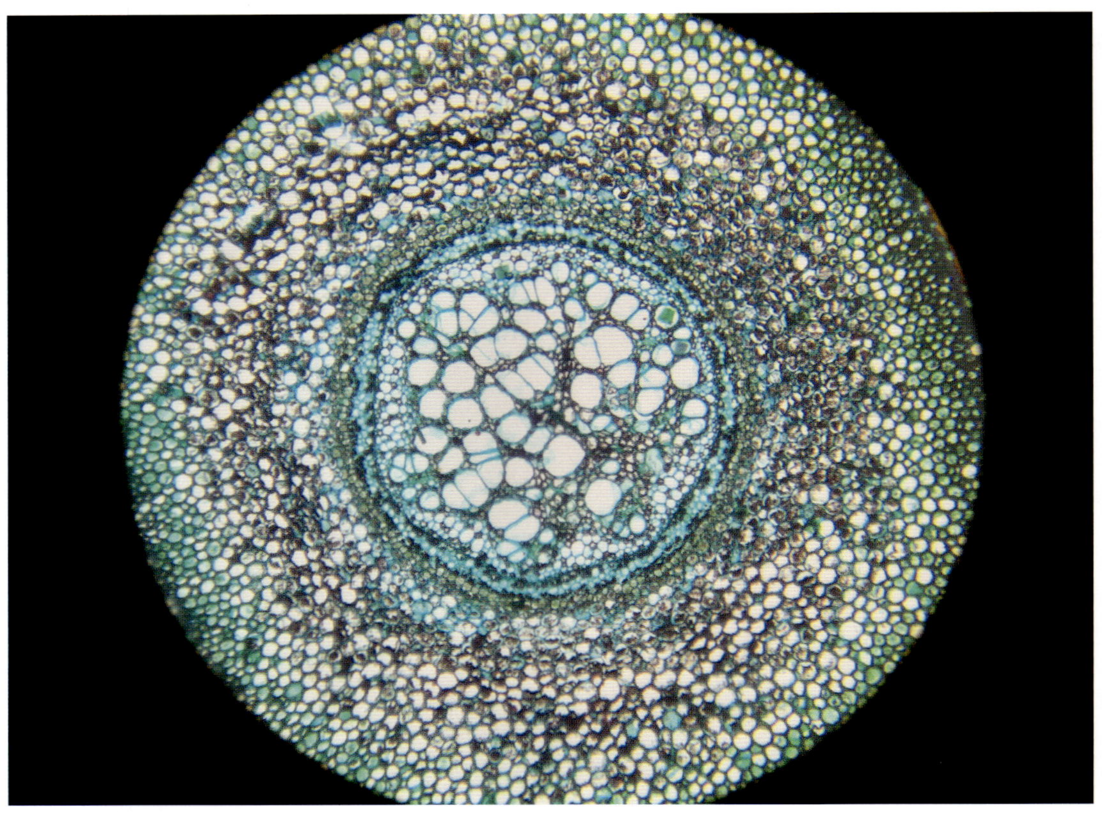

Preparing A Slide

Slides are thin, rectangular sheets of glass or plastic that are used to mount a specimen. There are two types of slide: flat and concave. As the name suggests, flat slides are flat on both sides, while concave slides have one or more shallow indentations on one side and are used for liquids.

The slide specimen is placed at the center of the slide and a cover slip is used to hold it in place (a cover slip is simply an extremely thin square sheet of glass that is smaller than the slide itself, but larger than the specimen). The cover slip protects the specimen from dust and other contamination and can be permanently affixed to the slide using a sealant such as glue if the specimen is to be kept. There are four main methods used to place a specimen on a slide: dry mounting, wet mounting, squashing, and smearing, as outlined opposite.

Above: Using a cellphone attached to a microscope via an adaptor is by far the easiest way to shoot micro subjects. The drawback is the heavy vignetting around the edge of the photo, although this can be cropped out later if desired.

Dry Mounting

Dry mounting is used when the specimen is completely dry, such as hair, skin cells, or insect wings. The specimen is maneuvered into place using tweezers or needles and then covered with a cover slip. If a specimen is opaque it should be sliced thinly using a scalpel and the slice placed on the slide.

Wet Mounting

Wet mounting is a less permanent method of preparing a slide and is commonly used for specimens that require water, such as microscopic living organisms. A liquid—typically water or brine—is used, and the surface tension of this liquid is usually enough to keep the cover slip in place. To create a semi-permanent slide you can use petroleum jelly around the edge of the cover slip as a sealant.

Squashing

Similar to wet mounting, squashing is used when the specimen itself is partially liquid. With the specimen placed on the slide, it is squashed down gently with the cover slip until excess fluid has been expelled.

Smearing

This mounting method is used for liquid specimens such as blood. A pipette is used to add the specimen to the slide. A second slide is then used to carefully smear the specimen so that it forms a thin, translucent layer across the first slide. A cover slip is then placed over the specimen.

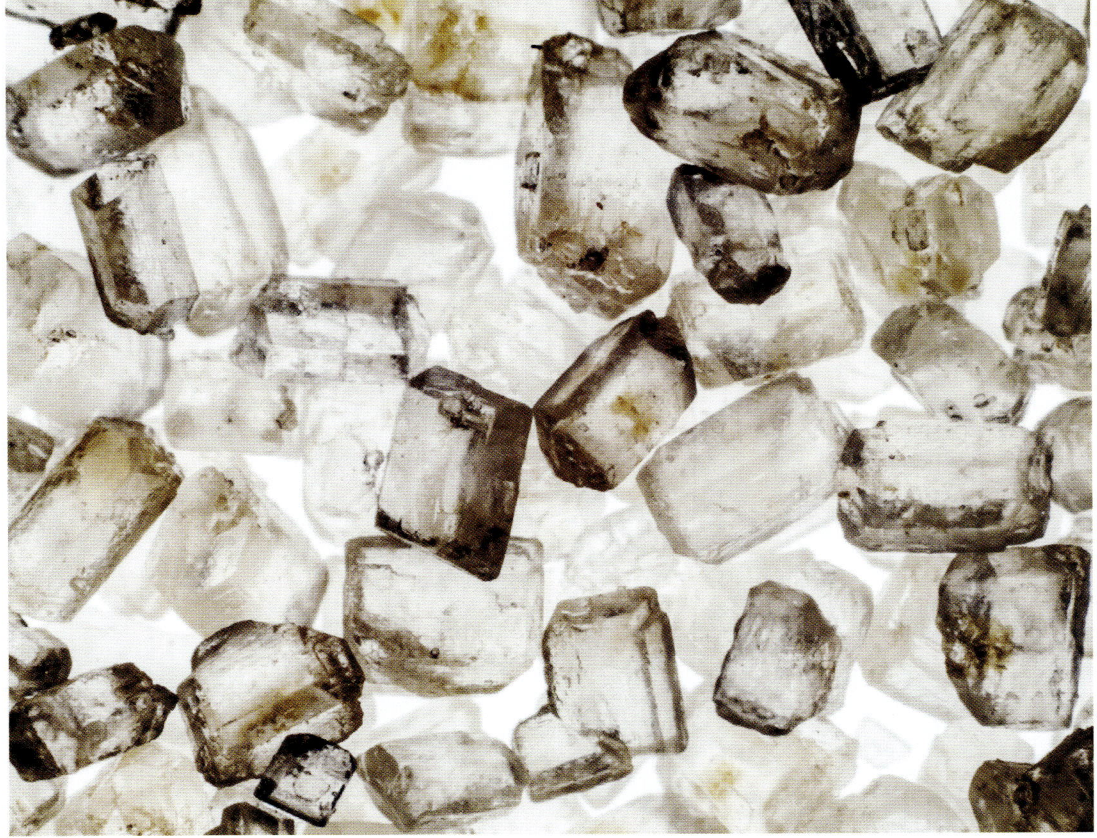

Tips

Depth of field is extremely narrow when shooting through a microscope, so your specimens should be sliced as thinly as possible.

Translucent subjects can be made more visible by staining them, using special dyes in a variety of colors, such as Gentian violet, fuchsin (a red dye), or methylene blue.

A polarized light source will reveal colors in crystalline subjects due to refraction.

Left: Loose particles—such as sugar, seen here—need to be dry mounted on a slide. To make the dry mount more permanent (and to stop the particles from slipping out from under the cover slip) you can seal the edges of the cover slip with narrow strips of masking tape.

Profile: Viktor Sykora

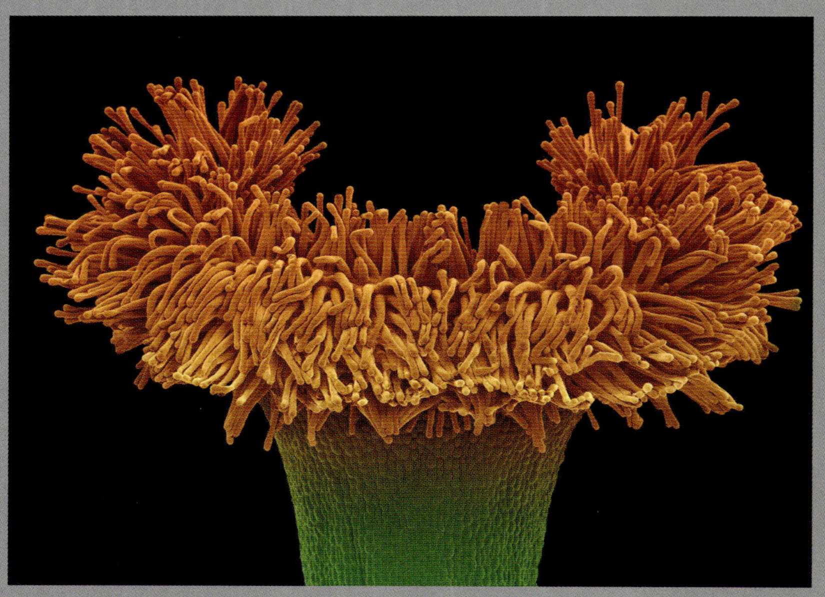

Above:

Begonia crassicaulis—flower detail.
A false-colored scanning electron
micrograph. Magnification 30x.

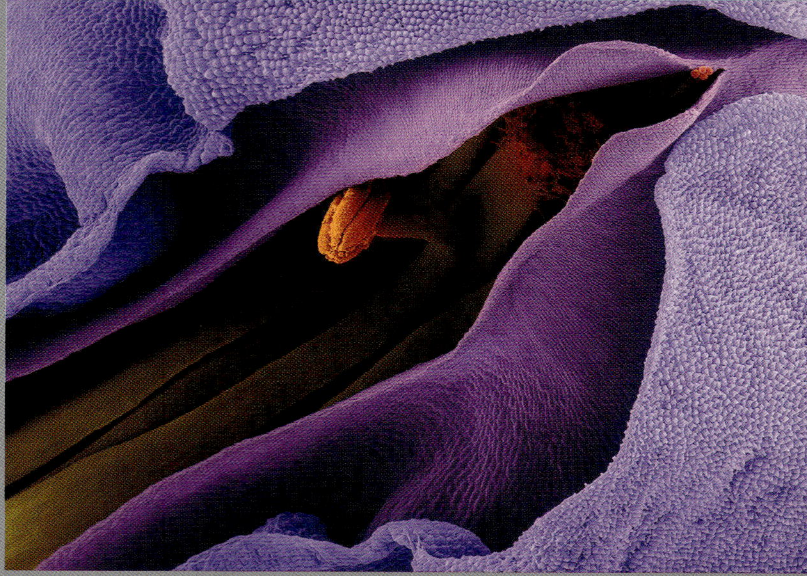

Above:

Vicia—flower detail. A false-colored
scanning electron micrograph.
Magnification 30x.

BIOGRAPHY

Viktor Sykora graduated from the Faculty of
Science, Charles University in Prague and
currently works at the University's First Faculty
of Medicine. In his spare time he specializes in
scientific photography and photomicrography.
He has had 17 solo exhibitions in the Czech
Republic and dozens of group exhibitions,
mainly in the USA, Great Britain, and the
Czech Republic. He is also the author of two
photography books—*Secrets of Plants* (2009)
and *Invisible Human World* (2014)—and has
won dozens of awards for his photographs
in international competitions.

www.viktorphoto.eu

Q) What is your specialty?
A) My main specialty is photomicrography, which
is essentially photography through a microscope.

**Q) What is it about your specialty that
fascinates you?**
A) With a microscope I can see even the most
ordinary things in a new way—I can discover
structures and sites that, due to their small
dimensions, remain hidden from most people.

Q) What equipment do you regularly use?
A) I use two distinctly different microscopy
techniques, which require special equipment.
The first (and the simpler one) is light microscopy,
which requires a microscope with a camera
adaptor, a camera, and a light source.

The second method I use is scanning electron
microscopy. I don't need a camera for the electron
microscope because the ray of light (photons) is
replaced with a beam of accelerated electrons
and a system of optical lenses is replaced with
electromagnetic lenses. However, I cannot do
this without the facilities and equipment in a
specialized lab.

Q) How do you prepare your subjects?
A) My preparation varies depending on the
technique I'm using. For light microscopy, I don't
have to do much modification to the subject, which
is one of the great advantages of this technique.

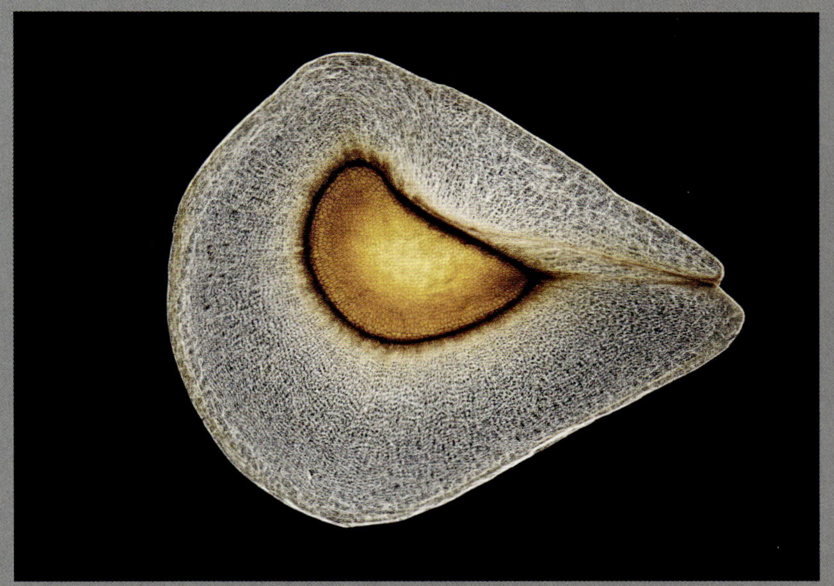

Cardiocrinum cordatum—seed.
Light microscopy (darkfield
illumination). Magnification 10x.

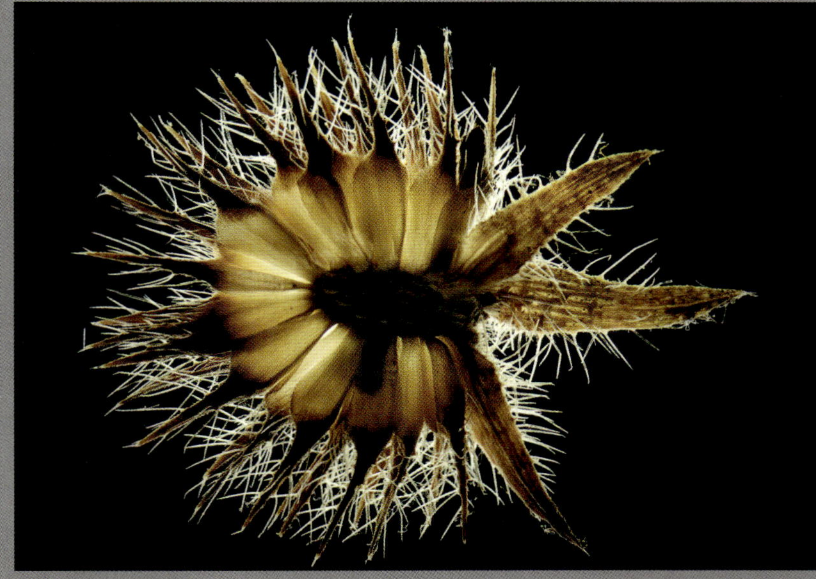

Virga pilosa—infructescence
consisting of achenes. Light
microscopy (darkfield illumination).
Magnification 10x.

However, preparing the subject for scanning by electron microscope is more complicated. Usually, sample preparation involves fixation with a fixing agent, dehydration, drying, sticking to the sputter target, and increasing the surface conductivity by coating the object with a layer of gold, platinum, or an alloy of platinum and palladium. This process can take two to three days.

Q) How do you light your subjects?
A) With light microscopy I use a combination of lighting from below (through the object), from the side and from above. The angle, intensity, and combination depend on the object being photographed.

Q) How important is postproduction to you?
A) In photomicrography it is almost impossible to avoid the presence of various artifacts in the image, especially unwanted particles that are not related to the photographed object. For this reason, postproduction is essential.

In the case of electron microscopy pictures, the situation is even more complicated, as images are produced in black and white. If you want a color photograph, the only option is to "colorize" the sample using appropriate software. This kind of work is very time consuming and in some cases can take several hours.

Q) What is your top tip?
A) My advice is simple and applies to more than just photomicrography: try to find your own way and be patient and persistent.

Chapter 6
Subjects

One fascinating aspect of photography is that no two photographers are ever wholly alike. Even photographers who shoot similar subjects are different in subtle ways: if you took ten photographers to the same location the results would be ten very different sets of images.

Macro photography is no exception to this rule. There is an infinite number of macro subjects that can be photographed and there is an infinite number of ways to photograph them. This chapter will guide you through some of the broader categories in macro shooting, including popular subjects such as insects and plants. Successfully shooting these subjects is partially about understanding the mechanics of creating a successful image— focusing, exposure, and so on—but it is also, perhaps more importantly, about having an empathy and passion about your chosen subject. Only when those are present will you produce your best photos.

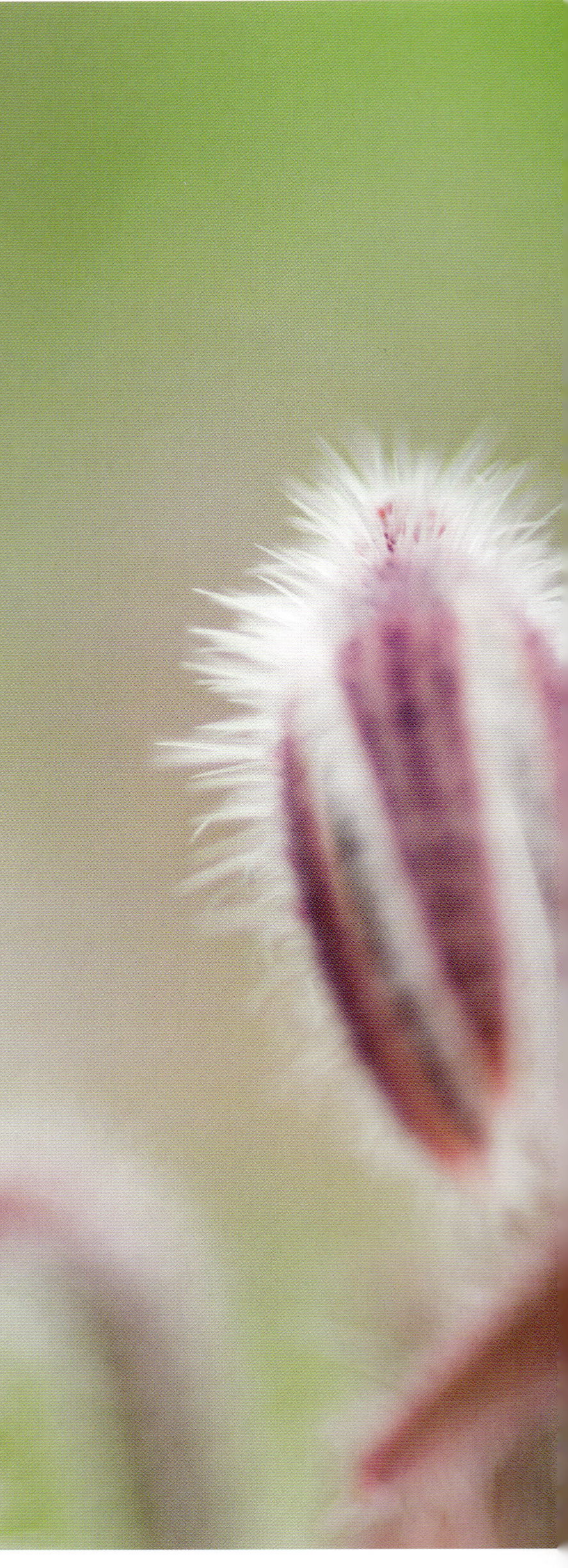

Right: Dead, mounted insects are easy to photograph, as they don't move. However, despite the difficulties of shooting fast-moving creatures I'd still rather face those challenges to produce images that (literally) have more life to them.

Focal length: 100mm macro lens

Aperture: f/4.5

Shutter speed: 1/400 sec.

ISO: 400

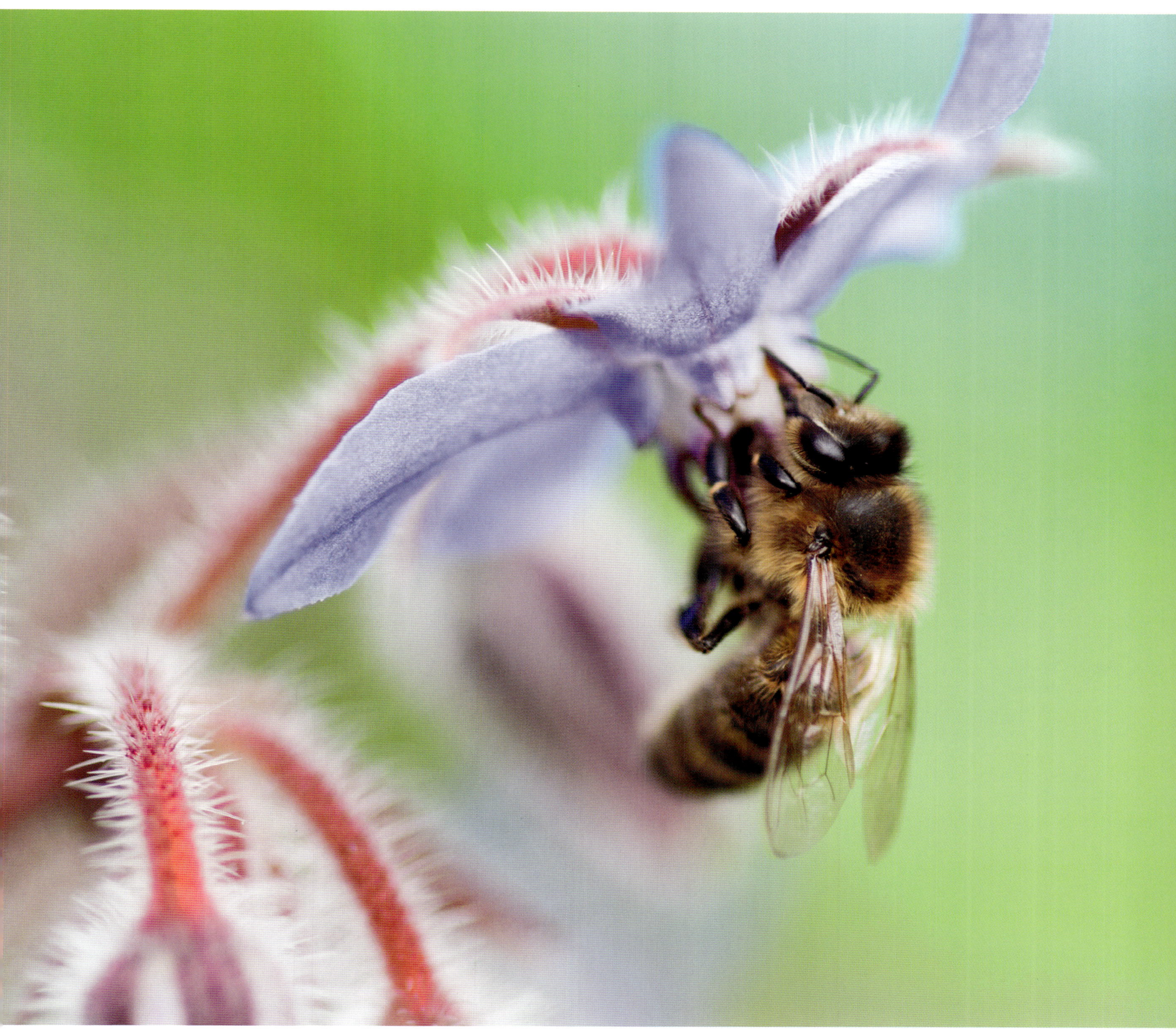

Plants & Flowers

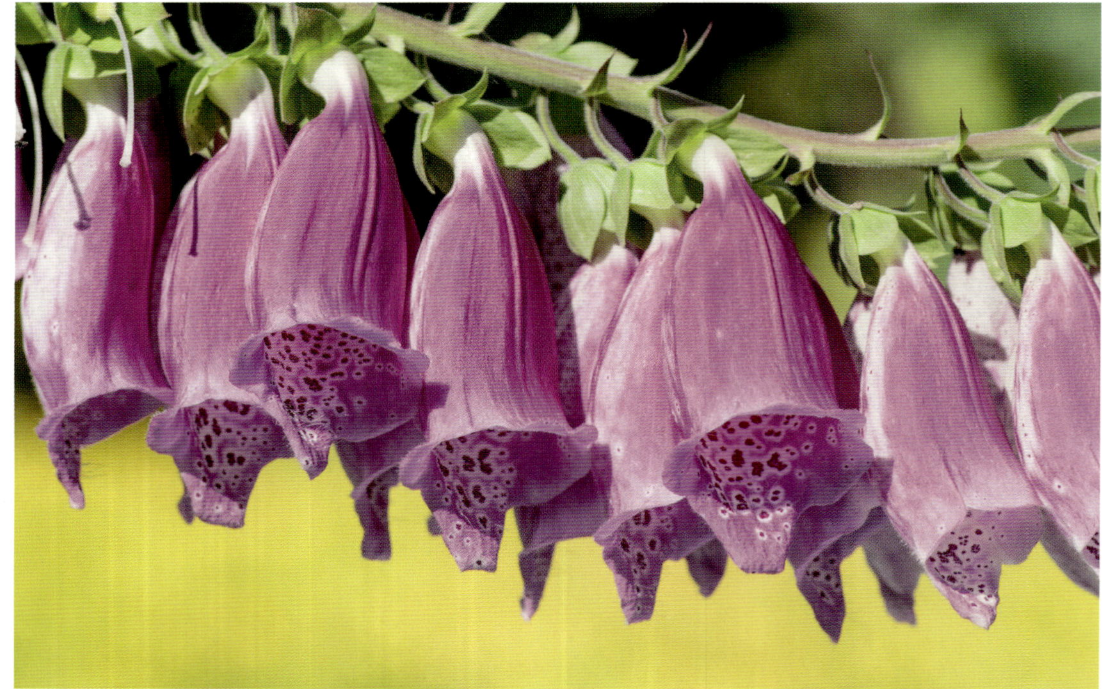

Plants are highly seasonal in temperate zones, changing over the course of the year as both the temperature and light levels alter. This is especially true of flowering plants that die back in the winter before blooming again with the onset of spring.

Getting to know the rhythms of the seasons is vital when shooting plants outdoors; it is all too easy to miss a vital stage of a plant's yearly cycle if care is not taken (shooting cut flowers indoors, or plants growing in controlled environments is one way to circumvent some of the limitations of the winter months).

Flowering plants can also change over the course of a day. The flowers of heliotropic plants follow the direction of the sun from sunrise to sunset and some flowers close up when light levels drop. A variation of this behavior is leaf heliotropism when the leaves of the plant track the daily movement of the sun.

Plants to one degree or another are also affected by wind. Lighter plants can move considerably in any wind above a light breeze. Deliberately using a longer shutter speed will create a sense of this movement by blurring flowers and foliage, but to ensure sharpness the plant will need to be sheltered—open reflectors, camera bags, or even your own body all make effective wind blocks.

Wild locations—and even some gardens—can be chaotic places, with much visual distraction. Shooting with a wide aperture will help to limit the depth of field and this can reduce this complexity to more pleasing proportions. This does, however, mean that the point of focus will need to be carefully thought about: where you focus will largely depend on what you think is the most interesting aspect. With flowers there are a number of possibilities: the edges of the petals are one

potential focus point; the tips of the stamens—the pollen-producing structures found at the center of flowers—are another.

DIFFUSION TENT

Small or delicate plants benefit from soft light rather than hard light. Shooting on an overcast day is one way to achieve the right conditions; diffusion or light tents are another.

A diffusion tent is a translucent structure that can be temporarily placed over the plant to soften the light. A hole in one of the sides enables you to position the camera lens and shoot inside the tent.

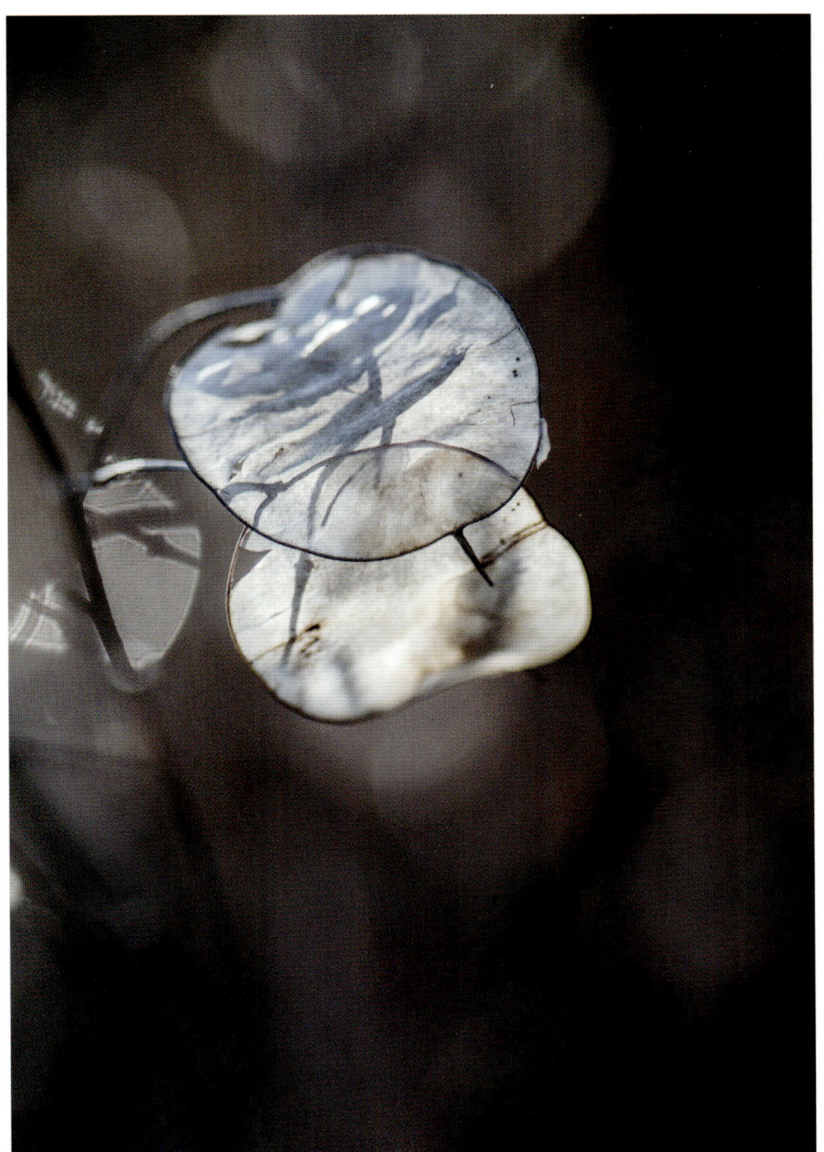

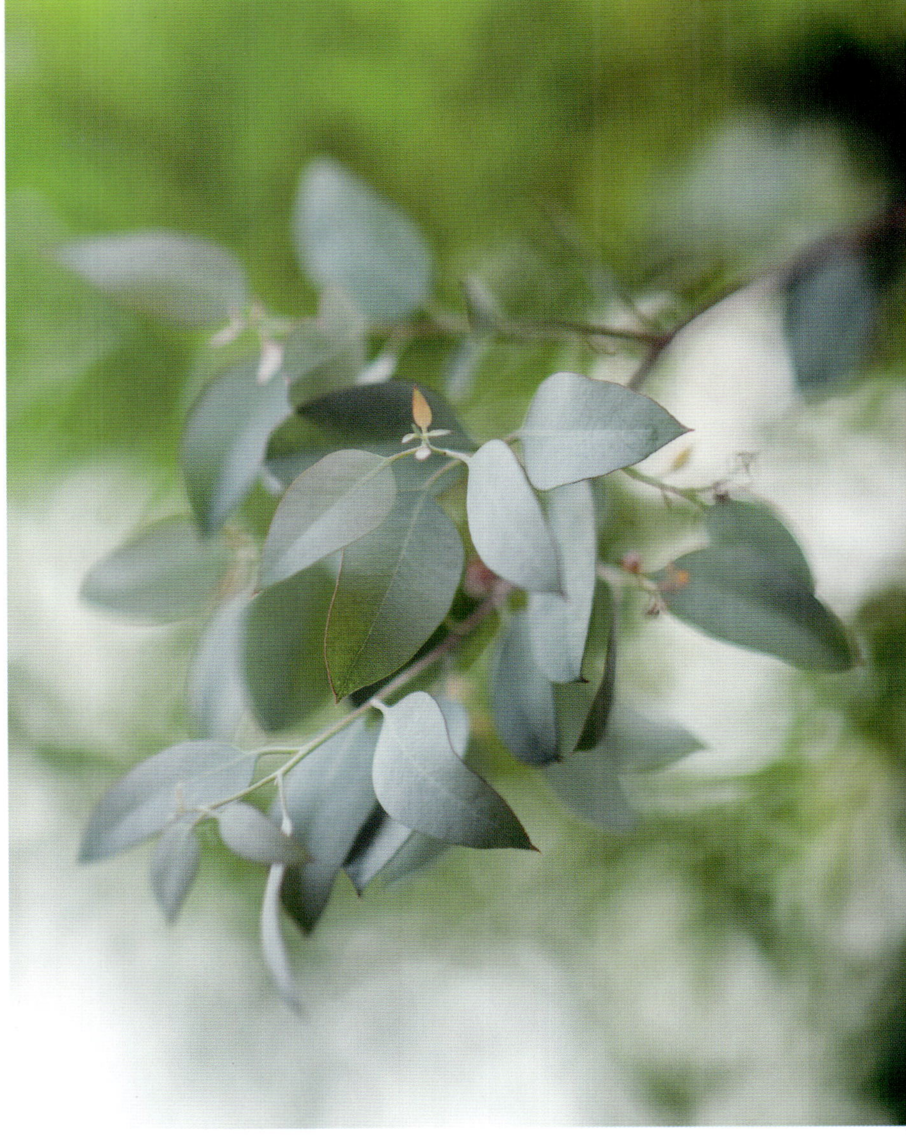

Above: The seasons affect the range of colors and subjects found in gardens. Winter is typically the most subdued season both in terms of color and available subjects, but it's a great opportunity to look for seed heads backlit by the low winter sun, particularly translucent seed heads, such as honesty.

Focal length: 100mm macro lens

Aperture: f/4

Shutter speed: 1/1600 sec.

ISO: 400

Above: Shooting at the maximum aperture setting on an 85mm f/1.8 lens produced a wafer-thin depth of field. This meant that the focus had to be very precise, so the correct set of leaves on this eucalyptus tree were sharp.

Focal length: 85mm

Aperture: f/1.8

Shutter speed: 1/800 sec.

ISO: 200

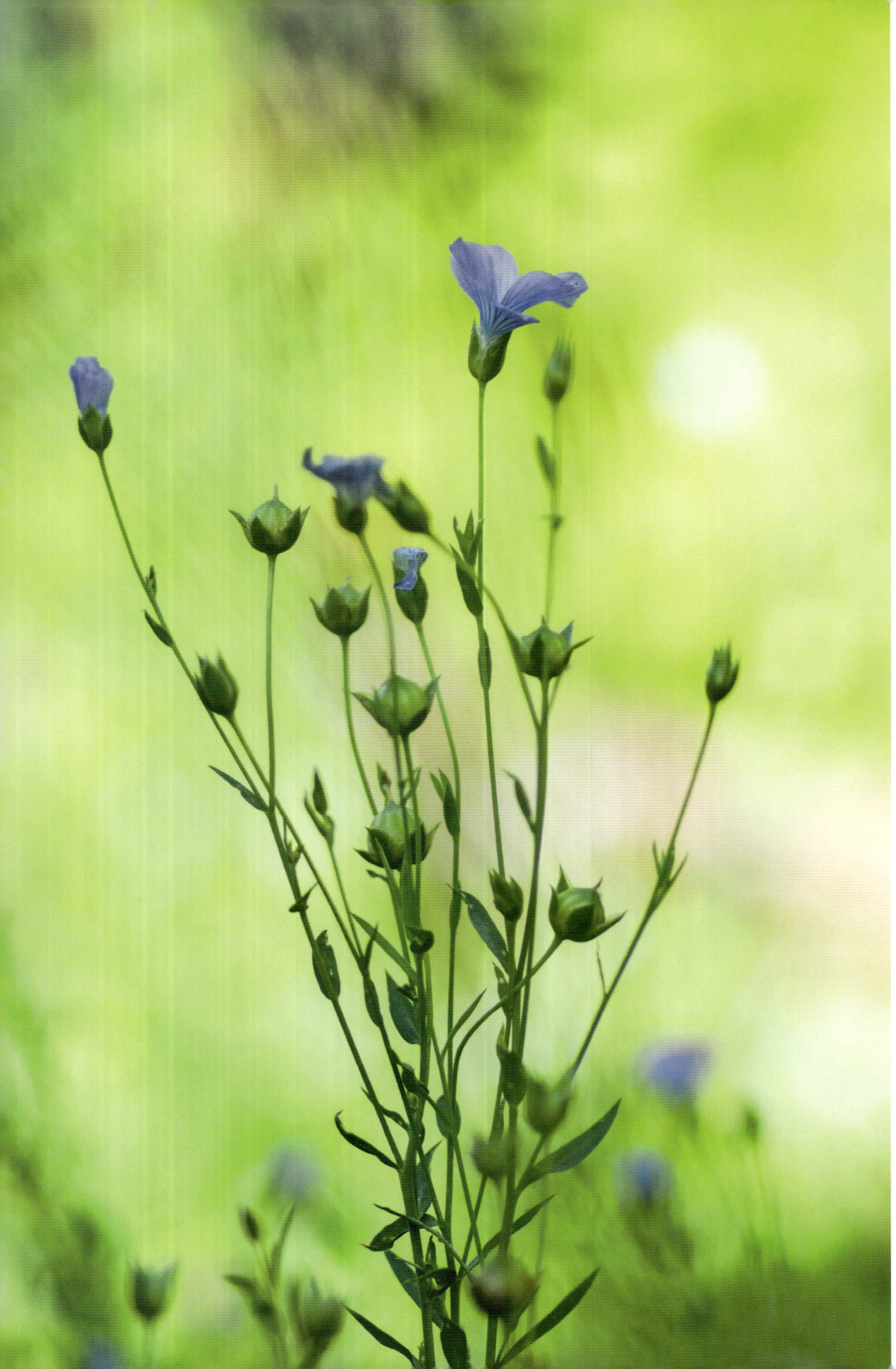

Left: Late spring and early summer sees plant life at its most verdantly colorful. The flax flowers in this image were in shade, but the background was in full sunshine. The slight coolness of the shadow light was sympathetic to the blues and greens of the plant. I left the white balance set to Daylight so that this delicate coolness wouldn't be lost.

Focal length: 100mm macro lens

Aperture: f/3.2

Shutter speed: 1/2500 sec.

ISO: 400

Ethics

Photographers have a duty of care to the natural world. When shooting natural subjects, such as flowers and insects, you should always prioritize the welfare of the subject (and its surroundings) over your photography. Natural subjects should not be harmed in order to make a photograph better. This includes being careful not to crush plants with either your feet or equipment such as your camera bag. If possible, do not disturb virgin ground—particularly in sensitive environments—and try to stay on recognizable paths.

Many countries have laws that protect the welfare of plants and animals, and these should be adhered to (the penalties for flouting the law are often strict and may result in custodial sentences). It is a good idea to learn about your subject's behavior and overall lifecycle too. This will allow you to shoot at times when the subject is less likely to be disturbed. Using longer focal length lenses will be helpful as these will enable you to keep your distance from the subject.

Below: Tripods can do a lot of damage to an environment, particularly when shooting flowers that carpet a large area. To shoot these snowdrops I had to place my tripod legs in amongst other flowers, taking special care not to knock or crush them.

Focal length: 100mm macro lens

Aperture: f/5.0

Shutter speed: 1/320 sec.

ISO: 200

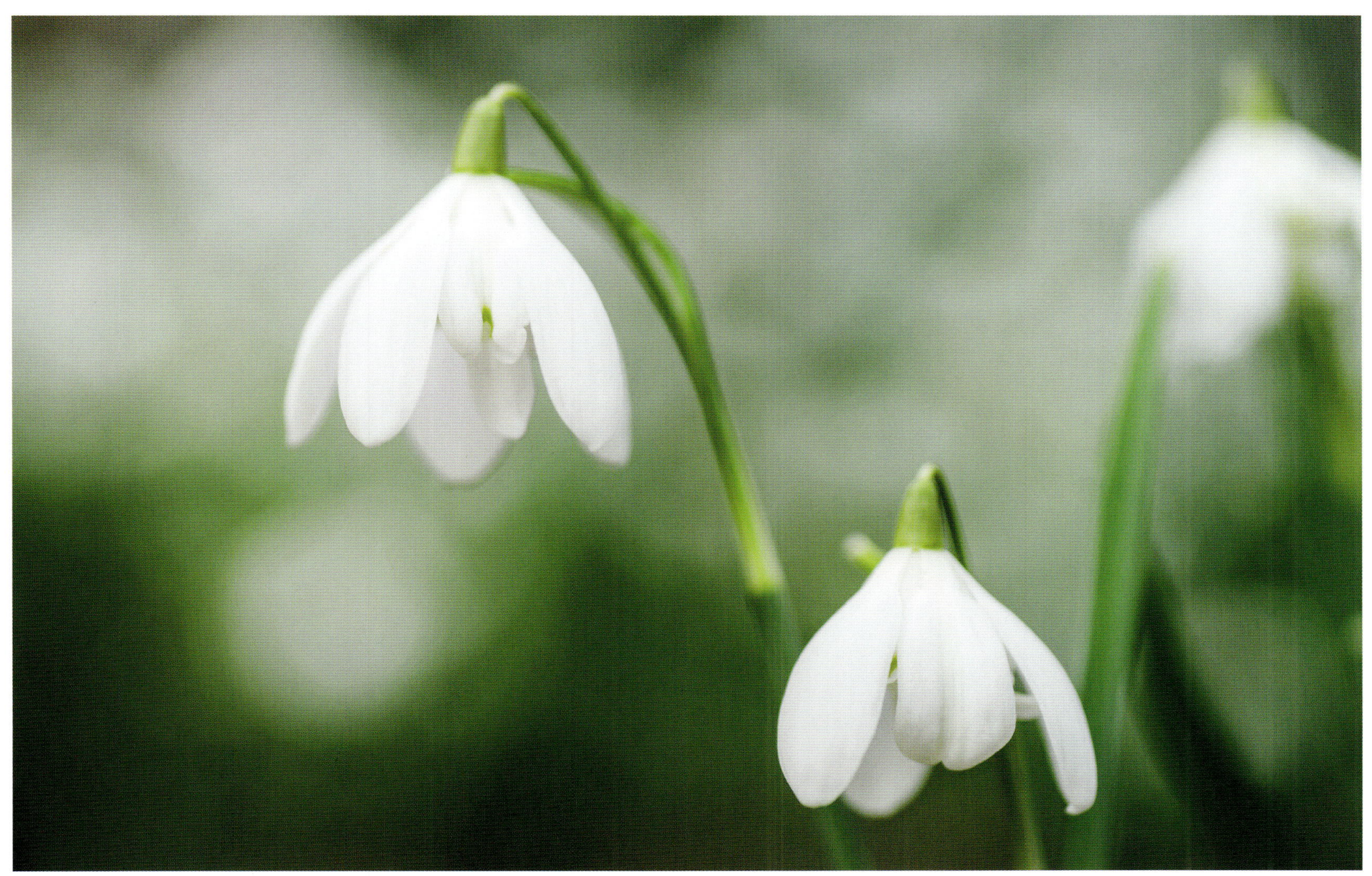

Fungi

The sculptural forms of fungi make them an interesting and rewarding photographic subject. Fungi can be found all year round, but it is the damp months of autumn when they are at their most common. The best place to find fungi is in woodland and in shady areas. Unlike plants, fungi do not photosynthesize, so low-light levels are less of a hindrance to growth. Of course, this isn't ideal for photography, so shooting fungi usually requires the use of a tripod to deal with the often necessary long shutter speeds.

The most immediately recognizable types of fungi are mushrooms and toadstools. These can literally appear overnight, so it is worth revisiting woodland on a regular basis during the autumn months. One problem with mushrooms and toadstools that grow in woodland is that their upper surfaces are often coated in leaf litter or dirt. This requires some very gentle gardening to make the most of your chosen subject.

Although it is tempting just to shoot the top of the mushroom or toadstool, do not neglect the gills under the cap. The gills are often highly photogenic, despite being inconveniently placed. A reflector—or even a sheet of aluminum foil— can bounce light up underneath to light the gills, and if you can't physically position your camera to photograph the gills, consider placing a mirror underneath and shoot the reflection. Note, however, that standard mirrors are not ideal for this, as the glass surface of the mirror will cause a double reflection. A mirror with the silvered surface on top is a better option, although these can be hard to find and are easily scratched.

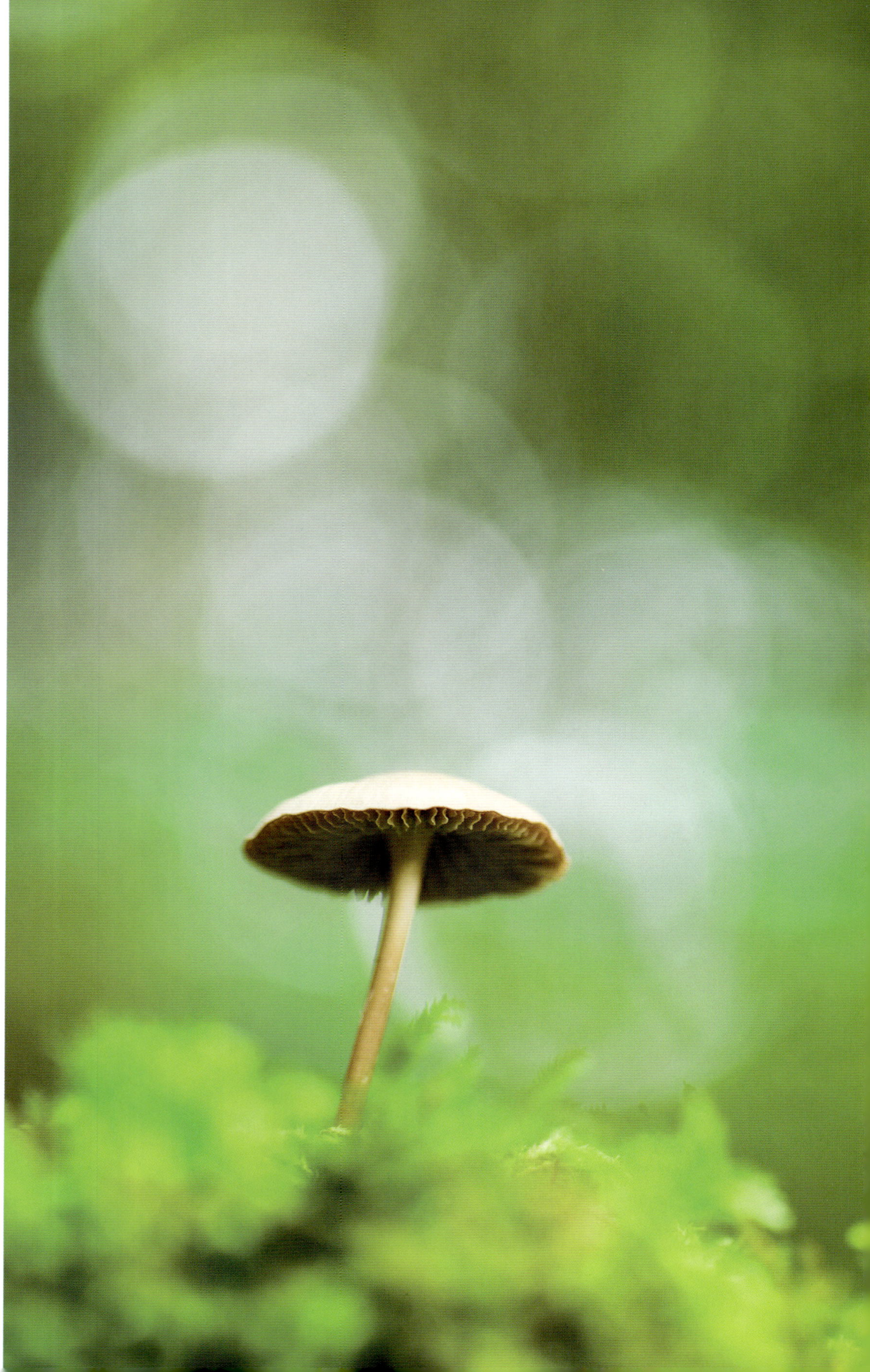

Right: In woodland, shooting fungi from a low angle with the camera tilted upward and using a large aperture can produce large, attractive out-of-focus highlights. Check the histogram to ensure these highlights aren't overexposed.

Focal length: 100mm macro lens

Aperture: f/4.5

Shutter speed: 1/5 sec.

ISO: 100

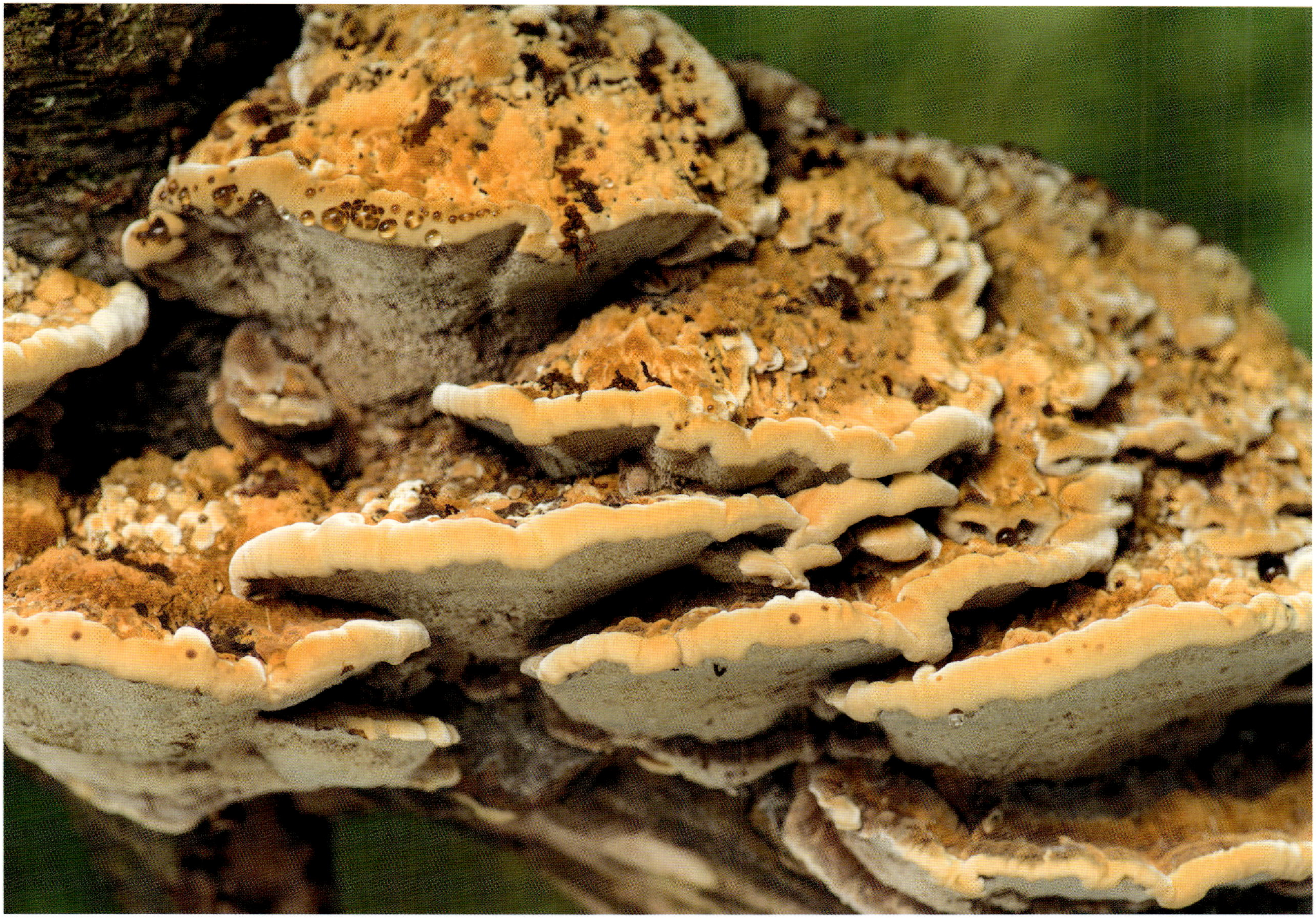

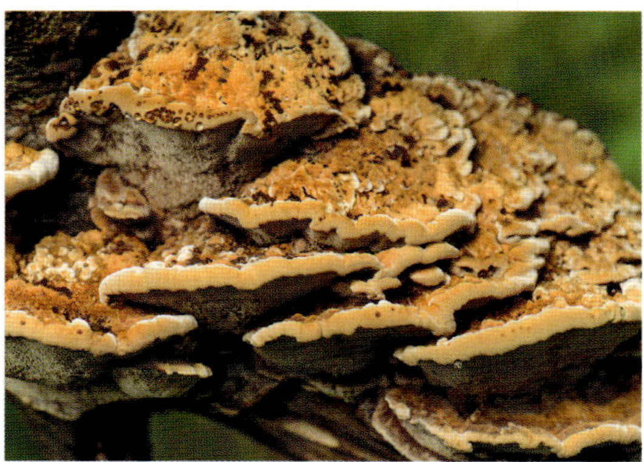

Above & left: Bracket fungi are found on tree trunks and can grow to a considerable size. Due to their shelf-like shape they are often far more brightly lit on top than below, which even in the soft light of an overcast day can cause problems with contrast (left). The simplest solution is to use a reflector held below—and out of shot—to bounce light underneath the fungi (above).

Focal length: 100mm macro lens

Aperture: f/9

Shutter speed: 1/60 sec.

ISO: 500

GARDENING

"Gardening" is the name photographers give to the act of tidying up a scene by clearing away dirt and dead plant material. Uprooting live plants that may mar a shot is not something that should be done.

Insects

Insects are everywhere, which makes them an easy-to-find macro subject. However, while they are easy to find they can be frustratingly difficult to photograph. Photographing insects requires a good understanding of photography from exposure to focusing. You will also benefit from a knowledge of the behavior of your invertebrate subjects. Bringing these two things together will increase your chance of success.

Below: Bees are fascinating insects to both watch and photograph. When they are collecting pollen they can be almost oblivious to what is happening around them. This makes them relatively easy to photograph compared to more skittish insects such as butterflies.

Focal length: 100mm macro lens (with 36mm extension tube)

Aperture: f/29

Shutter speed: 1/250 sec.

ISO: 400

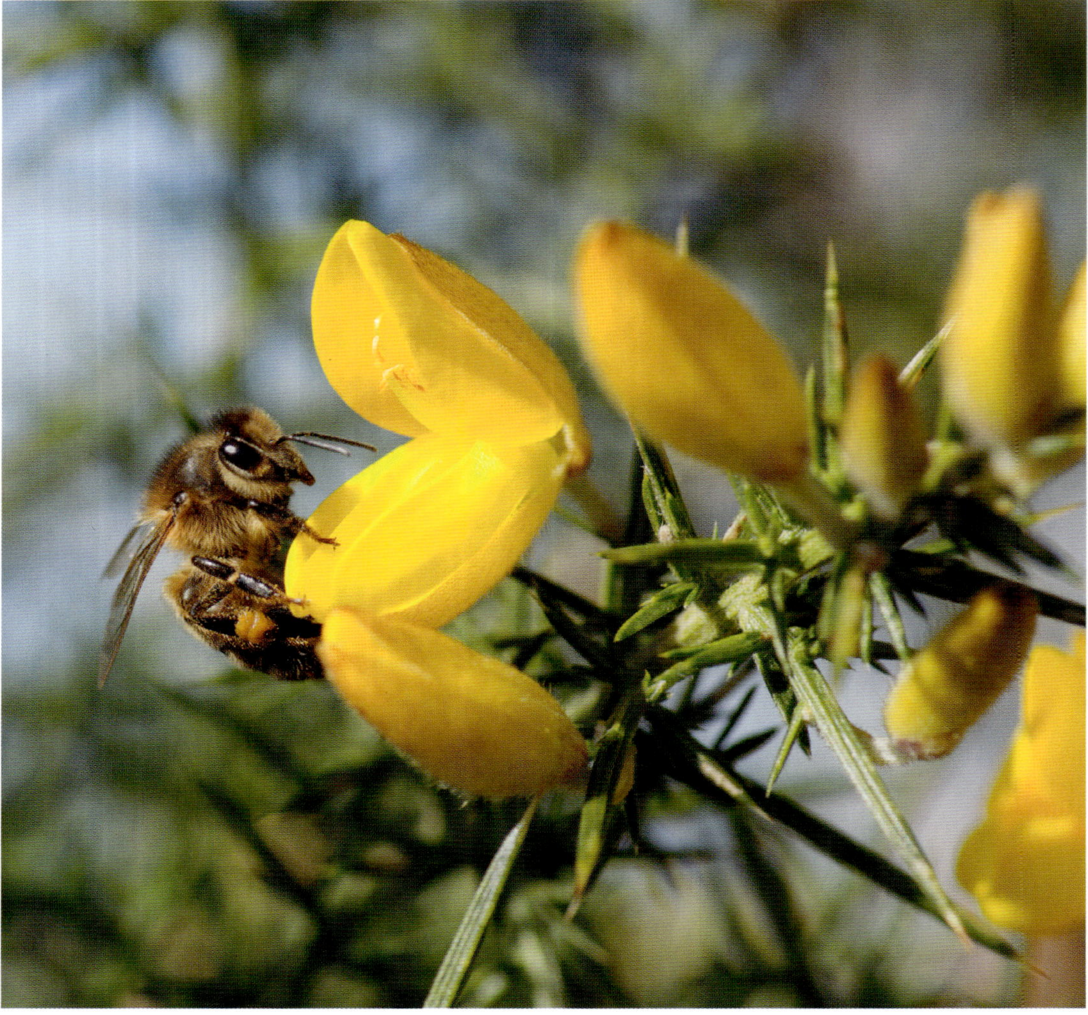

Behavior

Insects cannot generate their own body heat like mammals and birds can. This means they often need warmth from the sun to increase their metabolic rate. This is particularly true of fast-moving flying insects, such as butterflies, bees, and dragonflies (insects that live in colonies, such as ants, derive needed heat from the sheer mass of insects in the colony). Insects are therefore more sluggish early in the morning, making them easier to find and shoot. Insects such as butterflies can often be found sunning themselves on plant stems in the morning, having roosted through the night in situ (looking for roosting spots at sunset will save time the following morning).

Pollinating insects, such as bees, often have very predictable behavior. During the summer months bees fly around patches of flowers, working their way around each flower in turn. Predictable behavior such as this makes it easier to set your camera up on a tripod and wait for an opportune moment to shoot. As insects can be skittish and easily spooked, longer focal length lenses will help you to keep your distance, but move in slowly to your intended subject and do not make any sudden movements.

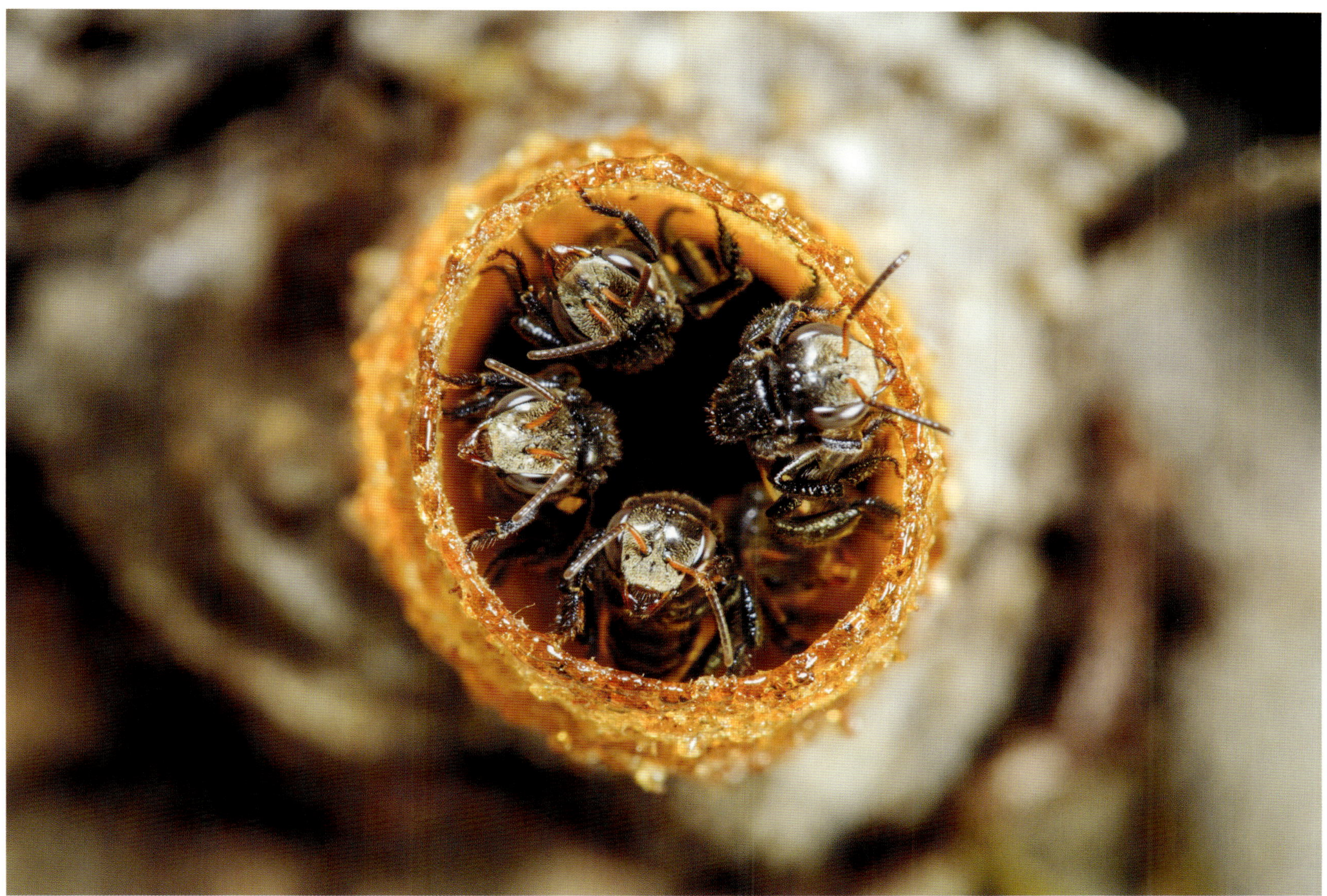

Habitat

There is no right habitat for all insects; different types of insects prefer different conditions. Meadows and land that has been left to go wild are good places to find and photograph insects, but they are not the only places. In woodland you may find fewer insect types such as butterflies, but you will increase your chances of photographing ants and spiders. Damp, dark places—under logs and stones, for example—are the habitat of creatures such as pill bugs.

The larval stage of insects such as dragonflies is spent underwater. Even when the adult dragonfly finally emerges into the air it still spends much of its life near water; ponds and lakes are therefore a good place to spot them during the summer months. These are also the locations where you will find insects such as pond skaters that spend their adult life skimming across the surface of still water. Buying a comprehensive guide to insects and their habitats will help you to both find and identify them.

Above: Communal insects, such as these stingless bees, live in constructed nests or hives that can be used to add context to a shot. It is important not to disturb the nest or distress the insects so that they react adversely to your presence.

Focal length: 100mm macro lens

Aperture: f/11

Shutter speed: 1/250 sec.

ISO: 400

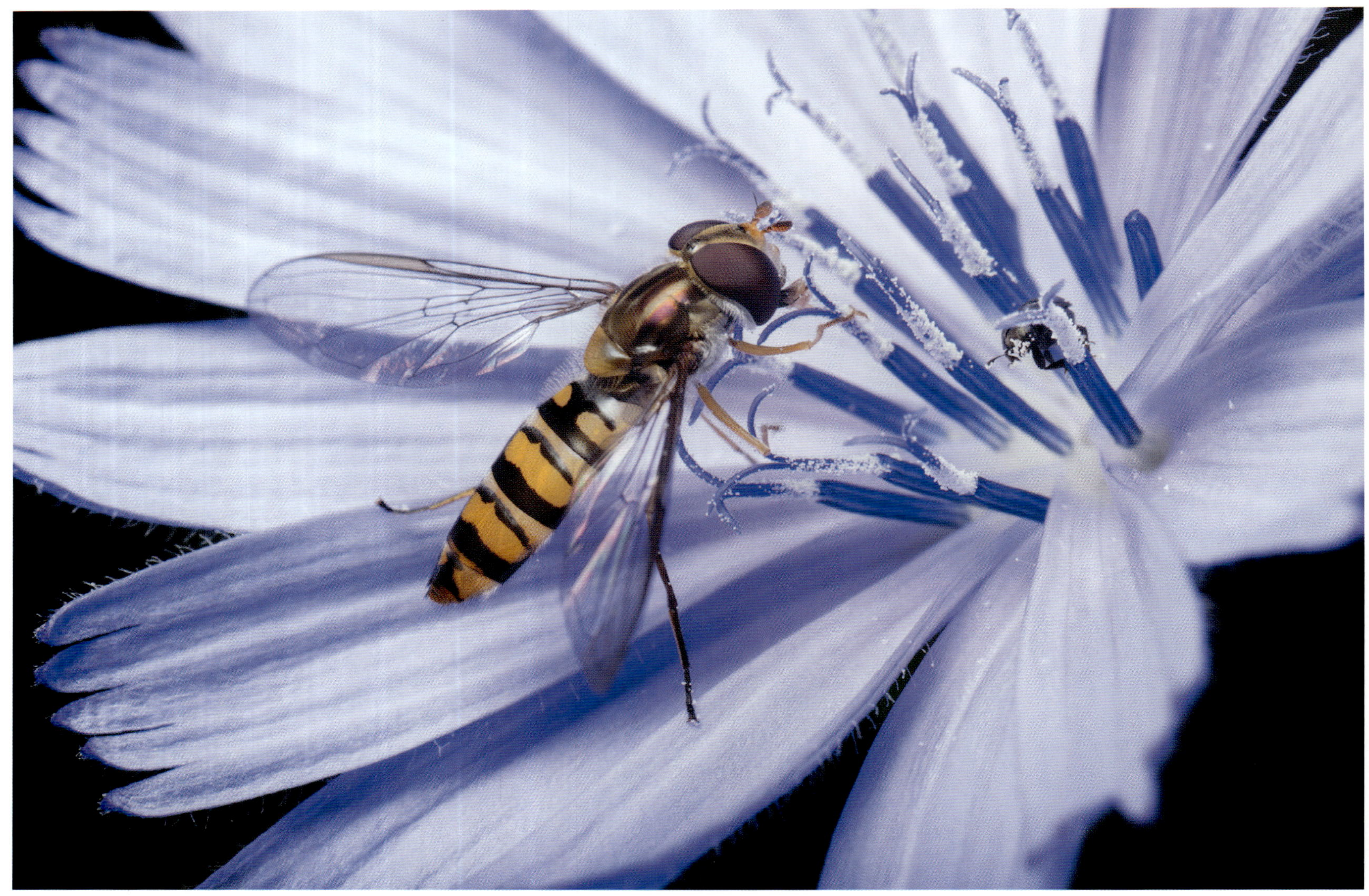

Above: Hoverflies are fast-moving insects that rarely seem to stay still. To ensure that any movement was frozen I used flash with the sync speed set to the camera's maximum. Combined with an aperture of f/29, this had the happy effect of underexposing the background, which was lit purely by the ambient light.

Focal length: 100mm macro lens (with 36mm extension tube)

Aperture: f/29

Shutter speed: 1/250 sec.

ISO: 400

Right: Depth of field can be an issue even when using small apertures. This makes it far more important to choose the right focus point compared to more conventional photography. With insects, such as this robber fly, you would typically focus on the eyes to ensure they are the sharpest part of the image.

Focal length: 100mm macro lens (with extension tube)

Aperture: f/16

Shutter speed: 1/250 sec.

ISO: 400

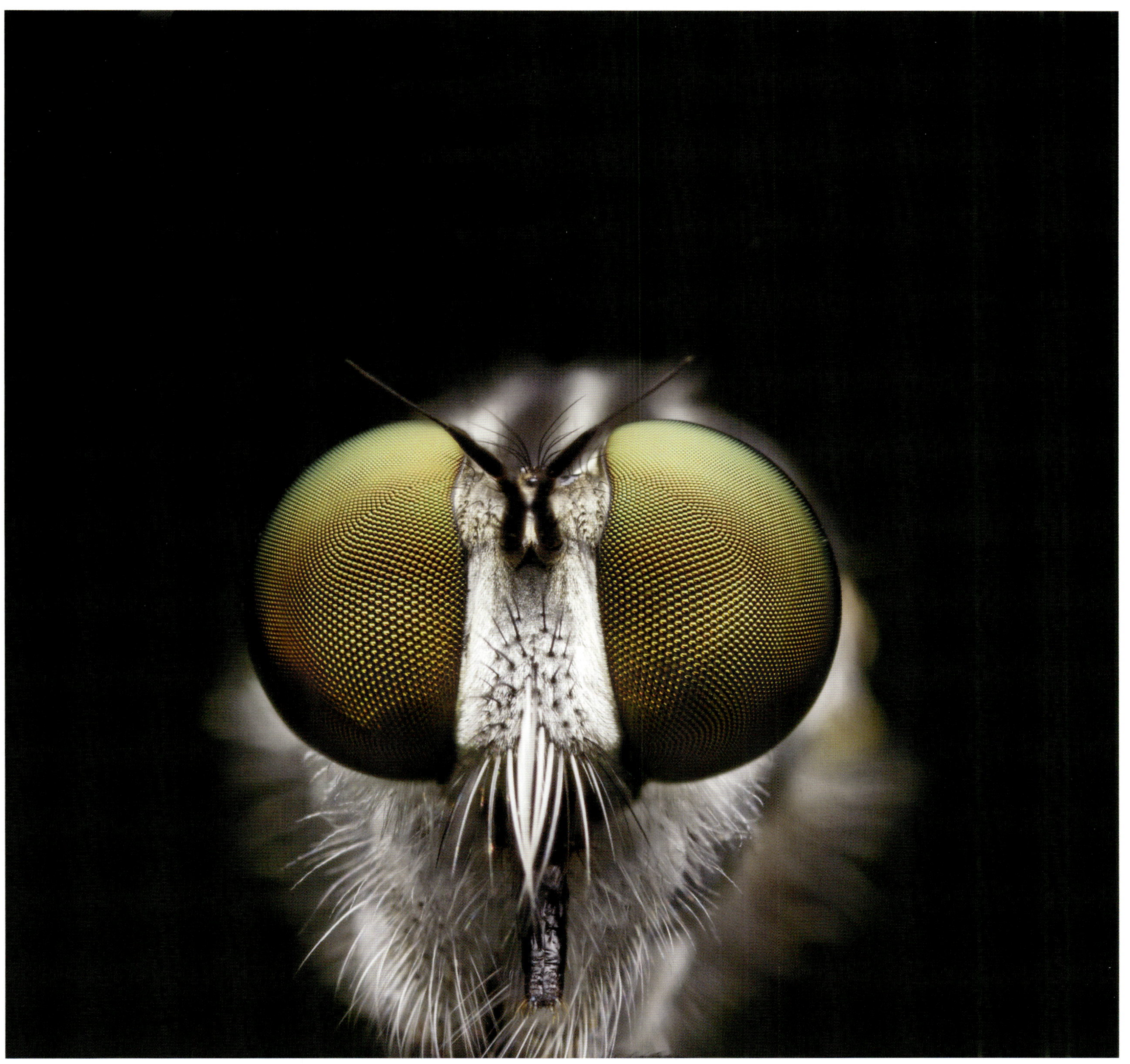

Sharpness

The hardest aspect of shooting insects is achieving a reasonable degree of sharpness. There is often a trade-off between maintaining a fast shutter speed and using a small aperture to maximize depth of field. Increasing the ISO is an option, but this is also subject to compromise and will largely depend on the high ISO capabilities of your camera.

The most important part of an insect is arguably its eyes, so focusing on the eyes should be your first priority. Whether you then need to maximize depth of field will depend on the orientation of the insect relative to the camera. Insects that are side-on to the camera will require less depth of field than shots where the insect is facing the camera. Moving so that the insect is side-on is therefore one solution if you need to prioritize shutter speed over depth of field.

Using flash is a very useful way to solve both the shutter speed and depth of field problem. The short burst of light from a flash will instantly freeze movement, while setting the camera to the sync speed will also maximize sharpness by avoiding camera shake. Using flash will also let you use smaller apertures than the ambient light conditions might otherwise allow.

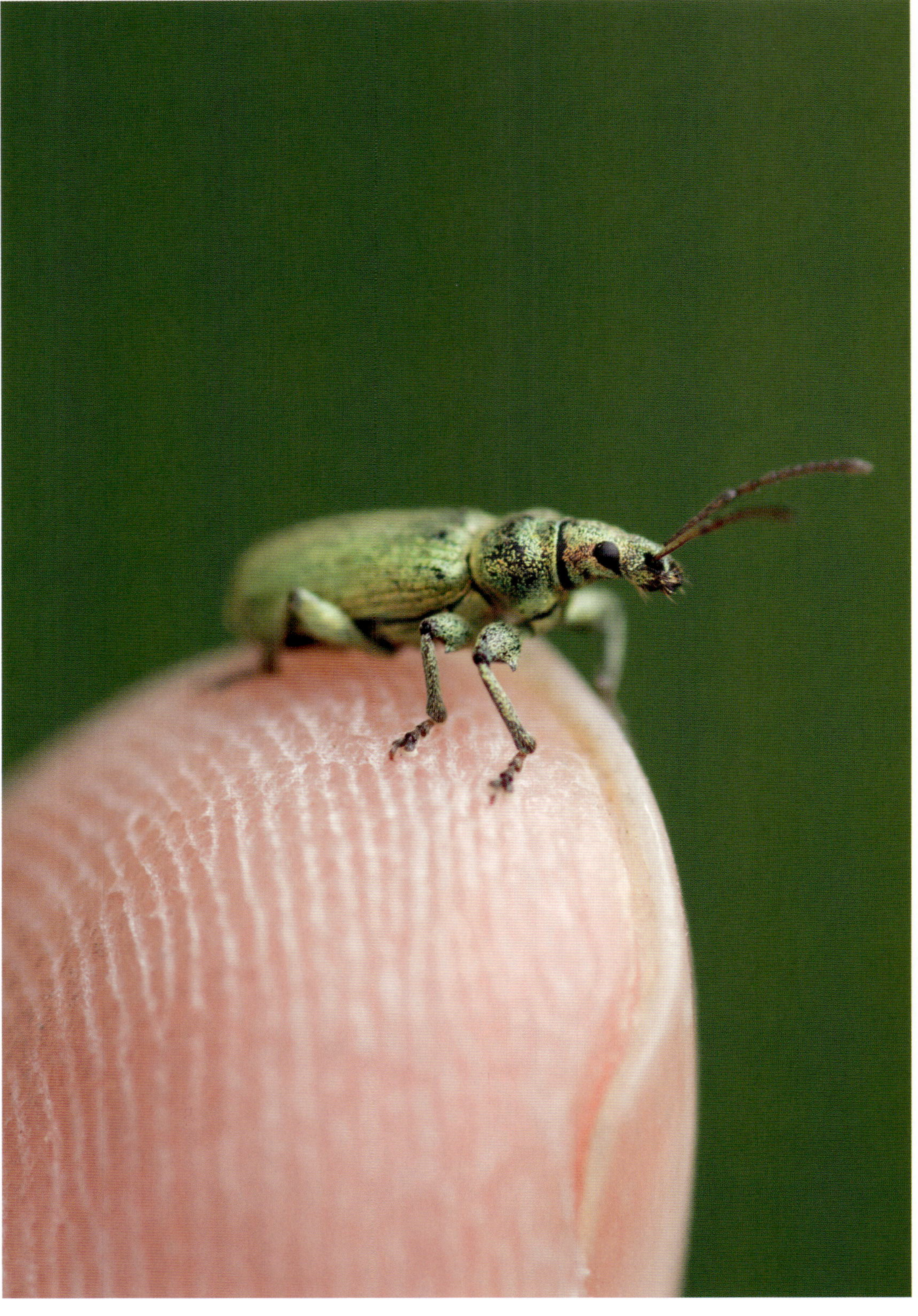

Right: Less-skittish insects can be a joy to photograph. In fact, the problem I had with this nettle weevil was finding a safe way to remove it from my finger! Focus was set on the weevil's eyes and a relatively large aperture setting was used to allow a faster shutter speed and blur out the background, helping the weevil to stand out clearly.

Focal length: 100mm macro lens

Aperture: f/9

Shutter speed: 1/400 sec.

ISO: 400

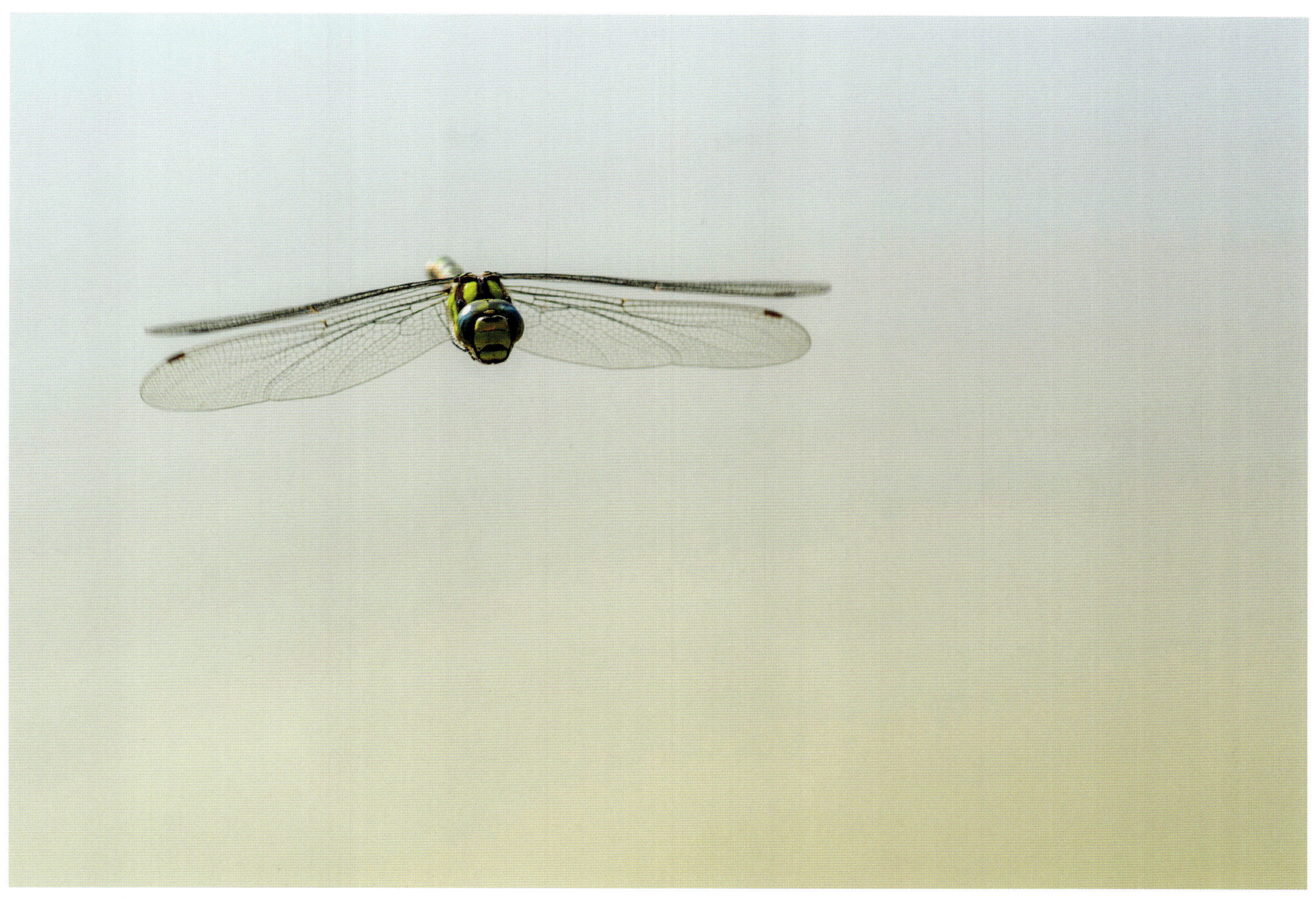

Tips

The weather has a big influence on which insects are visible: blustery days will make it less likely that flying insects will take to the air, for example. Rain is also a deterrent for flying insects, although damp weather will make invertebrates such as slugs and snails more prevalent.

Early morning dew can form on larger insects overnight, creating the appearance of a jewel-like coat. This will remain on their bodies until the rising sun warms the insects and they begin to move.

Still Life

A still-life photograph is one that features objects arranged either by you or a third party. The range of possible subjects that could be included under the umbrella term of still life is vast: it includes food, domestic items, toys, and natural objects brought into the studio.

There are two main factors to consider when shooting a still life: light and composition. Exposure is arguably a lesser consideration, as the shutter speed is largely irrelevant (a still life is static and shooting handheld isn't recommended); ISO should be at its lowest setting (for the best image quality); and the aperture should be set to deliver the right depth of field for the shot you are after.

How a still life is composed will largely depend on the number of elements in your shot. One element is simple: you only have to decide how large you want the subject in the frame and how this relates to the background.

More than one element is slightly more complicated. You need to decide how each element relates to the others; their relative size in the frame; whether they are spaced apart or whether there is overlap; which element is in the foreground and which in the background; and whether they are lit evenly or whether lighting emphasizes one or more elements compared to the rest.

How you light your still life image will again depend on your subject(s). For most subjects, soft, even lighting is preferable, although some sense of form through shadow should be retained. However, hard lighting can be used to create a chiaroscuro effect that is atmospheric and adds a sense of mystery to an image.

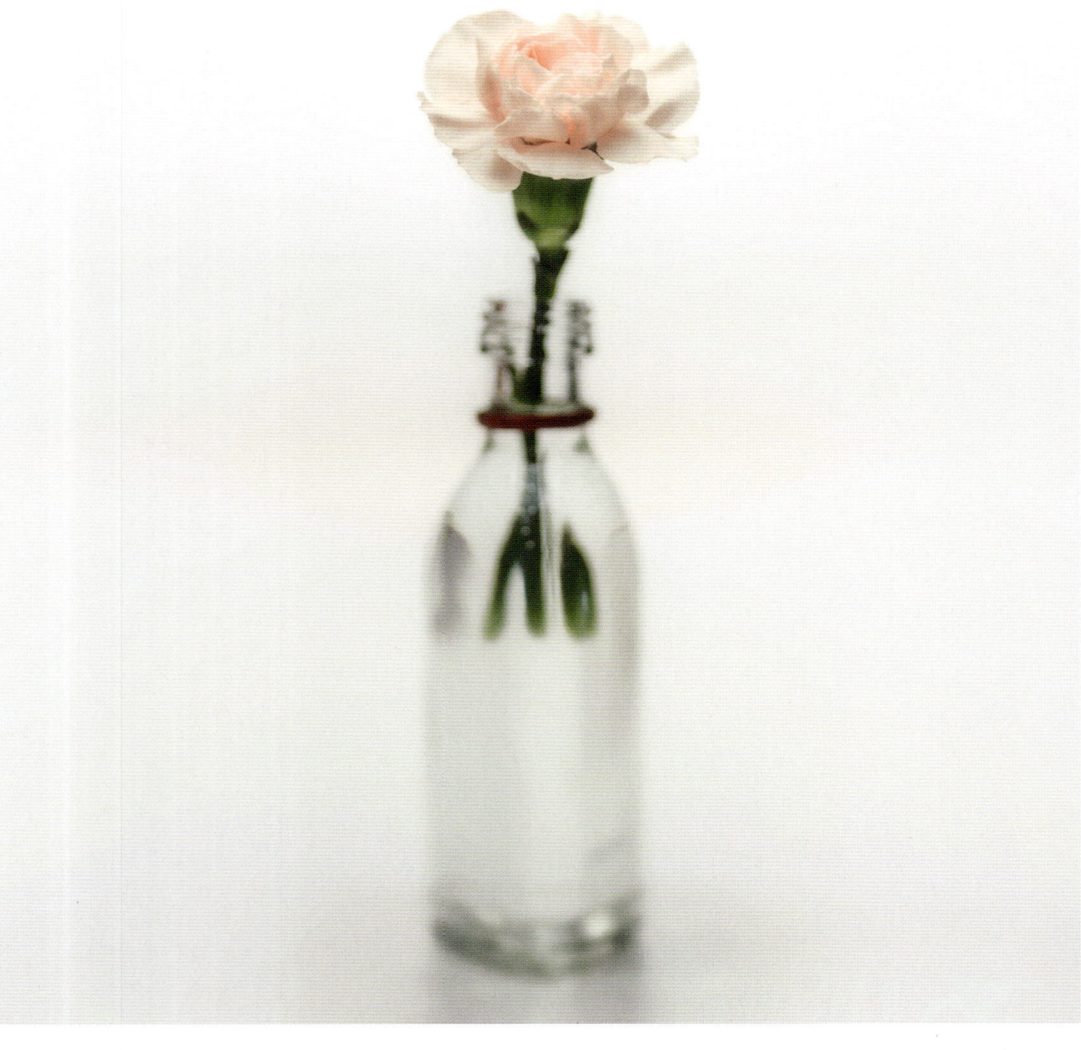

CHIAROSCURO

Chiaroscuro is a painting technique that uses high contrast between the highlights and the shadows in a painting to define the form of the subject. The Dutch artist Rembrandt was a noted user of the technique.

Above: Shooting in a studio lets you control the light as desired. The lighting in this shot was softened as much as possible by firing a flash through a 30in (75cm) softbox placed almost directly above the subject. This produced an near-shadowless light that I felt delivered a suitably romantic atmosphere.

Focal length: 100mm macro lens

Aperture: f/3.3

Shutter speed: 1/250 sec.

ISO: 100

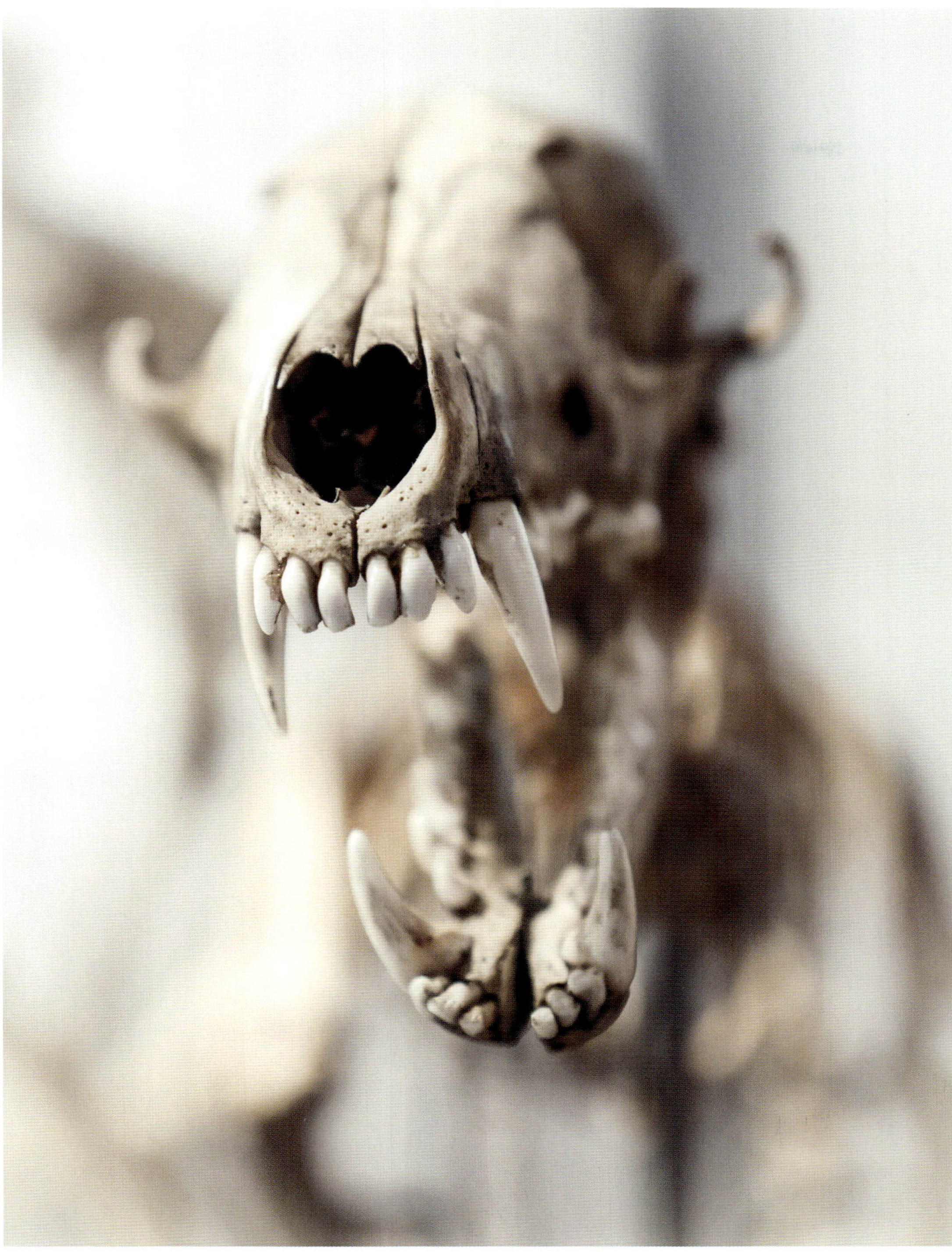

Tips

Use a longer focal length so you can put some distance between the camera and the still-life setup. This will produce a more natural perspective than a wide-angle lens.

For maximum impact fill the frame with your subject.

Think about the background and how it relates to your subject. A contrasting color or a visually complex background may draw the eye away from your subject.

Abstract

Close-up and macro photography is ideally suited to the creation of abstract photography. Excluding details that identify an object—including environmental context—mean it is possible to produce imagery that is difficult to read, but still fascinating to look at.

There are a number of factors to be thought about when creating abstract imagery. One of these is the focal point. A focal point in an image is arguably the most important part of the picture, as it is the ultimate destination of the eye as it scans the picture. Usually, the focal point would be the subject, but abstract images don't necessarily have or need a focal point.

Images with repetitive patterns—such as the cheese grater below—are interesting because the pattern appears as though it could stretch on forever outside the image space. If it is identifiable, a focal point may also reduce the abstract nature of the image.

Color is another important factor. Vibrant colors are more immediately striking than pastels or desaturated colors and hold the interest for longer. An image that is a mix of bold and subdued colors can feel unbalanced unless they are carefully arranged around the image space.

Shape and line also need to be considered. Square geometric shapes feel solid and bold, while curves are more subtle and graceful, and can be used to guide the eye through an image. Combining the two in an image adds contrast.

Subjects such as peeling paint or rusty iron will make visually interesting abstract images because of their texture, but the key to success with texture is light. Flat lighting will flatten the texture so use side or top lighting to add depth by creating highlights and shadows.

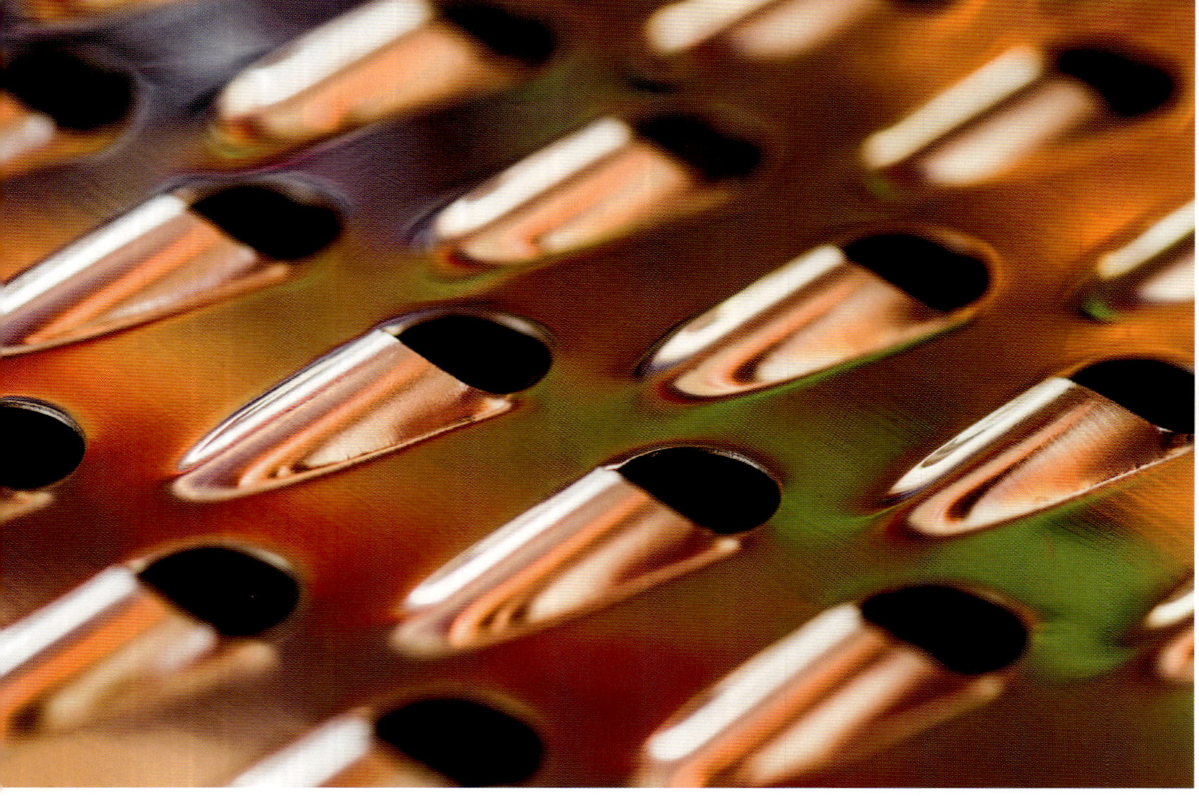

Left: Light can be used to increase the abstraction of an image. The colors in this close-up of a cheese grater were created by bouncing light from a flash off a colorful greetings card onto the surface of the grater. Because the metal of the cheese grater wasn't a perfect mirror, no detail from the card can be seen.

Focal length: 100mm macro lens

Aperture: f/14

Shutter speed: 1.5 sec.

ISO: 100

Right: Four very different approaches to shooting abstract imagery, including vibrant color and texture (top left), subdued color and texture (top right), shape (bottom left), and complementary colors (bottom right).

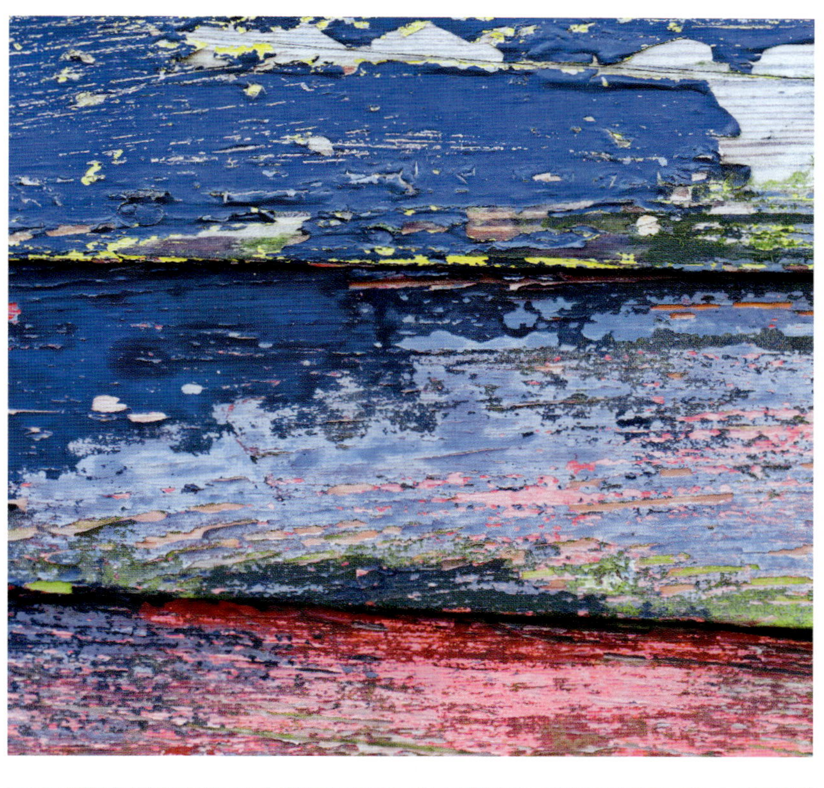
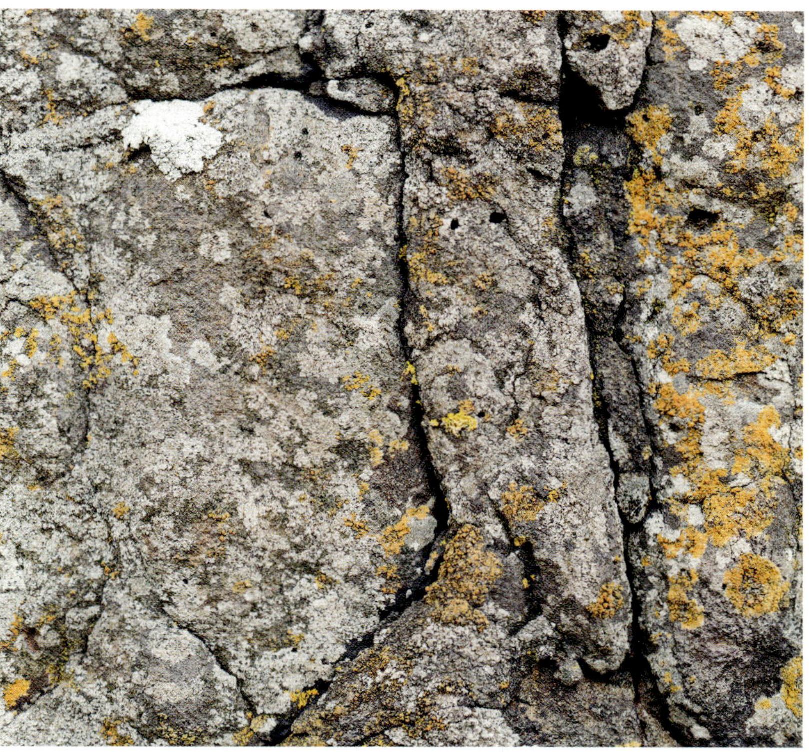
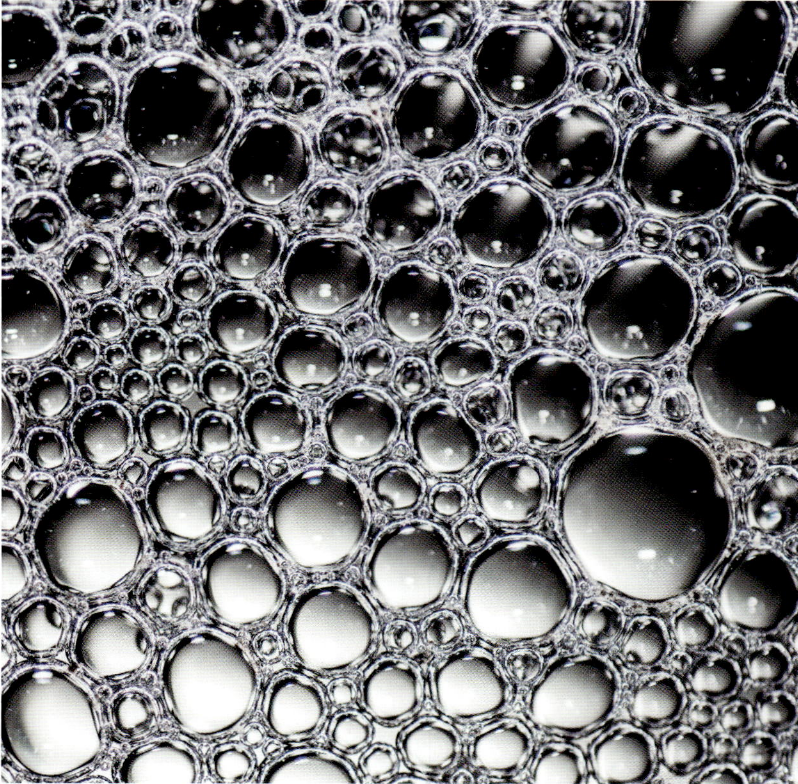
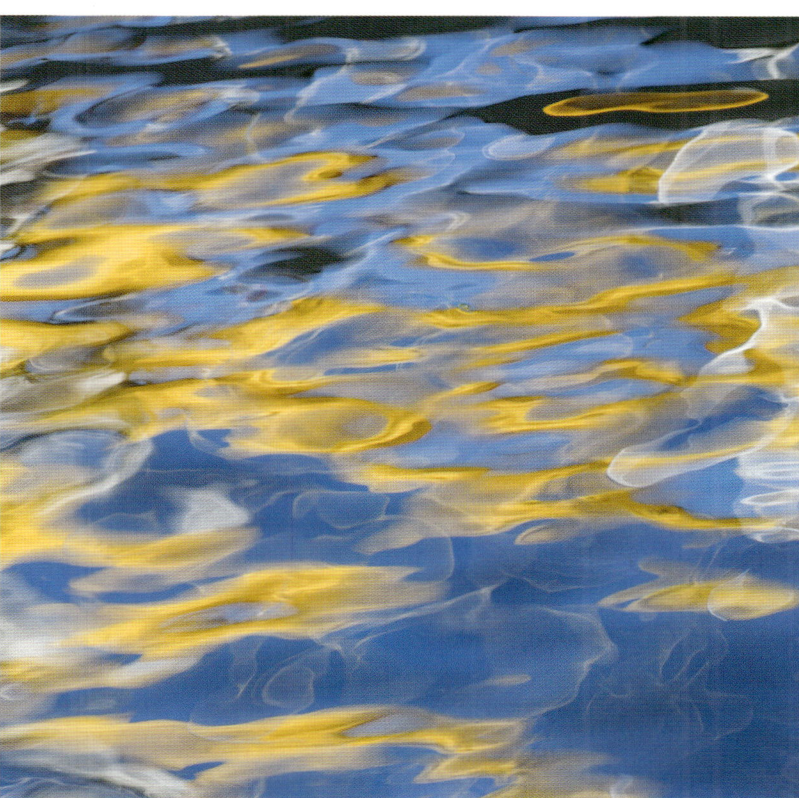

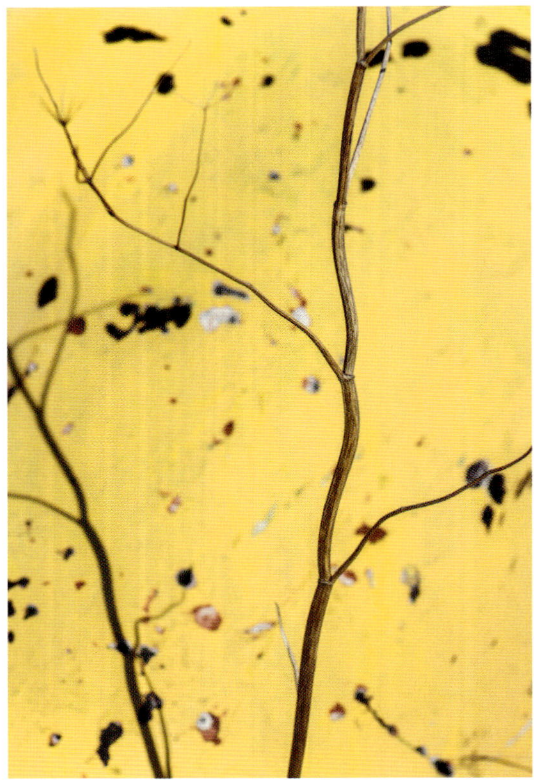

Above: A great way to start to produce an abstract image is to exclude any contextual detail. This is easier to achieve with a longer focal length lens than a wider one. Here, a 100mm lens was used to fill the frame with the background wall without an edge showing.

Focal length: 100mm macro lens

Aperture: f/8

Shutter speed: 1/800 sec.

ISO: 100

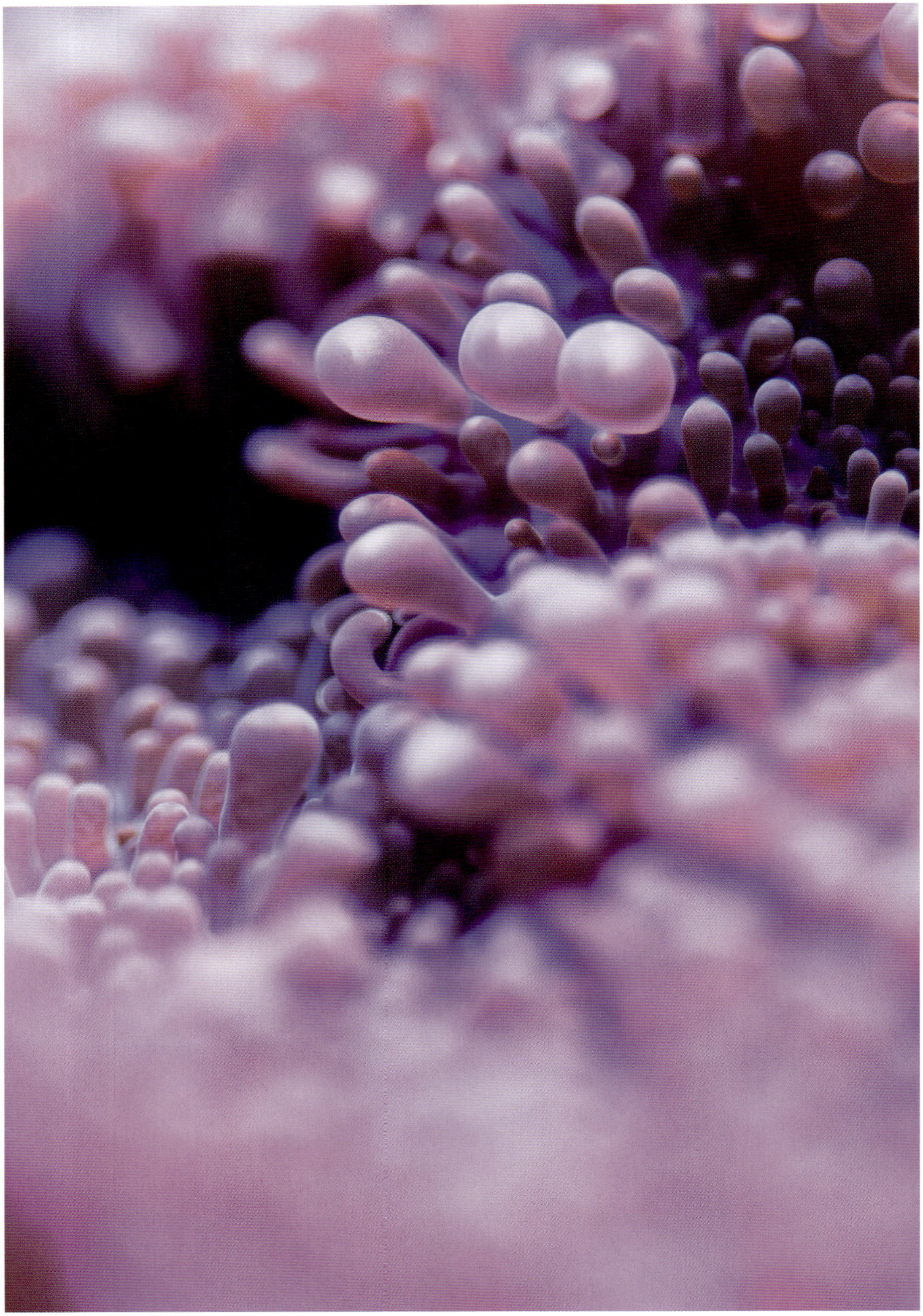

Right: Some subjects are difficult to recognize unless you are an expert in a particular field. By composing tightly on these coral polyps in an aquarium I was able to create a slightly surreal image, helped by the unusual lighting in the subject's tank.

Focal length: 100mm macro lens

Aperture: f/5.3

Shutter speed: 1/40 sec.

ISO: 800

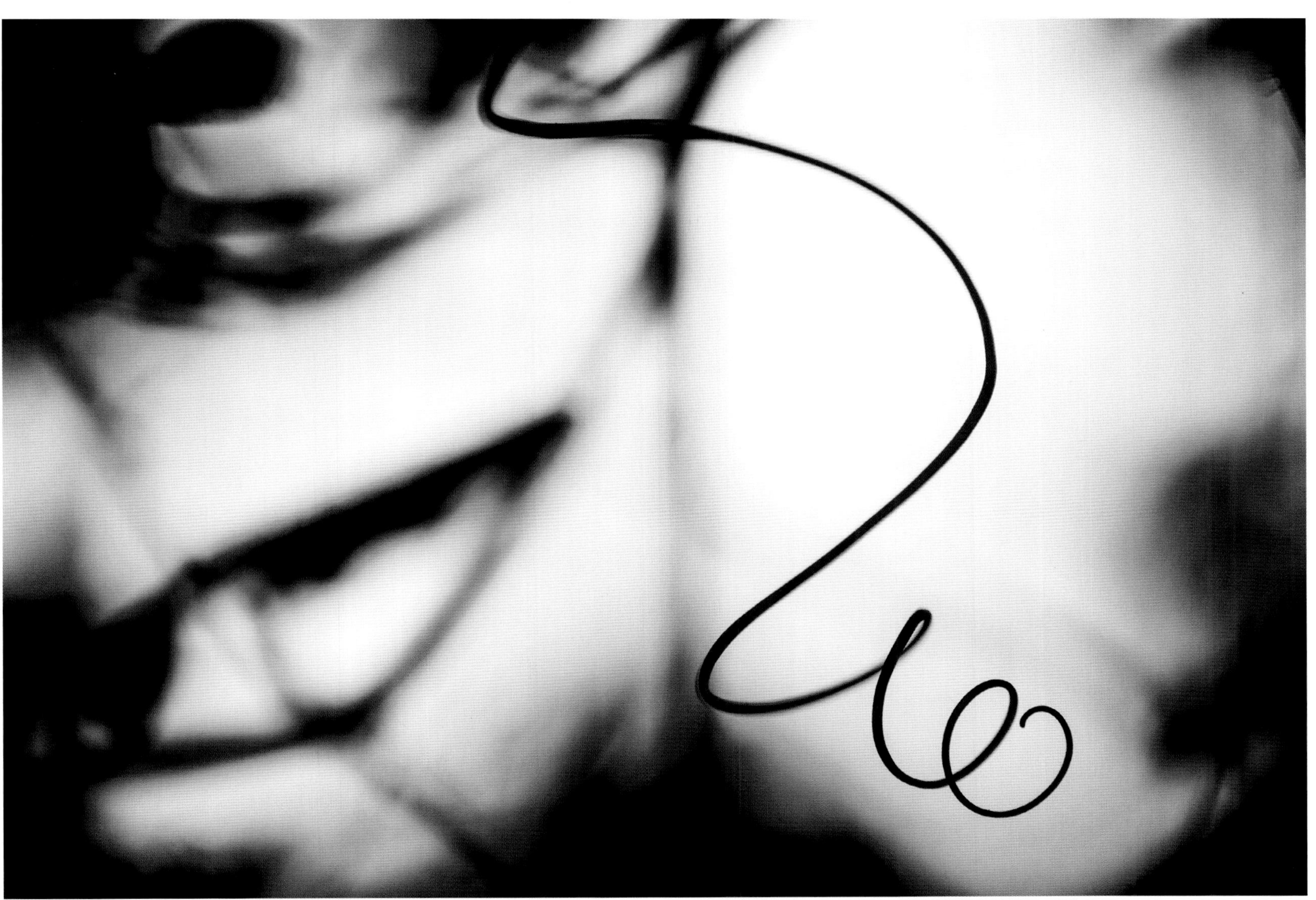

Above: Backlighting your subject and shooting it in silhouette adds a more abstract effect. The key is to keep the composition simple and avoid having too many confusing, overlapping elements. When shooting this English mandrake creeper I also minimized the depth of field so it was only the creeper that was sharp.

Focal length: 100mm macro lens

Aperture: f/6.3

Shutter speed: 1/4000 sec.

ISO: 400

Profile: Terry Border

BIOGRAPHY

Terry Border grew up in Indianapolis in the US, and went to nearby Ball State University where he majored in Fine Art Photography. He then spent 12 years in the field of commercial photography, assisting and photographing all kinds of people and things.

He started shooting his idiosyncratic vignettes in 2006, and now makes children's books in this style full time.

www.terryborder.com

Q) What is your specialty?
A) My specialty is creating figures out of everyday objects and/or food items, and using them to form amusing narratives.

Q) What is it about your specialty that fascinates you?
A) Coming up with the concept is the thing I enjoy most. The second is bringing the scene alive with some (hopefully!) dramatic lighting. Many times I like to show the shapes of things with a key light off to the side and slightly behind the main subject. I like shadows and showing some depth.

Q) What equipment do you regularly use?
A) I use a Canon camera and a nice Canon macro lens, as well as other Canon lenses that allow me to focus fairly close. I use Photogenic flash units that I've had for years, but the one thing I couldn't do my job without are the honeycomb grids that I use to direct my lights. When shooting small objects it's fairly easy to over-light a scene. I try to narrow the key light so I can control the light and mood.

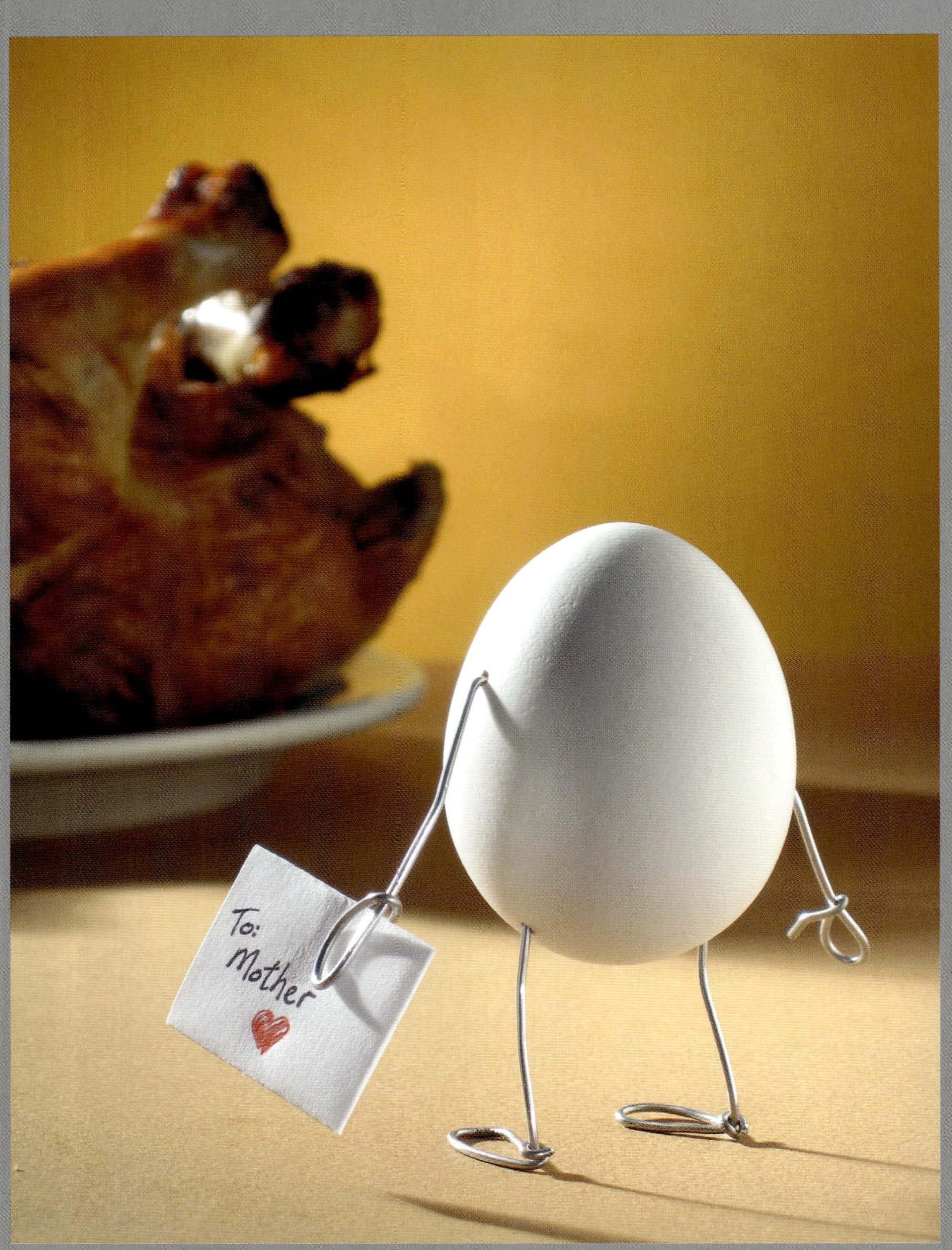

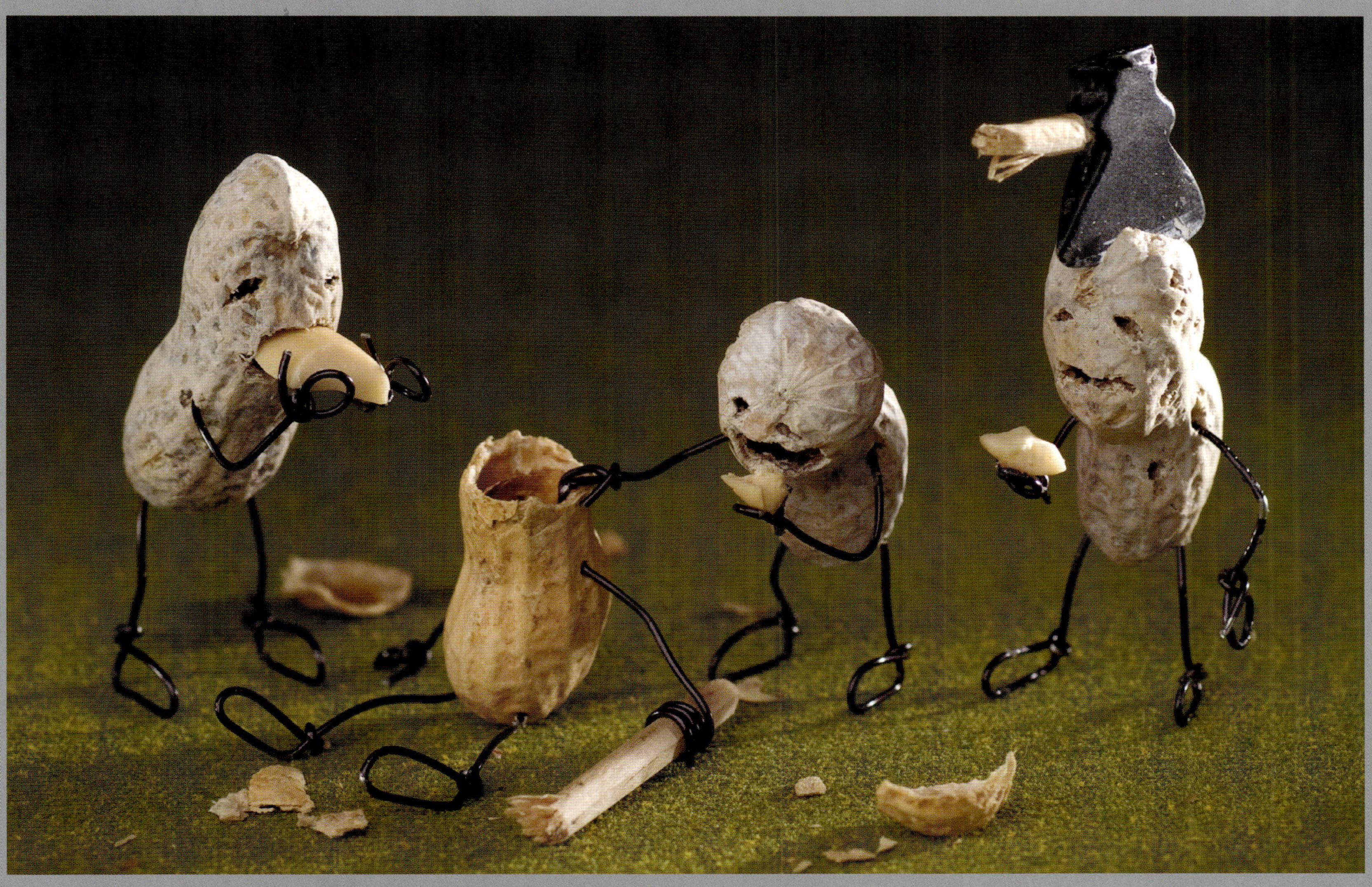

Left:
Belated
Focal length: 23.1mm
Aperture: f/4.9
Shutter speed: 1/4 sec.
ISO: 50

Above:
Zombies Are Nuts
About Brains
(exposure unrecorded)

Q) How do you plan a photography session?
A) I sketch ideas down and think about what kind of props I'll need and how I'll need to set things up. Then I drink a bunch of coffee that I hope will force me into the studio and begin!

Q) How do you light your subjects?
A) Artificial lighting is what I use 98% of the time. Like I said, I'm a control freak!

Q) How important is postproduction to you?
A) I'll use software to clean up any dust or whatever, and sometimes for a little color correction, but I try to keep it to a minimum.

Q) What is your top tip?
A) Stay in control of your light, even when you're shooting something small. Also, be prepared to shoot the same thing three-dozen times before you're absolutely thrilled with it!

Chapter 7
Postproduction

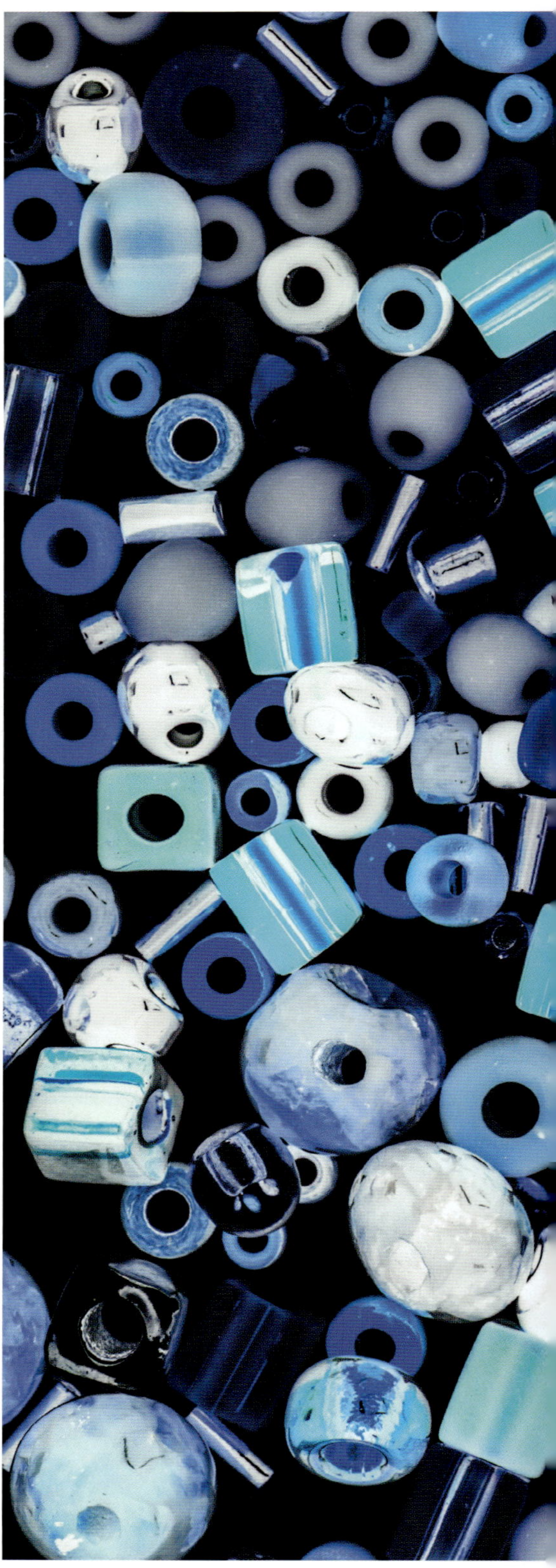

Shooting Raw invariably means there will be some postproduction work to do after exposure. This can be restricted to minor tweaks to color or contrast, or it can involve the wholesale change of an image so that the finished piece bears little resemblance to the original exposure. There is no right or wrong answer—just your own preferred way of producing a finished image.

The key is starting with a Raw file that gives you a good foundation for postproduction work. This means one that's correctly exposed and ideally with the correct WB (although WB can be adjusted in postproduction, it saves time if little or no adjustment is required).

Right: It is generally better to think about what you want to achieve with an image before you make an exposure, but that doesn't mean there's no room for creativity and experimentation afterward. This shot of beads on a lightbox started off as a fairly conventional shot until I nverted the colors to produce the more abstract negative effect seen here.

Focal length: 100mm macro lens

Aperture: f/18

Shutter speed: 1/15 sec.

ISO: 100

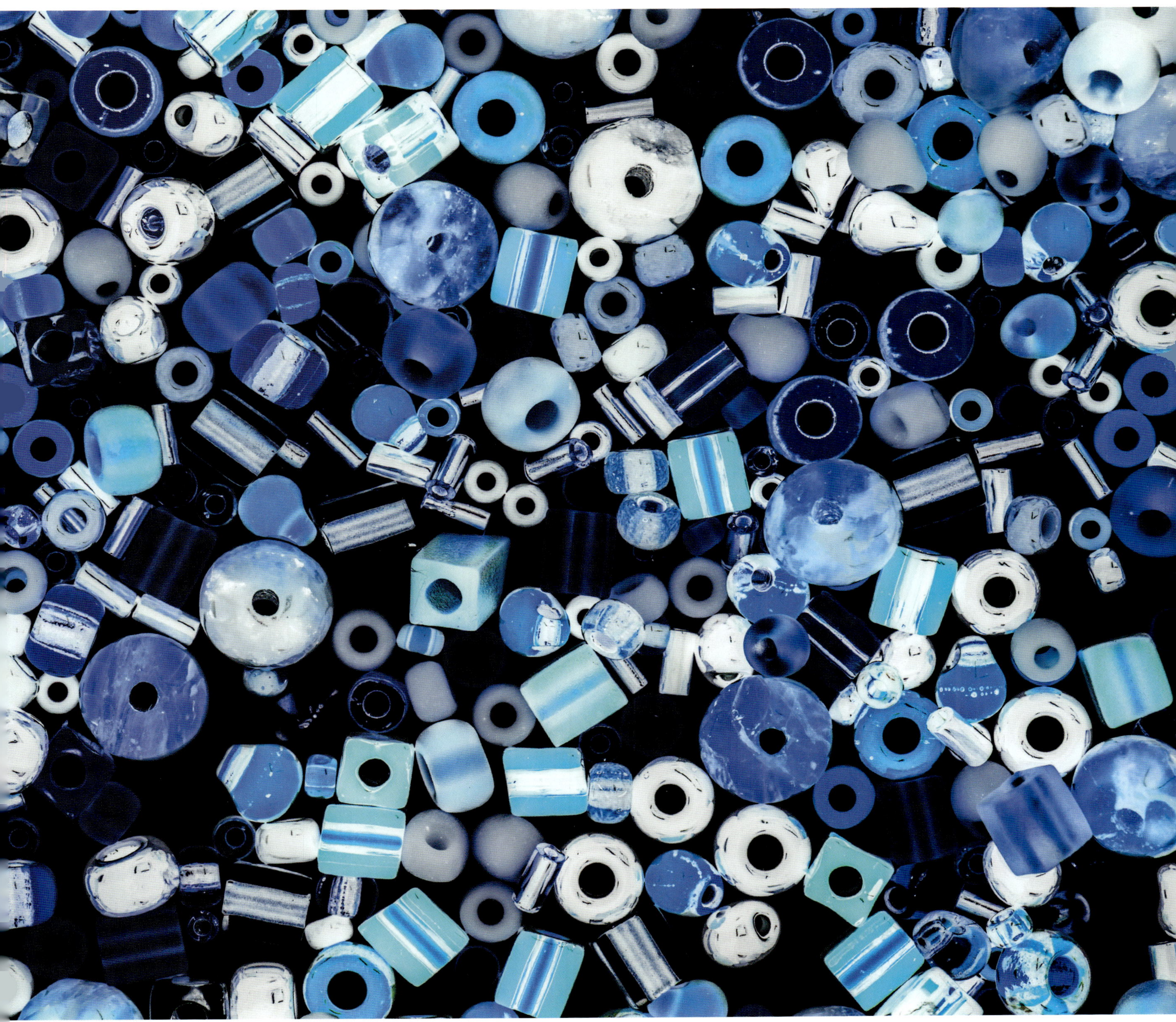

Software

There are plenty of options when it comes to postproduction software. Cameras often come with a manufacturer's own free Raw software, which is generally good, but not necessarily the best software available. Adobe is the name most closely associated with postproduction software, with both Photoshop and the photography-specific Lightroom available as a package on a monthly subscription basis.

However, despite Adobe's dominance there are other postproduction software packages that could be considered, such as Phase One's Capture One and DxO's OpticsPro. Both packages are available on a free 30-day evaluation basis.

DAM

Adobe Lightroom and similar programs are built around the idea of Digital Asset Management (DAM), which makes it easier to manage hundreds or thousands of images. The DAM side of the software (as opposed to the pure postproduction side) helps to automate routine tasks such as renaming images, adding keywords and descriptions to images, and moving images around your computer.

Adding keywords and descriptions to images is particularly useful as it lets you find your photographs easily using the software's search facility. Good DAM software should also allow you to adjust one image and then apply those adjustments to other photographs.

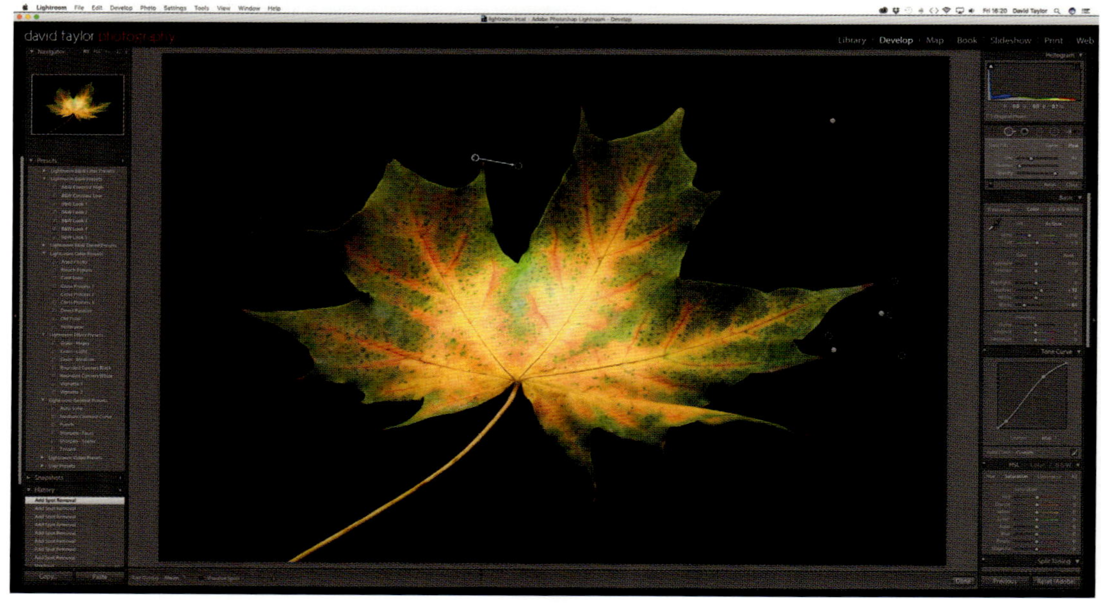

Above: Adobe Lightroom is designed specifically for photographers and combines image editing with DAM tools.

Global Vs. Local Adjustments

There are essentially two types of adjustment that you can make to an image: global and local. A global adjustment is one that affects the entire image. This includes applying tools such as white balance and exposure. Local adjustments are those that are targeted at specific areas of an image, such as cloning out dust spots. Note, however, that tools such as white balance and exposure can also be applied locally, so there is some overlap.

How far you alter your images is very much a matter of personal preference. The key is to think about what you want to achieve before you start so that unnecessary (and potentially damaging) alterations are made to your images. In most instances global adjustments are applied first, followed by local adjustments to give the image a final "polish." The main consideration is that an adjustment made to the image early in postproduction should not then be cancelled out by a later adjustment. This is particularly true if you are adjusting JPEG images, as the more they are altered the more they will degrade.

Right: I use Adobe Lightroom, which shows the history of adjustments in the Develop module. This image essentially had five basic alterations made: lens profile correction, noise reduction, contrast, and color adjustment (which are all global adjustments), followed by spot removal (a local adjustment) to clean up blemishes on the match.

Focal length: 100mm macro lens

Aperture: f/10

Shutter speed: 1/250 sec.

ISO: 100

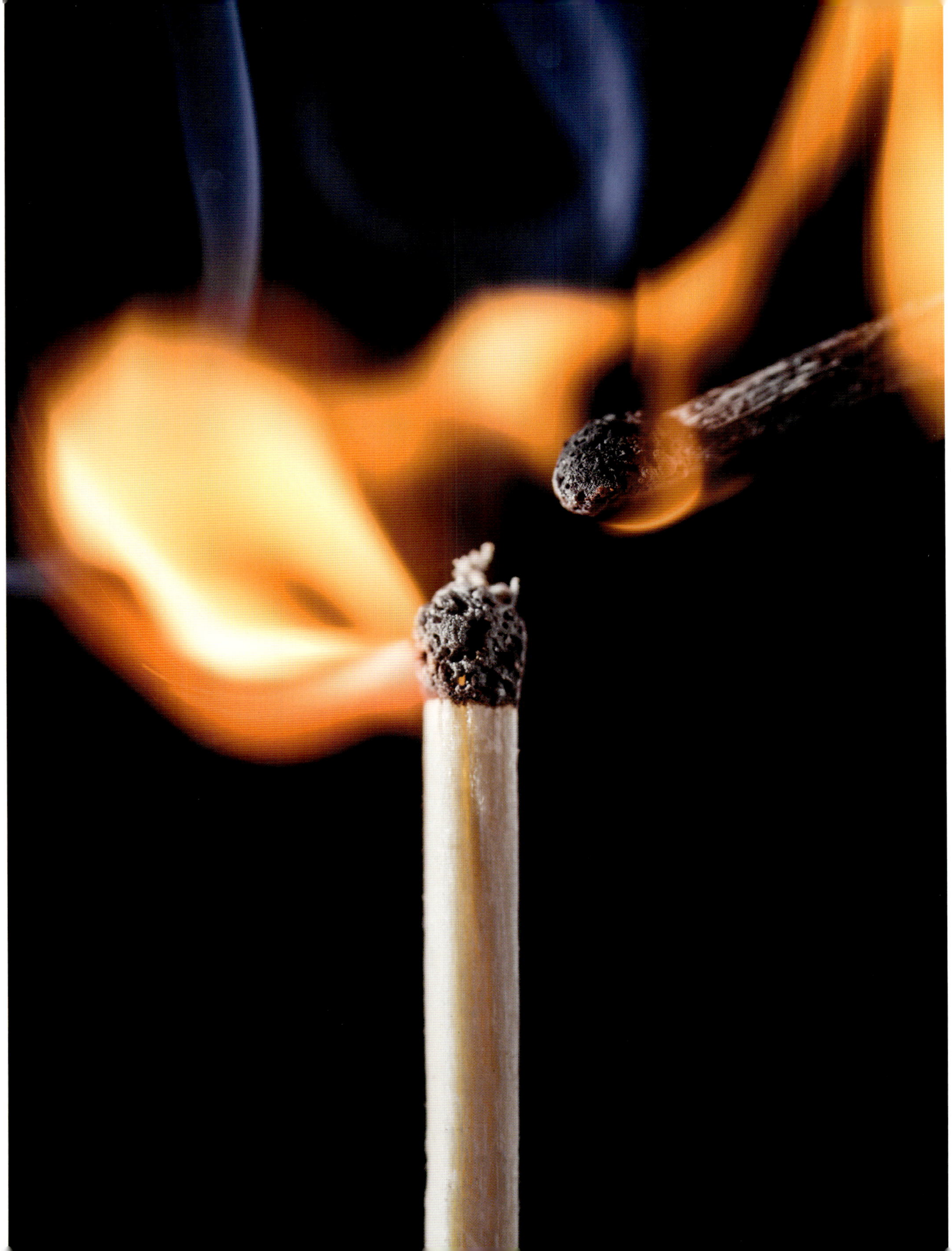

Tonal Adjustments

If you shoot Raw, your images will invariably need some form of tonal correction, which includes changes to contrast, color saturation, and/or WB. The adjustments described below are common to most postproduction software, although the names may be subtly different.

Brightness/Contrast

The Brightness tool is generally a slider that lets you darken or lighten your image. It is a slightly older (and cruder) version of the Exposure tool described below and is not found in some newer postproduction software. The Brightness control typically sits alongside a Contrast slider as well, as brightness adjustments often necessitate a change in the contrast (and vice versa).

White Balance

Shoot Raw and you can alter the WB setting in postproduction, allowing you to either correct an image's color temperature or adjust it for creative purposes. Most postproduction software will let you adjust WB using a range of presets (similar to those found on your camera) or more precisely via a slider (the range of values on the slider varies between programs, but is typically in the region of 2000–12,000K).

Some software will also let you click on any part of an image to use as a WB target. In this instance, a simple way to use the selection tool is to shoot two shots—one with a neutral surface (such as white paper or an 18% gray card) under the same lighting as your subject, and the second with your subject only. You can use the first shot to set the correct white balance (by setting the neutral surface as the WB target) and then apply the resulting WB setting to the main image.

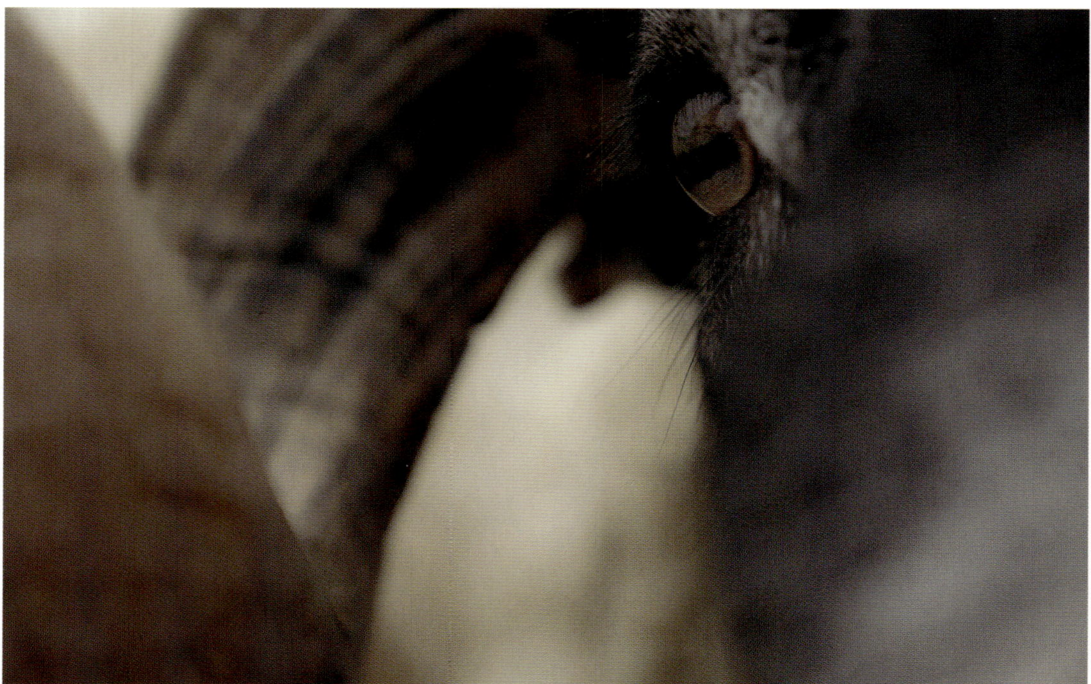

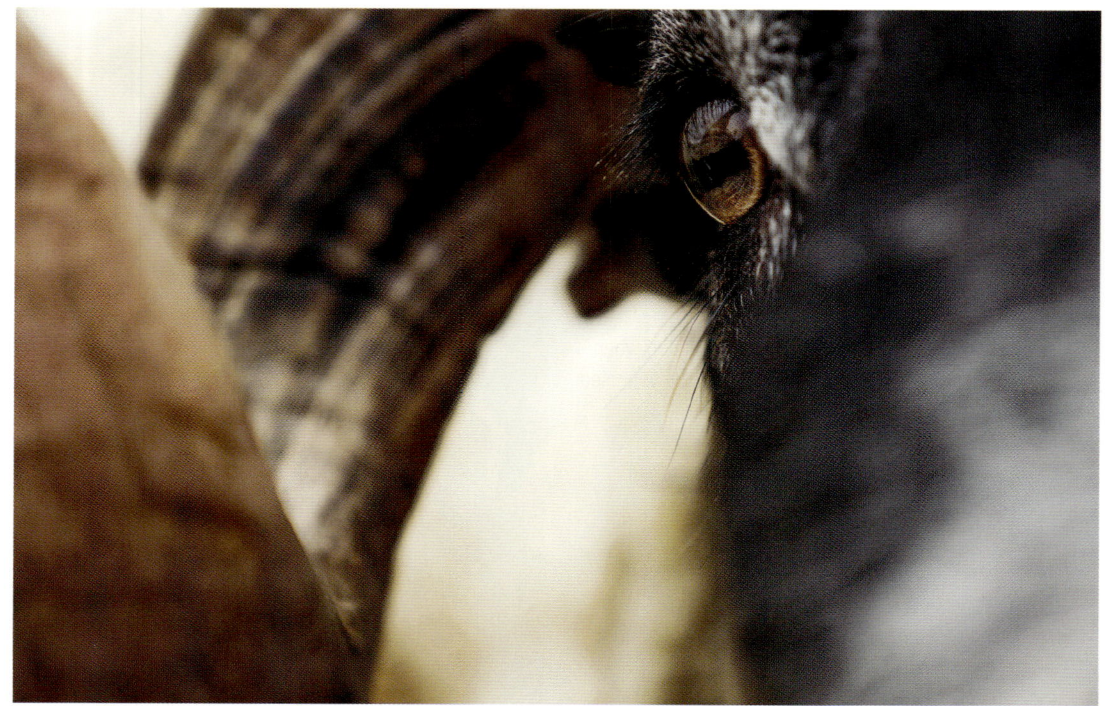

Exposure

The global or local brightness of images can be adjusted using the Exposure tool. This typically works in a similar way to exposure compensation on a camera, with images adjusted in stops using a slider. This offers you a very simple way to make quick changes to an image's brightness, and it is especially useful if you used the ETTR exposure technique and need to normalize an image.

However, care should be taken when lightening exposures in postproduction, as 1-stop of positive exposure adjustment is roughly equivalent to a 1-stop increase in ISO, which can exacerbate image noise. There is more scope for adjustment if the image was shot at ISO 100, but less room to maneuver at higher ISO settings.

Levels

The Levels tool is a step up from both Brightness/Contrast and Exposure in terms of the control you have over the tonal range of an image. Levels can be used to adjust the contrast in an image, by sliding control points that alter where the black point and the white point of an image are. By bringing the black and white points closer together, the overall contrast of the image is increased; pull them further apart and contrast is lowered.

You can also lighten images using the midtone control point: sliding it left, toward the black point, will lighten an image; sliding it right, closer to the white point, will darken an image.

Highlights & Shadows

The Highlights and Shadows tools let you lighten the shadows or darken the highlights in an image without significantly affecting the midtones. The Shadow slider can be thought of as a postproduction fill light, although care should be taken not to over lighten an image, as this may start to introduce noise into the image (too much lightening can also make an image look over processed and unnatural).

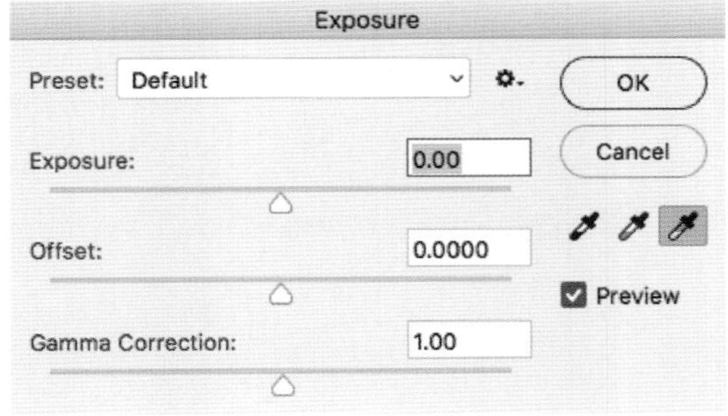

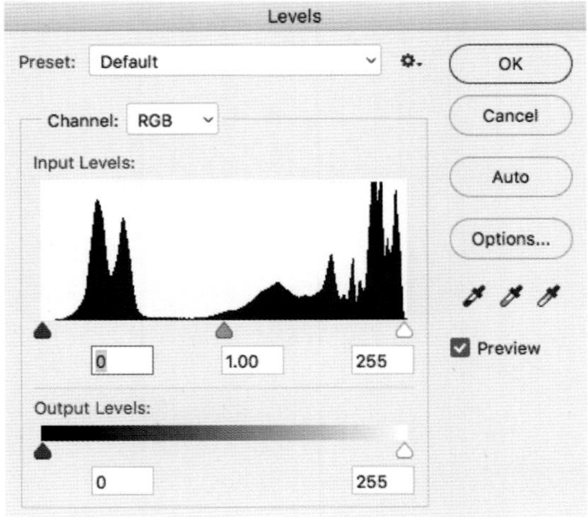

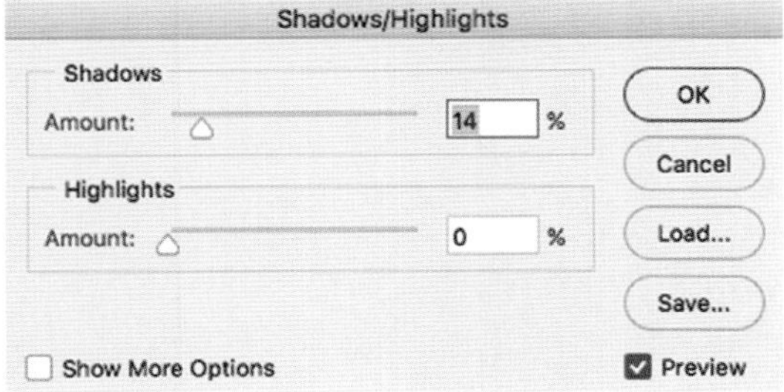

Left: Raw files can look flat and slightly desaturated when you import them onto your computer, particularly if you used a neutral picture parameter at the time of shooting. This image of a sheep's eye was also flat from being shot on a dull, overcast day. To go from the image on the left to the one on the right required three simple adjustments: a slight increase in exposure, an increase in contrast, and a boost to the color saturation.

Focal length: 35mm

Aperture: f/2.8

Shutter speed: 1/640 sec.

ISO: 200

Curves

The Curves tool is probably the least intuitive tonal adjustment tool, but arguably it is also the most useful. With the Curves tool you can adjust specific areas of an image's tonal range with far more control than with Levels. The Curves tool starts as a diagonal line running from the bottom left of a square box up to the top right. Along the bottom edge of the box is a grayscale gradient known as the Input that runs from black on the left through to white on the right. Vertically up the left edge of the box is the Output gradient that runs from black at the bottom to white at the top.

To adjust the Curve you click to add one or more control points to the diagonal line. When a control point is moved, the tones in the image that correspond to the tones below the control point on the Input gradient are altered to match the tones to the left of the control point on the Output gradient: move a control point upward and the relevant tones in the image are lightened; move the control point down and they are darkened.

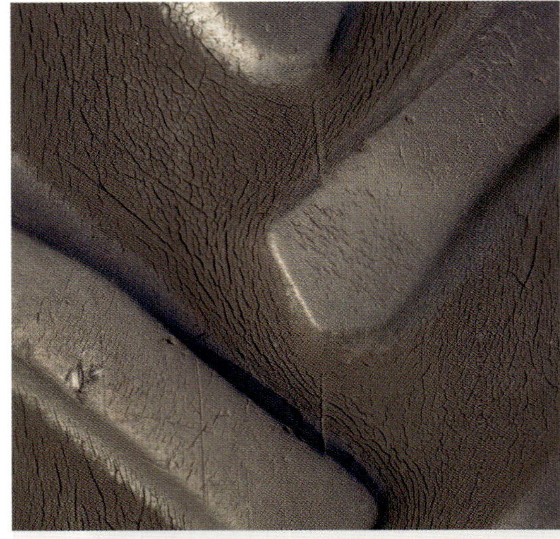

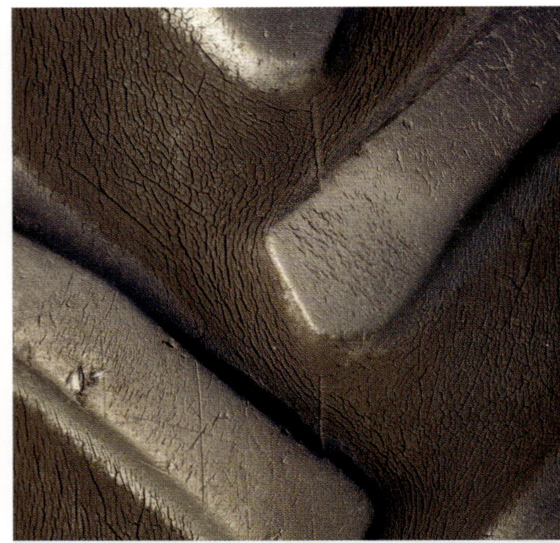

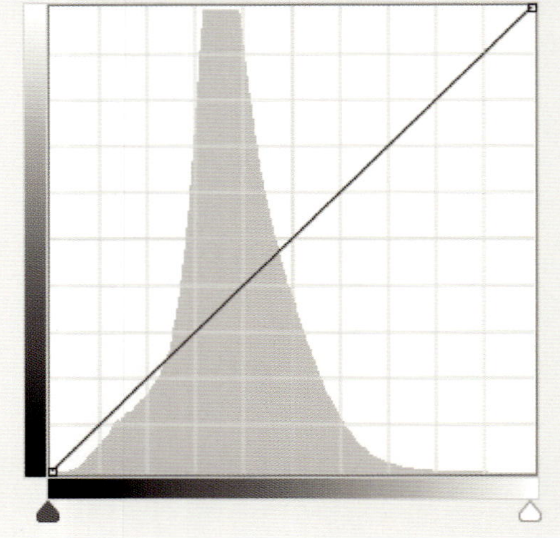

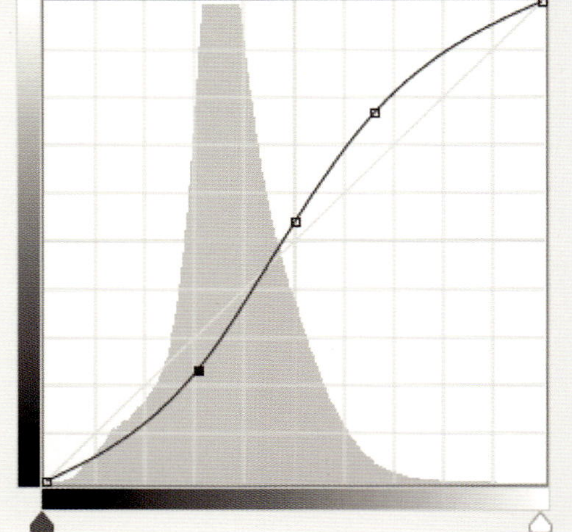

Above: Curves can be used to adjust exposure. It can also be used to alter contrast. Changing the curve to an "S" shape (above right) increases contrast by darkening the shadows and lightening the highlights. An inverted S-shape curve will reduce contrast by applying the opposite correction—lightening shadows and darkening highlights.

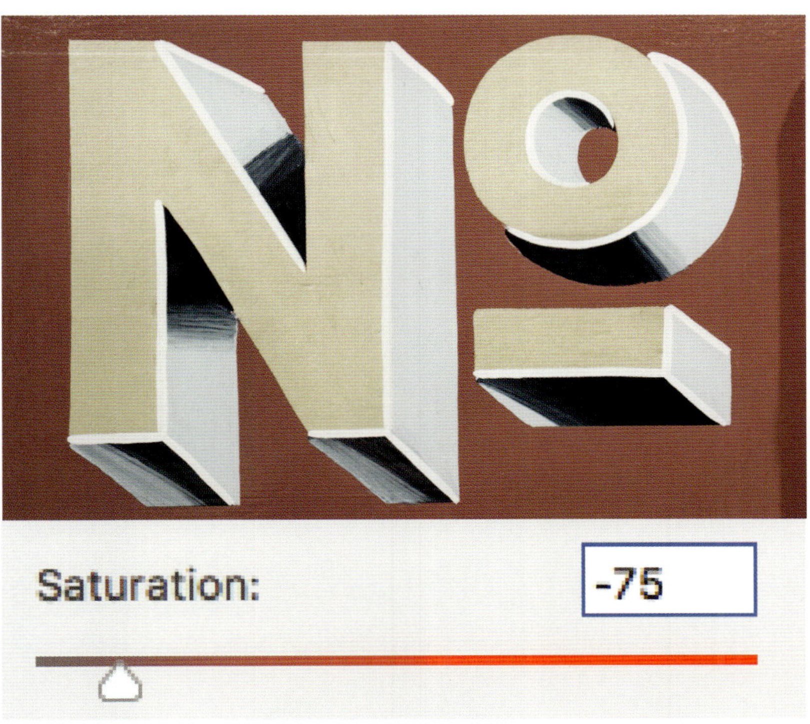

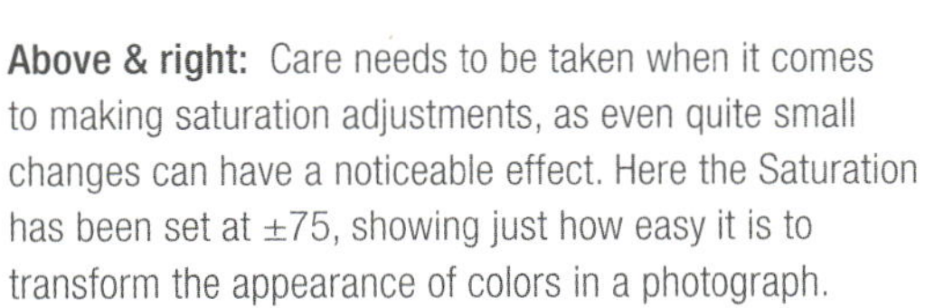

Saturation: -75

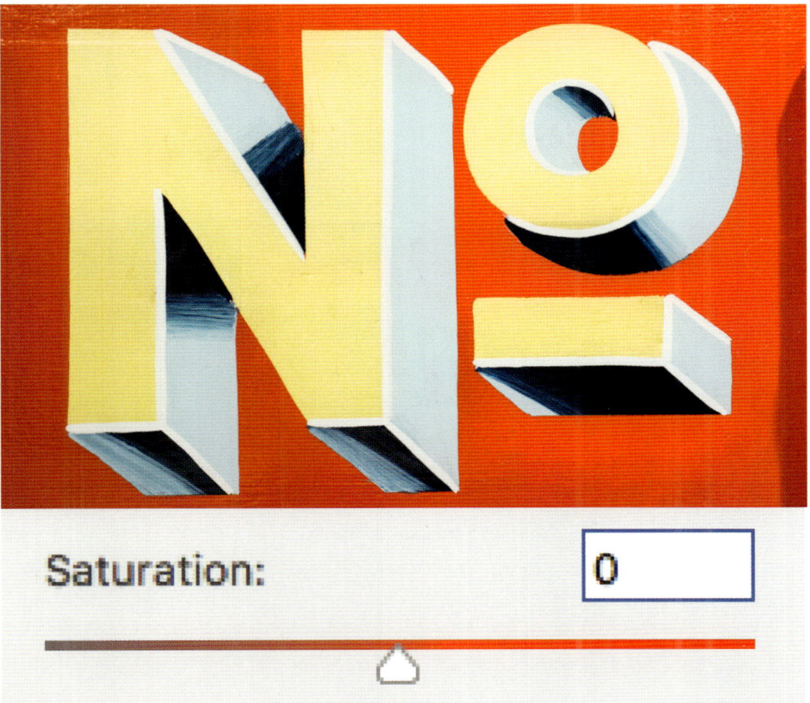

Saturation: 0

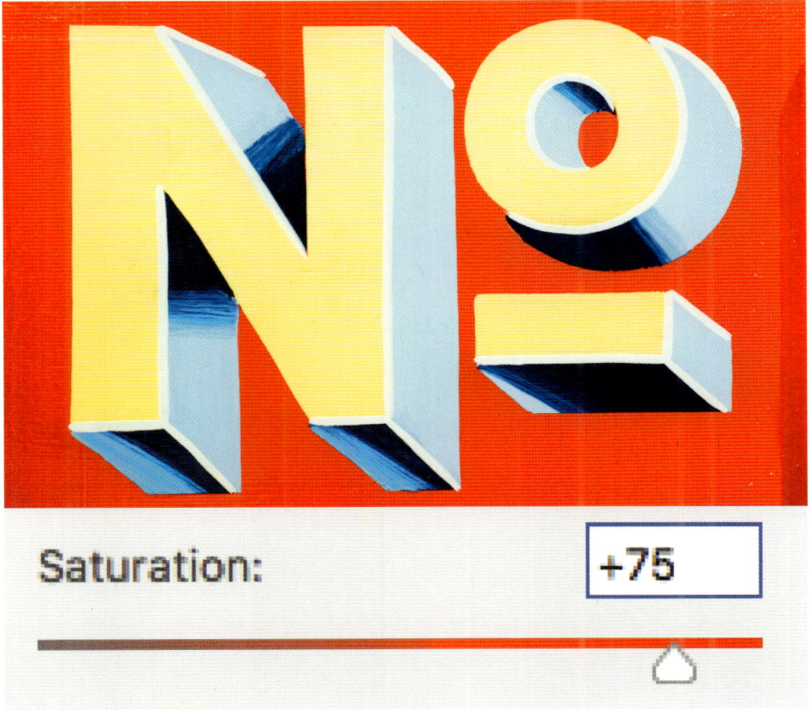

Saturation: +75

Above & right: Care needs to be taken when it comes to making saturation adjustments, as even quite small changes can have a noticeable effect. Here the Saturation has been set at ±75, showing just how easy it is to transform the appearance of colors in a photograph.

Focal length: 35mm

Aperture: f/2.8

Shutter speed: 1/20 sec.

ISO: 400

Saturation

Saturation adjustments change the intensity of the colors in the image. If the saturation is decreased, colors will appear less vibrant; if an image is desaturated completely it becomes black and white. An increase in saturation makes the colors in an image appear more vibrant and pure. However, a high saturation increase can make an image look cartoonish and unnatural.

Other Adjustments

Cloning

The Clone tool (along with related tools, such as Patch and Healing) is incredibly useful for macro photographers. One problem with shooting close-up imagery is that surface blemishes on subjects are more readily apparent than when the subject is photographed from a greater distance. Surface blemishes typically include scratches, hairs, and dust that were either impossible to fix or were not noticed at the time of shooting. The Clone tool can be used to remove these, as well as marks caused by dust on the camera's sensor. It can also be used to remove any other unwanted distractions in images, such as supporting structures—fishing line for instance—that you may have used to orientate your subject correctly for the camera.

The Clone tool is typically a round brush that can be varied in size. Some software also lets you adjust the "hardness" of the brush, enabling you to switch between a soft edge that is useful for subtle, feathered repairs and a harder edge that is better suited to tasks such as dust spot removal. You can also change the opacity of the brush: a lower opacity makes the brush more transparent, which enables you to gradually build up a repair through repeated clicks of the mouse.

The Clone tool works by taking the pixels from an unblemished area of an image and applying them to a blemished area. When you use the Clone tool you first need to select a "target" area of the image that most closely matches the area you want to repair in terms of color, texture, and brightness. Once selected you then paint over the unblemished area and your software will copy the pixels across from your target area. This process is repeated across the image until all the repairs have been completed.

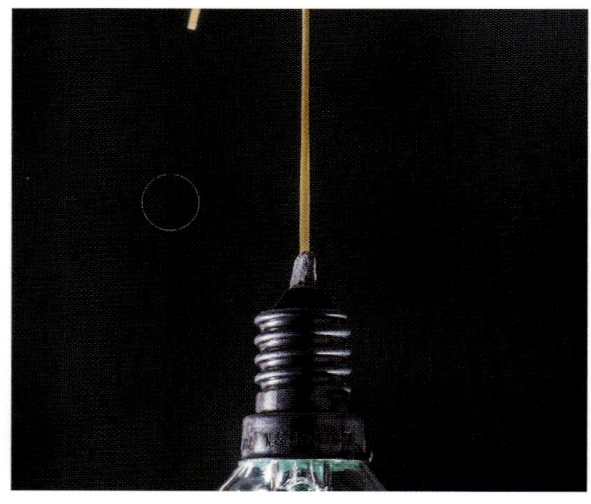

A

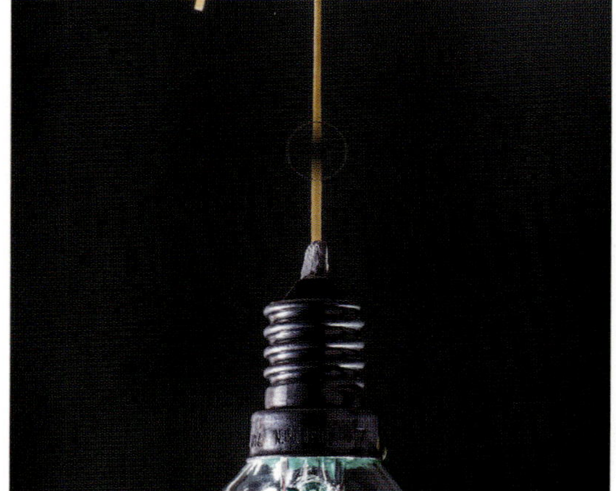

B

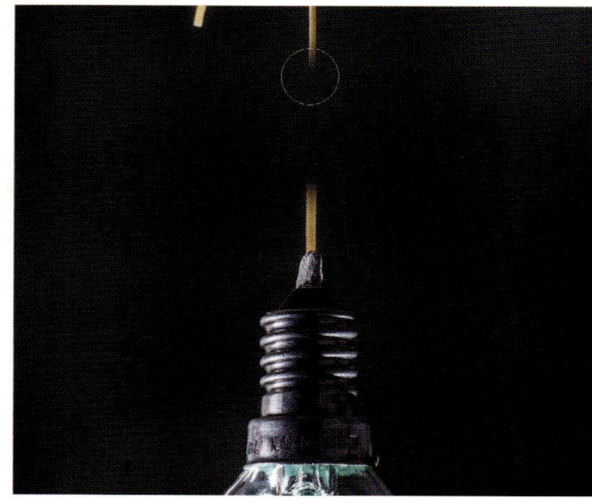

C

Right: The Clone tool is generally used to remove unwanted details in an image. To create this shot I hung a lightbulb in mid-air using a rubber band, which I always intended to remove. After shooting, I selected an area of background (A) and painted out the band (B and C). The base of the lightbulb required a similar treatment, but with a smaller, harder brush to carefully paint around the electrical contact. The entire image was then rotated through 180 degrees (opposite page).

Focal length: 100mm macro lens

Aperture: f/16

Shutter speed: 1/250 sec.

ISO: 50

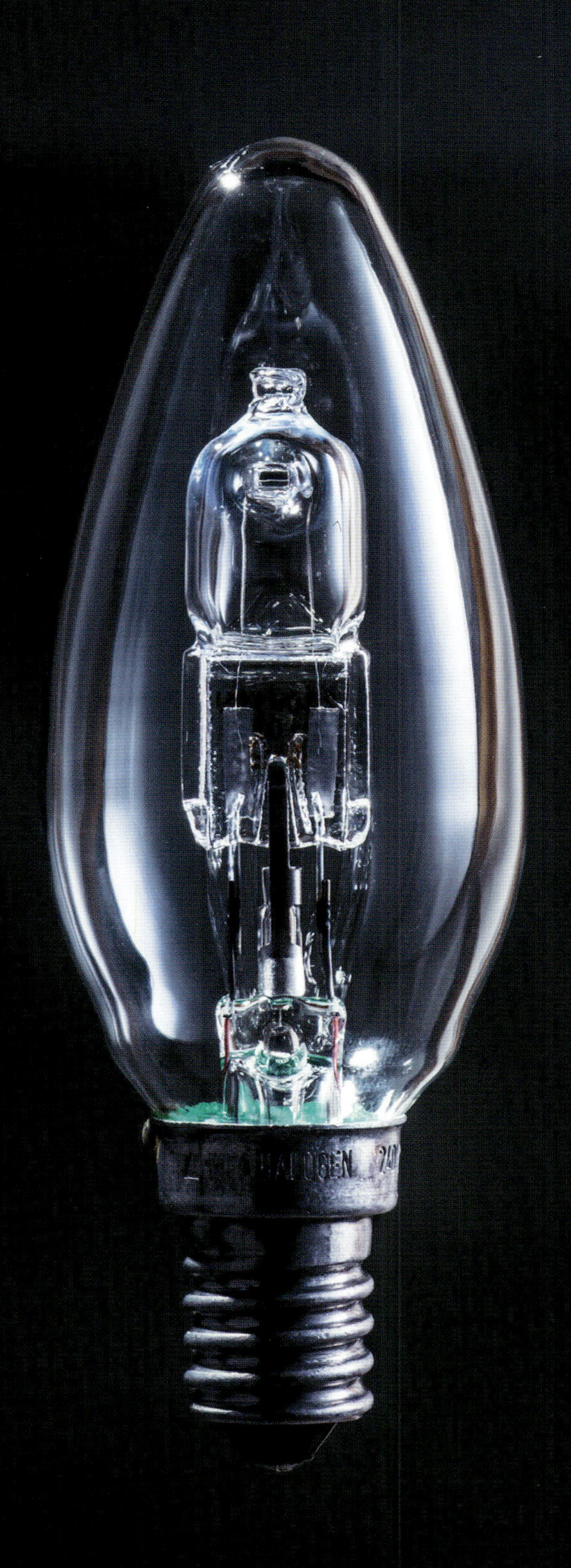

Cropping

Cropping is a simple, but effective way to reframe a shot by trimming away unwanted areas. It is analogous to zooming in on an important detail by altering the focal length at the time of shooting. Cropping also lets you reshape an image, so rather than being tied to the sensor's fixed aspect ratio (such as 3:2 for most DSLRs or 4:3 for Micro Four Thirds cameras) you can select from a series of preset aspect ratios or crop in a freeform way.

The limitation to cropping is that every time you crop an image you are reducing the number of pixels it contains. For some purposes—such as preparing an image to upload to the Internet—this is a relatively small concern, but it can reduce your options when it comes to the maximum size at which you can print the image.

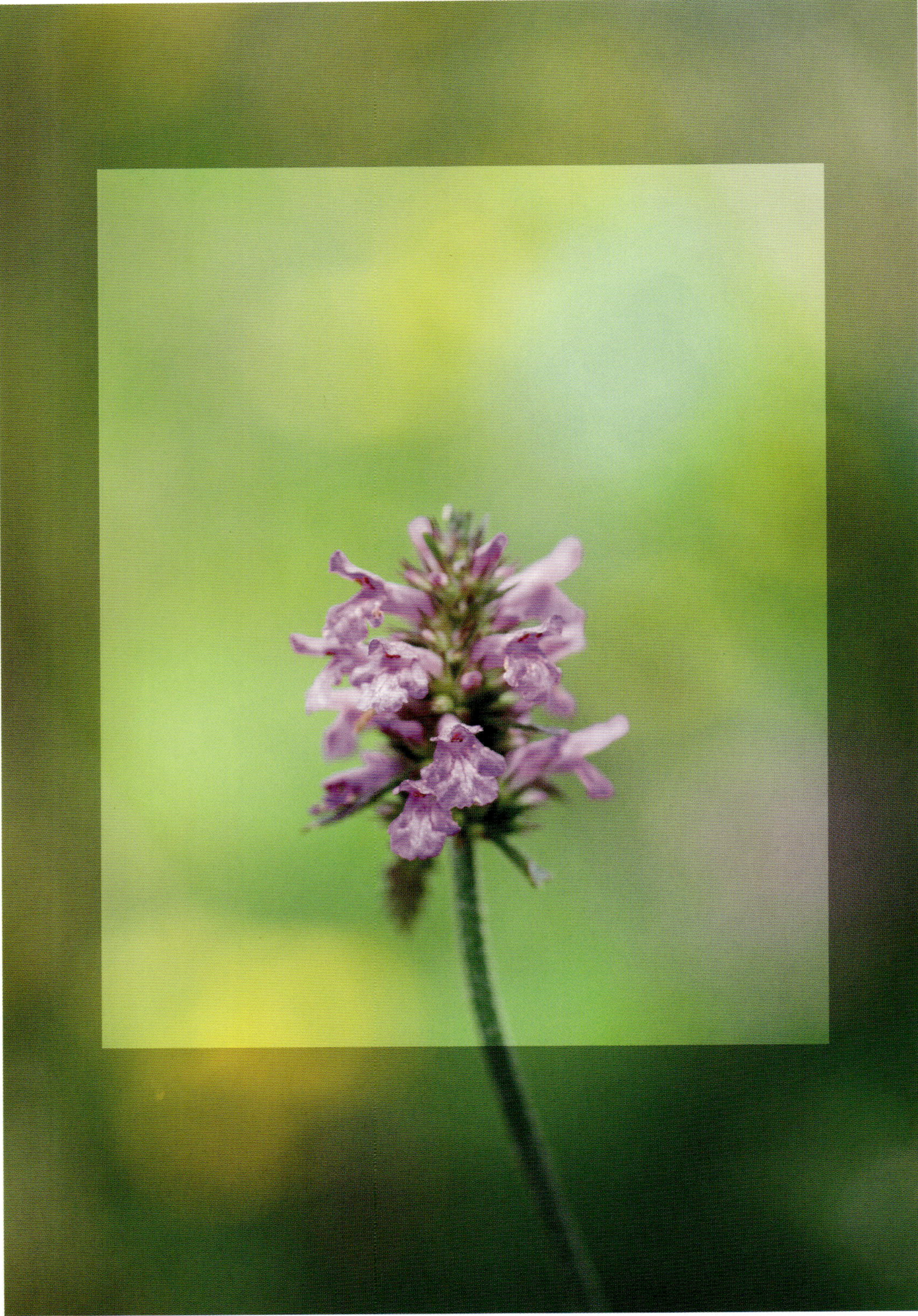

Right: Cropping is particularly useful if you cannot physically get close to a subject or zoom in further. I cropped this shot to the smaller (lighter) rectangle in the center for this very reason.
Focal length: 100mm macro lens
Aperture: f/5.6
Shutter speed: 1/250 sec.
ISO: 400

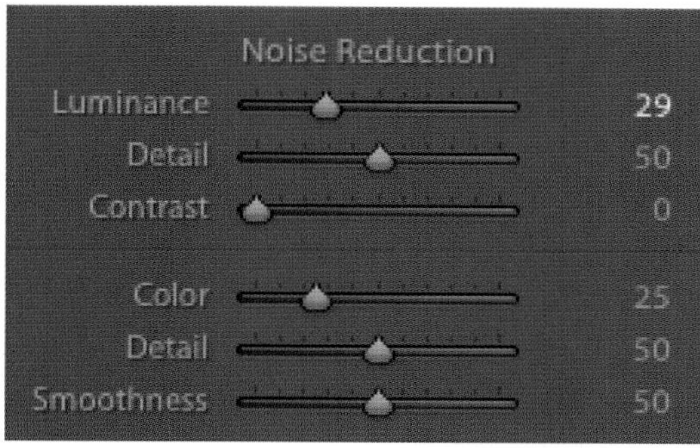

Above: There is a compromise to be made when removing noise. If you remove noise too aggressively, fine textural details in your subject will also be smoothed away, leaving an image looking unnaturally smooth. It is often better to leave a small amount of noise in an image—particularly luminance noise. It is also worth noting that noise reduction can be applied both globally and locally. By making careful selections you can remove noise locally, so you can reduce its appearance in areas of even tone (which suffer most from the appearance of noise), while leaving more detailed and important areas alone.

Noise Reduction

When you use a high ISO setting and/or a long exposure time of 30+ seconds, noise can start to have a negative impact on your images. To combat this, most cameras feature some sort of noise reduction function, but this is only relevant when dealing with high ISO noise and when shooting JPEGs—it doesn't tackle long exposure noise, or affect Raw files.

There are two types of noise: luminance and color ("chroma") noise. Of the two, luminance noise is the least objectionable, as it gives images a grainy texture that can make a digital image look slightly less sterile.

Chroma noise, however, is seen as unattractive blotches of color—often red or purple—that are scattered randomly across an image. Chroma noise becomes highly visible when a camera is set close to its maximum ISO values, or when a dramatically underexposed image is normalized. Both types of noise can usually be tackled separately in postproduction.

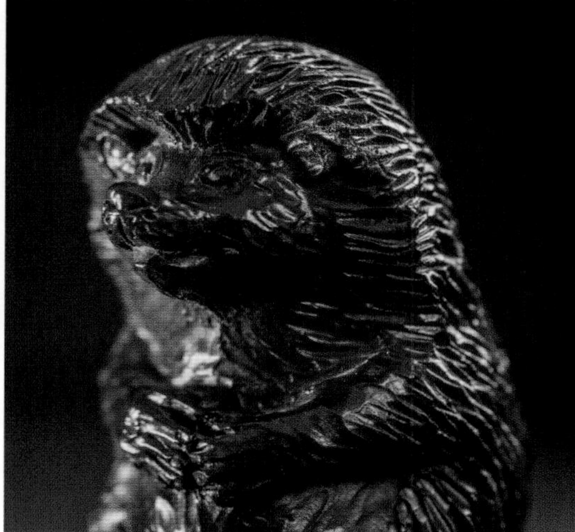

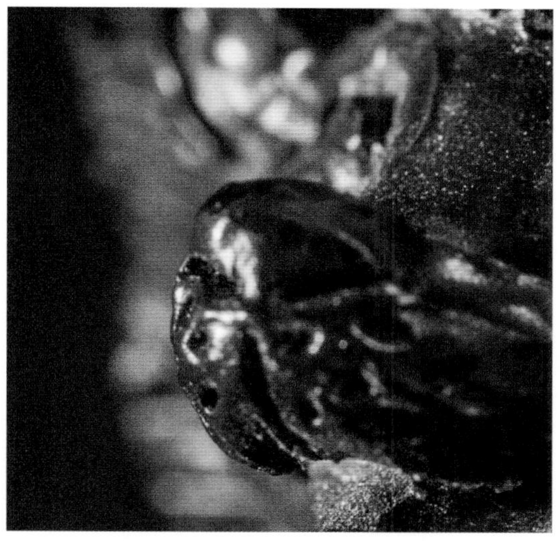

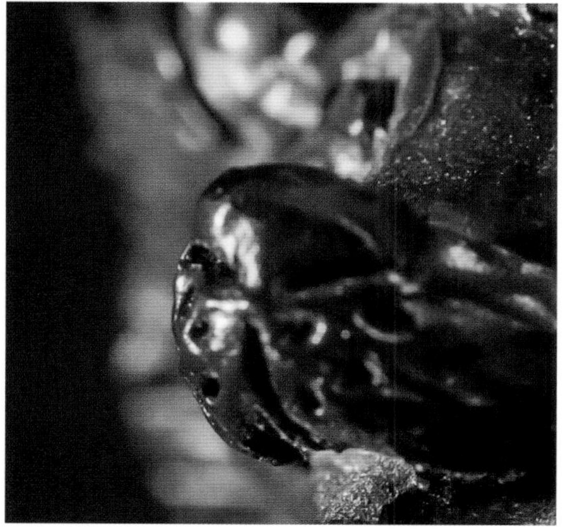

Sharpening

Postproduction software sharpens an image by increasing the amount of contrast between edges in the image.

There are two occasions when an image might be sharpened. The first is known as "capture sharpening." Many camera sensors use an anti-aliasing filter to deliberately soften an image in order to reduce the problem of moiré—an interference pattern caused by high-frequency subjects such as woven fabrics. Capture sharpening is used to counter this.

The second type of sharpening is known as "output sharpening," and is applied to an image according to how it is going to be used. Images destined for use on a website or significantly shrunk in size typically need far less output sharpening than images that will be printed. This is partly because inks spread slightly when you make a print (softening an image further) and partly because prints tend to be presented at a larger size (emphasizing any underlying softness).

The degree of sharpening, whether capture or output, can be varied according to need or taste. However, too much sharpening can result in ugly halos appearing along the edges in the image.

Left: The visibility of High ISO noise is greatly reduced when the resolution of an image is lowered (top). However, view an image at 100% (center) and the effects of high ISO noise are all too visible. Applying a judicious amount of noise reduction helps reduce high ISO noise (bottom), but the key is to balance the removal of noise with the loss of fine detail in the subject. If you apply too much noise reduction the surface of your subject can look unnaturally smooth.

Focal length: 100mm macro lens

Aperture: f/11

Shutter speed: 1/6 sec.

ISO: 3200

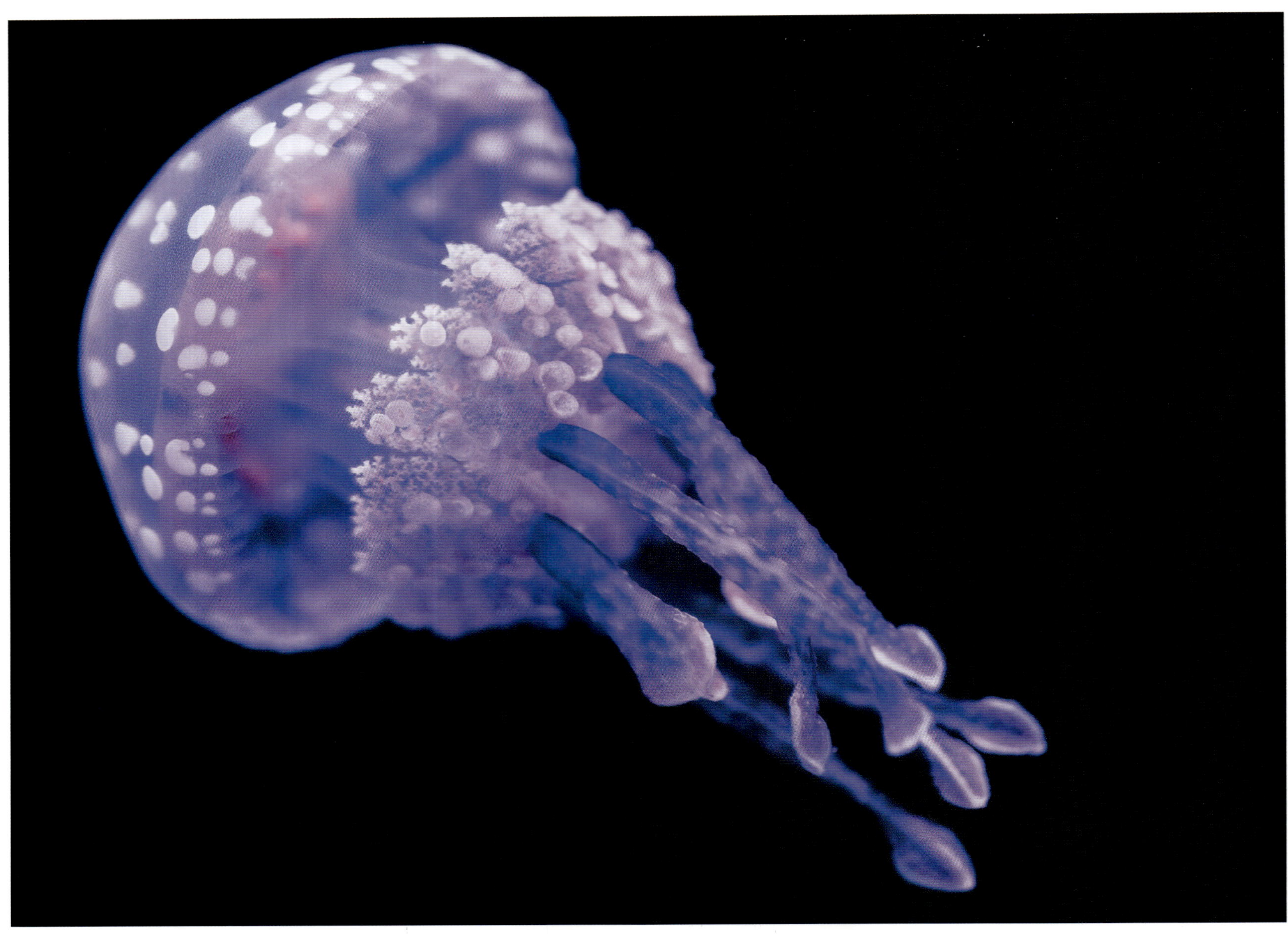

Above: Some images require more postproduction than others. This seemingly simple shot required extensive work, which included the removal of heavy image noise—from the use of a high ISO—and sympathetic sharpening. As the image was shot in an aquarium through glass, it also needed several blemishes removed to make it appear more natural.

Focal length: 100mm macro lens

Aperture: f/3.8

Shutter speed: 1/125 sec.

ISO: 3200

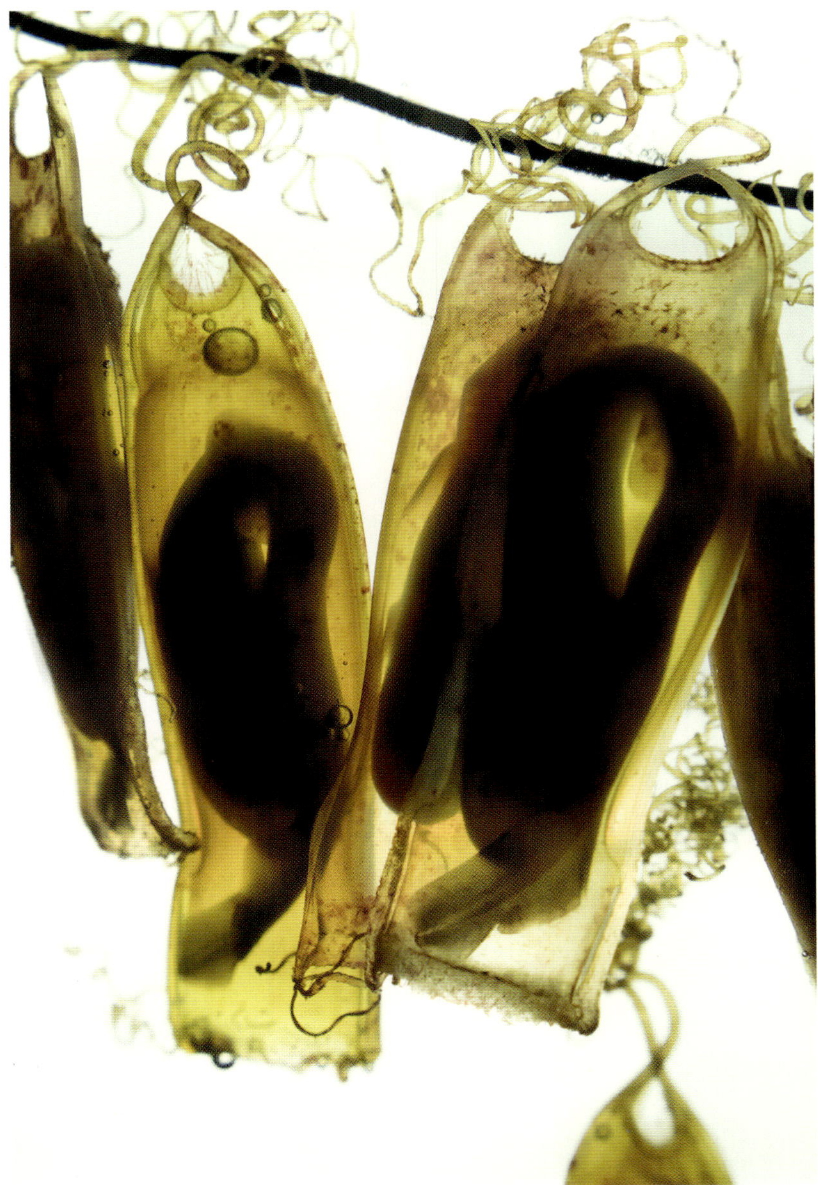

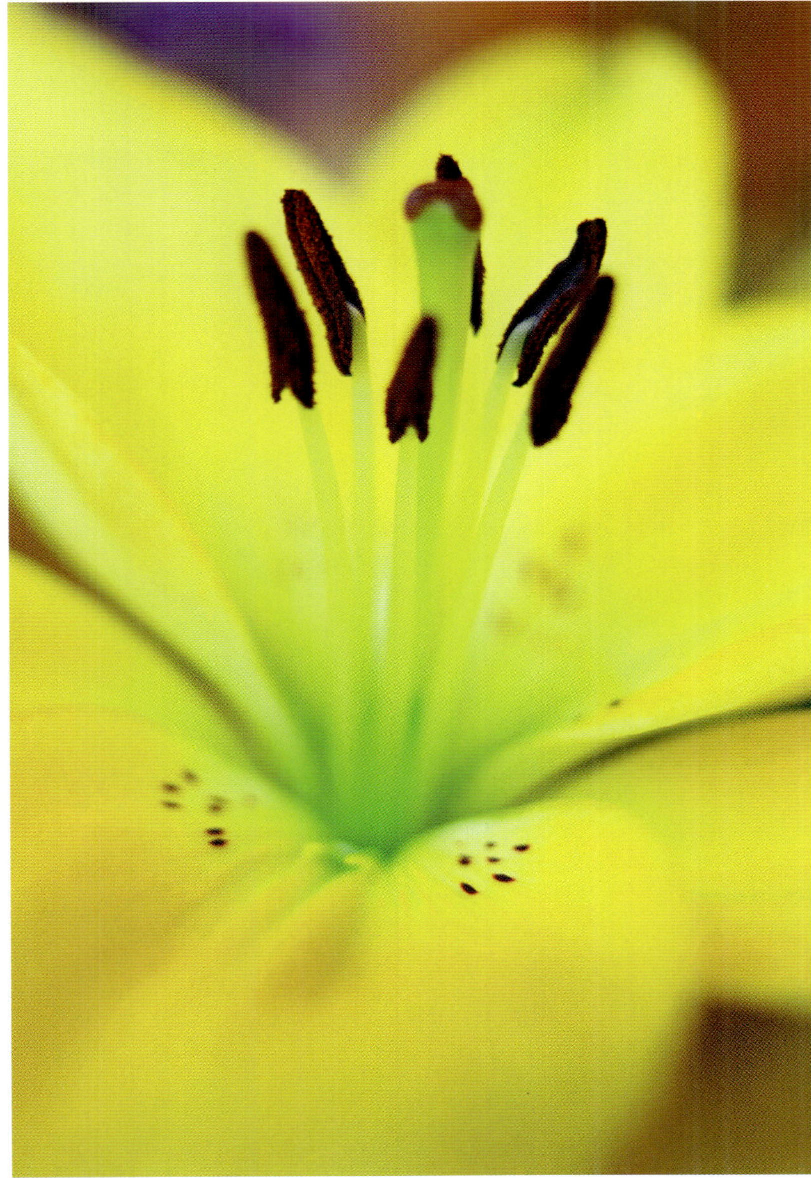

Above: The key to successful postproduction is knowing when to stop and keeping your adjustments to a minimum to maximize image quality. This image is noisy due to the unavoidable need for a high ISO at the time of shooting. However, I'm happy to live with the noise and not smother the details in the image further than necessary.

Focal length: 35mm

Aperture: f/4.5

Shutter speed: 1/320 sec.

ISO: 1600

Above: Scanned images, whether from film or print, or of a subject directly captured on the scanner itself, also need a certain degree of postproduction work. Scanning at the maximum color depth available will increase the scan time and file size, but as with a Raw file it will give you more room for postproduction adjustments.

Exposure details unrecorded

Black & White

Black-and-white photography is as valid to macro photography as it is to landscapes or portraiture. The key is to shoot subjects that will be enhanced by the visual esthetics of black and white: subjects that rely on color for impact, such as vibrant flowers, probably won't benefit from being converted to shades of gray.

Lighting also has an influence on whether a photo is ripe for conversion to black and white, with images that are high in contrast, with bright highlights and deep shadows, generally being the best candidates for black-and-white conversion.

There are two ways to shoot black and white. The first is to select the "Black and White" (or "Monochrome") picture parameter on your camera before you shoot; the second is to shoot in color and then convert the image to black and white during postproduction.

Of these options, the second is generally preferable, as it gives you more control over the conversion process. If you shoot Raw, you can shoot black and white in-camera, but "unpick" this conversion in postproduction and effectively start again from scratch. This luxury isn't available if you shoot black-and-white JPEGs.

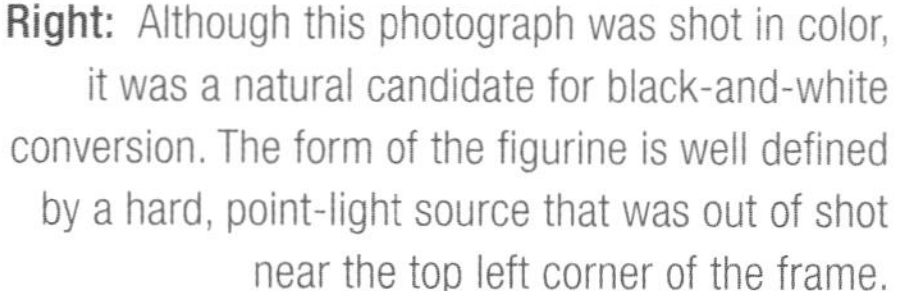

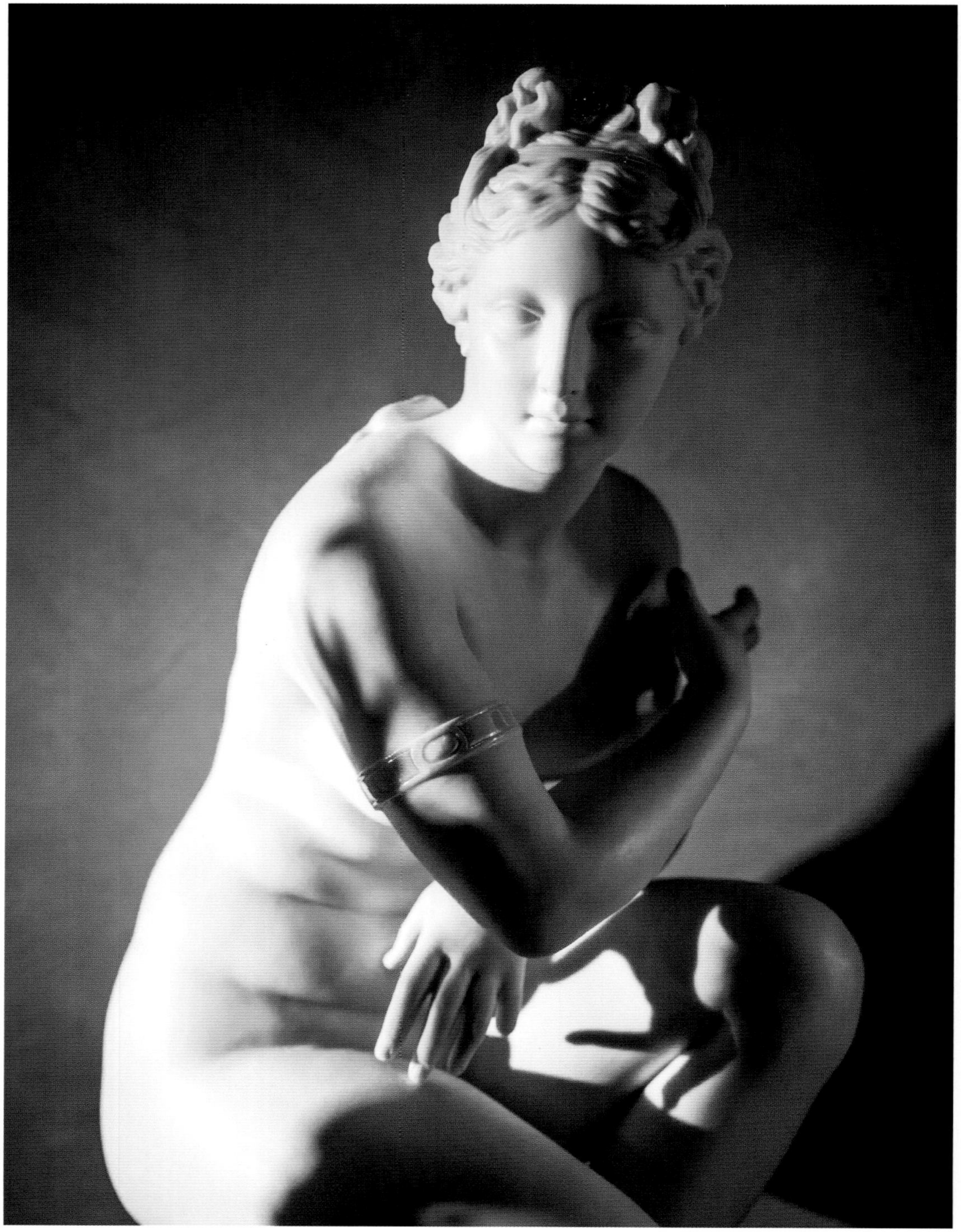

Right: Although this photograph was shot in color, it was a natural candidate for black-and-white conversion. The form of the figurine is well defined by a hard, point-light source that was out of shot near the top left corner of the frame.

Focal length: 23mm

Aperture: f/2.8

Shutter speed: 1/60 sec.

ISO: 200

Filtration

There is one big problem with simply converting a color image to black and white: colors such as mid-red or mid-blue, which look radically different in a color image, will appear as the same mid-gray tone in black and white. The result is that images can look flat and lifeless, making it difficult to distinguish one element in a scene from another.

The solution is to use colored filters. This can be either physical filters used over the lens at the time of shooting or "virtual" filtration that is applied in-camera or during postproduction. Both work on the same principal, which is that the filter (or filter effect) adjusts the tonal range by transmitting colors similar to it and blocking colors on the opposite side of the color wheel. This has the effect of lightening colors in the image that are similar to the filter, while darkening the opposite colors, separating the tones in the process.

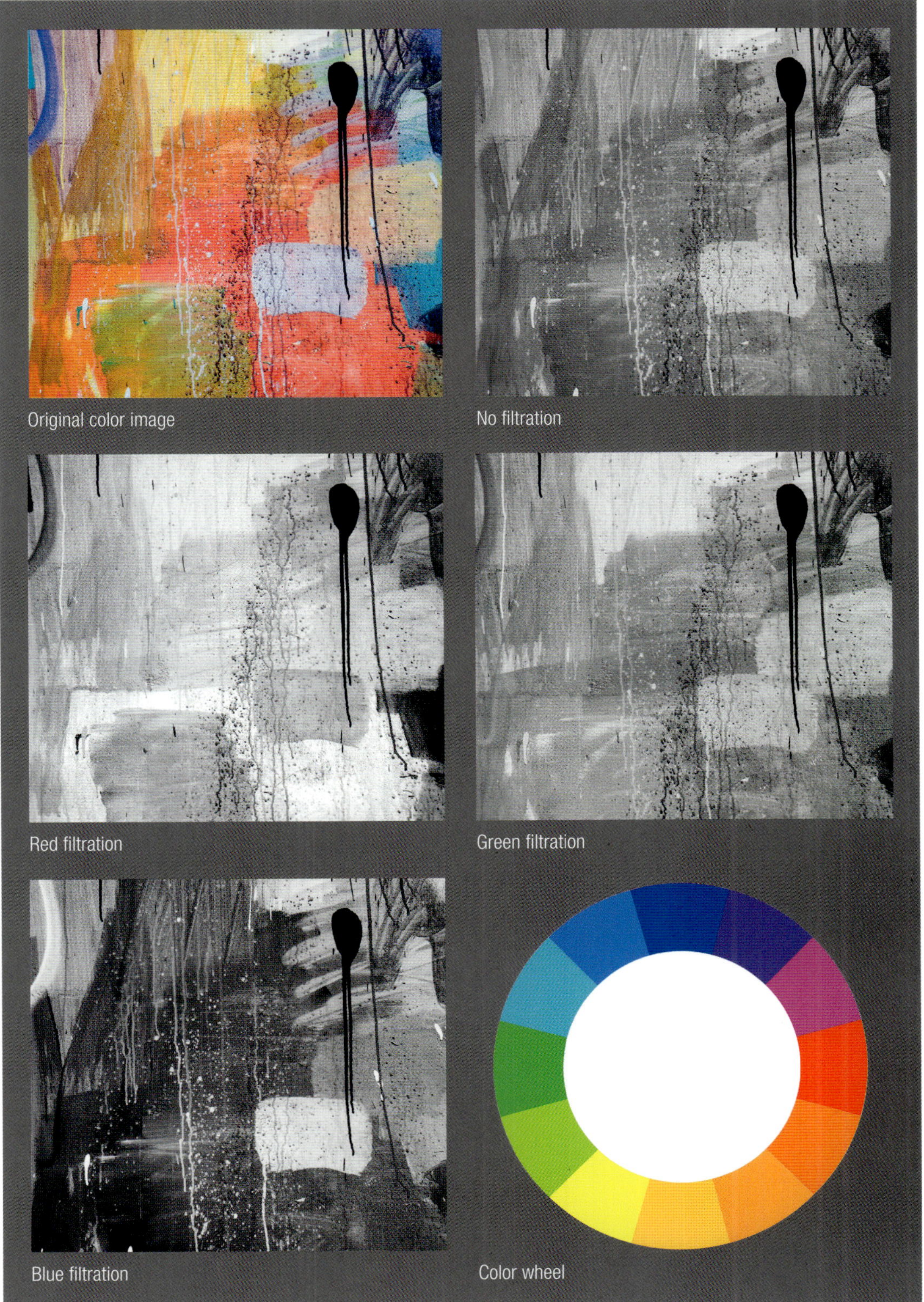

Original color image

No filtration

Red filtration

Green filtration

Blue filtration

Color wheel

Profile: Nordin Seruyan

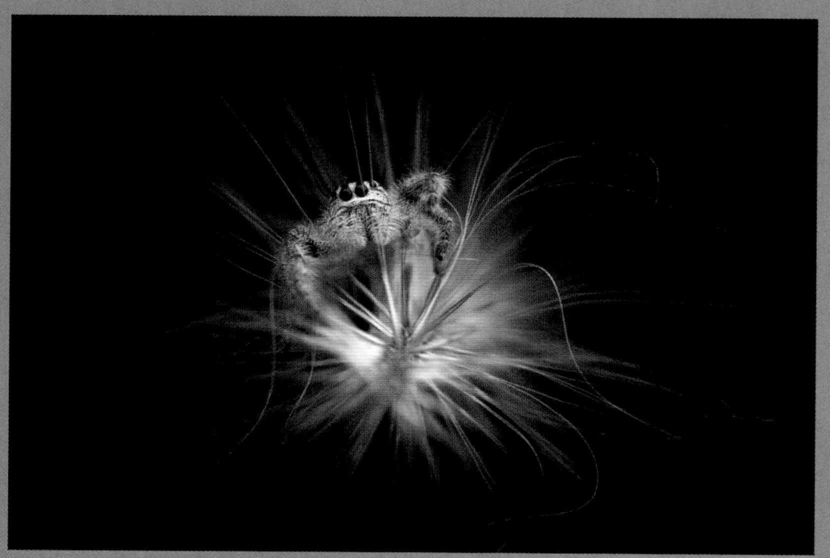 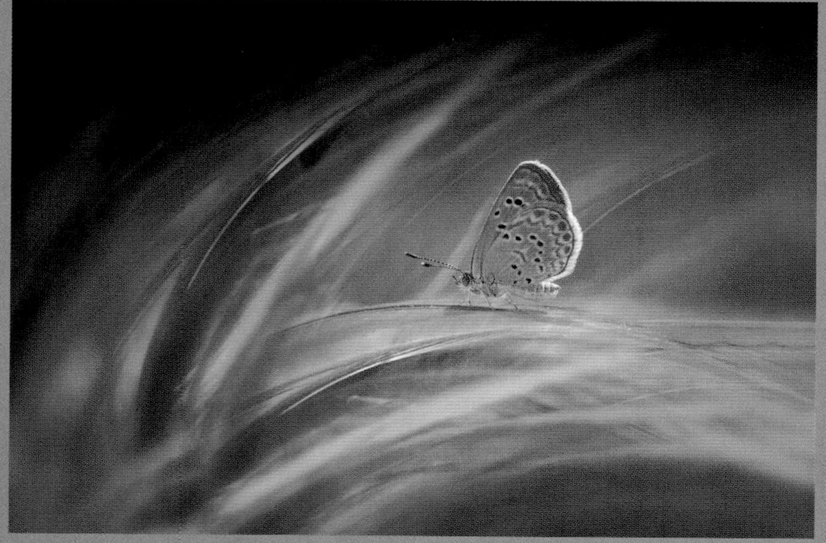

BIOGRAPHY

Nordin Seruyan was born and raised in a small town in central Borneo, Indonesia. He is a self-taught photographer whose interest in macro photography started in 2011. Since then he has won numerous awards and his work has appeared in magazines around the world.

https://1x.com/member/nordin_seruyan

Above:
Focal length: 105mm macro lens
Aperture: f/8
Shutter speed: 1/100 sec.
ISO: 200

Above right:
Focal length: 105mm macro lens
Aperture: f/7.1
Shutter speed: 1/320 sec.
ISO: 200

Q) What is your specialty?
A) I like to photograph live insects outdoors—for me, dead insects are not attractive. As there are a lot of insects in and around my house, there's always something to photograph. Sometimes I shoot them where I find them, but other times I'll move them, photograph them, and then let them go.

Q) What is it about your specialty that fascinates you?
A) I like my macro images to have a story or an interesting composition. From the story, I hope people will always remember the image as mine—I don't want people to tire of seeing my work.

Q) What equipment do you regularly use?
A) I use Nikon D3000 and D7100 DSLRs with a Nikkor 105mm Micro lens.

Q) How do you plan a photography session?
A) I generally don't plan my shoots—I just go out and see what there is to photograph.

Q) How do you light your subjects?
A) I prefer natural light, as the images it creates are also natural. I tend to shoot early in the morning or late in the afternoon, but I will also shoot during the day if the sun is not too intense. I simply use the available light, without reflectors or modifiers of any kind.

Q) How important is postproduction to you?
A) I shoot Raw and convert all my files in Adobe Photoshop using a simple and fast process that I've developed. For certain images, further postproduction work is very important, especially when it comes to preventing images looking too similar to one another.

Q) What is your top tip?
A) To get interesting pictures, try to avoid copying photographs you've seen before: create your own artwork, with its own story. Also, never feel satisfied with your results—you can always learn more and do better!

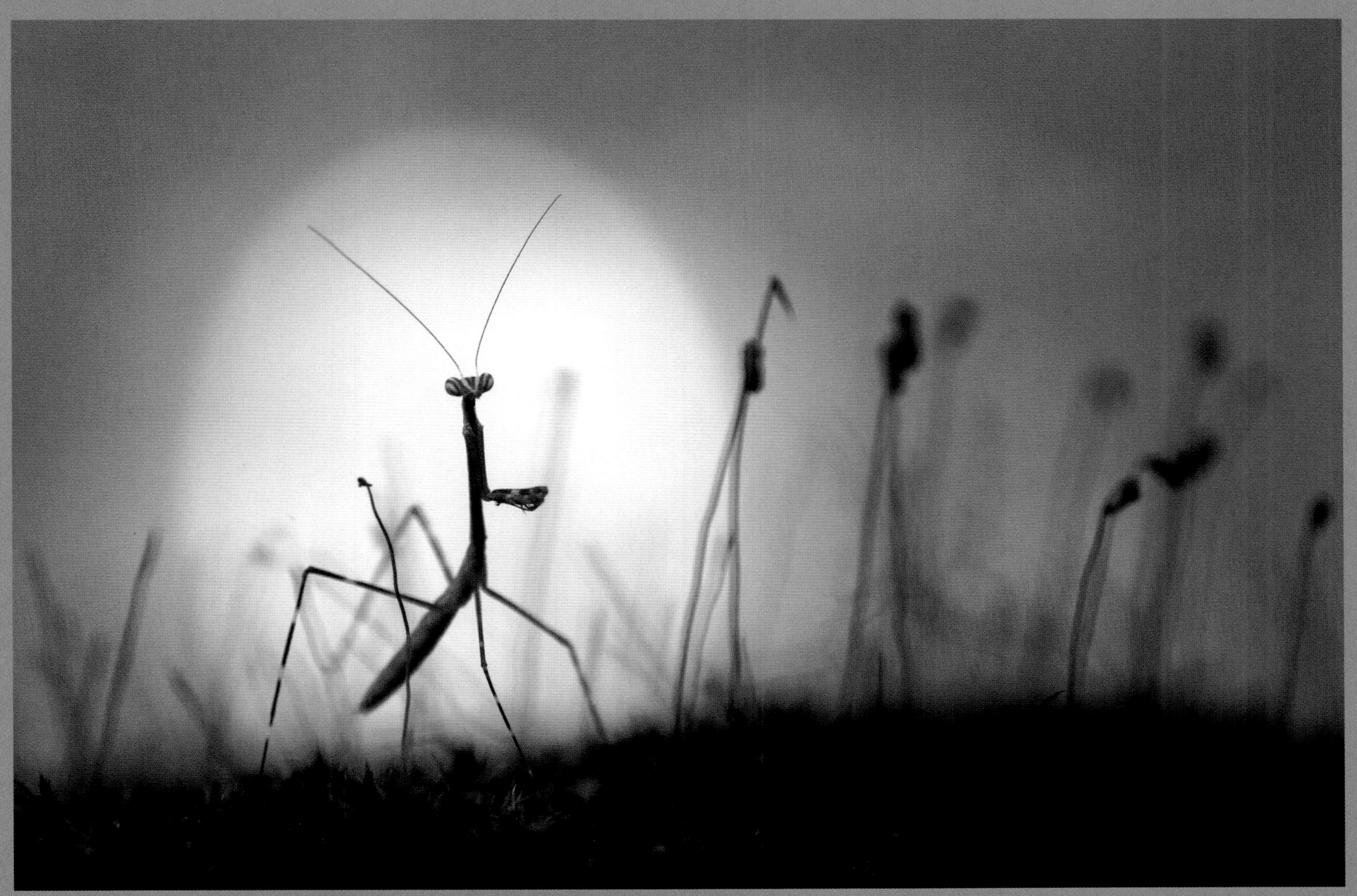

Above:
Focal length: 105mm macro lens
Aperture: f/7.1
Shutter speed: 1/500 sec.
ISO: 200

Glossary

Aberration An imperfection in a photograph, usually caused by the optics of a lens.

AEL (automatic exposure lock) A camera control that locks in the exposure value, allowing a scene to be recomposed.

Angle of view The area of a scene that a lens takes in, measured in degrees.

Aperture The opening in a camera lens through which light passes to expose the sensor. The relative size of the aperture is denoted by f/stops.

Autofocus (AF) A reliable through-the-lens focusing system allowing accurate focus without the photographer manually turning the lens.

Bracketing Taking a series of identical pictures, changing only the exposure, usually in ⅓-, ½-, or 1-stop increments.

Buffer The in-camera memory of a digital camera.

Camera shake Image fault caused by camera movement during exposure.

Center-weighted metering A metering pattern that determines the exposure by placing importance on the light meter reading at the center of the frame.

Chromatic aberration The inability of a lens to bring spectrum colors into focus at a single point.

Color temperature The color of a light source expressed in degrees Kelvin (K).

Compression The process by which digital files are reduced in size. Compression can retain all the information in the file (lossless compression), or "lose" data for greater levels of file-size reduction (lossy compression).

Contrast The range between the highlight and shadow areas of a photo, or a marked difference in illumination between colors or adjacent areas.

Depth of field (DOF) The amount of an image that appears acceptably sharp. This is controlled primarily by the aperture: the smaller the aperture, the greater the depth of field.

Digital sensor A microchip consisting of a grid of millions of light-sensitive cells. The more cells, the greater the number of pixels and the higher the resolution of the final image. The two most commonly used types of digital sensor are CCD (Charge-Coupled Device) and CMOS (Complementary Metal-Oxide Semi-conductor).

Diopter Unit expressing the power of a lens.

Distortion A lens fault that causes what should be straight lines in an image to bow outward from the center (referred to as barrel distortion) or inward (referred to as pincushion distortion).

dpi (dots per inch) Measure of the resolution of a printer or scanner. The more dots per inch, the higher the resolution.

DPOF Digital Print Order Format.

Dynamic range The ability of the camera's sensor to capture a full range of shadows and highlights.

Evaluative metering A metering system where light reflected from multiple subject areas is calculated based on algorithms.

Exposure The amount of light allowed to hit the digital sensor, controlled by aperture, shutter speed, and ISO. Also, the act of taking a photograph, as in "making an exposure."

Exposure compensation A control that allows intentional over- or underexposure.

Fill-in flash Flash combined with daylight in an exposure. Used with naturally backlit or harshly side-lit or top-lit subjects to prevent silhouettes forming, or to add extra light to the shadow areas of a well-lit scene.

Filter A piece of colored or coated glass, or plastic, placed in front of the lens.

Focal length The distance, usually in millimeters, from the optical center of a lens to its focal point.

Focus stacking A technique that increases the effective depth of field of a photograph by merging multiple shots taken at different focus settings.

fps (frames per second) A measure of the time needed for a digital camera to process one photograph and be ready to shoot the next.

f/stop Number assigned to a particular lens aperture. Wide apertures are denoted by small numbers (such as f/1.8 and f/2.8), while small apertures are denoted by large numbers (such as f/16 and f/22).

Highlights The brightest part of an image.

Histogram A graph representing the distribution of tones in a photograph.

Hotshoe An accessory shoe with electrical contacts that allows synchronization between a camera and a flash.

Hotspot A light area with a loss of detail in the highlights. This is a common problem with flash photography.

Incident light reading Meter reading based on the light falling onto the subject.

Interpolation A way of increasing the file size of a digital image by adding pixels, thereby increasing its resolution.

ISO The sensitivity of the digital sensor measured in terms equivalent to the ISO rating of a film.

JPEG (Joint Photographic Experts Group) JPEG compression can reduce file sizes to about 5% of their original size, but uses a lossy compression system that degrades image quality.

LCD (Liquid crystal display) The flat screen on a digital camera that allows the user to compose and review digital images.

Macro A term used to describe close focusing and the close-focusing ability of a lens. Technically, an image at a reproduction ratio of 1:1 ("life size") or greater.

Megapixel One million pixels is equal to one megapixel.

Memory card A removable storage device for digital cameras.

Metering The act of measuring the light falling on a scene to determine the exposure required.

Mirrorless Common name given to a camera that doesn't have a reflex mirror (*see* SLR). The photographer views a live image streamed from the digital sensor to an LCD.

Monochrome A synonym for black-and-white photography.

Noise Interference visible in a digital image caused by stray electrical signals during exposure.

Overexposure A result of allowing too much light to reach the digital sensor during exposure. Typically, the highlights in an overexposed image burn out to pure white, while the shadows appear unnaturally bright.

PictBridge The industry standard for sending information directly from a camera to a printer, without the need for a computer.

Pixel Short for "picture element." The smallest bit of information in a digital photograph.

Predictive autofocus An AF system that can continuously track a moving subject.

Prime A lens with a fixed focal length.

Raw The file format in which the raw data from the sensor is stored without permanent alteration being made.

Red-eye reduction A system that causes the pupils of a subject's eyes to shrink, by shining a light prior to taking the main flash picture.

Remote switch A device used to trigger the shutter of the camera from a distance, to help minimize camera shake. Also known as a "cable release" or "remote release."

Resolution The number of pixels used to capture or display a photo.

RGB (Red, Green, Blue) Computers and other digital devices understand color information as combinations of red, green, and blue.

Rule of thirds A rule of composition that places the key elements of a picture at points along imagined lines that divide the frame into thirds, both vertically and horizontally.

Shadows The darkest part of an image.

Shutter The mechanism that controls the amount of light reaching the sensor, by opening and closing.

SLR (Single Lens Reflex) A camera that directs the image projected through the lens to the viewfinder using a reflex mirror.

Spot metering A metering pattern that places importance on the intensity of light reflected by a very small portion of the scene, either at the center of the frame or linked to a focus point.

Teleconverter A supplementary lens that is fitted between the camera body and lens, increasing its effective focal length.

Telephoto A lens with a large focal length and a narrow angle of view.

TIFF (Tagged Image File Format) A universal file format supported by virtually all relevant software applications. TIFFs are uncompressed digital files.

TTL (Through The Lens) metering A metering system built into the camera that measures light passing through the lens at the time of shooting.

Underexposure The result of allowing too little light to reach the digital sensor during exposure. Typically, the highlights in an underexposed image will appear muddy and the shadows will be dense and lacking in detail.

Viewfinder An optical system used for composing and sometimes for focusing the subject.

White balance A function that allows the correct color balance to be recorded for any given lighting situation.

Wide-angle lens A lens with a short focal length and, consequently, a wide angle of view.

Zoom A lens with a variable focal length.

Useful Websites

Photographers

David Taylor www.davidtaylorphotography.co.uk

General

Digital Photography Review www.dpreview.com
On Landscape www.onlandscape.co.uk

Photographic Equipment

Canon www.canon.com
Fujifilm www.fujifilm.com
Lastolite www.lastolite.com
Leica www.leica-camera.com
Nikon www.nikon.com
Nissin www.nissindigital.com
OM Digital Solutions www.om-digitalsolutions.com
Panasonic www.panasonic.net
Ricoh/Pentax www.ricoh-imaging.com
Sigma www.sigma-photo.com
Sony www.sony.com
Tamron www.tamron.com
Tokina www.tokinalens.com
Venus Optics www.venuslens.net
Zeiss www.zeiss.com

Photography Publications

Ammonite Press www.ammonitepress.com
Black & White Photography Magazine www.thegmcgroup.com
Outdoor Photography Magazine www.thegmcgroup.com

Printing

Epson www.epson.com
Hahnemühle www.hahnemuehle.de
HP www.hp.com
Ilford www.ilford.com
Kodak www.kodak.com
Lexmark www.lexmark.com
Marrutt www.marrutt.com

Software & Actions

Adobe www.adobe.com
Affinity affinity.serif.com
Apple www.apple.com
Corel www.corel.com
DxO www.dxo.com
Exposure Software www.exposure.software
Phase One www.phaseone.com
Photomatix www.hdrsoft.com
PhotoPills www.photopills.com

Index

Acknowledgments

No person is an island, and a book is never written in isolation. In writing this book I had the help,
advice, and support of a number of people, all of whom deserve a profuse thank you or two. In no
particular order they are: Chris Gatcum, editor extraordinaire who made sure that this book actually
made sense; Jason Hook at Ammonite Press, who commissionec the title; Luke Herriott, who
designed it; and the six contributors—Chris, Ross, Polina, Viktor, Terry, and Nordin—
who have helped make the book more visually interesting.

I'd also like to thank Elaine and Nic at the Dilston Physic Garden for etting me photograph the flora
and fauna there over the summer of 2016; Sue and Brian Brown; my parents Bill and Carol for everything;
and last (but not least) my wife Tania, to whom this bcok is dedicated.

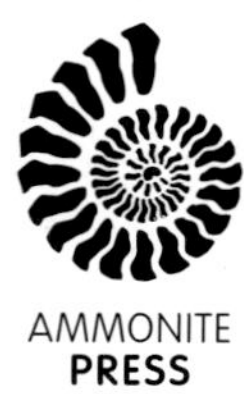

AMMONITE
PRESS

www.ammonitepress.com